MOUNTAIN BIKE!

Maine

1/20/98

MOUNTAIN BIKE!

A GUIDE TO THE CLASSIC TRAILS

SARAH L. HALE AND DAVID GIBBS

Menasha Ridge Press

© 1998 by Sarah L. Hale and David Gibbs
All rights reserved
Printed in the United States of America
Published by Menasha Ridge Press
First edition, first printing

Library of Congress Cataloging-in-Publication Data:
Hale, Sarah L., 1970–
Mountain bike! Maine: a guide to the classic trails/
Sarah L. Hale and David Gibbs.—1st ed.
   p.   cm.—(America by mountain bike)
Includes index.
ISBN 0-89732-266-5 (pbk.)
1. All terrain cycling—Maine—Guidebooks.
2. Bicycle trails—Maine—Guidebooks.
3. Maine—Guidebooks.
I. Gibbs, David, 1961–.   II. Title.   III. Series: America by mountain bike series.
GV1045.5.M2H35   1998
917.4104'43—dc21   98-11035
CIP

Photos by the authors unless otherwise credited
Maps by Brian Taylor at RapiDesign
Cover and text design by Suzanne Holt
Cover Photo by Dennis Coello

Menasha Ridge Press
700 South 28th Street
Suite 206
Birmingham, Alabama 35233

All the trails described in this book are legal for mountain bikes. But rules can change—especially for off-road bicycles, the new kid on the outdoor recreation block. Land access issues and conflicts between bicyclists, hikers, equestrians, and other users can cause the rewriting of recreation regulations on public lands, sometimes resulting in a ban of mountain bike use on specific trails. That's why it's the responsibility of each rider to check and make sure that he or she rides only on trails where mountain biking is permitted.

CAUTION

Outdoor recreational activities are by their very nature potentially hazardous. All participants in such activities must assume the responsibility for their own actions and safety. The information contained in this guidebook cannot replace sound judgment and good decision-making skills, which help reduce risk exposure, nor does the scope of this book allow for disclosure of all the potential hazards and risks involved in such activities.

Learn as much as possible about the outdoor recreational activities in which you participate, prepare for the unexpected, and be cautious. The reward will be a safer and more enjoyable experience.

CONTENTS

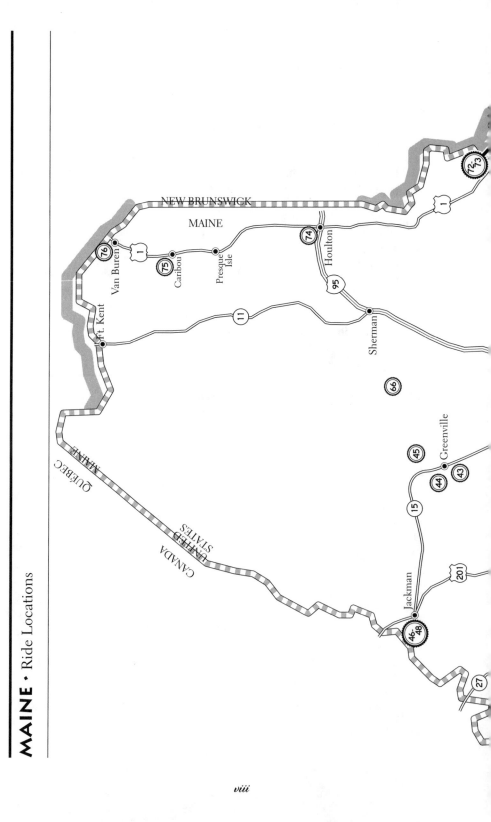

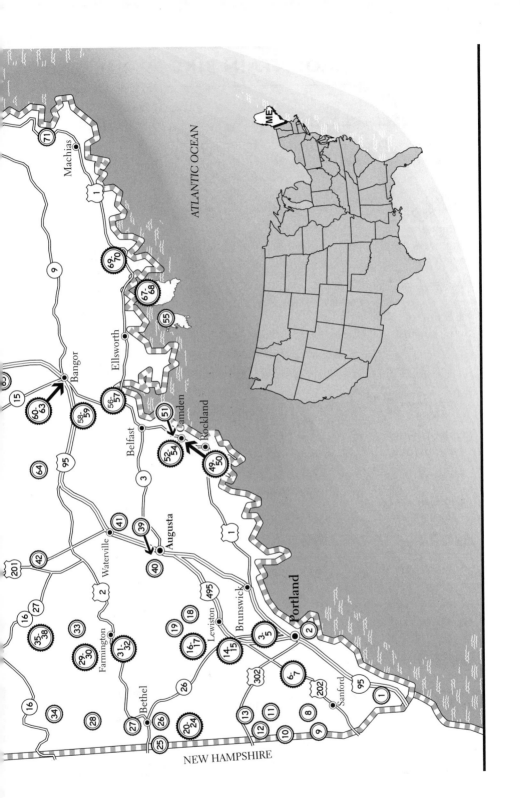

AMERICA BY MOUNTAIN BIKE   MAP LEGEND

Ride trailhead

Primary bike trail — **Direction of travel** — **Steep hill** — **Optional bike trail and trailhead** — **Other trail** — **Hiking only trail**

Interstate highways (with exit no.) — **US routes** — **State routes** — **Other paved roads** (Taylor Rd.) — **Unpaved, gravel, or dirt roads** (4WD) (may be 4WD only)

US Forest Service roads — **Cities** (Portland) — **Towns or settlements** (Mt. Vernon) — **Lake** (Dam) — **Intermittent stream** — **Perennial stream**

Approximate scale in miles (0 ½ 1 MILES) — **True north** (N) — **Public lands*** (WILDERNESS AREA) — **State or county border**

- ✈ Airport
- 🏹 Archeological or historical site
- 🚢 Boat ramp
- ▲ Campground (CG)
- ≡ Cattle guard
- Cemetery or gravesite
- Church
- Cliff, escarpment, or outcropping
- Drinking water

- Fire tower or lookout
- Falls or rapids
- Food
- Gate
- House or cabin
- Lodging
- Mountain or butte
- Mountain pass
- Mountain summit (elevation in feet) 3312
- Mine or quarry

- Observatory
- Park office or ranger station
- ⊼ Picnic area
- Power line or pipeline
- Rest rooms
- Spring
- Stable, corral, or ranch
- Swimming area
- Transmission towers
- Tunnel or bridge

Remember, private property exists in and around our national forests.

LIST OF MAPS

ACKNOWLEDGMENTS

Our thanks are due to the many people who assisted us throughout the year we spent researching, riding, and writing about these trails. The enthusiasm of friends who accompanied us and the friendliness and interest of people we met on our travels constantly reminded us who this book is really for: people who possess a love of the outdoors, a passion for two-wheeled travel, and an interest in the natural resources and history of Maine.

In particular, we would like to thank the Tuesday-night riding group: Bill, Cynthia, Jeff, Katie, Laurie, Mary, Rick, T.W., and the many other riders who led us along trails throughout the greater Portland area. Thanks also to Joe and Amy Montefusco for enduring less-than-perfect conditions in Carrabassett Valley, and to first-time riders Steven and Paula for their company in Rangeley. We could not have enjoyed our trip to Jackman without the hospitality of the Pinettes or the assistance of Al and Walter Szarka. Our appreciation to Karine Morin for providing us with a refreshing, out-of-state perspective on riding in Maine, and for hours of painstaking proofreading. And thanks to Cassie and Harold Gibbs for offering us a home-away-from-home.

We are both indebted to our respective employers, the City of Portland and Chintz-N-Prints, for enabling us to take the time we needed to wander the far reaches of the state. Of course, none of this would have been possible without Dennis Coello, to whom we shall be forever grateful for the opportunity to deepen our love of mountain biking and our appreciation for the state of Maine.

Finally, we would like to dedicate this book to MacDonald and Elizabeth Murphy, from whom we have received frequent encouragement, and in whose stories and experience we have seen an indomitable spirit of adventure and a lifelong respect for the land. It is in the footsteps of people such as these that we now ride.

FOREWORD

Welcome to *America by Mountain Bike*, a series designed to provide all-terrain bikers with the information they need to find and ride the very best trails around. Whether you're new to the sport and don't know where to pedal, or an experienced mountain biker who wants to learn the classic trails in another region, this series is for you. Drop a few bucks for the book, spend an hour with the detailed maps and route descriptions, and you're prepared for the finest in off-road cycling.

My role as editor of this series was simple: First, find a mountain biker who knows the area and loves to ride. Second, ask that person to spend a year researching the most popular and very best rides around. And third, have that rider describe each trail in terms of difficulty, scenery, condition, elevation change, and all other categories of information that are important to trail riders. "Pretend you've just completed a ride and met up with fellow mountain bikers at the trailhead," I told each author. "Imagine their questions, be clear in your answers."

As I said, the *editorial* process—that of sending out riders and reading the submitted chapters—is a snap. But the work involved in finding, riding, and writing about each trail is enormous. In some instances our authors' tasks are made easier by the information contributed by local bike shops or cycling clubs, or even by the writers of local "where-to" guides. Credit for these contributions is provided, when appropriate, in each chapter, and our sincere thanks goes to all who have helped.

But the overwhelming majority of trails are discovered and pedaled by our authors themselves, then compared with dozens of other routes to determine if they qualify as "classic"—that area's best in scenery and cycling fun. If you've ever had the experience of pioneering a route from outdated topographic maps, or entering a bike shop to request information from local riders who would much prefer to keep their favorite trails secret, or know how it is to double- and triple-check data to be positive your trail info is correct, then you have an idea of how each of our authors has labored to bring about these books. You and I, and all the mountain bikers of America, are the richer for their efforts.

You'll get more out of this book if you take a moment to read the Introduction explaining how to read the trail listings. The "Topographic Maps" section will help you understand how useful topos will be on a ride, and will also tell you where to get them. And though this is a "where-to," not a "how-to" guide, those of you who have not traveled the backcountry might find "Hitting the Trail" of particular value.

In addition to the material above, newcomers to mountain biking might want to spend a minute with the glossary, page 356, so that terms like *hardpack, single-track,* and *waterbars* won't throw you when you come across them in the text.

Finally, the tips in the Afterword on mountain biking etiquette and the land-use controversy might help us all enjoy the trails a little more.

All the best.

Dennis Coello
St. Louis

PREFACE

W e have lived in Maine for a combined period of more than 30 years. In this time, we have traveled throughout Maine by bicycle, paddled its waterways by canoe and kayak, and backpacked many miles of its extensive network of hiking trails. During the year we spent riding, camping, and doing research for this book, we revisited some of our favorite places in the state and made new tracks as well. In so doing, we came to appreciate not only the remarkable landscape that Maine has to offer, but also the sport of mountain biking. To really experience Maine you must venture off the beaten track, and there is no better vehicle than a mountain bike with which to begin the adventure!

Maine has a rugged appeal, and from its uneven coastline to its highest mountains and largest lakes, it celebrates a landscape of diversity: a landscape that is as colorful as the changing seasons, as disparate as the people who settled here, and as rich as the history that has been recorded here. Because the state covers an area so large, Maine can be an intimidating place to explore. In fact, for many people the state consists of a narrow corridor along the coast: a shoreline of fingerlike peninsulas and steep cliffs that is epitomized by small towns like Kennebunkport, Boothbay Harbor, and Camden. However, like the gradual movement of early settlers, many explorers of the state do eventually turn their attention from the coast and follow the paths of Maine's grand valleys upriver to the mountains, lakes, and forests.

In the year that we spent traveling the trails and back roads of the state by mountain bike, we learned that, despite its vast area, Maine is surprisingly accessible. The weathered landscape encourages exploration and provides opportunities for all levels of adventure. In fact, people have been vacationing in

Maine since the mid-1800s. Wealthy families, escaping the hot, stuffy summer climate of Boston, New York, and Philadelphia came to enjoy the fresh, cool air on the coast. Sportsmen represented some of the state's first outdoor recreationalists, and they came to fish or to hunt deer, moose, and bear in the Maine woods.

For the sport of mountain biking, Maine's network of abandoned old roads—now scenic single- and double-track trails—allow access to vast areas that were once cleared and cultivated. Furthermore, the decline of the railroad in Maine in the late 1930s and 40s has provided the substructure for the development of miles of multi-use recreational trails. The variety of terrain available to mountain bikers is tremendous. There are areas like Mount Desert Island that have been carefully preserved and tamed, and others, like the rugged and remote wilderness of the Wild River, that have recovered from development and fire and are slowly returning to their natural state.

The rides that we have selected for this guidebook represent a wide range of geographic regions and provide access to some of the most beautiful areas of the Maine landscape. It is our hope that they will give both visitors and "Maineacs" alike a starting point from which to further explore and experience the state of Maine.

REGIONAL SETTING

Maine is the northeasternmost state of the United States and encompasses an area that extends east from the foothills of the White Mountains to the Atlantic Ocean, and north to the Canadian provinces of Quebec and New Brunswick. Elevations range from sea level at the Atlantic Ocean to 5,267 feet atop Mount Katahdin, located just north of the geographic center of the state at Katahdin Iron Works. Within Maine, a state almost as big as all of the other New England states combined, the geologic variations in the structure of the underlying rocks have created a landscape that is both interesting and inviting to outdoor explorers.

Two events in geologic history have had the greatest impact on Maine's topography. The first, some 350 to 400 million years ago, was the collision of the North American and European tectonic plates. The impact caused the plates to buckle, creating huge mountain ranges. In some places, molten rock was forced upward by heat and pressure, and volcanoes were formed. This uplift of the crust caused rivers to run more quickly and to erode the landscape at a faster rate. The previously flat land was gradually carved into a series of sharp valleys. Slowly, the European and North American plates began drifting apart, and the Atlantic Ocean was formed.

Since then, nine cycles of glacial advance and withdrawal not only carved deeper valleys but rounded off the hills and mountain peaks. Deposits of sand and gravel left by the last retreating glacier changed the drainage of the land, leading to the formation of lakes and ponds. Water from the melting glacier drained toward the ocean, flooding the valleys and lowlands. The resulting coastline, which is often referred to as the drowned coast, is dotted with thousands of islands. The underlying topography of the state is therefore largely a product of glacial sculpting. The landscape that has evolved since that time is a mosaic of medium-sized mountains, wide river valleys, abundant forests, and rocky coastline that reflects not only its geologic past but also its subsequent human occupation. It is a landscape that betrays the history of its settlement and use from the time of its first inhabitants.

THE PEOPLE AND CHANGES IN THE LAND

Native Americans occupied the land that is now Maine as soon as the glaciers receded, some ten to twelve thousand years ago. The first known inhabitants of the area were the early Native Americans known as the Red Paint People, so called because their burial sites all contained deposits of red ochre paint. Huge piles of oyster and clam shells, evidence of another group of people referred to as the Oyster Shell People, have been uncovered on the coast. Very little is known about these early inhabitants, but it is thought that they summered on the coast and moved inland for the winter. Their successors were the Abenakis, or "people of the dawn," a branch of the Algonquin Nation that included four tribes: the Androscoggins, Kennebecs, Penobscots, and Passamaquoddies. They carried on the seasonal way of life of the Oyster Shell People, gathering berries and fishing on the coast in the summer and moving inland for the winter to hunt and trap and to fish in the lakes and rivers.

In the sixteenth century, explorers from Europe traveled west looking for Norumbega, a mythical land of riches. The first European documented to have landed was John Cabot (Giovanni Caboto), an Italian mariner whose explorations in the service of King Henry VII of England were part of the European effort to find passage to the Indies. Eight years later, in 1534, Jacques Cartier claimed land on the Gaspé peninsula of present-day Quebec for the French. Although it was roughly 60 years later that the first settlements were attempted, the French and the English were to remain the key players in the colonization of this part of the New World.

Colonization was to have a huge impact on the landscape of much of New England. Where the Native Americans had developed a harmonious relationship with the land, carefully harvesting its bounty to ensure the continuity of the resources they depended upon, the early Europeans regarded the area and its seeming abundance as a commodity to be manipulated for profit. Not only were the natural resources of the area used to sustain the colonists who moved to the region, but fish, lumber, and many other resources were exported and traded on a worldwide market. The European relationship to the land was also governed by a lifestyle that was fundamentally rooted in permanent settlement and almost wholly dependent upon agriculture. Gradually, the colonists worked to order and cultivate the savage wilderness that they saw the land to be. The natural balance of the landscape was severely altered as land was cleared, as property lines were established, and as stone fences were constructed to clear fields of rocks and to provide enclosures for livestock.

The transition of the land from forest to cultivated field interfered with the way of life of the indigenous peoples. The Native Americans, who had not lived on the land according to the rules of ownership, were forced from the places they had depended upon for food. In the conflicts that erupted between them and the European settlers, the Native Americans eventually fell prey to epidemics brought from Europe and suffered huge losses in the hostilities that raged from 1675 to 1763 between the French and the English.

With British dominance established in New England after the French and Indian War, the number of colonists on the coast increased. The successful development of Maine was closely linked to the land's availing natural features: The seemingly endless forest provided lumber for trade and the construction of houses; the fisheries off the coast were a rich source of food; and the many rivers and streams provided abundant sites for waterpower and encouraged the construction of mills. However, increasing prosperity also changed the relationship between the colonists and their mother country. Under the reign of George III, Britain began to pursue the taxation of the colonies with vigor. The colonists, who had no representation in Parliament, resisted and finally revolted.

Maine prospered after the Revolutionary War, becoming the primary producer of lumber and wood products in the country. In 1820 Maine became the 23rd state to join the Union, and in the mid-1850s it was known as the wooden shipbuilding capital of the United States. As the world market for timber decreased, the pulp and paper industry developed as a more economically viable business. Railroads contributed to the rise in industries like granite quarrying, iron and copper mining, ice harvesting, and potato growing in Aroostook County. Gradually, from an economy dependent upon agriculture and fishing, Maine industrialized. Today, the state is more densely forested than it was at the time of the Civil War, and evidence of the abandoned farms of the early communities can be found deep in the woods. On many of the rides in this book, traces of once-prosperous industries can be seen at old quarry sites and mining pits, and along old railroad routes. They remain as a testament to the many and varied uses of the land, and reminders for all of us that respect for the land we ride over is the first step to its preservation.

Mount Agamenticus features a variety of challenging terrain.

FLORA AND FAUNA

Much of the land that was cleared in Maine in the nineteenth century has since returned to forest. Today, forests cover 90 percent of the state. Although there are 76 species of trees represented in the Maine woods, softwoods like white pine, balsam fir, spruce, and hemlock account for most of the forested land. In the fall, however, it is the colorful foliage of the hardwoods (birch, oak, maple, and beech) situated on the high ridges that draws thousands of "leaf peepers" to the state.

The woods provide a sheltered habitat for a variety of plant life. Many ferns, flowers, and mushrooms thrive in the northern climate. Much of Maine's wildlife also finds its home in the forest and includes white-tailed deer, racoons, woodchucks, rabbits, squirrels, porcupines, and more than 20,000 black bears. Despite their numbers, it is not all that common to see a bear in the Maine woods. Black bears are shy creatures, primarily vegetarian, and usually react to humans in the wilderness by quickly disappearing. More common are the pheasants and grouse that inhabit areas of dense undergrowth. It is quite likely that you will startle many of these birds on your rides.

In addition to its forests, Maine boasts thousands of lakes and ponds, and miles of rivers and streams. Waterfowl is common in these areas and includes the common loon, well known for its impressive diving and fishing skills as well as its eerie, haunting cries. On the fringe of these areas are the bogs and wetlands, literally teeming with a variety of plant and animal life. The Maine state animal is the moose, which is often seen on the densely wooded shores of lakes and ponds. Beavers, perhaps the most common of the local animals, are inhabitants of small ponds and streams. Their lodges are impressive constructions, as are their dams, which often cause flooding across low-lying trails.

The Down East coast is dominated by blueberry barrens, which produce 98 percent of the low-bush blueberries in the country. Aroostook County's claim to fame is the potato, and in the summer white and purple potato-plant blossoms cover tens of thousands of acres.

SPECIAL ISSUES AND TIPS FOR SAFE, ENJOYABLE RIDING

Weather: Maine is recognized for being one of the most healthful states in the nation. Summer temperatures average a pleasant 70° F and winter temperatures a tolerable 20° F. Despite these agreeable averages, the weather in Maine is best described by a well-known northern New England saying: If you don't like the weather, wait an hour. Indeed, the weather follows patterns as changeable as the seasons. Spring is a season that teases: warm temperatures one day can be followed by bitter cold the next. For riders, spring is a fine time for connoisseurs of mud. The combination of thawing ground and frequent rainfall creates soggy conditions and mud of a variety of consistencies and depths. Many trails are best left to dry out at this time of year, so that deep rutting in the soft ground doesn't result in their long-term deterioration. Rail trails, of which Maine has many, are usually well drained and offer great spring riding. Rides along these abandoned railroad beds make for excellent preseason training, along routes with relatively little change in elevation.

Spring and summer are often bridged by bug season, when the rainfall of late spring and the warmer temperatures of early summer conspire to produce huge populations of biting insects. At the same time, the gradual leafing-out of the trees and first warm temperatures of the year draw people to the trails. Gradually, temperatures climb and days lengthen. Summer temperatures in Maine can rise above 90° F, and humidity levels can become as stifling as the crowds of summer visitors. Thunderstorms are more prevalent in the summer, particularly in the mountains. The Down East Coast and Aroostook County beckon at this time of year, offering both cooler temperatures and fewer tourists.

Autumn is probably the finest season Maine has to offer to mountain bikers. Cooler temperatures and fewer insects combine with the splendid show of fall foliage to create truly exhilarating days. The western mountains are a popular destination at this time of year, where the stunning blue of the lakes reflects mountainsides festive with the red, yellow, and orange hues of changing fall foliage. Down East, the blueberry barrens in the state rival even the maples and turn the countryside into a carpet of brilliant scarlet.

By November the last leaves drop to the ground and the contours of the land are once again revealed in drab shades of brown and gray. Shorter days curtail evening rides, except for those riders who don headlights and equip their bikes with lamps. By the end of December snow is in the air and on the ground. Winter does not necessarily mark the end of the biking season, however. Hundreds of miles of snowmobile trails can be easily explored with the addition of studded tires and layers of warm clothing. Riders should prepare for winter riding with care, as cold temperatures, windchill, and fewer hours of daylight create conditions that can become dangerous. Extra clothing is a necessity, as are plenty of food and water.

Fording Rivers: Several rides included in this guidebook require that you ford a river or a stream. Safe river crossings involve picking the right time and the right place and using the proper technique. It is not always safe to ford a river or a stream, particularly in spring or after a heavy rainfall. Always turn back and choose an alternative route if the water level is higher than your thighs or, in swift water, when the water reaches your knees. A few simple strategies can make fording a river a safer task:

Don't necessarily cross at the narrowest point on the river; water usually runs more slowly and is shallowest at the widest parts of the river.

Never remove your shoes, as you can easily break an ankle or a foot if you slip.

Remove only your socks before wading in, especially in cooler temperatures, so that you have something dry to put on your feet for the rest of the ride.

Face slightly downstream and move diagonally in that direction.

Carry your bike in such a way that you can easily release it in the event you slip and fall.

Always plant both feet firmly before taking your next step.

Look ahead at the bank you are moving toward — not down at the rushing water.

Equestrian Encounters: As a cyclist, you must always yield to horses and their riders. This is fairly easy when they approach you from the opposite direction; you just stop and pull off the trail to give them space to pass by. It is important to stop riding in these cases, even when the road or trail you are on is wide enough for both of you. But what about when you're coming up behind them? We have learned, through trial and error, that when approaching horses and riders from behind it is always best to call out to both the rider and the horse. Make sure both creatures know you're coming before you proceed. Horses can be spooked by shiny metal bikes, and a soft, reassuring word will usually quell their fears.

Hunting Season: The primary hunting season in Maine runs from September to November, depending on the game species. All hunting is prohibited on Sundays. For up-to-date information on specific opening and closing dates, contact:

Maine Department of Inland Fisheries and Wildlife
41 State House Station
Augusta, ME 04333-0041
(207) 287-8000

The Department also has a 24-hour recording that provides up-to-the-minute information on hunting in Maine. Phone (207) 287-8003.

As a rider, sharing the woods with hunters can be a frightening prospect. At the same time, the primary hunting season in Maine coincides with some of the best and most beautiful riding conditions. Despite the fact that your actual risk of injury is extremely slight, a few simple precautions can further lessen the chance that you will be mistaken for a deer: Make plenty of noise as you ride; deck yourself out in as much blaze-orange gear as you can get your hands on (our collection includes helmet covers, ankle reflectors, vests, and gloves); and avoid wearing anything white. Luckily, most riding apparel is designed with high visibility in mind.

Bugs: In setting out on a ride, being prepared for biting insects is the first step in accepting that you will be sharing the woods with them. On a bike, chances are good that you will be moving along quickly enough to avoid getting bitten. However, chances are also good that, at some point, you'll need to stop and take a break or (agony) stop to wait for someone in your group. Along with the traditional repellents designed to ward off vicious attacks, there are a growing number of natural and herbal concoctions designed to deter insects. Most products are readily available at local general stores. Also, evidence points to black flies and mosquitos being attracted to dark colors. Choose white or light-colored clothing, which will also facilitate the detection of ticks.

In Maine, mosquitos, black flies, and midges (no-see-ums) can be fierce in May and June, especially after a wet spring. Although ticks are not as common in Maine as they are in states farther south, they do seem to be increasing in numbers. Wood ticks, most common in areas of tall grass, are relatively large in size (about the size of lentils) and slow to attach themselves to a host. Usually you will be able to pick them off your skin or clothing after a ride. Deer ticks can be more of a problem. They can be as small as the head of a pin and are therefore much more difficult to detect. Deer ticks, if they bite and stay attached for an extended period of time, can transmit Lyme disease. Symptoms of the disease include fatigued joints, fever, headache, muscle soreness, and vomiting. Often, a ringed rash will develop around the bite. If you experience these symptoms, seek medical attention. Antibiotics are an effective treatment against the disease that, if left untreated, can cause serious health problems.

Food and Water: Whenever you head out for a ride, carry more food and water than you think you will need. There is only one feeling better than being able to offer a depleted cyclist a granola bar or a gulp of water, and that is actually receiving the favor yourself. The fact is, no matter how fit you are, your body is going to need refueling at some point along the ride. Although many of the rides in this guidebook cross or pass by brooks and streams, all water should be filtered and treated before consuming. If you ride in the winter, fill your water bottles with warm water, so that it doesn't freeze. In cold temperatures, many people neglect to properly hydrate themselves. Your body will not be able to function properly and stay warm without adequate amounts of food and water.

Map and Compass: Don't wait until you're lost to learn how to use these tools! Mountain biking and mountain bike trails are full of surprises: The stream you intended to cross may be too high to ford; a beaver dam may have flooded a trail and made it impassable; or logging operations may have eliminated trails or created new ones. The fact is, you never know when you may need to choose an alternative route home. The most useful maps, and the ones that we refer to in this book, are the 7.5 minute series USGS (United States Geological Survey) topographic maps. With a topographic map and a compass you will be able to pinpoint your position and make your way to a chosen destination. The topographic map will also provide you with crucial information on just how difficult the trip might be. Plus, both tools are relatively inexpensive, small, lightweight, and easy to pack. Note that the compass declination in Maine is approximately 18° west. This means that true north (map north) is 18° clockwise from the compass needle.

The DeLorme Mapping Company, based in Yarmouth, Maine, is an excellent source for all topographic maps we refer to in this book. In addition, DeLorme publishes a book of maps called the *Maine Atlas and Gazetteer.* Many of the trails we have described are included in the *Gazetteer,* which is also an extremely useful aid in finding the trailheads. The DeLorme Mapping Company is located on ME 1 in Yarmouth, directly across from a Tourist Information Center. Requests for the *Maine Atlas and Gazetteer* or any topographic map can be addressed to:

DeLorme
P.O. Box 298
Yarmouth, ME 04096
(207) 846-7000

New technology has recently provided cyclists with an alternative to the map and compass system of navigation. The Global Positioning System (GPS) involves a hand-held or bike-mounted device that allows users to find their exact location, within 300 feet or so, by displaying their precise latitude and longitude. For cyclists, this system can be used as an electronic compass. You take a reading, plot it on your map, and presto! You know exactly where you are. You can also program a ride into the unit, which will then indicate when you veer from your intended route. Even for those riders willing to make the investment in a GPS unit, however, a compass is still the best way to determine direction.

Family rides: Mountain biking is something almost everybody can do. As a result, more and more families are planning day trips and biking vacations. We have included several rides in this guidebook that will particularly appeal to groups in which a combination of abilities is represented. These rides are characterized by terrain that requires little or no technical skill and only a moderate level of fitness. Many of these rides are out-and-back affairs, allowing riders to turn back at any time. Several of the rides also feature good picnicking sites or points of interest on the way.

For a list of rides we recommend for families or groups of riders of mixed abilities and fitness levels, see page xxviii in the Ride Recommendations for Special Interests section. In addition to these rides, there are good family and group rides to be enjoyed at Acadia National Park and Moosehorn National Wildlife Refuge. In southern Maine, Back Country Excursions of Maine offers guided tours for all ages and abilities. For further information, contact:

Back Country Excursions of Maine
RFD 2, Box 365
Limerick, ME 04048
(207) 625-8189

Land-Use Controversy: Although Maine covers an area almost as large as the other five New England states combined, the state has one of the smallest percentages of publicly owned land in the country. As a result, issues of land access and use are very real concerns, particularly as Maine has relatively few established trails for mountain bikers. It is not without some hesitation that we have included several of our favorite discoveries and rides in this guidebook, for fear that they will one day fall into the category of rides that have been closed due to overuse or abuse. At the same time, it is not without a great deal of regret that we have chosen not to include other, more well-known destinations either because of restricted access or because they have become sites of contentious debate. We have tried to identify routes that, to the best of our knowledge, traverse areas where public access is allowed. These areas include public land, public right-of-ways, and places where access is implied by virtue of heavy use by mountain bikers, all-terrain vehicle riders, and snowmobilers. The risk we run in publishing some of these rides is not that hundreds more riders will head out to enjoy them (we hope they will), but that some riders will act irresponsibly, offend landowners or other trail users, ride in a destructive manner, and ultimately force the closure of such trails to all mountain bikers.

In Maine, the Snowmobile Association has worked hard to create and maintain literally hundreds of miles of trails for snowmobiles. This group and the network of trails they have successfully managed are an inspiration for mountain bike riders. If we want to continue riding in Maine, we must contribute in some way to the maintenance of the areas in which we ride. If you are interested in becoming more involved with the development of off-road cycling in your area, contact your local bike store or get in touch with the Bicycle Coalition of Maine, an organization advocating bicycling safety, education, and access throughout the state. You can contact the Bicycle Coalition of Maine by phone at (207) 288-3028 or by mail at PO Box 654, Bar Harbor, ME 04609. We urge you to help us and all the advocates for Maine's land to protect these rides from abuse and guarantee their use for years to come.

Here's wishing you safe and happy trails!

Sarah L. Hale and David Gibbs

Family

17 Hebron-to-Canton Rail Trail
22 Evergreen Valley
38 Bigelow Preserve
42 Solon-to-Bingham Rail Trail
60 Kenduskeag Stream Park Trail
    (first 2.25 miles)
62 Penobscot Experimental Forest
65 South Lagrange–to-Medford
    Rail Trail
67 Paradise Hill
71 Edmunds Township
72 Goodall Heath–to–Barn
    Meadow
73 Snare Meadow

Novice & Beginner

12 Fryeburg (first, 5-mile loop)
17 Hebron-to-Canton Rail Trail
18 Androscoggin River Trail
    (first 4 miles)
22 Evergreen Valley
27 Sunday River Mountain Bike
    Park (beginner trails)
34 Rangeley Lake
35 Sugarloaf/USA (beginner trails)
38 Bigelow Preserve
39 Summerhaven Use Area
42 Solon-to-Bingham Rail Trail
43 Greenville Junction–to–Shirley
    Mills Rail Trail
45 Mount Kineo
46 Attean Township Logging
    Roads
55 Isle au Haut
57 Monroe
60 Kenduskeag Stream Park Trail
62 Penobscot Experimental Forest
64 Corinna-to–Dover-Foxcroft
    Rail Trail
65 South Lagrange–to-Medford
    Rail Trail
67 Paradise Hill
68 The Heart of Acadia
71 Edmunds Township
72 Goodall Heath–to–Barn
    Meadow
73 Snare Meadow
74 Houlton-to–Phair Junction
    Rail Trail
76 Van Buren–to-Stockholm Rail
    Trail (as a point-to-point)

Intermediate

1   Mount Agamenticus
2   Hinckley Park
3   Atherton Hill
4   Bruce Hill
5   Bradbury Mountain State Park
9   Wiggin Mountain
10 Porterfield
11 Boston Hills
12 Fryeburg (second, 8-mile loop)
14 Mount Apatite
15 Lost Valley
19 Bear Mountain
20 Waterford
21 Cold River Valley
24 Virginia Lake
26 Mount Abram Valley
27 Sunday River Mountain Bike
    Park (intermediate trails)
35 Sugarloaf/USA (intermediate
    trails)
36 Poplar Stream
37 Carrabassett River Trail
40 Vienna Mountain
47 Rancourt Pond
48 Sandy Bay Loop
51 Camden Hills State Park
53 Appleton Ridge
54 Frye Mountain
56 Mount Waldo
58 Common Hill
59 Dixmont Hills
61 Caribou Bog
63 University Woods
66 Baxter Perimeter Road

(continued)

RIDE RECOMMENDATIONS FOR SPECIAL INTERESTS (*continued*)

69 Schoodic Mountain
70 Donnell Pond

76 Van Buren–to-Stockholm
   Rail Trail (as an out-and-back)

Advanced

13 Shawnee Peak
16 Streaked Mountain
23 Albany Mountain
25 Highwater Trail
27 Sunday River Mountain
   Bike Park (expert trails)

29 Little Blue Mountain
35 Sugarloaf/USA (expert trails)
41 Waterville Ridge Loops
44 Little Squaw Mountain
50 Camden Snow Bowl
56 Mount Waldo (summit climb)

Loops

2 Hinckley Park
4 Bruce Hill
6 North Hollis Loop
7 Killick Pond
9 Wiggin Mountain
10 Porterfield
16 Streaked Mountain
20 Waterford
21 Cold River Valley
23 Albany Mountain
24 Virginia Lake
29 Little Blue Mountain
30 Center Hill
32 Troll Valley
33 Wire Bridge
34 Rangeley Lake
37 Carrabassett River Trail
39 Summerhaven Use Area
41 Waterville Ridge Loops
44 Little Squaw Mountain

47 Rancourt Pond
48 Sandy Bay Loop
49 Pleasant Mountain
50 Camden Snow Bowl
52 Hope
53 Appleton Ridge
54 Frye Mountain
55 Isle au Haut
56 Mount Waldo
57 Monroe
61 Caribou Bog
63 University Woods
67 Paradise Hill
68 The Heart of Acadia
71 Edmunds Township
72 Goodall Heath–to–Barn
   Meadow
73 Snare Meadow
75 Aroostook Valley Trail

Out-and-Backs

11 Boston Hills (paved loop option)
14 Mount Apatite (paved loop option)
17 Hebron-to-Canton Rail Trail
18 Androscoggin River Trail (paved
   loop option)
19 Bear Mountain (paved loop option)
22 Evergreen Valley
25 Highwater Trail (dirt and paved
   road loop option)
28 Sawyer Notch

31 West Farmington–to-Jay Rail Trail
36 Poplar Stream
38 Bigelow Preserve
40 Vienna Mountain (paved loop
   option)
42 Solon-to-Bingham Rail Trail
43 Greenville Junction–to–Shirley
   Mills Rail Trail
46 Attean Township Logging Roads

(*continued*)

RIDE RECOMMENDATIONS FOR SPECIAL INTERESTS (*continued*)

51 Camden Hills State Park
60 Kenduskeag Stream Park Trail
62 Penobscot Experimental Forest
65 South Lagrange–to-Medford
    Rail Trail

69 Schoodic Mountain
70 Donnell Pond
76 Van Buren–to-Stockholm Rail
    Trail

Point-to-Points

26 Mount Abram Valley
64 Corinna-to–Dover-Foxcroft
    Rail Trail

66 Baxter Perimeter Road
74 Houlton-to–Phair Junction
    Rail Trail

Multiday Tours

46 Attean Township Logging Roads
66 Baxter Perimeter Road

75 Aroostook Valley Trail

Wildlife Viewing

17 Hebron-to-Canton Rail Trail
22 Evergreen Valley
44 Little Squaw Mountain
46 Attean Township Logging Roads
47 Rancourt Pond
70 Donnell Pond

71 Edmunds Township
72 Goodall Heath–to–Barn Meadow
73 Snare Meadow
75 Aroostook Valley Trail
76 Van Buren–to-Stockholm Rail
    Trail

Great Scenery

13 Shawnee Peak
16 Streaked Mountain
18 Androscoggin River Trail
21 Cold River Valley
22 Evergreen Valley
23 Albany Mountain
24 Virginia Lake
25 Highwater Trail
26 Mount Abram Valley
27 Sunday River Mountain Bike Park
29 Little Blue Mountain

34 Rangeley Lake
35 Sugarloaf/USA
37 Carrabassett River Trail
40 Vienna Mountain
42 Solon-to-Bingham Rail Trail
44 Little Squaw Mountain
55 Isle au Haut
66 Baxter Perimeter Road
67 Paradise Hill
68 The Heart of Acadia
70 Donnell Pond

Single-Track

2 Hinckley Park
5 Bradbury Mountain State Park
15 Lost Valley
18 Androscoggin River Trail
    (2-mile section)
21 Cold River Valley (sections)
23 Albany Mountain (4 miles)
25 Highwater Trail
29 Little Blue Mountain

35 Sugarloaf/USA
41 Waterville Ridge Loops
50 Camden Snow Bowl
51 Camden Hills State Park
    (Summer Bypass Trail)
61 Caribou Bog (sections)
63 University Woods
70 Donnell Pond

MOUNTAIN BIKE!
Maine

INTRODUCTION

Each trail in this book begins with key information that includes length, configuration, aerobic and technical difficulty, trail conditions, scenery, and special comments. Additional description is contained in 11 individual categories. The following will help you to understand all of the information provided.

Trail name: Trail names are as designated on United States Geological Survey (USGS) or Forest Service or other maps, and/or by local custom.

At a Glance Information

Length/configuration: The overall length of a trail is described in miles, unless stated otherwise. The configuration is a description of the shape of each trail—whether the trail is a loop, out-and-back (that is, along the same route), figure eight, trapezoid, isosceles triangle, decahedron . . . (just kidding), or if it connects with another trail described in the book. See the Glossary for definitions of *point-to-point* and *combination*.

Aerobic difficulty: This provides a description of the degree of physical exertion required to complete the ride.

Technical difficulty: This provides a description of the technical skill required to pedal a ride. Trails are often described here in terms of being paved, unpaved, sandy, hard-packed, washboarded, two- or four-wheel-drive, single-track or double-track. All terms that might be unfamiliar to the first-time mountain biker are defined in the Glossary.

For both the aerobic and technical difficulty categories, authors were asked to keep in mind the fact that all riders are not equal, and thus to gauge the trail in terms of how the middle-of-the-road rider—someone between the newcomer and Ned Overend—could handle the route. Comments about the trail's length, condition, and elevation change will also assist you in determining the difficulty of any trail relative to your own abilities.

Scenery: Here you will find a general description of the natural surroundings during the seasons most riders pedal the trail, and a suggestion of what is to be found at special times (like great fall foliage or cactus in bloom).

Special comments: Unique elements of the ride are mentioned.

Category Information

General location: This category describes where the trail is located in reference to a nearby town or other landmark.

Elevation change: Unless stated otherwise, the figure provided is the total gain and loss of elevation along the trail. In regions where the elevation variation is not extreme, the route is simply described as flat, rolling, or possessing short steep climbs or descents.

Season: This is the best time of year to pedal the route, taking into account trail conditions (for example, when it will not be muddy), riding comfort (when the weather is too hot, cold, or wet), and local hunting seasons.

Note: Because the exact opening and closing dates of deer, elk, moose, and antelope seasons often change from year to year, riders should check with the local Fish and Game department, or call a sporting goods store (or any place that sells hunting licenses) in a nearby town before heading out. Wear bright clothes in fall, and don't wear suede jackets while in the saddle. Hunter's-orange tape on the helmet is also a good idea.

Services: This category is of primary importance in guides for paved-road tourers, but is far less crucial to most mountain bike trail descriptions because there are usually no services whatsoever to be found. Authors have noted when water is available on desert or long mountain routes, and have listed the availability of food, lodging, campgrounds, and bike shops. If all these services are present, you will find only the words "All services available in . . ."

Hazards: Special hazards like steep cliffs, great amounts of deadfall, or barbed-wire fences very close to the trail are noted here.

Rescue index: Determining how far one is from help on any particular trail can be difficult due to the backcountry nature of most mountain bike rides. Authors therefore state the proximity of homes or Forest Service outposts, nearby roads where one might hitch a ride, or the likelihood of other bikers being encountered on the trail. Phone numbers of local sheriff departments or hospitals have not been provided because phones are almost never available. If you are able to reach a phone, the local operator will connect you with emergency services.

Land status: This category provides information regarding whether the trail crosses land operated by the Forest Service, Bureau of Land Management, a city, state, or national park, whether it crosses private land whose owner (at the time the author did the research) has allowed mountain bikers right of passage, and so on.

Note: Authors have been extremely careful to offer only those routes that are open to bikers and are legal to ride. However, because land ownership changes over time, and because the land-use controversy created by mountain bikes still has not completely subsided, it is the duty of each cyclist to look for and to heed signs warning against trail use. Don't expect this book to get you off the hook when you're facing some small-town judge for pedaling past a "Biking Prohibited" sign erected the day before you arrived. Look for these signs, read them, and heed the advice. And remember there's always another trail.

Maps: The maps in this book have been produced with great care, and, in conjunction with the trail-following suggestions, will help you stay on course. But as every experienced mountain biker knows, things can get tricky in the backcountry. It is therefore strongly suggested that you avail yourself of the detailed information found in the 7.5 minute series USGS (United States Geological Survey) topographic maps. In some cases, authors have found that specific Forest Service or other maps may be more useful than the USGS quads, and tell how to obtain them.

Finding the trail: Detailed information on how to reach the trailhead, and where to park your car, is provided here.

Sources of additional information: Here you will find the address and/or phone number of a bike shop, governmental agency, or other source from which trail information can be obtained.

Notes on the trail: This is where you are guided carefully through any portions of the trail that are particularly difficult to follow. The author also may add information about the route that does not fit easily in the other categories. This category will not be present for those rides where the route is easy to follow.

ABBREVIATIONS

The following road-designation abbreviations are used in the *America by Mountain Bike* series:

CR   County Road
FR   Forest Service road

I-   Interstate
IR   Indian Route
US   United States highway

State highways are designated with the appropriate two-letter state abbreviation, followed by the road number. Example: ME 117 = Maine State Highway 117.

Postal Service two-letter state codes:

AL	Alabama	MT	Montana
AK	Alaska	NE	Nebraska
AZ	Arizona	NV	Nevada
AR	Arkansas	NH	New Hampshire
CA	California	NJ	New Jersey
CO	Colorado	NM	New Mexico
CT	Connecticut	NY	New York
DE	Delaware	NC	North Carolina
DC	District of Columbia	ND	North Dakota
FL	Florida	OH	Ohio
GA	Georgia	OK	Oklahoma
HI	Hawaii	OR	Oregon
ID	Idaho	PA	Pennsylvania
IL	Illinois	RI	Rhode Island
IN	Indiana	SC	South Carolina
IA	Iowa	SD	South Dakota
KS	Kansas	TN	Tennessee
KY	Kentucky	TX	Texas
LA	Louisiana	UT	Utah
ME	Maine	VT	Vermont
MD	Maryland	VA	Virginia
MA	Massachusetts	WA	Washington
MI	Michigan	WV	West Virginia
MN	Minnesota	WI	Wisconsin
MS	Mississippi	WY	Wyoming
MO	Missouri		

TOPOGRAPHIC MAPS

The maps in this book, when used in conjunction with the route directions present in each chapter, will in most instances be sufficient to get you to the trail and keep you on it. However, you will find superior detail and valuable information in the 7.5 minute series United States Geological Survey (USGS) topographic maps. Recognizing how indispensable these are to bikers and hikers alike, many bike shops and sporting goods stores now carry topos of the local area.

But if you're brand new to mountain biking you might be wondering "What's a topographic map?" In short, these differ from standard "flat" maps in that they indicate not only linear distance, but elevation as well. One glance at a "topo" will show you the difference, for "contour lines" are spread across the map like dozens of intricate spider webs. Each contour line represents a particular elevation, and at the base of each topo a particular "contour interval" designation is given. Yes, it sounds confusing if you're new to the lingo, but it truly is a simple and wonderfully helpful system. Keep reading.

Let's assume that the 7.5 minute series topo before us says "Contour Interval 40 feet," that the short trail we'll be pedaling is two inches in length on the map, and that it crosses five contour lines from its beginning to end. What do we know? Well, because the linear scale of this series is 2,000 feet to the inch (roughly 2 ¾ inches representing 1 mile), we know our trail is approximately ⅖ of a mile long (2 inches × 2,000 feet). But we also know we'll be climbing or descending 200 vertical feet (5 contour lines × 40 feet each) over that distance. And the elevation designations written on occasional contour lines will tell us if we're heading up or down.

The authors of this series warn their readers of upcoming terrain, but only a detailed topo gives you the information you need to pinpoint your position exactly on a map, steer yourself toward optional trails and roads nearby, plus let you know at a glance if you'll be pedaling hard to take them. It's a lot of information for a very low cost. In fact, the only drawback with topos is their size—several feet square. I've tried rolling them into tubes, folding them carefully, even cutting them into blocks and photocopying the pieces. Any of these systems is a pain, but no matter how you pack the maps you'll be happy they're along. And you'll be even happier if you pack a compass as well.

In addition to local bike shops and sporting goods stores, you'll find topos at major universities and some public libraries where you might try photocopying the ones you need to avoid the cost of buying them. But if you want your own and can't find them locally, write to:

USGS Map Sales
Box 25286
Denver, CO 80225

Ask for an index while you're at it, plus a price list and a copy of the booklet *Topographic Maps*. In minutes you'll be reading them like a pro.

A second excellent series of maps available to mountain bikers is that put out by the United States Forest Service. If your trail runs through an area designated as a national forest, look in the phone book (white pages) under the United States Government listings, find the Department of Agriculture heading, and then run you finger down that section until you find the Forest Service. Give them a call and they'll provide the address of the regional Forest Service office, from which you can obtain the appropriate map.

TRAIL ETIQUETTE

Pick up almost any mountain bike magazine these days and you'll find articles and letters to the editor about trail conflict. For example, you'll find hikers' tales of being blindsided by speeding mountain bikers, complaints from mountain bikers about being blamed for trail damage that was really caused by horse or cattle traffic, and cries from bikers about those "kamikaze" riders who through their antics threaten to close even more trails to all of us.

The authors of this series have been very careful to guide you to only those trails that are open to mountain biking (or at least were open at the time of their research), and without exception have warned of the damage done to our sport through injudicious riding. My personal views on this matter appear in the Afterword, but all of us can benefit from glancing over the following International Mountain Bicycling Association (IMBA) Rules of the Trail before saddling up.

1. *Ride on open trails only.* Respect trail and road closures (ask if not sure), avoid possible trespass on private land, obtain permits and authorization as may be required. Federal and State wilderness areas are closed to cycling.
2. *Leave no trace.* Be sensitive to the dirt beneath you. Even on open trails, you should not ride under conditions where you will leave evidence of your passing, such as on certain soils shortly after rain. Observe the different types of soils and trail construction; practice low-impact cycling. This also means staying on the trail and not creating any new ones. Be sure to pack out at least as much as you pack in.
3. *Control your bicycle!* Inattention for even a second can cause disaster. Excessive speed can maim and threaten people; there is no excuse for it!
4. *Always yield the trail.* Make known your approach well in advance. A friendly greeting (or a bell) is considerate and works well; startling someone may cause loss of trail access. Show your respect when passing others by slowing to a walk or even stopping. Anticipate that other trail users may be around corners or in blind spots.
5. *Never spook animals.* All animals are startled by an unannounced approach, a sudden movement, or a loud noise. This can be dangerous for you, for others, and for the animals. Give animals extra room and time to adjust to you. In passing, use special care and follow the directions of horseback riders (ask if uncertain). Running cattle and disturbing wild animals is a serious offense. Leave gates as you found them, or as marked.
6. *Plan ahead.* Know your equipment, your ability, and the area in which you are riding—and prepare accordingly. Be self-sufficient at all times. Wear a helmet,

keep your machine in good condition, and carry necessary supplies for changes in weather or other conditions. A well-executed trip is a satisfaction to you and not a burden or offense to others.

For more information, contact IMBA, P.O. Box 7578, Boulder, CO 80306, (303) 545-9011.

HITTING THE TRAIL

Once again, because this is a "where-to," not a "how-to" guide, the following will be brief. If you're a veteran trail rider these suggestions might serve to remind you of something you've forgotten to pack. If you're a newcomer, they might convince you to think twice before hitting the backcountry unprepared.

Water: I've heard the questions dozens of times. "How much is enough? One bottle? Two? Three?! But think of all that extra weight!" Well, one simple physiological fact should convince you to err on the side of excess when it comes to deciding how much water to pack: a human working hard in 90-degree temperature needs approximately ten quarts of fluids every day. Ten quarts. That's two and a half gallons—12 large water bottles, or 16 small ones. And, with water weighing in at approximately eight pounds per gallon, a one-day supply comes to a whopping 20 pounds.

In other words, pack along two or three bottles even for short rides. And make sure you can purify the water found along the trail on longer routes. When writing of those routes where this could be of critical importance, each author has provided information on where water can be found near the trail—if it can be found at all. But drink it untreated and you run the risk of disease. (See *Giardia* in the Glossary.)

One sure way to kill the protozoans, bacteria, and viruses in water is to boil it. Right. That's just how you want to spend your time on a bike ride. Besides, who wants to carry a stove, or denude the countryside stoking bonfires to boil water?

Luckily, there is a better way. Many riders pack along the inexpensive and only slightly distasteful tetraglycine hydroperiodide tablets (sold under the names Potable Aqua, Globaline, and Coughlan's, among others). Some invest in portable, lightweight purifiers that filter out the crud. Unfortunately, both iodine *and* filtering are now required to be absolutely sure you've killed all the nasties you can't see. Tablets or iodine drops by themselves will knock off the well-known *Giardia*, once called "beaver fever" for its transmission to the water through the feces of infected beavers. One to four weeks after ingestion, giardia will have you bloated, vomiting, shivering with chills, and living in the bathroom. (Though you won't care while you're suffering, beavers are getting a bum rap, for other animals are carriers also.)

But now there's another parasite we must worry about—*Cryptosporidium.* "Crypto" brings on symptoms very similar to *giardia,* but unlike that fellow protozoan it's equipped with a shell sufficiently strong to protect it against the chemical killers that stop *giardia* cold. This means we're either back to boiling or on to using a water filter to screen out both *giardia* and crypto, plus the iodine to knock off viruses. All of which sounds like a time-consuming pain, but really isn't. Some water filters come equipped with an iodine chamber, to guarantee full protection. Or you can simply add a pill or drops to the water you've just filtered (if you aren't allergic to iodine, of course). The pleasures of backcountry biking—and the displeasure of getting sick—make this relatively minor effort worth every one of the few minutes involved.

Tools: Ever since my first cross-country tour in 1965 I've been kidded about the number of tools I pack on the trail. And so I will exit entirely from this discussion by providing a list compiled by two mechanic (and mountain biker) friends of mine. After all, since they make their livings fixing bikes, and get their kicks by riding them, who could be a better source?

These two suggest the following as an absolute minimum:

tire levers
spare tube and patch kit
air pump
Allen wrenches (3, 4, 5, and 6 mm)
six-inch crescent (adjustable-end) wrench
small flat-blade screwdriver
chain rivet tool
spoke wrench

But, while they're on the trail, their personal tool pouches contain these additional items:

channel locks (small)
air gauge
tire valve cap (the metal kind, with a valve-stem remover)
baling wire (ten or so inches, for temporary repairs)
duct tape (small roll for temporary repairs or tire boot)
boot material (small piece of old tire or a large tube patch)
spare chain link
rear derailleur pulley
spare nuts and bolts
paper towel and tube of waterless hand cleaner

First-aid kit: My personal kit contains the following, sealed inside double Ziploc bags:

sunscreen
aspirin

butterfly-closure bandages
Band-Aids
gauze compress pads (a half-dozen 4" × 4")
gauze (one roll)
ace bandages or Spenco joint wraps
Benadryl (an antihistamine, in case of allergic reactions)
water purification tablets / water filter (on long rides)
Moleskin / Spenco "Second Skin"
hydrogen peroxide, iodine, or Mercurochrome (some kind of antiseptic)
snakebite kit

Final Considerations: The authors of this series have done a good job in suggesting that specific items be packed for certain trails—raingear in particular seasons, a hat and gloves for mountain passes, or shades for desert jaunts. Heed their warnings, and think ahead. Good luck.

Dennis Coello

SOUTHERN MAINE

Southern Maine was the first area in Maine to be settled and is therefore filled with evidence of the early history of the region. For mountain bikers, this means rides that follow the lines of stone fences along wooded trails that were once town and county roads. The fences are a mystery to anyone unfamiliar with the changes in the land that took place after the British colonization of New England. These days, they appear to divide the forest. However, during the settlement of the area, much of the land was cleared for agriculture. The stone fences not only stood as property lines, but also served to enclose livestock. After the Civil War, many farms were abandoned, and the land slowly returned to its former wooded state. Evidence of once-prosperous farms can still be found along these old roads, however. As you ride, you will no doubt discover the crumbling remains of cellar holes, small cemeteries, and apple trees that once stood as part of large orchards.

TOURISM

Southern Maine forms the gateway into the state for the bulk of tourists heading north from as far down the east coast as Florida. In 1947, construction began on the Maine Turnpike, which now links Maine's tourist and industrial economy with the rest of New England. Prior to the construction of roads and interstates, a combination of train and steamboat provided access for the many people who came to summer in Maine in order to escape the oppressive heat of cities like Boston, New York, and Philadelphia.

Maine's tourist trade was boosted by the increased leisure time available to

The perfect finale
to a day of riding:
sunset on the coast.

the middle class and by the arrival of the automobile. The concept of Maine as "Vacationland" gradually evolved and produced a flood of leisure and sporting goods. This is epitomized in the success of the now internationally known catalog company L.L. Bean. Today, tourism follows timber as the second largest industry in Maine, and visitors arriving through the southern part of the state are greeted with the bold claim: "Maine: The Way Life Should Be."

Portland is the largest city in Maine. The city's motto, resurgam ("I shall rise again"), could not be more appropriate, considering its history. In the seventeenth century it was not only destroyed twice by Native Americans, but it also fell at the hands of the British. Nevertheless, Portland developed into a bustling port and flourished even through the Civil War. Then on July 4, 1866, the city was once again destroyed, this time by fire. Undaunted, the city rebuilt, replacing its previously wooden buildings with brick.

Today, Portland is a city filled with restaurants, brew pubs, coffee houses, art galleries, museums, and bike shops!

RIDE 1 · Mount Agamenticus

Length/configuration: 11.5-mile figure eight

Aerobic difficulty: Moderate to advanced

Technical difficulty: Mixed; generally intermediate-level terrain with several extremely challenging sections

Scenery: Wooded and wetland area characterized by many streams, small ponds, and reservoirs

Special comments: Bring a map and a compass! There are literally miles of additional trails to explore

The area surrounding Mount Agamenticus has become a mecca for mountain bikers in southern Maine, and for good reason: there are excellent trails heading in all directions from both the summit and the foot of the mountain. This ride is made up of an upper loop of 2.5 miles, a lower loop of 7 miles, and a connecting trail (which you will ride twice), 2 miles long. The total distance is 11.5 miles and features challenging single- and double-track trails that cover the wooded and hilly terrain below the summit of the mountain. The trail surface varies from smooth, grassy double-track, to rocky, rooted, and eroded single-track. This ride is suitable for intermediate and advanced riders who possess a good level of physical fitness. Good route-finding skills are also recommended, as there are literally dozens of side trails to explore that do not even make it onto the topographic map for the area.

Mount Agamenticus is a 691-foot monadnock that rises high above the coastal plains of southern York County. The name "Agamenticus" is the Abnaki Indian name for the river that creates York's harbor. It is said that Aspinquid, a Pawtucket Indian, was buried on the mountain in a ceremony that involved the sacrifice of more than 6,000 animals. You can visit the monument commemorating the event by taking an optional side trip, up a short but grueling climb that takes you to the top of the mountain. You will also be rewarded with a refreshing breeze and a view that extends to the western Maine mountains in one direction and the Maine coastline in another. In the history of the settlement of northern New England, Mount Agamenticus played an important role as one of the primary navigational landmarks for early sailors. More recently, this site continues to be significant for reasons other than the excellent mountain biking opportunities it offers: an unusually diverse representation of both northern and southern plant species makes the mountain an important natural resource. Recognition of the area's unique and diverse flora and fauna will undoubtedly influence its future use by cyclists.

General location: York County, 4 miles west of Interstate 95.

Elevation change: This ride includes many short climbs and descents. You will gain a modest 230' throughout the entire ride. You can make up for this relatively slight gain, however: the ride up to the summit of Mount Agamenticus is a short 0.5-mile climb that will earn you an additional 340'.

Season: Though the trails around Mount Agamenticus are used all year, it is best to avoid damaging them during the mud season in early spring. The months from June through October usually offer the best riding conditions.

Services: All services are available in York.

Hazards: At times these secluded trails can be tricky to follow, especially in autumn when fallen leaves will probably obscure the tracks of previous riders. Familiarize yourself with the roads that border the area and with the many nearby lakes and ponds, and use these to orient yourself. The trails are also used by hikers, equestrians, all-terrain vehicles, and snowmobiles.

Rescue index: You will rarely be more than 3 miles from assistance.

Land status: The 5,000 acres surrounding and including Mount Agamenticus are owned by a number of different landowners, including the York and Kittery water districts, the Town of York, and private owners. Some of the land has recently been purchased by Land for Maine's Future. Though informal access currently exists for the many trails in the area, developing plans for the management of the area may impact the use of the area by cyclists.

Maps: The USGS quadrangle for Mount Agamenticus is York Harbor. However, very few of the single-track trails on this ride are mapped, and the topographic map will be more useful in delineating natural boundaries like ponds, lakes, and roads than in depicting the actual trails.

Finding the trail: Take Exit 1 off I-95 at York Village and follow signs to US 1. Turn left on US 1 and drive north for 3.5 miles before turning left onto Mountain Road. You will cross the interstate and come to a **T** intersection. Turn right and continue to follow the main road past several small side roads. When you reach a road on the right, signed to Mount Agamenticus Park, pull off into a small, dirt parking area on the right. If no parking is available in this lot, turn right and drive to the summit of Mount Agamenticus, where you will find more parking spaces.

RIDE 1 · Mount Agamenticus

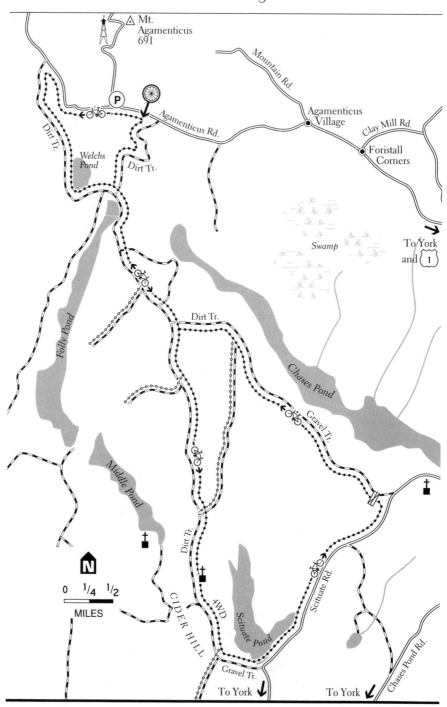

Mount Agamenticus features a variety of challenging terrain.

Source of additional information:

Berger's Bike Shop
241 York Street
York, ME 03909
(207) 363-4070

Notes on the trail: From the small parking area at the base of the mountain, begin riding westward on the unpaved portion of Mount Agamenticus Road. Keep your eyes peeled for the first four-wheel-drive road on the left. You will have to turn sharply onto this road, which heads downhill. You will ride down a short, rocky, and eroded section of the road before crossing a stream. As you ride out of the stream bed, begin looking for a double-track trail that branches off to the left at the top of a small rise. Turn left here for some rocky, technical riding through the woods. You will pedal past a rather boggy pond on the right. Beyond this pond, the trail becomes narrower and more difficult to follow.

After crossing another stream, there may be some flagging tape marking a subtle, uphill bend in the trail to the right. At the crest of this slight hill, a short, steep descent will lead you to Welchs Pond on the left. Keeping the pond on your left, follow the trail through an opening in an old stone fence. This fence marks the beginning of a section of trail that winds through old pasture, past several piles of old stones, and across several more old fences.

Follow the main trail until a reservoir appears in front of you. This is Folly Pond. Keeping the water on your right, follow a narrow trail that runs along the top of the dam at the edge of the pond. Although you will notice a much wider trail at the base of the dam, be sure to follow the trail closest to the water's edge. There is a short distance of fairly technical riding beyond the dam, as the trail climbs up the bank from the water's edge. You will come to a spur on the right that drops back down to the water, but follow the main trail as it swings to the left away from the water and continues in a southerly direction.

This next portion of the ride follows a wide jeep trail through the woods. You will pass a trail heading uphill on the right and another, less obvious trail branching off to the left. Keep to the main trail until you reach a Y intersection in an area that, though still wooded, is slightly more open. It is to this intersection that you will return at the completion of the lower loop. Bear right to begin the loop, following the trail that reenters the heavy forest. Traveling a short distance on this trail will bring you to a T intersection. Turn left (the trail on the right narrows significantly after about half a mile, continuing on a single-track trail). Follow the trail around to the left, passing a rough jeep trail over your right shoulder. You will come to a Y intersection shortly after. Here, the right-hand trail zigzags up and over a small knoll, to drop down to a water reservoir. The ride continues by following the left-hand trail, which descends to a T intersection. Turn right. You will begin to notice that an extensive network of stone fences distinguishes this portion of the ride. Pass a trail branching off on the left and, almost immediately, you will come to a tiny cemetery on the left. Beyond the cemetery, the trail forks. Bear left. You will pass numerous old stone foundations throughout this area, which was once considerably more developed than it is now.

Pass a grassy trail turning up to the right and continue to a Y intersection. Bear right and ride through an opening in a stone fence. You will pass a few grassy trails branching off on the left and, a short distance farther, will come to an intersection with a well-worn dirt road. Bear left and cross a small stream. Bear left again almost immediately, at a small clearing, and then bear right, passing a trail on the left that heads up to Scituate Pond. Follow the road out to a T junction with the paved Scituate Road and turn left.

You will ride on pavement for 1.25 miles, after which you must look for and turn left onto the unpaved, gated access road for the York Water District. You will follow the access road for almost 2 miles, avoiding all side trails. The road gradually deteriorates into a double-track trail that reconnects with the first Y intersection of the ride to complete the loop. Bear right here to retrace your way back toward the dam on Folly Pond.

As you approach the pond, you will ride past the short spur that drops down to the water (now on your left). Follow the trail as it creeps closer to the water. You can drop down to the dam along the way you came up, or you can bear right along what actually appears to be a more obvious trail. If you choose the latter route you will drop steeply down a bank and come to a **T** intersection with a wide, muddy trail. Turning left will take you back to the dam (visible from this intersection), and turning right continues the ride. The route is obvious from this point, but it also traverses some of the most technically difficult terrain of the ride. In addition to several large, muddy holes, you will cross a small stream and negotiate two short, extremely steep and eroded hills before climbing up to Mount Agamenticus Road. Turn left on the road to return to your vehicle, or if you've still got energy to burn, head up either the paved road or one of the trails to the summit of Mount Agamenticus.

RIDE 2 · Hinckley Park

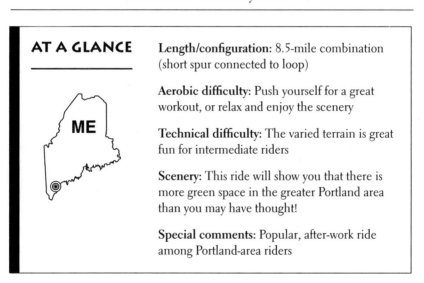

AT A GLANCE

Length/configuration: 8.5-mile combination (short spur connected to loop)

Aerobic difficulty: Push yourself for a great workout, or relax and enjoy the scenery

Technical difficulty: The varied terrain is great fun for intermediate riders

Scenery: This ride will show you that there is more green space in the greater Portland area than you may have thought!

Special comments: Popular, after-work ride among Portland-area riders

Hinckley Park is just the starting point for this 8.5-mile ride along an amazing network of trails in South Portland. This ride is a long loop that begins and ends with a short spur. For riders of intermediate skill level, the varied terrain covered on this ride provides an excellent balance of technical challenge and effortless cruising. Narrow single-track trails are linked by short stretches of pavement to miles of undulating terrain beneath power lines and hard-packed woods trails. Due to the complicated and sometimes difficult-to-identify trail junctions, even the most advanced rider should allow a couple of hours to complete this ride.

This is a mountain biker's tour of South Portland and a certain cure for the city blues. Popular with Portland-area riders, this ride is a convenient after-work jaunt. You will begin it at Hinckley Park, following some single-track trails out to a paved road. Upon reentering the woods, you will spin through a beautiful stand of pines and follow a hard-packed woods trail out to a power line. After cruising along a smooth, grassy jeep road, the trail links up with a section of rough single-track that zigzags down through the woods to a small stream. A slightly wider woods trail leads to more riding beneath power lines, which provides access to a trail system in Cape Elizabeth: a network of hard-packed, narrow trails running through a beautiful forest. A breezy descent through a grassy field ends at the paved Sawyer Road. Ducking back into the woods again, you will ride between tall pines before returning to some woods trails and the beginning of the loop.

General location: South Portland and Cape Elizabeth.

Elevation change: Some short, steep drops and ascents and several miles of undulating terrain beneath power lines makes this a challenging ride without any significant gain in elevation.

Season: This trail can be ridden year-round, although it is wise to let the ground dry out before riding it in the spring and to allow snowmobiles to pack the trails before tackling it in the winter.

Services: All services are available in nearby Portland.

Hazards: This route is an unmarked circuit used by many local riders. Because it is intersected by many trails, it can be a tough one to follow. If you can, ride this trail with someone who knows it, or meet up with an organized ride through one of the bike shops mentioned below. Also, wear bright clothing: not only are there several road crossings along this trail, but many walkers, joggers, hunters, skiers, and other riders regularly use this trail.

Rescue index: You will be riding through and around several well-developed residential areas, and well-traveled roads will always be nearby.

Land status: This ride begins in South Portland's Hinckley Park, but does continue along undeveloped private land, under power lines, and to Cape Elizabeth's network of multi-use trails. Though the route is used by many riders, be alert for changes to the trails, including detours and closures.

Maps: A street map of the greater Portland area will provide an overview of the area and will probably include more up-to-date information than the USGS quad, which is Portland West.

Finding the trail: From Portland, cross the Casco Bay Bridge into South Portland and drive down Waterman Drive, keeping in one of the middle lanes. Bear left on Broadway and quickly move to the right-hand lane. Turn right at the first traffic light, onto ME 77 South. Turn right at the first light

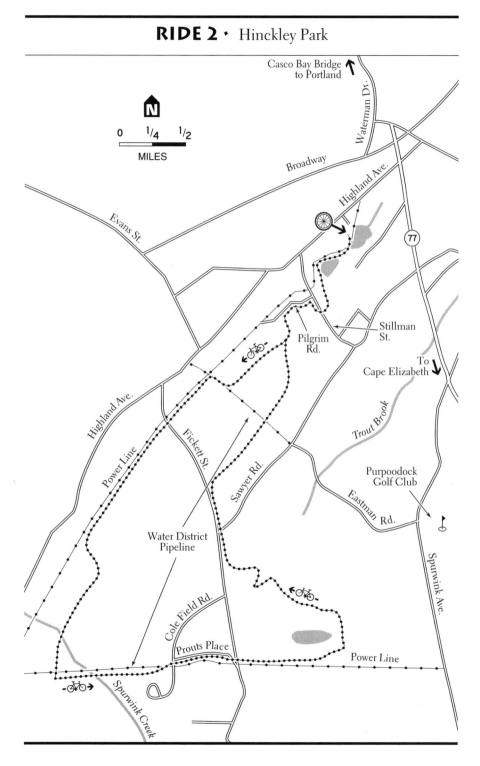

and continue along Highland Avenue for about one mile, before reaching the entrance to Hinckley Park on the left. Because the parking area is so small, car pooling is a must.

Sources of additional information: Many of the bike shops in Portland have information about riding in the greater Portland area and also offer weekly mountain bike rides. Try contacting Back Bay Bicycle at 333 Forest Avenue, (207) 773-6906; Cycle Mania at 59 Federal Street, (207) 774-2933; or Allspeed Bicycle and Ski at 1041 Washington Avenue, (207) 878-8741.

Notes on the trail: From the parking circle, start up the dirt road that leads to the power substation and look to your left for a small trail that follows the fence around the substation. Keeping the fence on your right and a small pond on your left, follow the trail that runs alongside the power lines. At a wet area at the base of a hill, bear left and follow a smaller set of power lines up a hill. As you come up to the edge of the woods at the top of the hill, turn right and ride along a narrow single-track trail, which will bring you to a side entrance of the park and a paved road.

Turn right on the road and then take the first left up Pilgrim Road. Pilgrim Road passes through a new residential area. After house #108, look to the left for an indistinct single-track trail leading straight into the woods. Keep to the right as you pass through this stand of pines; if you venture to the left you will find yourself crossing a stream into an open pasture.

Follow the trail through the woods, avoiding any side trails. When you reach a wet, boggy area to the left of the trail, bear right down a trail that is the water district right-of-way. You will soon reach another set of power lines. Turn left and follow the trail beneath the power lines. After a short distance, cross a paved road and continue following a wide, grassy jeep trail. When you come to a trail perpendicular to the one you've been riding along (at which point there is no definitive trail straight ahead of you) look for a narrow single-track trail shooting off to the left at an angle of about 45°. This narrow path quickly takes you down a hill, across a small stream (watch for a sudden drop-off), and up steeply into a recently cut area. Pick your way through the slash and felled trees and descend to negotiate a washed-out ravine and streambed.

Just beyond this stream, you will reach a T intersection. Looking to your left, you will notice a red roof and a small Christmas tree farm; turn right away from this opening and onto a wider woods trail. One section of this trail is prone to flooding, and you will ride over logs placed across the trail, corduroy-style. Beyond this area, bear left at the first fork you come to. After just 0.1 mile you will see a small stream ahead of you and some power lines just beyond it. Turn left and follow the trail to the power lines. The trail crosses beneath the power lines and continues alongside them on the other

Squeezing through
"Pinball Alley" in
Cape Elizabeth.

side. After just 0.5 mile, you will find yourself on the paved Cole Field Road
at its intersection with Prout's Place.

Ride up Prout's Place, admiring the grand homes that line the street, and
duck back onto a small trail following the power line right-of-way. Cross a
paved road and then an old section of once-paved road before reconnecting
with the trail beneath the power lines. After some distance, as the undulating
terrain beneath the power lines begins to descend through an area thick with
sumacs, the trail will cross to the other side of the power lines and then enter
the woods on a grassy jeep road. When you come to a **T** intersection in front
of a farm, turn left on a dirt road. You will pass a pond on your left before
reentering the woods.

The next turn is not very obvious. After about a quarter mile, look for a trail
branching off on the left. This trail is marked by two trees, one on each side,
both faintly marked with a blaze of orange. If you miss this turn, you will follow a trail from which you will quite quickly be able to make out some homes

on the right. If you reach this point, turn around and pedal back, carefully looking for the missed trail. The next landmark is a stone fence, beside which you will ride until you come to a **T** intersection. Turn right and ride to the edge of a field. Ride down the left side of the field, along a narrow track that descends through the field before crossing a small stream and ending at the paved Sawyer Road. Turn right up Sawyer Road and ride straight past its bend to the right, continuing along Fickett Street.

From Fickett Street, look for and ride past two rusted old water valves before turning into the woods on the right. The trail you pick up here is fairly wide, running through the middle of a stand of pines. At a **T** intersection, turn left and then turn right almost immediately to ride down "pinball alley": a narrow trail between closely spaced pines. Bear left out of "pinball alley" and cross a stone fence. At a small open area, bear right at a fork in the trail. You will quickly reach an intersection with the first woods trail you began on. Turn right and make your way back to the side entrance to Hinckley Park via Pilgrim Road. Back at the park, you can retrace your route to the parking circle, or take some time to explore some of the other trails in the park and return a different way.

RIDE 3 · Atherton Hill

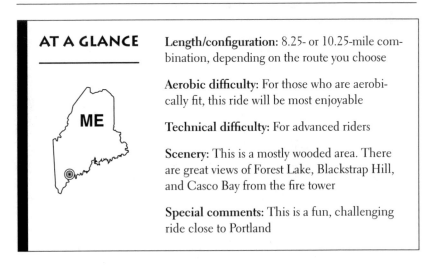

AT A GLANCE

ME

Length/configuration: 8.25- or 10.25-mile combination, depending on the route you choose

Aerobic difficulty: For those who are aerobically fit, this ride will be most enjoyable

Technical difficulty: For advanced riders

Scenery: This is a mostly wooded area. There are great views of Forest Lake, Blackstrap Hill, and Casco Bay from the fire tower

Special comments: This is a fun, challenging ride close to Portland

This ride to the top of Atherton Hill is one of the most popular among Portland-area riders. Most of the ride follows overgrown four-wheel-drive roads through heavily shaded forest. However, a short loop up and around Atherton Hill provides access to an abandoned Maine Forest Service fire tower, from which a superb 360° view can be enjoyed on clear days. Mount Washington dominates the view to the west, and Casco Bay defines the eastern horizon. On hot and humid days, the climb to the top of the fire tower is also worth the effort because of the breeze that usually blows at the top.

This ride is a challenging one and requires both technical expertise and aerobic fitness. The terrain is fairly rocky and interspersed with only a few short, smooth interludes beneath pine trees. There are also two severely eroded sections of the trail that only very skilled riders should attempt. The ride is an out-and-back endeavor, with a choice of two different loops up to the fire tower on top of Atherton Hill. Depending upon the loop you choose, the total mileage for this ride is 8.25 or 10.25 miles. In addition, there are many side trails worth exploring. Riders in good physical condition should allow at least a couple of hours to complete the ride.

General location: Windham, 10 miles northwest of Portland.

Elevation change: From the trailhead, you will climb a series of short hills before gradually ascending to the fire tower on Atherton Hill at approximately 580'. Total elevation gain is about 380' for the shorter option, and slightly more for riders pedaling the longer loop.

Season: The trails around Atherton Hill should be dry enough to ride by late May. As with many trails in the greater Portland area, high usage can be particularly destructive to the trails after heavy rainfall or in the early spring. Use your best judgment and consider the long-term effects your wet-weather riding may have. It is also possible to explore this ride in the winter, with studded tires and after snowmobile traffic has packed down the snow.

Services: All services are available in both Portland and North Windham.

Hazards: There are two severely eroded sections along this trail that only skilled riders should attempt. The first occurs as you approach the power lines on a rough four-wheel-drive road. The second, and the most severe, occurs on the trail that descends from the fire tower to the southern slope of Atherton Hill.

Rescue index: You will begin this ride in a residential neighborhood and will remain within 3 miles of these homes.

Land status: This ride begins on snowmobile trails with informal year-round access. The ride also makes use of the trails beneath a power line and a Forest Service access road to the fire tower on Atherton Hill. The ride, frequently pedaled by mountain bikers, does cross private property, and riders must respect any changes in access and any posted signs.

Maps: The USGS map for this area is Cumberland Center. Although many of the trails along this ride are not marked on the map, it will clearly

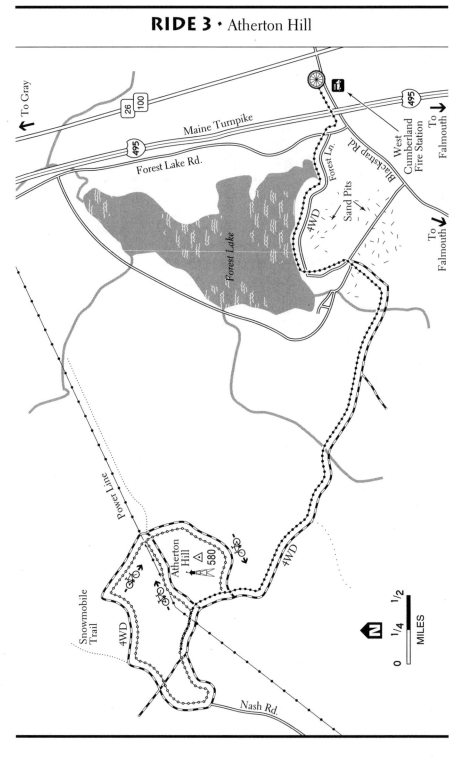

identify the landmarks that serve as boundaries to the area in which you will be riding.

Finding the trail: From Portland, travel north on ME 100/26. After driving out of Falmouth, crossing the town line into Cumberland, turn left onto Blackstrap Road at a crossroad marked by a flashing light. Turn left again almost immediately, into a parking area provided for the West Cumberland Community Field. Be sure not to park in the way of the fire station next to the park.

Sources of additional information: All of the Portland-area bicycle shops will have some information on this ride. For more specific information, contact New England Mountain Bike in the Falmouth Shopping Center on US 1 at (207) 781-4882.

Notes on the trail: From the parking area, turn left onto Blackstrap Road and ride across the bridge over the Maine Turnpike. Bear right immediately after the bridge and then turn left onto Forest Lane. This road changes to a gravel surface as Forest Lake becomes visible to your right. Continue along this road until you reach a three-way intersection at a gravel pit that marks the trailhead.

From the road, ride down the steep drop into the gravel pit straight ahead of you. If you are doubtful about the direction in which you should head, ride toward the radio tower just visible above the trees. Cross the pit and follow a loose, sandy trail up to a **T** intersection at the edge of a wooded area. Turn left and then follow the trail around to the right, over some partially exposed old tires. At this point, the trail leaves the perimeter of the gravel pit and enters the woods.

Following the most distinct trail through the woods, you will have to negotiate some loose rock up a fairly steep climb that covers the first mile of the ride. You will reach a small clearing at the top of this climb, beyond which the trail splits. Bear right. You will descend slightly to cross a rocky streambed that is followed by a tough climb up an eroded slope on the other side. After a short run along a twisting section of trail crisscrossed by roots, be prepared for a short drop down the first severely eroded portion of this trail. Continue straight beyond this point, though there is a rough, grassy road branching off to the left. When you come to a **T** intersection, turn left to begin either of the loops up to the fire tower; the trail to the right is the one you will come down after reaching the top of Atherton Hill.

At the power lines, you have the option of turning up to the right and climbing a steep ledgy section of trail that follows the power lines, or of crossing beneath the power lines and following the trail that continues into the woods beyond them. The latter is an option that will add approximately 2 miles to the length of the ride. The routes reconnect just a short distance

Fall leaves cover the trail to Atherton Hill.

farther up on the power line. For the shorter of the two options, turn right and follow a path beneath the power lines. After a short distance, the trail crosses beneath the power lines again. At this point, there is a trail on the right, leading into the woods through a small opening, and a trail on the left, which is where the longer loop reconnects with the trail. The ride continues through the small opening in woods.

If you chose to ride the longer loop, you will have crossed beneath the power lines and picked up the trail continuing into the woods on the other side. Crossing some exposed rock, you will reach a clearing that was once the site of a schoolhouse. Continuing beyond this point, you will reach a junction with the unpaved portion of Nash Road. Turn right and pedal along this road to a crossroad: go straight and enter the woods on a double-track trail. Almost immediately the road splits. Bear right onto the less-maintained trail, and cross over a culvert through which a small stream passes. You will begin climbing over exposed and loose rock. At the next split, bear right again. Ride past a small cleared area on the left and, after the road has dipped down, bear right at the next fork. This trail will quickly connect you to the power lines. Upon reaching the power lines, ride up so that you are between the two rows of lines. This is where the loop options intersect. Continue straight, through the narrow opening in the trees.

Beyond the narrow opening, the trail continues straight, past a trail branching off on the left and along a broad path covered with pine needles. You will follow this trail as it swings to the right over the collapsed remains of a stone wall. Zigzag through the woods before reaching the fire tower in a small clearing. This is a great rest stop, and on clear days, riders who make the climb to the top of the fire tower will be rewarded with a panoramic view of the surrounding area.

To complete the loop, follow the trail that passes in front of the fire tower and reenter the woods to descend the southern slope of Atherton Hill. Use extreme care when you begin this descent, as one area of the trail is severely eroded. The trail will reconnect with the four-wheel-drive road at a fork. Bear left and retrace your route back to Forest Lake.

RIDE 4 · Bruce Hill

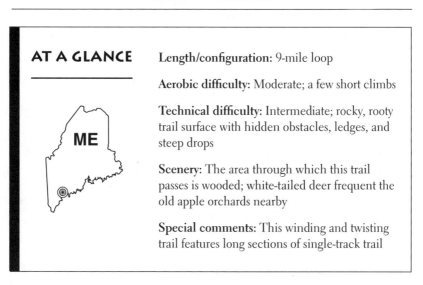

AT A GLANCE

Length/configuration: 9-mile loop

Aerobic difficulty: Moderate; a few short climbs

Technical difficulty: Intermediate; rocky, rooty trail surface with hidden obstacles, ledges, and steep drops

Scenery: The area through which this trail passes is wooded; white-tailed deer frequent the old apple orchards nearby

Special comments: This winding and twisting trail features long sections of single-track trail

The climb up Bruce Hill that begins this ride continues to create a loop of approximately nine miles, including an optional spur that cuts down to the small pond at the foot of Bruce Hill. The ride follows single- and double-track trails that are used in the winter by snowmobiles. Intermediate riders with a moderate level of fitness should allow a few hours to complete this ride. Convenient to all of the greater Portland area, this ride makes a terrific after-work jaunt.

General location: Bruce Hill is located a few miles north of Cumberland Center.

Elevation change: This ride is characterized by a series of short climbs and descents.

Season: Good riding conditions for this ride begin in June and continue through October.

Services: There is a general store in Cumberland Center, but assistance related to bicycle needs must be sought in Falmouth or Portland.

Hazards: None.

Rescue index: You will never be more than 1 mile from homes on this ride.

Land status: Private land. The trail follows the route of a snowmobile trail. Please respect private property signs.

Maps: The USGS quad for this ride is Cumberland Center.

Finding the trail: From the Portland area, drive north on ME 9 toward Cumberland Center. Continue straight at a four-way intersection with Blanchard Road and Tuttle Road. Approximately 1 mile beyond this intersection, turn left onto Greely Road. Drive to the end of Greely Road and pull over to the side to park. Because there is very limited space for parking vehicles, try to arrange car pooling if you are riding with a group.

Sources of additional information: None.

Notes on the trail: From the cul-de-sac at the end of the paved portion of Greely Road, begin riding up the unpaved continuation of the road. You will ascend Bruce Hill over a short section of ledge. After cresting the hill, look for an old woods road branching off on the right. Turn right and begin following this road. A stone fence parallels the road on the right and you will ride through a forest of mixed growth that may show signs of recent logging activity. When you come to a power line, turn right.

After only 0.1 mile on the power line, bear left onto a fairly obvious trail that branches off from the power line. After passing some wrecked cars, you will come to a pasture and a clearing. Turn right and follow the trail down the right-hand side of the pasture. Bear right where the trail appears to fork into another woods road. You will rejoin the power line just a short distance beyond this junction. Follow the trail beneath the power line for slightly less than 1 mile. You will ride through a sandy section of trail and past some houses to the left of the trail before reaching an intersection with a trail that shoots off into the woods on the right. This trail looks like an ATV trail and comes just before the power lines cross ME 9.

You will come to a small brook, where the trail veers left and then swings right to reach a snowmobile bridge that provides access across the brook.

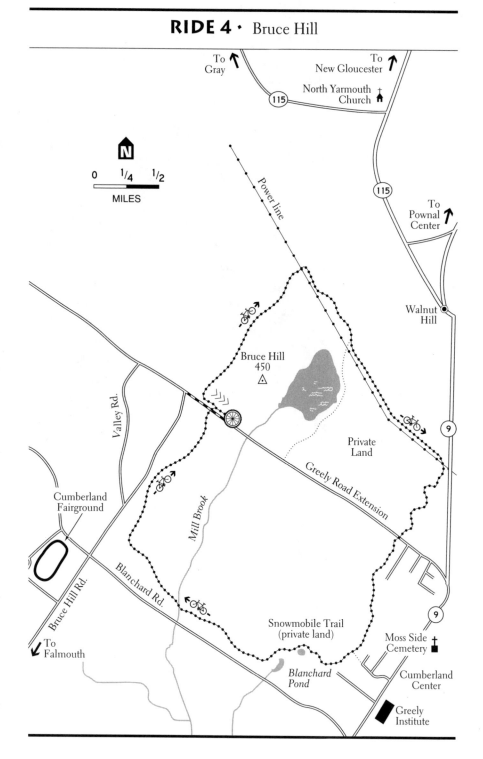

To
Gray

To
New Gloucester

North Yarmouth
Church

115

N

0   1/4   1/2

MILES

Power line

115

To
Pownal
Center

Walnut
Hill

Bruce Hill
450

Private
Land

Greely Road Extension

9

Valley Rd.

Cumberland
Fairground

Mill Brook

Bruce Hill Rd.

Blanchard Rd.

Snowmobile Trail
(private land)

Moss Side
Cemetery

Cumberland
Center

9

To
Falmouth

Blanchard
Pond

Greely
Institute

Splashing through
a small brook
in Cumberland.

Shortly beyond this stream, you will reach Greely Road. Cross the road and pick up the trail on the other side. Signs posted for snowmobiles may direct you toward Blanchard Road. This portion of the ride traverses a trail that, though relatively flat, is muddy and crisscrossed with roots. At a fork in the trail, bear right (the left fork will lead you into a housing development). At a small pond located quite close to Blanchard Road, turn right. The trail merges with a dirt road and passes through a pasture. Keeping to the right-hand edge of the pasture, ride until you see several homes ahead of you. Look for a snowmobile trail that turns sharply into the woods on the right. Follow this trail, which becomes a narrow double-track trail. You will climb the south slope of Bruce Hill and come to the beginning of the loop. Turn right to return to your vehicle.

RIDE 5 · Bradbury Mountain State Park

AT A GLANCE

ME

Length/configuration: 6.5-mile figure eight

Aerobic difficulty: Moderate

Technical difficulty: For intermediate riders; rocky single-track trails with short, steep climbs and descents

Scenery: Spectacular view of the Maine coastline

Special comments: Pretty ride through one of the first state parks to welcome mountain bikers

---

Making use of all the trails open to mountain bikers at Bradbury Mountain, this 6.5-mile ride traces a figure eight across the middle of the park. The result is a ride that takes you over ever-changing terrain: from the smooth woods roads of the Knight Woods Loop to the more challenging single-track that clings to the dips and climbs that characterize the Boundary Trail. Riders with intermediate technical skills will enjoy this ride immensely, and because of the configuration and relatively short distance covered, it is also suitable for adventurous beginners.

Bradbury Mountain State Park covers 440 acres of forested land that is rich not only in plant and animal life but also in history. As you begin your ride along the Northern Loop Trail, look for the cattle pound on the right. Built by early settlers to enclose stray cattle, sheep, and pigs, the stone structure remains nearly intact. The stone fences that now mark the park boundaries are evidence that the land around the mountain was once cleared for fields and pasture. Terraces are also still visible on the mountain from the time when the Cotton family, its first European settlers, cultivated grapes on its slopes. Even before these settlers arrived, the Wabanakis used to camp on the mountain on their trips from New Gloucester to the coast. The exposed, glacier-sculpted summit of Bradbury Mountain is indeed an excellent vantage point from which to look out to sea. Visitors who make it to the summit will be treated to spectacular views extending all the way to the coast. In the spring and fall, hawks and eagles can be seen riding the thermals over the mountain.

General location: Bradbury Mountain State Park is located in the town of Pownal, 5 miles from the Freeport-Durham exit off Interstate 95.

Elevation change: The summit of Bradbury Mountain is 485' above sea level. The Boundary Trail features short, steep climbs over undulating terrain. The Tote Road Trail climbs steadily up a more moderate grade to the summit; there is no significant change in elevation for the remainder of the trail.

Season: Trails are open to mountain bikers when conditions permit. It is a good idea to call the park to confirm trail openings. Summer and fall will be the best seasons in which to ride.

Services: The picnic areas in the park include tables, grills, and a shelter. Camping is also permitted throughout the year. Water is available at the park, and there is a country store in Pownal Center. Your closest resource for bike parts and service is L.L. Bean in Freeport.

Hazards: The trails at Bradbury Mountain are shared with hikers, to whom bikers must yield at all times. Erosion control is also a significant concern at the park. Because of this, and due to the steep drops that surround many of the trails, it is very important that riders stick to the marked trails.

Rescue index: All the trails at Bradbury Mountain stay within 2 miles of the park headquarters.

Land status: State park.

Maps: A map of all the trails at Bradbury Mountain State Park is available at the park headquarters.

Finding the trail: Bradbury Mountain is just 5 miles from Freeport. Take Exit 20 off Interstate 95 and turn inland toward ME 125 and ME 136 (away from US 1). Turn left immediately at a **T** intersection and follow the Pownal Road around a sharp bend to the right. Continue straight for 4 miles (the Pownal Road runs into Elmwood Road) until you reach a blinking light at a four-way intersection in Pownal Center. Turn right here, onto ME 9. The entrance to Bradbury Mountain State Park is just 0.5 mile on the left. You will want to pick up a trail map and pay the modest park fee, and then bear right to make your way to the upper parking lot.

Source of additional information:

Bradbury Mountain State Park
528 Hallowell Road
Pownal, ME 04069
(207) 688-4712

Notes on the trail: From the parking lot, ride toward the playing field (away from the park headquarters) and begin riding along the Northern Loop Trail as it follows the perimeter of the playing field. At the first trail junction, approximately 1 mile into the ride, turn left up the Ski Trail. After a short climb you will reach a four-way intersection with the Northern Loop Trail

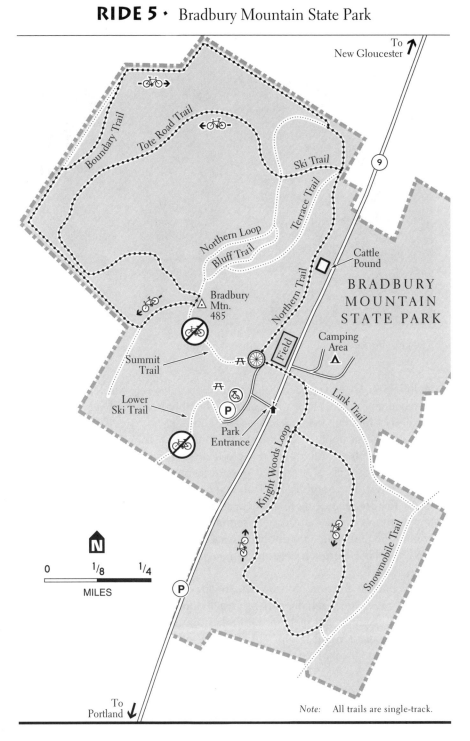

To
New Gloucester

Boundary Trail

Tote Road Trail

Ski Trail

9

Terrace Trail

Northern Loop

Bluff Trail

Cattle
Pound

BRADBURY
MOUNTAIN
STATE PARK

Bradbury
Mtn.
485

Northern Trail

Camping
Area

Summit
Trail

Field

Lower
Ski Trail

Link Trail

Park
Entrance

Knight Woods Loop

Snowmobile Trail

N

0   1/8   1/4

MILES

P

To
Portland

Note: All trails are single-track.

The morning sun kisses the top of Bradbury Mountain.

and the Tote Road Trail. Continue straight onto the Tote Road Trail, which is signed and marked with white blazes. The Tote Road Trail curves around Bradbury Mountain before leading to the summit.

From the summit, drop down to the Boundary Trail, which is marked with orange blazes. After a short, technical section over undulating terrain scattered with rocks and exposed roots, a ledge and a stone fence create a sharp corner. The South Ridge Trail branches off here, but you will want to follow the Boundary Trail to the right as it runs alongside an old stone fence that marks the park boundary. Continue to follow the trail all the way around the park boundary until you reach a T intersection with the Northern Loop Trail. Turn left here and retrace the beginning of the ride back to the parking lot.

To continue the ride and complete the lower loop of the figure eight, look to your left as you reach the parking area and follow a trail to the road. Cross the road carefully and pick up the Link Trail on the other side. Bear right onto the Knight Woods Loop, which can be ridden in either direction, and then return to the parking area.

RIDE 6 · North Hollis Loop

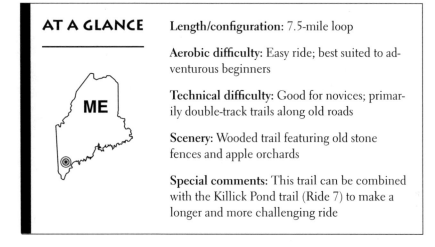

AT A GLANCE

Length/configuration: 7.5-mile loop

Aerobic difficulty: Easy ride; best suited to adventurous beginners

Technical difficulty: Good for novices; primarily double-track trails along old roads

Scenery: Wooded trail featuring old stone fences and apple orchards

Special comments: This trail can be combined with the Killick Pond trail (Ride 7) to make a longer and more challenging ride

The North Hollis ride is a 7.5-mile loop along primarily old roads and woods trails. The terrain is an excellent introduction to the basics of off-road riding: a few wet areas and some short stretches on rocky, eroded terrain provide some technical challenge for beginning-level riders without the ardors of dramatic elevation changes. Because of its close proximity to Killick Pond, this loop can be combined with the Killick Pond ride to create a longer excursion.

Old farmland and pasture dominate the landscape on this ride. Many of the trail junctions are old road intersections, distinguished by the remains of old stone fences. Forest has reclaimed the land since the fields and pasture were abandoned. Apple trees, particularly when they are in blossom in the spring, provide clues to the location of old farms, which often included orchards. In the fall, these trees attract plenty of deer, when fallen apples provide an easily accessible source of food.

General location: North Hollis.

Elevation change: This ride features nothing more than gradually rolling terrain.

Season: Spring through fall.

Services: There is a general store in North Hollis. The nearest location for bike services is Gorham Bike and Ski on ME 25 in downtown Gorham (phone (207) 839-2770).

Hazards: Due to recent cutting in this area, this ride may change somewhat in its surrounding features. Also, use care crossing ME 117, which can be especially busy in the summertime.

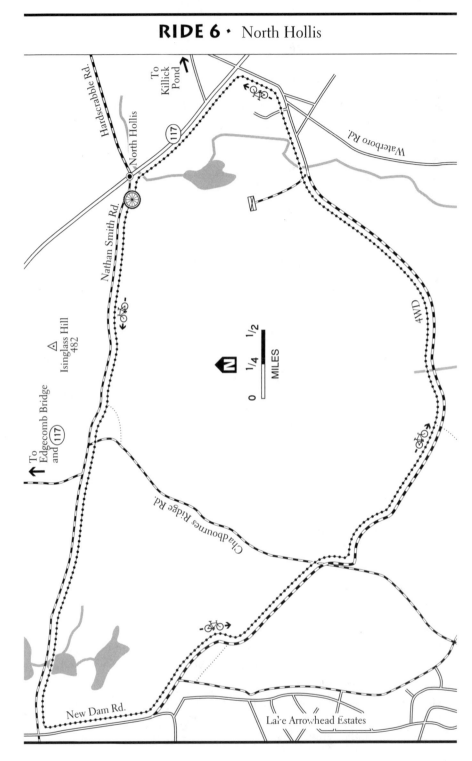

Majestic pines
tower above the
trail in North
Hollis.

Rescue index: You are never far from homes along this ride.

Land status: Old roads and snowmobile trails.

Maps: The USGS 7.5 minute quadrangle is Limington, Maine. Most of the ride is also depicted in the DeLorme Mapping Company's *Maine Atlas and Gazetteer* (map 2, section A-4).

Finding the trail: From the Portland area, head west on ME 25 to Gorham. Just outside downtown Gorham, turn south onto US 202 and drive to Hollis Center. In Hollis Center, turn up ME 117. After about 4 miles, you will come to a crossroads marked by a blinking light. Continue straight and, less than 1 mile beyond the light, turn left on Nathan Smith Road. You can drive a short distance down the road, pulling over to park on the side of the road.

Source of additional information:

Gorham Bike and Ski
12 Main Street
Gorham, ME 04038
(207) 839-2770

Notes on the trail: Begin riding down the unpaved Nathan Smith Road. Continue straight past a trail branching off to the left, just before a small clearing. Continue straight again at the junction of another trail that joins the road on the left. At the next fork in the trail, bear left (if you bear right at this junction, you will eventually reach ME 117). Continue straight at a four-way trail intersection. You will pass through a swampy area.

When you reach the paved Old Portland Road, at its intersection with New Dam Road, turn left. After approximately 0.4 mile, just before the road curves gently to the right, look for a trail branching off the road on the left. As you turn onto this trail, you will notice the remains of a stone fence on the left and, through the trees, houses to your right. At a fork in the trail just after a slightly rocky incline, bear left. Stone fences line both sides of this portion of the trail, which is also a little grassier. Pass a trail on the right, and notice an old stone foundation on the right side of the trail just beyond that intersection. The trail passes some tall pines on the right and then a clear-cut area on the left. At this clear-cut lot, ride toward a large boulder and follow the trail out to a dirt road.

Turning right on the dirt road, look on the left for a snowmobile sign and orange blazes that mark another old road. Turn left down this road, and when you come to a three-way intersection continue straight toward Hollis. After riding through another area of logging activity, the trail merges with a dirt road. Ride up the road, crossing a bridge, and continue to an intersection with a paved road. Turn left and then turn left again, riding a short distance on ME 117 to return to the trailhead.

RIDE 7 · Killick Pond

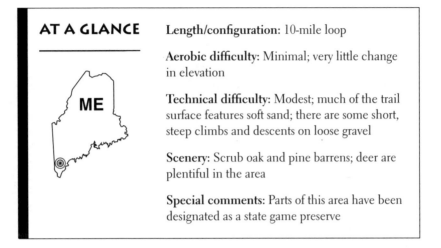

AT A GLANCE

Length/configuration: 10-mile loop

Aerobic difficulty: Minimal; very little change in elevation

Technical difficulty: Modest; much of the trail surface features soft sand; there are some short, steep climbs and descents on loose gravel

Scenery: Scrub oak and pine barrens; deer are plentiful in the area

Special comments: Parts of this area have been designated as a state game preserve

This loop around Killick Pond is an easygoing, 10-mile ride, with several miles of side trails to explore. The ride follows a combination of rough dirt roads and snowmobile trails, with a short stretch on pavement. Although sand makes some sections of this ride challenging, the overall terrain is manageable for riders of all abilities. Furthermore, the ride features only a modest gain in elevation and therefore requires only a moderate level of physical fitness.

The area surrounding Killick Pond is unique for its sandy soil and pine barrens. The woods around the pond are a mixture of pines and young oaks, a combination that tells something of the history of the land. Devastating fires have repeatedly swept through the area, including a major fire in 1947. Since then, large-scale agricultural development has put a lot of pressure on the area. As a result, the Department of Inland Fisheries and Wildlife has acquired the area around the pond. The wetlands adjacent to the pond and the forested shoreline provide a home to deer and waterfowl. Eagles are often spotted here as well. The roads and snowmobile trails that wander through the area offer plenty of opportunities for exploring. One landmark of particular note is an old airstrip that you will ride past on the latter half of the ride. This is connected with the National Guard training facility located at this site. There are numerous side trails branching off the airstrip and some interesting buildings to explore.

General location: Killick Pond is located in the town of Hollis and lies approximately 15 miles west of the city of Portland.

Elevation change: The name "Killick Plains," which describes the area around Killick Pond, accurately reflects the generally flat terrain. There are no substantial changes in elevation throughout this ride.

Season: Early summer through fall is the best time of year to explore this ride, given that the mosquitos can be fierce in the spring.

Services: There is a general store in North Hollis. Bicycle parts and service are available at any of the many bike shops in the greater Portland area. The closest source for such needs is Gorham Bike and Ski on ME 25 in downtown Gorham (phone (207) 839-2770).

Hazards: Sections of this trail are quite sandy. The best way to ride in sand is to decrease your tire pressure and relax your grip on the handle bars. Ticks are plentiful in the area; be sure to examine yourself thoroughly after completing your ride.

Rescue index: Residential development in the area around Killick Pond guarantees that you will never be more than a few miles from assistance.

Land status: Killick Pond is part of a wildlife management area overseen by the Department of Inland Fisheries and Wildlife. Parts of this trail may also pass through private property.

Maps: The USGS quad for this area is Limington, Maine.

Finding the trail: From the Portland area, drive west on ME 25 through Westbrook and Gorham. At the junction of ME 25 and ME 112, bear left onto ME 112, which is also named the Dow Road. After about 5.5 miles, you will reach a crossroad; turn right onto ME 22. After little more than a mile, turn left at another crossroad onto ME 35 heading south. Cross the Saco River and, as ME 35 makes a sharp turn to the left, continue straight. This road turns to dirt. After a small rise, the area opens out into an agricultural field (potatoes were growing when we passed by); turn right just before the field, and travel along a dirt road that skirts the perimeter of the field. Bear right at a fork and make your way to a single pole line. You should find ample parking just in front of the sign for Killick Pond.

Source of additional information:

Maine Department of Inland Fisheries and Wildlife
41 State House Station
Augusta, ME 04333-0041

Notes on the trail: Ride down the dirt road, passing the sign for Killick Pond on your right. At a split in the road, turn right and ride along a firm section of double-track that follows the bank of a stream. This portion of the trail is carpeted with pine needles. At an open field, follow the perimeter out to a paved road. This is Sand Pond Road; turn left. When you reach the entrance to the unpaved Killick Mills Pond Road, bear left. Notice the sandy terrain, very different from the moist, hard-packed trail at the beginning of the ride. As you come up a slight rise, turn right onto Old Coach Road. At a white trailer

RIDE 7 · Killick Pond

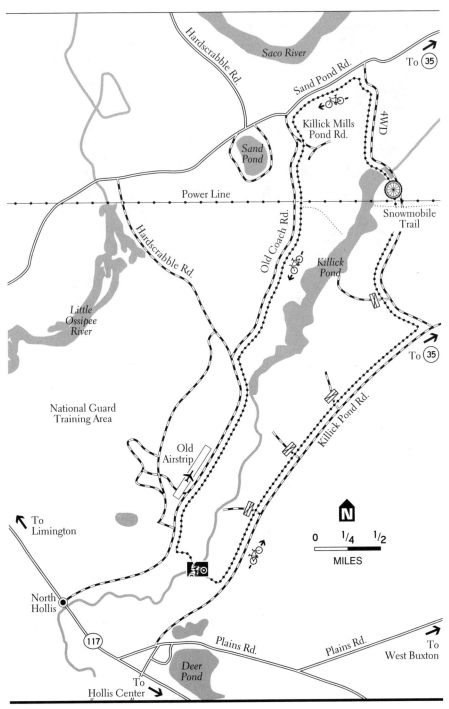

A sandy trail through the pine barrens of Killick Plains.

house, which also has a paddock for horses, bear right onto a narrower trail that reaches and crosses the same single pole line that marked the trailhead.

Beyond the power line, the trail reenters the woods. After a mile, you will reach a wider dirt road: Hardscrabble Road, which is also signed for snowmobiles as ITS 89. Turn left onto this road. A short distance will bring you to what we fondly refer to as the "Desert of Hollis": a barren, sandy area that boasts a small airstrip. It is worth exploring this area, as there is a vast network of side trails, most of which reconnect with Hardscrabble Road at some point. To resume the ride, however, continue along Hardscrabble Road until you see a narrow trail on the left. This junction should be signed for snowmobiles, and the left turn is marked as ITS 89 South, heading toward Hollis, Bar Mills, and Alfred. This is a tunnel-like section of trail that resembles a luge run with sand, instead of ice and snow, as its base. You will cross the stream that runs out of Killick Pond over a snowmobile bridge. Shortly beyond this point you will reach a **T** intersection. Turn left and continue up the dirt road. When you reach another dirt road, signed for Killick Pond, turn left onto it and return to the trailhead.

RIDE 8 · Sawyer Mountain

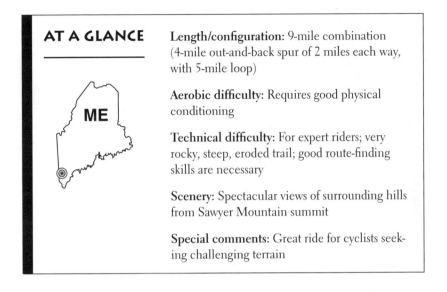

AT A GLANCE

Length/configuration: 9-mile combination (4-mile out-and-back spur of 2 miles each way, with 5-mile loop)

Aerobic difficulty: Requires good physical conditioning

Technical difficulty: For expert riders; very rocky, steep, eroded trail; good route-finding skills are necessary

Scenery: Spectacular views of surrounding hills from Sawyer Mountain summit

Special comments: Great ride for cyclists seeking challenging terrain

The summit of Sawyer Mountain can be reached on this 9-mile ride, but not without a struggle. Although an old town road leads up and over the top of the mountain, both the ascent and descent feature a rough and severely eroded surface that requires excellent bike handling skills. A portion of the loop also follows a snowmobile trail through the woods. Not only is this a challenging section of single-track, but the trail can be tricky to follow in summer months when foliage and thick undergrowth obscure the trail.

This ride can be experienced in a number of ways. Our trail notes describe the route we took, which begins and ends on an old town road that branches off ME 117 and connects to a loop around the western slope of Sawyer Mountain. Tackling the ride in this fashion makes for a 9-mile excursion that includes a short side trip up to the summit of the mountain. We have noted an alternative parking area on the map, making it possible to ride the loop and the side trip up Sawyer, while avoiding the most severely eroded sections of the road between ME 117 and the summit of the mountain. Regardless of the route you choose, this ride requires the skills of an advanced rider in good physical condition.

For the most part, you will be in the woods throughout this ride. A small clearing at the top of Sawyer Mountain does offer some good views, and you will also be able to look up at the mountain from the orchard at its base. The single-track trail that loops back up the mountain covers land that was once farmed. You will ride among a myriad of stone fences, and past old well sites and overgrown stone foundations.

General location: Sawyer Mountain lies northwest of Limington.

Elevation change: The trailhead from ME 117 is at about 490'. From there, you will climb steadily and steeply to 1,120'. The side trip to the summit of Sawyer Mountain continues up to 1,200'. From the top of the mountain, you will descend to 460' just before Emerys Corner. You will then climb slightly to 640' before dropping to 500'. From there, you will climb back up to 1,120' before descending to the trailhead and ME 117. Total elevation gain for the ride is 1,510'.

Season: Late spring through fall offer the best riding conditions.

Services: There is a small shopping center in North Limington at the junction of ME 25 and ME 11. The nearest bike shop is Gorham Bike and Ski, 12 Main Street, Gorham, (207) 839-2770.

Hazards: The road up and over Sawyer Mountain is steep and severely eroded, with a lot of loose rock and a number of deep gullies. This is also a popular road with all-terrain vehicle riders.

Rescue index: You will never be more than a few miles from homes throughout this ride.

Land status: Old roads and a snowmobile trail.

Maps: There are three USGS quads for this ride: Cornish, Limerick, and Limington. A portion of the ride is also depicted in DeLorme's *Maine Atlas and Gazetteer* (map 4, sections D-4, D-3, and E-3).

Finding the trail: From the Portland area, follow ME 25 heading west. At the junction of ME 25 and ME 11 in North Limington, turn left onto ME 11. At the crossroad in Limington, turn right onto ME 117. Follow ME 117 through a sharp left turn and up a small hill. As ME 117 begins to swing to the right, a small dirt road continues straight ahead. Turn left into the pullout on the side of the road. Your ride begins up that dirt road.

Sources of additional information: None.

Notes on the trail: From ME 117, begin pedaling up the dirt road. You will notice a stone fence on your left and probably some land share signs. Also, just a short distance from where you parked, you will pass a junction of snowmobile trails on the right. Continue straight, passing a grassy road on the left and beginning up a rocky, eroded hill. This rough stretch gradually breaks into more even terrain, though you will continue to climb. You will pass a road on the right and a small cemetery before reaching a junction with a gated road on the left. Bear right here and then immediately bear left, avoiding a vague trail that leads back down the hillside, to continue uphill. From

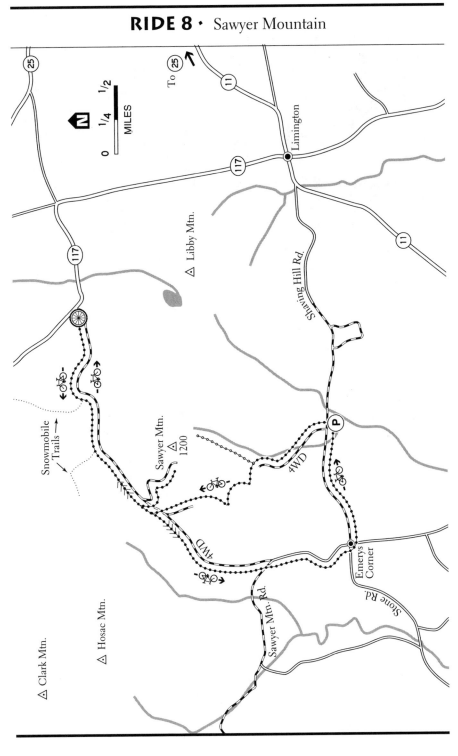

A well-earned descent from Sawyer Mountain.

here, the climb intensifies and you will negotiate a rather beastly eroded section of the road. Continue on, passing another snowmobile junction on the right that leads to Cornish.

At the crest of the hill, the trail begins to descend. However, at this point there is also a trail continuing up on the left. This is the out-and-back side trip to the top of Sawyer and may be signed as Mountain Top. The trail first climbs over some exposed rock before winding along a grassy path through sumac and pine. The trail ends at a small, grassy clearing at the summit of Sawyer Mountain. On clear days, it is possible to take in some great views from this vantage point.

Retrace your route to the previous intersection and turn left down the hill toward Limerick. This rough descent eventually merges into a dirt road that then becomes paved. Don't make any turns until you reach Emerys Corner, a crossroad at the edge of Three Hills Orchards. Turn left at this crossroad and follow a dirt road that runs through the middle of the orchard and then re-enters the woods. Ride past an old road on the left and, after a short descent, look for a second road on the left. If the snowmobile signs are still posted, this road will be signed to Sawyer Mountain; turn left. There is a small clearing across from the road, an alternative parking area should you choose to begin the trail from here.

Stone fences still run alongside this abandoned old road. At a fork, stay straight between these walls, avoiding a trail that branches off to the right. As you continue up a gradual climb, keep your eyes peeled for a cluster of old stone foundations on the left. The trail you are looking for bears left here at an angle of about 45° to the main road. You will be ducking into the woods among these foundations. As you pass an old well opening on the right, the trail becomes more obvious, running between two stone fences. If you miss this turn, the road you are riding up veers to the right and continues for about a mile before petering out in the woods. It makes an interesting side trip, however, revealing much about the past agricultural activity of the area.

Up the southern slope of Sawyer Mountain, you will be riding along an indistinct single-track trail that weaves across land that was once farmed and through openings in old stone fences. The trail will take you up the mountain to a snowmobile trail junction that is signed as Round Top to the left, and Sawyer Mountain to the right. Bear right here, descending slightly as you ride along an indistinct path around a small knoll. Past the knoll, look for an opening in a stone fence on the left. Proceed through this opening and turn right to ride alongside the fence. Gradually, you will need to bear to your left, across this old pasture (now grown in with trees) and through another stone fence into an area of young saplings and onto a more obvious, grassy path. Follow this path to its junction with the old town road that goes up and over Sawyer Mountain. Turn right, climbing back up to the crest of the hill and then descending back to the trailhead.

RIDE 9 · Wiggin Mountain

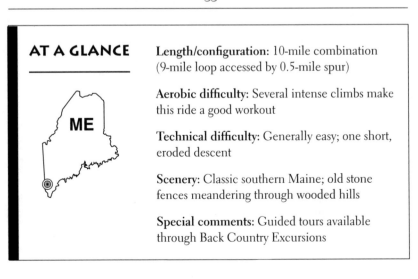

AT A GLANCE

Length/configuration: 10-mile combination (9-mile loop accessed by 0.5-mile spur)

Aerobic difficulty: Several intense climbs make this ride a good workout

Technical difficulty: Generally easy; one short, eroded descent

Scenery: Classic southern Maine; old stone fences meandering through wooded hills

Special comments: Guided tours available through Back Country Excursions

The wooded landscape of this rural area in southern Maine makes this ride a perfect city getaway. It begins up a short, half-mile spur that connects to a 9-mile loop and demands an intermediate technical ability and a moderate level of fitness. Along old and abandoned town and county roads, the trail follows the lines of old stone fences that recall earlier years, when the land was cleared for pasture. The terrain includes everything from steep climbs and tricky technical sections to long, easy, downhill stretches and beautiful scenery.

Parsonsfield is home to Back Country Excursions, a facility and service that offers guided tours, fabulous meals, cozy accommodations, and the opportunity to share the experience of exploring and enjoying the many trails available in this area. Cliff Krolick, owner and creator of B.C.E., offers single- and multi-day tours that are designed to meet the needs of mountain bikers of all skill levels, ages, and preferences. Behind the B.C.E. lodge, the "Rock–Log Palace" terrain garden gives riders the opportunity to practice or learn many different technical skills. Cliff includes breakfast and trail snacks for all his participants (the cookies alone are worth going for) and will see that you wrap up your ride with a trip to his wood-fired cedar hot tub.

General location: Parsonsfield.

Elevation change: Back Country Excursions is located at 700'. You will climb to 825' before traveling along undulating terrain to the foot of Wiggin Mountain. The climb up Wiggin Mountain is by far the most aerobically challenging portion of the ride and ascends to 1,120' in less than 1 mile. From this high point, you will embark upon a breathtaking descent that drops to 730'. From here, the trail is characterized by relatively modest changes in elevation. Total elevation gain is approximtely 1,010'.

Season: The trails in this area can be ridden throughout the year. Back Country Excursions will schedule tours all week long, year-round, and at your convenience.

Services: Apart from Back Country Excursions, the closest resources for cycling needs are to be found in either Sanford or the greater Portland area. Stores in Limerick, Kezar Falls, and Cornish should satisfy all other needs.

Hazards: There are many interconnecting trails and old roads in this area that may not be clearly marked on any map. If you choose to ride without a guide, a topographic map is essential. Be aware that some of the areas covered by this trail may at times be busy with logging activity.

Rescue index: Though you pass some homes at points along this route, you will be riding through woods where the chance of meeting another person may be slim. At the farthest, you will be 5 miles from assistance.

Land status: Though the network of trails in this area is made up of discontinued roads along which a public right-of-way still exists, much of the surrounding land is privately owned.

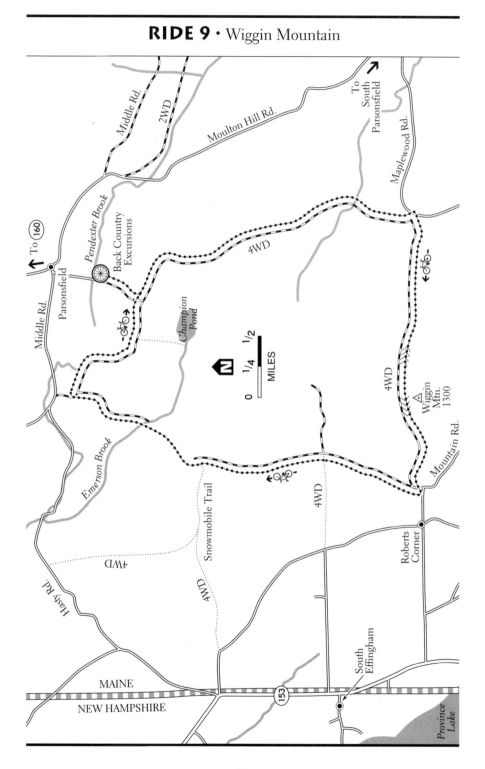

Maps: The USGS 7.5 minute series quadrangle for Wiggin Mountain is West Newfield.

Finding the trail: From Portland, take the Westbrook exit off the Maine Turnpike and follow ME 25 heading west through Gorham and Standish. After crossing the Saco River, turn left at the first traffic light onto ME 11 heading toward Limerick. You will travel on ME 11 for about 7 to 8 miles, passing 2 lakes on your right. At the top of the hill on Main Street in Limerick, turn right and then veer immediately to the left onto ME 160. After another 7 to 8 miles, look for a green sign for Province Lake. Past the sign, you will want to take the next left onto Merrill Hill Road. Drive up and over Merrill Hill and begin to slow down when you see a church on the right. Turn right just after passing the church, and immediately look and turn left (you will notice a white farmhouse nearby). After a quarter mile you will see a sign for Back Country Excursions, which is on the left side of the road. If you are not riding with a group from B.C.E., you will have to park your car up by the church and begin your ride from there.

Source of additional information:

Back Country Excursions of Maine
RFD 2, Box 365
Limerick, ME 04048
(207) 625-8189

Notes on the trail: We began this ride with Cliff Krolick on a chilly Saturday morning in October. If you organize a trip with Cliff, you will begin the ride from his doorstep. If, however, you have parked up by the church, you will need to follow the directions to Back Country Excursions and continue your ride from there.

Turning left out of Cliff's driveway, the ride begins with what B.C.E. fondly refers to as the "wake-up call." This initial climb features a few technically challenging sections before cresting at a **T** intersection that marks the beginning and end of the loop. Turn left and follow the trail along an old road bordered by old stone fences. After a steep descent and twist to the right, you will reach Moose Marsh. At a **T** intersection with the paved south road, turn right and continue along the pavement for a short stretch. Continue straight onto another dirt road and begin the most strenuous climb of the ride up Wiggin Mountain.

At the top of Wiggin Mountain there is a small, cleared area that makes a great refueling site. If you're lucky, this is where Cliff will dig out a bag of his famous cookies. The ride continues down Wiggin Mountain, a breezy cruise that more than makes up for the extended climb to the top. Follow the trail down to the left. You will descend Wiggin Mountain on a trail that has been well maintained and features a series of waterbars. If you are into "big air,"

Karine skillfully
negotiates the
descent from
Wiggin Mountain.

you will certainly have the opportunity to catch some here! At the bottom of
the hill, you will come to a **T** intersection with an improved road. Turn right
and continue following the road until it swings sharply to the right. At this
point, continue straight instead and follow an old road through a recently
logged area. The road descends gradually and then deteriorates into a rough
and eroded trail that requires excellent route-picking skills. Beyond the
roughest section of this trail you will come to a three-way intersection that
may be marked with snowmobile trail signs. Bear right here. You will cross a
stream and then pass through an open area before returning to the woods on a
gradually improving two-wheel-drive road.

When you reach an old road branching off to the right, turn right and follow the trail up a few short hills. After a short distance you will return to the
first junction at the top of the "wake-up call" hill. Turn left down the hill to
return to Back Country Excursions or your car.

RIDE 10 · Porterfield

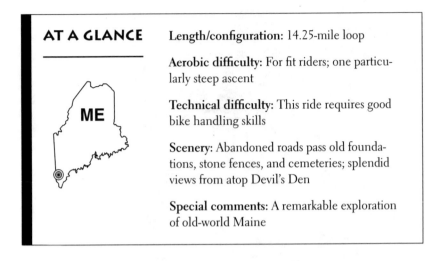

AT A GLANCE

Length/configuration: 14.25-mile loop

Aerobic difficulty: For fit riders; one particularly steep ascent

Technical difficulty: This ride requires good bike handling skills

Scenery: Abandoned roads pass old foundations, stone fences, and cemeteries; splendid views from atop Devil's Den

Special comments: A remarkable exploration of old-world Maine

This ride is a 14.25-mile loop along some of the most beautiful old roads in southwestern Maine. Don't let the word "road" dissuade you from exploring this area. You will pedal on pavement for just a short distance; the remaining roads were never paved and were abandoned long ago. They offer excellent double-track riding along surfaces that include smooth, grassy interludes and rocky, severely eroded slopes. The Porterfield area is isolated, the landscape rough and hilly; this terrain will present a challenge to intermediate riders and requires good cardiovascular fitness.

Porterfield is located just east of New Hampshire. Most of this ride follows abandoned old roads that are still accompanied by miles of stone fences. Old foundations and cemeteries are still visible from the trail and remain as evidence of what was once a thriving farming community. At the beginning and end of this ride, views of the Burnt Meadow Mountains are expansive. In the fall, these views are particularly spectacular, turning into a festive celebration of fall's vibrant colors. Part way through the ride, there is an optional side trip up a paved road to Buena Vista Estates, a development that is situated at the top of a hill that provides a spectacular view of the White Mountains, including Mount Washington, which is usually dusted with snow by early fall. The latter portion of the ride also provides riders with the opportunity to hike up a short trail to Devil's Den. A precipitous drop from this high knoll encourages a careful step but nevertheless provides an excellent vantage point from which to survey the surrounding area.

General location: Porterfield is in southern Oxford County. The closest large town is Fryeburg, just 12 miles to the north.

RIDE 10 · Porterfield

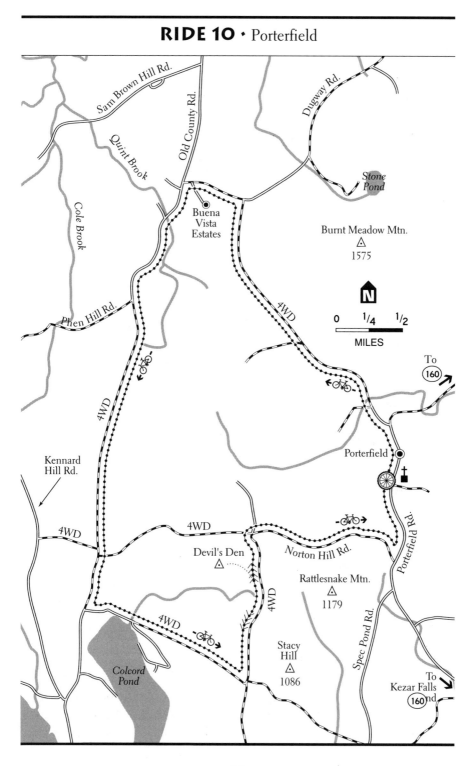

Elevation change: The trailhead for this ride is at about 540'. You will climb to 800' and then drop to about 740'. If you choose to ride up to Buena Vista Estates, you will climb to just over 860'. On the paved road, you will descend to 640' to cross Quint Brook and then begin a gradual climb to 860'. A quick drop to cross another small brook is followed by a steep climb to 900'. Beyond this point, the trail descends to Colcord Pond at 550'. From the pond, you will climb gradually to 800', enjoy a short descent to a crossroads at 770', and then climb to Devil's Den at 1,020'. You can choose to walk to the top of Devil's Den from this point: a further gain of 165' to the summit at 1,185'. The ride ends, forgivingly, with a blissful descent to the trailhead. Total elevation gain for this ride is about 1,150'.

Season: Summer and fall provide the best riding conditions for the Porterfield ride, but there is an active ski and snowmobile club that grooms the trails for wintertime use. With studded tires and some cold-weather gear, the ride is a breathtaking winter expedition.

Services: General stores in Hiram, Cornish, South Hiram, and Kezar Falls will satisfy your needs for food and water. Bike parts, however, may be hard to come by unless you're prepared to travel to Fryeburg, Bridgton, or Naples.

Hazards: The descent to Colcord Pond is steep, extremely rough, and strewn with loose rock.

Rescue index: You will not be more than 2 or 3 miles from homes along this ride.

Land status: Public right-of-ways still exist for these old roads, but be aware that the land they cross is private property.

Maps: The USGS 7.5 minute quads for this area are Kezar Falls and Brownfield. The ride is also depicted in DeLorme's *Maine Atlas and Gazetteer* (map 4, section C-1).

Finding the trail: From the Portland area, travel west on ME 25 all the way to Kezar Falls. After crossing the Ossipee River, bear right onto ME 160 north, through South Hiram. You will travel only 2.5 miles along ME 160, passing Stanley Pond and Trafton Pond on the right, before turning left onto Porterfield Road. Continue along Porterfield Road until you see a small cemetery on the right. You should be able to find a place to pull off the road just beyond the cemetery.

Sources of additional information: None.

Notes on the trail: From the cemetery, begin your ride by continuing along the paved Porterfield Road. Bear left at the first fork and then continue straight past Rounds Road, which branches off to the left. The road is unpaved from this point on, and after 1 mile it deteriorates to a less improved double-track jeep trail. Although the road seems to bear left and descend, be sure to bear right at the next fork, climbing slightly along fairly rocky terrain. You will pass a driveway and small camp on the left; continue straight until you reach a T intersection. Bear right. Past a swamp and a white house, you will come to a second T intersection. Turn left onto a more improved dirt road that climbs past a beautiful hillside pasture. When you reach a paved road, you must bear right and drop down to a T intersection with Old County Road to continue the ride. However, it is well worth making a short side trip by riding up the road to the left. This climb to Buena Vista Estates will reward you with a panoramic view of Mount Washington and other summits of the White Mountains. When we rode this trail in October, snow-covered Mount Washington created a striking background to the brilliant fall colors of the lower foothills.

From the hilltop, ride back down the hill to the T intersection with Old County Road. Turn left. You will ride on pavement for a full mile, first descending to cross Quint Brook and then continuing over small hills and several curves in the road. When you come to the unpaved portion of the road, continue straight past a house on the right and a dirt road branching off on the right. As you pass the Sugarloaf Tree Farm on your left, the road once again reverts to a double-track jeep trail.

Notice the stone foundations off the right-hand side of this trail and the stone fence still standing on the left. Continue straight, avoiding turnoffs that merely lead to dead ends. As you reach a junction with a grassy road on the left, pause to examine a beautiful old stone foundation at the corner of the intersection. A half mile farther, you will negotiate a rather steep climb. Just beyond this hill, you will reach a junction with a less grassy road. There is some trail activity to the left, but continue straight. A short distance farther you will also notice a road on the right that is well signed for winter snowmobile travel. After a steep and extremely rocky descent, turn left down a more improved dirt road. You will be able to see cabins and cottages along the edge of Colcord Pond. The road skirts the pond, which is on your right. At a small clearing on the left, you will begin to move away from the water. The road deteriorates soon after and continues to the left at a junction with a driveway.

You will climb steadily away from the pond. Old stone fences on either side of the road clearly identify the route. Ride straight past two trails that branch off to the left. After the second, notice many old, deep foundations to the right of the trail. A rough, rocky section of the road breaks into a smooth descent beneath the bowed branches of trees that create an almost tunnel-like passage. Past this stretch, an opening on the right reveals a spot where fieldstones are being collected near the site of an old cemetery. Just beyond, you will reach a crossroad. There is a cluster of trees at the center of this four-way

Ride back to
the past along
old roads in
Porterfield.

intersection. Bear left and then turn left up the first road that leads out of the
intersection. If the signs posted to guide snowmobile riders are still up, be
sure you begin riding up the trail that heads in the direction of Devil's Den,
Brownfield, and the New Hampshire trails.

This road is now a grassy trail, bordered on either side by stone fences.
Start up a fairly treacherous climb, and bear right at the first split in the trail.
You will continue to climb. At the crest of the hill, you may notice a sign on
the left that reads "Devil's Den Mount." This private way leads to the top of a
prominent hill. Day hikers are welcome, so leave your bike and hike up. Not
only is there a precipitous fall and cave at the top, but also a splendid view
that will make the previous climb seem well worthwhile.

To continue your ride, follow the road as it descends, and turn right at a
crossroad onto Norton Hill Road. Cruise down the next hill, taking in another gorgeous view of the Burnt Meadow Mountains. The next T intersection connects you with Porterfield Road. Turn left to return to your car.

RIDE 11 · Boston Hills

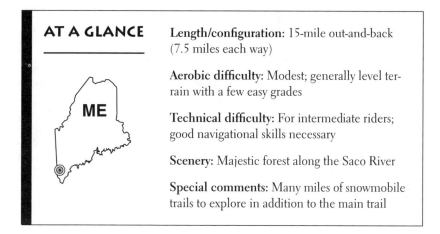

AT A GLANCE

Length/configuration: 15-mile out-and-back (7.5 miles each way)

Aerobic difficulty: Modest; generally level terrain with a few easy grades

Technical difficulty: For intermediate riders; good navigational skills necessary

Scenery: Majestic forest along the Saco River

Special comments: Many miles of snowmobile trails to explore in addition to the main trail

This is a 15-mile out-and-back ride on a combination of old logging roads and single- and double-track trails. The ride skirts the base of the Boston Hills, never gaining much in elevation. It meanders, much like the nearby Saco River, through generally low-lying woods. Intermediate-level riders in good physical condition will have no difficulties with this ride. Riders looking for a shorter alternative can opt to ride out to the Saco River and back, for a six- or a seven-mile round-trip.

After mosquito season, this ride is spectacular. The trees along the Saco River branch out gracefully and create a high, thick, leafy canopy through which sunlight is filtered into soft hues of green in the spring and summer. The ground cover beneath the trees is a sea of soft, tall ferns, which seem to part only to let the trail weave through the woods. The Saco River is equally picturesque and moves at a leisurely pace past small, white, sandy beaches on its banks. Although the trails on this ride get a great deal of use by snowmobiles in the winter, they seem to be visited by very few other travelers in the summer and fall.

General location: In Denmark; this ride falls in the middle of the triangle formed between the towns of Hiram, Fryeburg, and Bridgton.

Elevation change: Slight.

Season: The only time to avoid this ride is in the early spring, when the entire area is likely to be damp and overshadowed by clouds of mosquitos. There is an extensive network of snowmobile trails in and around the area, making for some fantastic winter riding.

Services: There is a general store in Denmark. The nearest bike shop is to the east, in Naples.

Hazards: There is no doubt that we encountered some of the most fierce mosquitos of the summer along the Saco River section of this trail. Be sure to carry bug repellent with you if you are riding here in the spring or early summer, when the bugs are at their worst.

Rescue index: You will be 3.75 miles from assistance at the halfway point along this trail.

Land status: Although a public right-of-way still exists along certain portions of this ride, you will also be riding on snowmobile trails and old logging roads through private land along the Saco River. Be considerate of the landowners and stay on the trails.

Maps: The most up-to-date map we could find for this area is in the most recent edition of *Maine Atlas and Gazetteer* (map 4, section B-3). The USGS 7.5 minute quad is Hiram, although the last update on this map was in 1964, and the trail documentation is therefore incomplete.

Finding the trail: From the Portland area, follow ME 25 west all the way to Cornish. In Cornish, bear right onto ME 117 and cross the Saco River. At the junction with ME 113, turn left and continue to Hiram. In Hiram, bear right to continue along ME 117. After approximately 5 miles, look for a dirt road on the left. Although easy to miss the first time around, this is the first and only dirt road on the left between Hiram and Denmark. Follow this road just until you come to a small cleared area on the right that serves as a parking area.

Sources of additional information: None.

Notes on the trail: Begin by riding away from the dirt road you drove in on. The trailhead is at the far end of the parking area and is identified by a large boulder. Pick up the double-track trail beyond this boulder. You will ride through an old clear-cut that gives you the only opportunity you will have on this ride to enjoy the scenery of the surrounding hills. Cross a snowmobile bridge and then continue straight at a fork in the road; turning right here will take you along a logging road into another clear-cut. Bear right at the next fork, coming face-to-face with a tranquil, lilly pad–laden pond. Pedal over the wide, metal grate that serves as a bridge over the outlet of the pond.

At the next fork in the trail, you can stay straight or bear to the right — both routes quickly reconnect. If you stay straight, you will come to a **T** intersection. Turn right unless you're interested in a very short detour down to the left, which will bring you to a gated bridge across the water. Once you ride back up to the **T** intersection, continue straight and you will very quickly see the other trail coming in on the right.

A small snowmobile bridge is the next landmark. Crossing it, you will enter a magnificent wood. Through this wood, you will reach an old channel of the Saco River, following its sandy bank for a short while before the

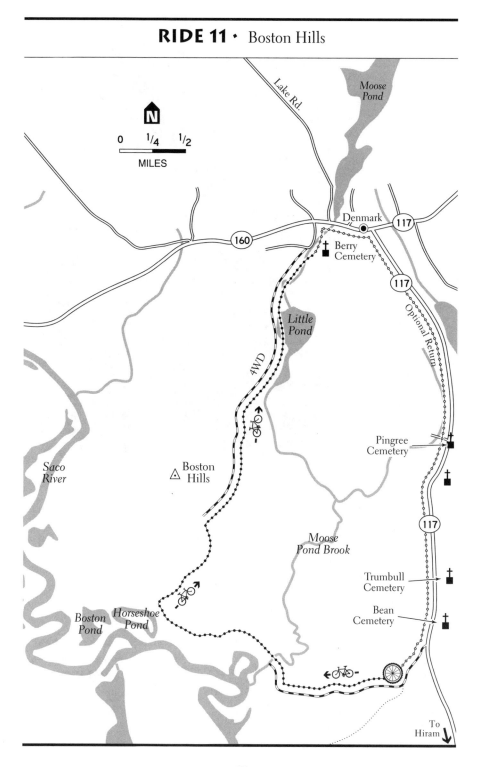

Tall, lush ferns grace the trail at the foot of the Boston Hills in Brownfield.

trail once again turns into the woods. A short distance farther, you will come to a trail junction that will most likely be signed for snowmobiles. Turn right, away from Brownfield and Fryeburg, and follow the signs toward Denmark Village and Bridgton (the direction from which you came will be signed as Sebago and Hiram). Just beyond this intersection, the snowmobile trail is rerouted because of a fallen tree. All trails here lead to the same spot: a small brook that shows evidence of once having been spanned by a small bridge. Cross the brook and continue to follow the trail on the other side.

Gradually, the trail widens into an old road. You will pass Little Pond on your right. A stone fence on the right, followed by a meadow and a house, signals the end of the trail, which continues for just a short distance farther before connecting to a road that leads into Denmark. Continue up to this intersection, which is also the site of an old mill, though a snowmobile bridge is now the only structure spanning the stream. Turn around here, and retrace your route back to the parking area.

RIDE 12 · Fryeburg

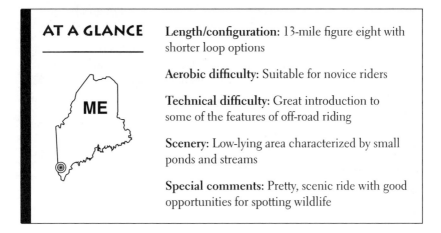

AT A GLANCE

Length/configuration: 13-mile figure eight with shorter loop options

Aerobic difficulty: Suitable for novice riders

Technical difficulty: Great introduction to some of the features of off-road riding

Scenery: Low-lying area characterized by small ponds and streams

Special comments: Pretty, scenic ride with good opportunities for spotting wildlife

There is some marvelous riding just south of Fryeburg, which highlights the many low mountains that rise up from the lush, low-lying area along the Saco River. This ride makes use of a combination of single- and double-track trails, as well as dirt roads, an old access road, and a short section of pavement. Several options are available to bikers on this ride, which features two overlapping loops. The first is an excellent five-mile circuit suitable for beginning-level riders. The second is a slightly more rigorous ride of eight miles and is more suitable for intermediate- and advanced-level riders. Each loop can be ridden alone for a less lengthy ride, or together as a figure eight of almost 13 miles.

Although not part of the Brownfield Bog Wildlife Management Area to the east of ME 5/113, the area traversed on this ride features similar, if slightly less wet, terrain. A combination of wetlands and wooded uplands creates a picturesque landscape that offers plenty of opportunities to spot wildlife. In 1947, the town of Brownfield was leveled by the great fire in Maine.

General location: This ride begins from the Maine Bird Dog Club Trial Area, just off ME 5/113 south of Fryeburg.

Elevation change: There is very little change in elevation on this ride, except for the trip up Tibbetts Mountain on the second loop. The access road up the mountain climbs to 620' and promptly descends back to the road at 495', for a total elevation gain of 125'.

Season: Riding is good from June through the fall, with the exception of periods of high rainfall, after which some sections of the ride may become too wet to traverse.

Services: Most services are available in Fryeburg, with the exception of bicycle-related needs. The closest bike store is Speed Cycle on US 302 in Naples (phone (207) 693-6118), situated at the southern tip of Long Lake approximately 15 miles east of the town of Fryeburg.

Hazards: There is a network of snowmobile trails throughout this area, and the ride crosses several bridges constructed for snowmobile traffic in the winter. These structures may be in various stages of disrepair, and it is advisable to check their soundness before trusting them to get you safely across brooks and streams.

Rescue index: You will remain within a few miles of either ME 5/113 or Haley Town Road. There is quite a bit of traffic on ME 5/113, and residences line both sides of Haley Town Road.

Land status: Sections of this ride utilize trails that cross land held by the Maine Bird Dog Club. In addition, the ride follows dirt roads and an old access road up Tibbetts Mountain.

Maps: With the exception of the trails running through the Bird Dog Club Trial Area, this ride is mapped out in DeLorme's *Maine Atlas and Gazetteer* (map 4, section B-1).

Finding the trail: From Fryeburg, head south on ME 5/113. About 3 miles out of town, you will pass the entrance to the Eastern Slopes Regional Airport on the right side of the road. Continue beyond this road and look for the next road on the right. This entrance is signed for the Maine Bird Dog Club Trial Area. Follow the road in, bearing right at a split, until you reach a clearing suitable for parking.

Sources of additional information: None.

Notes on the trail: The trail you want to begin riding on is a double-track jeep trail that runs along the left side of the clearing. You will quickly come to a split in this trail; bear right. A half mile into the ride, you will cross a brook. Just beyond this brook you will reach a clearing with a pond on the left. This is Clays Pond, and just below the dam, there is a narrow trail that descends and then climbs the bank on the other side. This is the trail on which you will return to complete the loop.

To continue the ride, travel north up an improved dirt road that leads out of the clearing, keeping the pond on your left. Bear left at the next trail junction (the trail on the right just loops up into a cleared, sandy area and reconnects with the trail a short distance ahead). Very shortly after this, there is a side road descending to the pond on the left; continue straight. One and a half miles into the ride, you will come to a **T** intersection. Turn left onto a dirt road and ride up to a second **T** intersection. This is Farnsworth Road, a wide, sandy road. Turn left again. You will pedal past the western shore of Clays

RIDE 12 · Fryeburg

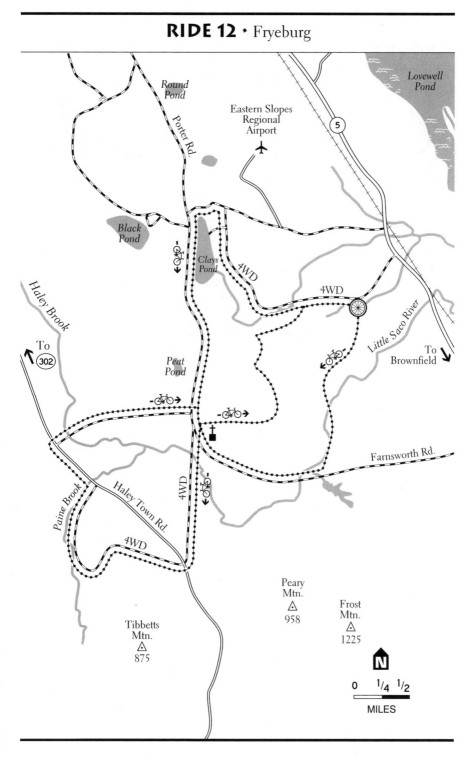

The "Bird Dog" club area.

Pond. Several side trails off to the right lead to Peat Pond and offer short but interesting side trips. Continuing on Farnsworth Road, stay straight at the intersection of a dirt road that branches off to the right. Shortly past this intersection, and just before Farnsworth Road swings around to the left, look for a narrow trail entering the woods on the left. This trail may be marked with snowmobile signs. You will be riding in the woods on this portion of the ride, gradually descending to a bog that offers excellent moose-viewing opportunities. After one mile, you will reach the western shore of Clays Pond.

Follow a trail that bears to the right and drops down the bank quite close to the dam on the edge of Clays Pond. This trail will take you across a drainage pipe and back up into a clearing on the other side of Clays Pond. This is the clearing that you passed through at the beginning of the ride. Bear right and retrace your route back to the very first trail junction. From this junction, you can continue straight and return to your car to complete the 5-mile loop, or you can bear right to continue riding and add another 8 miles to the ride.

If you choose to continue riding, you will follow a snowmobile trail into the woods. After about half a mile, bear left onto a trail that may be signed for East Brownfield and Denmark. Riding just 0.1 mile farther will bring you to a snowmobile bridge with a swamp on the right. When we rode this trail, the bridge was in an advanced state of disrepair. Depending on whether or not it has been repaired or replaced, you may need to dismount and carefully carry your bike across. Continue riding along the grassy double-track trail on the other side. You will pass a trail coming in on the left and then reach an intersection with a cluster of trees in the center. Continue straight and find yourself at an intersection with the unpaved Farnsworth Road.

Turn right onto Farnsworth Road, and ride over the bridge crossing the Little Saco River. Up a short hill, you will pass a cemetery on the right, and just beyond, the road will swing sharply to the right. At this corner, look for a cabin in the woods on the left and find a double-track trail descending past it. Follow this trail around to the right at a junction and cross a bridge over the Little Saco River. You will travel south on this trail, an old road, to its intersection with the paved Haley Town Road. Turn right and immediately look for Fire Lane 14G on the left side of the road. Turn left and begin a steady climb up the western side of Tibbetts Mountain. The road loops around to the right and then descends back to Haley Town Road less than 1 mile farther; turn left on the pavement.

From Haley Town Road, take the first right onto an unnamed dirt road. This road joins the Farnsworth Road after about 1 mile, at which point you will connect with the route of the first loop. Bear right at the junction, and immediately look for the snowmobile trail on the left that will traverse the bog and return you to the dam at the southern tip of Clays Pond. Turn right after crossing the dam and return to the trailhead along what should be a rather familiar route.

RIDE 13 · Shawnee Peak

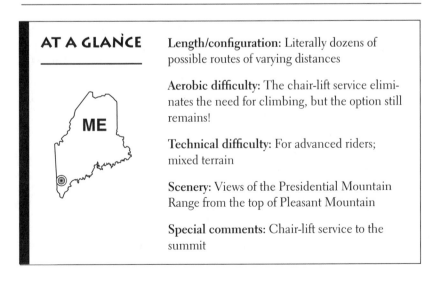

AT A GLANCE

Length/configuration: Literally dozens of possible routes of varying distances

Aerobic difficulty: The chair-lift service eliminates the need for climbing, but the option still remains!

Technical difficulty: For advanced riders; mixed terrain

Scenery: Views of the Presidential Mountain Range from the top of Pleasant Mountain

Special comments: Chair-lift service to the summit

ME

S hawnee Peak, located in Bridgton, Maine, offers experienced riders an exhilarating biking experience. Situated on Pleasant Mountain, Shawnee Peak's mountain bike park offers chairlift service up a 1,300-foot ascent to the summit at 1,900 feet. From there, riders have access to a variety of steep, mountainous terrain and can work their way down the mountain over a combination of existing ski trails and specially created bike paths. The park features a combination of rough, technically challenging terrain (40 percent), wide-open, grassy meadows (40 percent), and dirt roads (20 percent). The terrain is steep and variable, and is not recommended for beginning riders.

On the way up to the summit, riders will be treated to some of the most spectacular views in the area. Shawnee Peak is nestled on the shores of 12-mile Moose Pond and surrounded by a striking combination of mountains, meadows, and lakes. Ever-changing views include those of Mount Washington, the Presidential Range, and the dozens of lakes in the area. Shawnee Peak hosts a variety of summer events each year, including a NORBA-sanctioned mountain bike race.

General location: Shawnee Peak is situated on the north side of Pleasant Mountain, just west of the town of Bridgton.

Elevation change: The base of the chairlift at Shawnee Peak is at 600'. The lift carries riders and their bikes just shy of the summit of Pleasant Mountain at 1,900'. The elevation change is 1,300' for every ride you make down the mountain!

Season: The park is open weekends only, from late June through Labor Day. The season may be extended based on demand and weather, so be sure to call for up-to-the-minute information. Mid-week riding can be arranged in advance for large groups.

Services: Services available at the park include a chairlift service to the top of the mountain, bike and helmet rentals, small-scale bike repairs, an accessory shop, a snack bar, and a first-aid/safety patrol. Some overnight camping is allowed with advance notice. Lift-serviced hiking is also available.

Hazards: Much of the terrain at Shawnee Peak is rough and technically challenging. A helmet is required when you are biking the resort's trails.

Rescue index: There is a first-aid and safety patrol at Shawnee Peak. You will never be more than a mile or two from assistance.

Land status: Shawnee Peak is a privately owned and operated resort.

Maps: Trail maps are available at the base of the mountain, and may also be available at bike stores throughout the state.

Finding the trail: The Shawnee Peak Mountain Bike Park is located on Mountain Road, 6 miles west of downtown Bridgton, off US 302.

RIDE 13 · Shawnee Peak

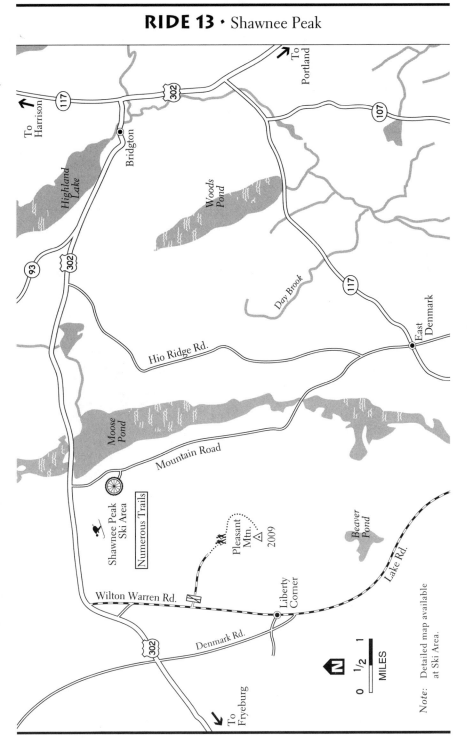

Sources of additional information: For current trail information call (207) 647-8444. Alternatively, you can access park information via e-mail at info@shawneepeak.com, or check out Shawnee Peak's Web site at www.shawneepeak.com.

Notes on the trail: There are any number of routes down the mountain; all you need is a trail map and the will to ride!

Information for the Shawnee Peak ride was provided by Amy Brown.

WESTERN MAINE MOUNTAINS
AND LAKES

The western mountains and lakes region stretches northeast from the New Hampshire border to the Kennebec River Valley. The mountains, a chain known as the Longfellows, stretch northeast across the state and form the northern extremity of the Appalachian Mountain Range. They reach their highest point at Mount Katahdin, 5,267 feet above sea level and the northern endpoint of the Appalachian Trail. Maine's mountains, though not high, are quite dramatic as they rise up from the significantly lower elevations of the surrounding countryside. Many are characterized by a sloping north side and a craggy, broken southern slope. This shape was caused by moving ice, which rode up the northern slopes, smoothing them, and then plucked away rock on the "downstream" side, leaving steep cliffs.

The region is bisected by the Appalachian Trail National Scenic Corridor, which is administered by the National Park Service. The Appalachian Trail was blazed by foresters in the 1920s. Today, the path is a 2,100-mile wilderness trail that connects Mount Katahdin in Baxter State Park to Georgia's Mount Springer. Two hundred and eighty-one miles of the trail pass through Maine and are considered to be the most wild and rugged terrain along the entire route. Many of the rides in this section cross the corridor, providing riders with the opportunity to meet and chat with "through hikers." Most through hikers, traveling from south to north, arrive in the region by late September.

Prior to the passage of modern-day hikers and backpackers, this was the area through which Benedict Arnold and his ragtag army marched on their way to Quebec during the Revolutionary War. Passing just north of the Bigelow Range in the heart of the region Arnold recorded this account in his journal on October 14, 1775: "Reached the third pond or lake; there the prospect is very beautiful and noble, a high chain of mountains encircling the pond, which is deep, clear and fine water, over which a forked mountain [Bigelow] which exceeds the rest in height bearing northwest, and covered with snow, in contrast with the others adds greatly to the beauty of the scene." Arnold and his troops went on to raise a flagpole at the site of what later became the town of Flagstaff, named in honor of that event. In 1950, when the Long Falls Dam was built and the Dead River flooded the town, the resulting reservoir was named Flagstaff Lake. The account of Arnold's expedition is displayed on a series of information boards throughout the region, and the beauty of the Bigelow Mountain Range he described has since been preserved through the creation of the Bigelow Preserve.

The major towns in the region include Fryeburg, Bethel, Rumford, Jay, and Farmington. Any of these towns can supply the basic necessities, and all except Fryeburg have bicycle shops.

FALL FOLIAGE

The best time of year to ride in Maine is in the autumn. The weather is cool; the biting insects have abated; and riders are treated to a spectacular display of color as the foliage responds to seasonal changes. Fall foliage is visible throughout the state, but nowhere is the color contrast more pronounced than in the western mountains.

The change starts occurring by the first week in September, when the swamp maples turn a brilliant red. The other trees follow throughout the month, at a speed that varies from year to year. Some years, the leaves change gradually, with each day's progression hardly noticeable. Other years, the trees seem to explode in color overnight. Peak color in the region usually occurs between the first and second week of October. There is no reliable way to tell in advance when the peak will occur. However, the Department of Conservation issues daily foliage reports to allow "leaf peepers" to determine the locations with the best viewing.

Why do the leaves change color? The process is a photochemical one that actually starts on June 21st, when the day length (photoperiod) is greatest. After June 21st, the daylight hours decrease and the production of chlorophyll by the leaves declines. Chlorophyll is the part of a leaf that makes it green. The pigments carotene and xanthophyll, which cause leaves to turn yellow, are always present in the leaf, but in the summer months they are usually masked by the green chlorophyll. With the decreased production of chlorophyll in the fall, the other pigments start to show. Furthermore, about two weeks before a leaf starts to change color, a layer of cells forms at the base of each leaf. This effectively limits the supply of nutrients to the leaf and causes chlorophyll production to cease altogether. The result is the rapid change in color.

Yellow is primarily seen in birches, witch hazels, maples, aspen, white ash, and beeches. The tannin in the leaves of oaks and beeches turns them brown. Reds are caused by a pigment called anthocyanin. This too is always present in the leaf and is revealed by the same process as the yellow xanthophyll. Bright sunlight is essential for anthocyanin production. This is why the best foliage colors seem to occur during years in which autumn is graced with sunny days and cool nights. The most vivid reds are found in sugar and red maples, northern red oaks, sumac, mountain ash, blueberries, and cranberries.

For information about fall foliage conditions, call the Maine Department of Conservation at (207) 287-4909.

RIDE 14 · Mount Apatite

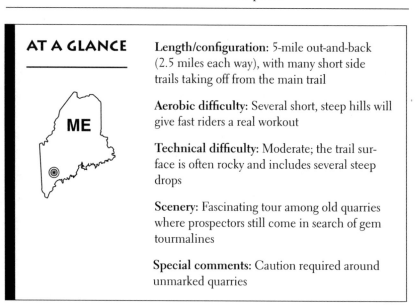

AT A GLANCE

Length/configuration: 5-mile out-and-back (2.5 miles each way), with many short side trails taking off from the main trail

Aerobic difficulty: Several short, steep hills will give fast riders a real workout

Technical difficulty: Moderate; the trail surface is often rocky and includes several steep drops

Scenery: Fascinating tour among old quarries where prospectors still come in search of gem tourmalines

Special comments: Caution required around unmarked quarries

This ride is a short out-and-back affair of five miles, although it is possible to create a loop if you don't mind finishing the ride on pavement. There are also numerous side trails worth exploring. Most of the ride covers moderately technical terrain, beginning up a rugged old mining road that climbs the south side of Mount Apatite. The ride then continues along a double-track trail that runs through woods, along open grassy clearings, and across a small stream. Allow a couple of hours for this loop, or join the many local riders who come here to spend as much time as they have playing on some of the best technical terrain in the area.

Mount Apatite is famous for the gem tourmalines that have been discovered in its vicinity. Local records tell the story of a young boy living at Haskell's Corner, south of Mount Apatite, who found a pretty green stone that he brought home and set on the mantel. Years later, the stone was noticed by Reverend Luther Hill, an itinerant phrenologist. His curiosity aroused, the Reverend searched the area and found the pegmatite patch now known as Mount Apatite. Mining activities have since turned up rich finds on Mount Apatite, including royal purple apatite and green tourmaline. There is currently at least one active mine in the area, which draws vacationing rock hounds and mineral collectors.

Gemstones are not the only treasures mined in this area, however. The most fascinating part of this ride takes you along the edge of a series of quarries. Several companies used to mine for feldspar here, a mineral used in making china. Most of these operations closed in the 1930s. Today, the quarry pits are filled with water, and the stillness of the pools is broken only by the sound of water dripping from the sheer rock above. It is worth exploring the many side trails that surround these deep quarries. Be cautious, though; it is easy to ride around the large boulders that often mark their edge.

General location: Mount Apatite lies southwest of Taylor Pond in Auburn.

Elevation change: This ride is characterized by a series of short climbs and descents.

Season: The best conditions for this ride begin in the late spring and continue through the fall.

Services: All services are available in the Lewiston-Auburn area.

Hazards: The quarries along this ride are deep, and many small trails will take you straight to their edge with little or no warning. The National Guard makes use of this area occasionally. If maneuvers are taking place, postpone your ride for another day.

Rescue index: You will never be far from assistance on this ride. There are often ballgames going on at the fields near the trailhead, and the area is bordered by both homes and roads.

Land status: Once a town park, this area is now managed by the National Guard.

Maps: We could find no adequate map of the trails and roads within this area. However, with the map we have provided and a general familiarity with some of the major geographic landmarks in the area, there is little chance of getting lost. The USGS quad for Mount Apatite is Minot.

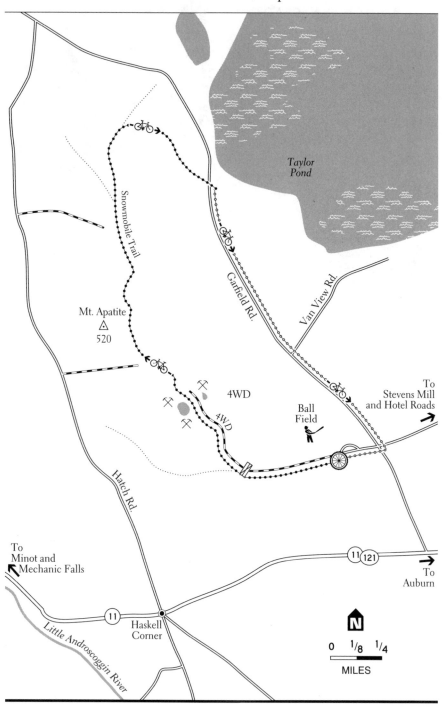

Taylor
Pond

Snowmobile Trail

Garfield Rd.

Van View Rd.

Mt. Apatite
520

4WD

4WD

Ball
Field

To
Stevens Mill
and Hotel Roads

Hatch Rd.

To
Minot and
Mechanic Falls

11 121

To
Auburn

11

Haskell
Corner

Little Androscoggin River

N

0   1/8   1/4

MILES

Blasting down an old mine road at Mount Apatite.

Finding the trail: From ME 4 in Auburn, travel west on ME 11/121. Turn north up Garfield Road and look for the entrance to Cliff Rydholm Park on your left. There is plenty of parking available in the lot beyond the two baseball diamonds.

Source of additional information:

Rainbow Bicycles
1225 Center Street
Auburn, ME 04210
(207) 784-7576 or (800) 244-7576

Notes on the trail: From the baseball diamonds you need to follow the road on which you came in. Keep the fence that encloses some National Guard facilities on your left, and the open, sandy area on your right. The road continues into the woods, and you may notice an old sign for the town park. Pass through a gate and continue along this road as it begins to climb. Follow the road around to the left at an intersection with another trail. In so doing, you will cross what looks like a small bridge over an old mining shaft and you will come to several quarries. The ride continues up some stairs (one quarry is directly on your left here), and turns first to the left and then to the right. The path you want to follow is the main snowmobile trail, signs for which will probably remain from the winter.

At the junction of snowmobile trails, avoid a steep descent to the clubhouse and continue along a grassy road into a cleared area. Follow the trail back into the woods. You will descend steeply to a small stream. The trail continues on the other side of the stream and comes out on Garfield Road, not far from Taylor Pond. At this point, you can either turn around and retrace the ride in the opposite direction, or turn right down the road and follow it back to the entrance to the playing fields.

RIDE 15 · Lost Valley

AT A GLANCE	
ME	**Length/configuration:** Numerous options to explore
	Aerobic difficulty: A network of trails offers riders of all fitness levels a chance to explore
	Technical difficulty: Trails are rated for difficulty
	Scenery: Wooded slopes
	Special comments: Fun riding within minutes of Lewiston-Auburn

Lost Valley is a great setting for your mountain biking pleasure. Located on a wooded 300-acre parcel just west of Auburn, Lost Valley is conveniently located in southern Maine. Mountain biking at Lost Valley includes a combination of a series of tote (or logging) roads and a network of single-track trails. The result is a unique trail system over wooded terrain, rolling hills, streams, and bridges. Recreational riders and mountain bike racers alike will enjoy the thrilling experience of mountain biking at Lost Valley—where there is something for everyone.

Lost Valley is also home to L.L. Bean's bicycling school. Several classes and clinics are organized every season, with programs available for both the beginning rider and the experienced cyclist. In addition, Lost Valley schedules a series of off-road races each year. Open to male and female racers between the ages of 7 and 60, the races are laid out over a three-mile loop. A timed downhill run follows each race. The "Lost Valley Challenge," scheduled each year, is a race that is part of the Maine Mountain Bike Championship Series sanctioned by NORBA. In the fall there is also a two-day event that features a guided tour, cross-country race, giant slalom race, "chariots of fat tire" race, bike pull, cookout, and awards party.

General location: Lost Valley is located just west of the city of Auburn and can be found on Perkins Ridge, overlooking Lake Auburn to the east and Taylor Pond to the south.

Elevation change: At the highest point on Perkins Ridge, riders will reach an elevation of almost 500'. Starting from the Brookside Trail along Lapham Brook at just under 300', this means an elevation gain of 200', without factoring in the rolling hills featured along many of the trails.

Season: The Lost Valley bike facility is open from early May through November. Hours of operation are 9 A.M. to 6 P.M.

Services: All services are available in the twin cities of Lewiston-Auburn.

Hazards: All of Lost Valley's trails are maintained by an experienced staff. No all-terrain vehicles are permitted at Lost Valley, and hunting is discouraged.

Rescue index: While at Lost Valley, you will not be more than a few miles from assistance. All riders are required to check in at the ticket counter upon arrival and to check out after riding.

Land status: Lost Valley is a private facility.

Maps: A trail map is available from the ticket counter.

Finding the trail: From the Maine Turnpike, take Exit 12 and turn right on ME 4. Take the first right, shortly afterward, onto Kitty Hawk Avenue, and follow it until you reach an intersection with Hotel Road. Turn right onto Hotel Road and continue straight to Young's Corner, which is located between the southern tip of Lake Auburn and the northern tip of Taylor Pond. Turn left here and follow the signs to Lost Valley.

Sources of additional information: For further information, or to get the Lost Valley race series schedule, you can contact Lost Valley at (207) 784-1561. For more information about the L.L. Bean bicycling school, call the L.L. Bean Outdoor Discovery Program at (800) 341-4341, ext. 6666.

Notes on the trail: With 8 interconnecting trails, riders at Lost Valley can enjoy miles of varied terrain. All the trails are rated according to difficulty. Brookside, one of the trails designated as moderate, was specifically designed and developed for mountain bikers in the summer and cross-country skiers in the winter. Brookside parallels Lapham Brook and follows a scenic route over double-track terrain, cutting through an evergreen forest. For the more daring rider, Mountain Vista is the most difficult trail at Lost Valley, and thrill seekers will find plenty of technical single-track terrain to take them up to the highest elevation on Perkins Ridge, with views overlooking Taylor Pond to the south.

Information for the Lost Valley Ride was provided by Matthew Erickson of Lost Valley.

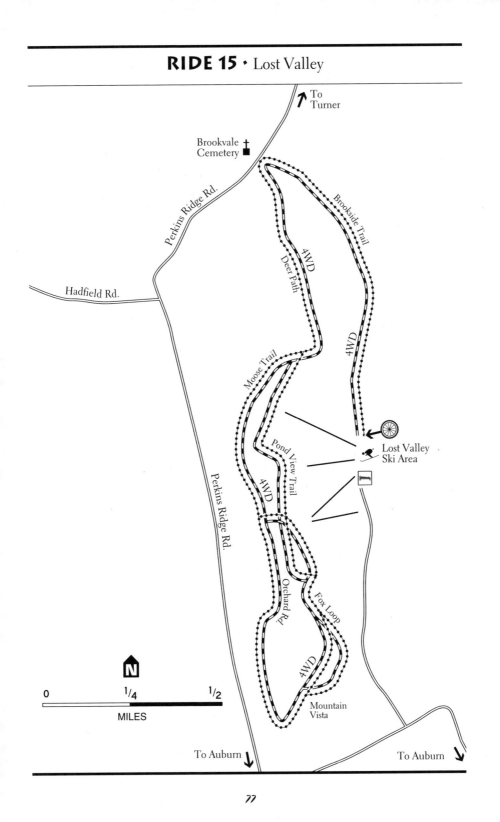

To
Turner

Brookvale
Cemetery

Perkins Ridge Rd.

Brookside Trail

4WD

Deer Path

Hadfield Rd.

Moose Trail

4WD

Pond View Trail

Lost Valley
Ski Area

Perkins Ridge Rd.

4WD

Orchard Rd.

Fox Loop

4WD

Mountain
Vista

N

0   1/4   1/2

MILES

To Auburn

To Auburn

RIDE 16 · Streaked Mountain

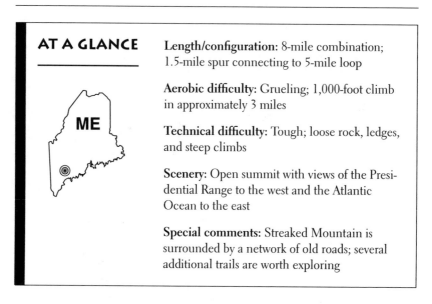

AT A GLANCE

Length/configuration: 8-mile combination; 1.5-mile spur connecting to 5-mile loop

Aerobic difficulty: Grueling; 1,000-foot climb in approximately 3 miles

Technical difficulty: Tough; loose rock, ledges, and steep climbs

Scenery: Open summit with views of the Presidential Range to the west and the Atlantic Ocean to the east

Special comments: Streaked Mountain is surrounded by a network of old roads; several additional trails are worth exploring

Streaked Mountain is one of the peaks in the eastern part of the Oxford Hills and is easily identified by its distinct, round summit and open ledges that provide expansive views in all directions. This is an 8-mile ride that begins and ends on a spur that connects to a 5-mile loop. The trail follows a series of old roads, as well as a beautiful stretch of single-track trail descending from the summit. Suitable for intermediate and advanced bikers, the ride features a strenuous climb to the summit of Streaked Mountain and some technical terrain along the descent.

The fire tower at the summit of Streaked Mountain was previously located on top of Speckled Mountain in the White Mountain National Forest. Flown to the site in 1987, it was reassembled and erected by a crew from the Maine Forest Service. However, along with all of the other fire towers in Maine, this one was abandoned in the early 1990s when it was determined that aircraft surveillance was a more cost-effective method for detecting fires. One of the authors was a member of the crew that replaced the tower and can remember several invigorating days spent atop the summit during the winter months of 1987.

General location: Streaked Mountain is located between the towns of South Paris and Buckfield, and it lies 15 miles northwest of the Lewiston-Auburn area.

Elevation change: The ride begins from Sodom Road at an elevation of 581' and climbs steadily to the summit of Streaked Mountain at 1,770'. Total elevation gain is 1,189'.

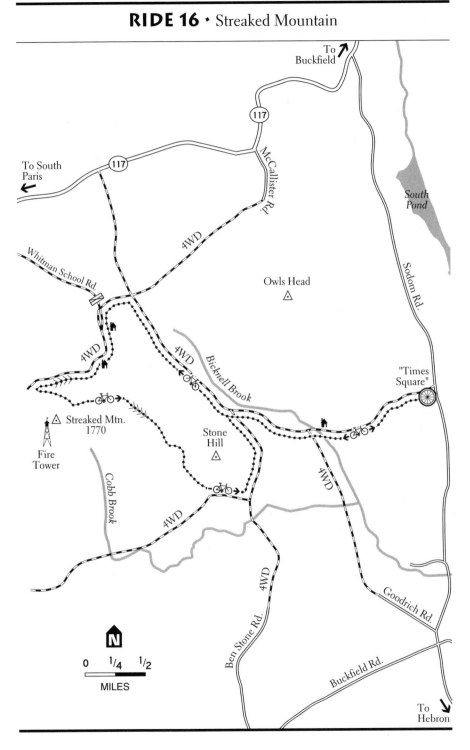

Season: This ride can be ridden from June through October, though mountain bikers should be aware that hunters will also be in the area in the fall.

Services: Lewiston-Auburn will be your best bet for bike-related supplies. Food and water are available at stores in both South Paris and Buckfield.

Hazards: There are many old woods roads that interconnect around the base of Streaked Mountain. Numerous intersections can make this ride a difficult one to follow. Be sure to travel with a topographic map, so that if you do stray from the trail you will be able to reorient yourself.

The ledges at the summit of the mountain are liable to be slippery when wet.

Rescue index: At the summit you will be 4 miles from assistance. Your nearest source for help will be the homes you pass on the way in.

Land status: The land around Streaked Mountain is privately owned, with public access still allowed on the old roads.

Maps: Refer to the USGS quads for Lake Auburn West, Oxford, and West Sumner.

Finding the trail: From Buckfield, turn south off ME 117 onto Sodom Road, just 1 mile west of the center of Buckfield. Stay straight on this road until you reach an intersection sometimes referred to as "Times Square." This junction is just 2.3 miles from ME 117 and is marked by a small island of trees. Park off the road, out of the way of logging operations.

Sources of additional information: None.

Notes on the trail: From "Times Square," begin pedaling on a woods road on the right (riding west). At a fork near Cobb Brook, bear right and ride up a two-wheel-drive dirt road that passes a farm and crosses Bicknell Brook several times. At the next intersection, turn right to begin the loop. You will return to this intersection from the left at the completion of the loop. Beyond this intersection, the road widens due to recent logging activity. Continue straight, past a wide, well-maintained road that branches off to the right. Shortly beyond this road, bear left at a Y intersection. Soon after, you will reach the junction with Whitman School Road. Bear left. You will ride past a house and open pasture on the left before the road swings around to the right. Continue straight past a small cabin on the left and climb through the woods. Then pedal over open ledges to the summit and the fire tower.

From the summit, begin riding back down the way you came, looking for an indistinct jeep trail on the right. This trail branches off from the main trail just a short distance from the summit and before the main trail reenters the woods. This jeep trail narrows to a single-track trail that follows a ridge that runs southeast from the summit. You will be riding over ledges through gradually more wooded slopes. The trail descends quite steeply in places, finally dropping down to a T junction with an old woods road. Turn left at this first intersection. You will continue to descend through the woods to a second **T** junction. Turn left again and continue straight until you reach the three-way intersection that marks the end of the loop. Turn right and retrace your route back to "Times Square."

RIDE 17 · Hebron-to-Canton Rail Trail

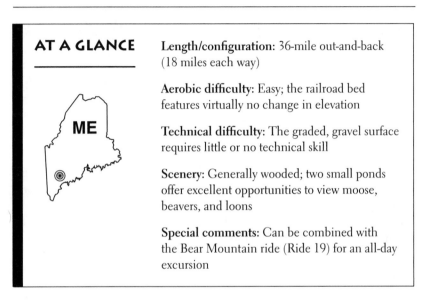

AT A GLANCE

Length/configuration: 36-mile out-and-back (18 miles each way)

Aerobic difficulty: Easy; the railroad bed features virtually no change in elevation

Technical difficulty: The graded, gravel surface requires little or no technical skill

Scenery: Generally wooded; two small ponds offer excellent opportunities to view moose, beavers, and loons

Special comments: Can be combined with the Bear Mountain ride (Ride 19) for an all-day excursion

Between Hebron and Canton, an abandoned railroad bed now provides miles of good riding through several small communities just north of Lewiston-Auburn. This ride can be as long as you choose. One-way, it is 18 miles from Station Road to Lake Anasagunticook, but you can turn around at any time for a shorter ride. Plan on spending the day if you choose to do the 36-mile round-trip. The riding is easy and follows the railroad bed over what is now a wide, hard-packed trail that requires no technical expertise. There are two short stretches of pavement in Buckfield and East Sumner, where the route has been interrupted by building and development. This ride can also be combined with Ride 19, for a side trip to Bear Mountain.

South of Buckfield, the trail passes South Pond. It is possible to watch and listen for loons at this pond that creates a scenic clearing in the midst of an otherwise wooded landscape. Just above Hartford Center you will also pass Bunganock Pond, where beavers have built a lodge on the east side of the trail and where moose can often be seen at the water's edge. Crossing a small, wooden bridge over the outlet of the pond during our ride, we disturbed a pile of water snakes that slowly uncoiled and slithered back into the water beneath our stares.

The Hebron-to-Canton Rail Trail crosses private land between East Sumner and Hartford Center. We recommend that you ride on ME 140 for this section of the ride, a short detour that eliminates the complications of trespassing on private property. The railroad bed is easy to reconnect with north of Hartford Center and continues traveling north to Lake Anasagunticook. However, this detour bypasses a very scenic portion of the old railroad. You may want to seek permission to ride this section of the trail by speaking with the owners. At the time we rode this trail, we stopped in at Half Barn Farm (located on the west side of ME 140, right next to the railroad bed) and spoke with the Gaynors.

General location: 10 miles north of Lewiston-Auburn, this ride follows an abandoned railroad bed from Hebron to Lake Anasagunticook just south of Canton.

Elevation change: You will be pedaling along an old railroad bed with virtually no change in elevation.

Season: This trail is open for year-round recreational use and offers riders the opportunity to enjoy the landscape as it constantly changes and renews through the cycle of the seasons. In the spring, there may be a series of long, deep puddles across the trail just beyond Hartford Center. These can be avoided by riding north up ME 140 to the first unpaved road on the right. This road will reconnect you to the railway bed at a point just 2 miles from its intersection with ME 140.

Services: All services are available in Lewiston-Auburn. In addition, there are several general stores in Buckfield, and a store in East Sumner that has a small restaurant that serves, among other things, excellent homemade pies and desserts.

Hazards: Be conscious of the fact that all-terrain vehicles also use this trail.

Rescue index: There are roads and homes within close proximity to this trail along its entire length.

Land status: An abandoned railroad bed. One portion of the railroad bed does pass through the property of Rusty and Ulrke Gaynor. It is necessary to secure permission from the Gaynors to cross through their land and to receive instruction on securing the gates that contain their livestock. The Gaynors' address is Half Barn Farm, RFD 1, Box 224, Canton, ME 04221. If you are unable to speak with the Gaynors, ride on paved ME 140 between East Sumner and Hartford Center.

Maps: The route of this abandoned railway is still marked on the DeLorme Mapping Company's *Maine Atlas and Gazetteer* (map 11, sections D-3, C-3, B-3, and B-4).

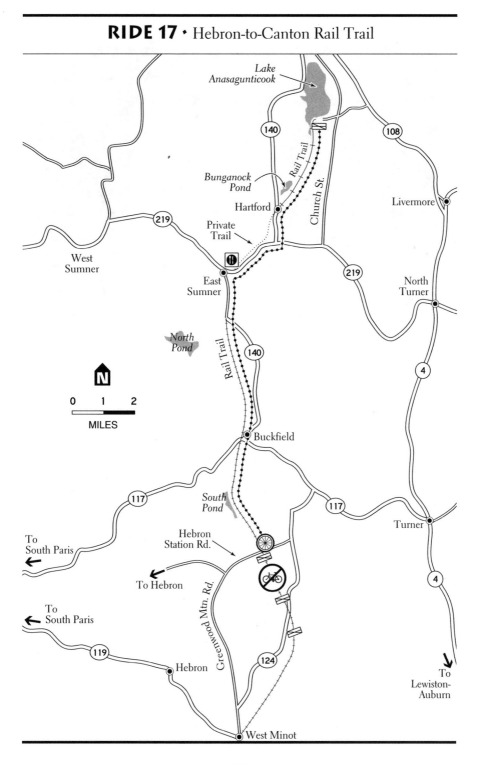

A dense grove of pines frames the abandoned railroad between Hebron and Canton.

Finding the trail: From Auburn, travel west on ME 11/121. Just beyond the town of Minot, turn right on ME 119. In West Minot, bear right on ME 124. You will actually drive over the railroad bed just a few miles south of the trailhead. Less than 2 miles farther, turn left onto Station Road. The railroad bed crosses Station Road near a baseball diamond and a small store. Park in the lot adjacent to the baseball diamond. You will have to cross Station Road to begin riding north up the trail.

Sources of additional information: None.

Notes on the trail: Riding north from Station Road, the trail is wide and hard-packed. Tall trees on either side of the trail create the sense of a long, narrow corridor that was once noisy with the sound of trains. These days, the trail can be virtually silent, and when you reach the east bank of South Pond, it is worth stopping to look or listen for loons. Beyond the pond, the trail enters Buckfield through the wider site of a now abandoned rail yard. Ride through the yard to reach ME 117, and turn right onto the paved road. Before you reach the center of Buckfield, you can pick up the trail on the left and ride over a snowmobile bridge that crosses the Nezinscot River. Beyond the bridge, continue straight and then turn right on a paved road. Look for the continuation of the trail on the left, just before the intersection with ME 140.

Follow the trail north from Buckfield. You will cross a small dirt road (Spring Road) and just south of East Sumner the trail ends at its intersection with ME 140. Ride up ME 140 to East Sumner, turning right at the T intersection with ME 219. If you have received permission from the Gaynors, turn left up the unpaved Town Farm Road and look for the trail heading back into the woods on the right. This stretch of the ride is beautiful and follows Bunganock Brook through some prime moose habitat. You will come to the fence that marks the Gaynor property. Being sure to leave all gates as you found them, continue behind Half Barn Farm until you reach a paved road, which is ME 140. Cross the road and reconnect with the trail on the other side. After a short distance you will reach a small bridge crossing the outlet of Bunganock Pond. Continue straight on the trail.

After several miles, you will reach the junction with the Bear Mountain trail on the right. From this point, the railroad bed descends slightly as it continues toward Lake Anasagunticook. Not far from the lake, boulders in the trail mark where it has been rerouted to the right. You will climb slightly and then descend as the trail curves around to the left and over a bridge that may be in an advanced state of disrepair. You will find yourself on an old town road, on which you want to continue straight, despite snowmobile signs that direct winter traffic to the right. This old road will connect you with the access road for Pine Shore Development. If you are feeling up to it, turn right on the access road and follow it out to Staples Hill Road (there is a baseball diamond across the street). Turn left onto Staples Hill Road and ride up Staples Hill to relax and enjoy the view from a grassy meadow that overlooks Lake Anasagunticook. Retrace your route to return to the trailhead.

RIDE 18 · Androscoggin River Trail

AT A GLANCE

Length/configuration: 18-mile out-and-back (9 miles each way) or 15-mile loop

Aerobic difficulty: Combination of easy cruising and fast, steep climbs and descents that make for a real workout

ME

Technical difficulty: Mixed; easy beginning, but latter part of the ride is for intermediate and advanced riders

Scenery: Pretty, wooded west bank of the Androscoggin River

Special comments: Exceptionally scenic trail easily accessible from Lewiston-Auburn

Along the west side of the Androscoggin River runs an unpretentious trail that gently drops to the water before turning inland just slightly to twist and roll across wooded hills, dells, and slopes. This ride can be ridden as an 18-mile out-and-back or, for a slightly less rigorous expedition, as a 15-mile loop. Either way, the ride includes broad, rolling double-track along the river's edge and twisted, technical single-track in the wooded slopes on the river's western bank. There is terrain for everyone to enjoy on this ride. Beginning riders will appreciate the moderate ground of the first part of the ride. Riders of intermediate and advanced skill levels will relish the more technical topography of the latter half.

The Androscoggin River has had a significant impact on the nearby cities of Lewiston and Auburn. The river, which finds its source in Umbagog Lake, flows toward the twin cities on its way to join the Kennebec at Merrymeeting Bay. The two cities are divided by the Lewiston Falls on the Androscoggin, where a series of dams were built to harness the falls. The power generated was used to support the textile mills and shoe factories in both towns, industries that boomed in the nineteenth century. Many factories employed French Canadians after the Civil War, casting the seeds for the bicultural society that still distinguishes Lewiston-Auburn from other cities in Maine. The shoe and textile industries eventually suffered because of changes in labor markets and the economy.

RIDE 18 · Androscoggin River Trail

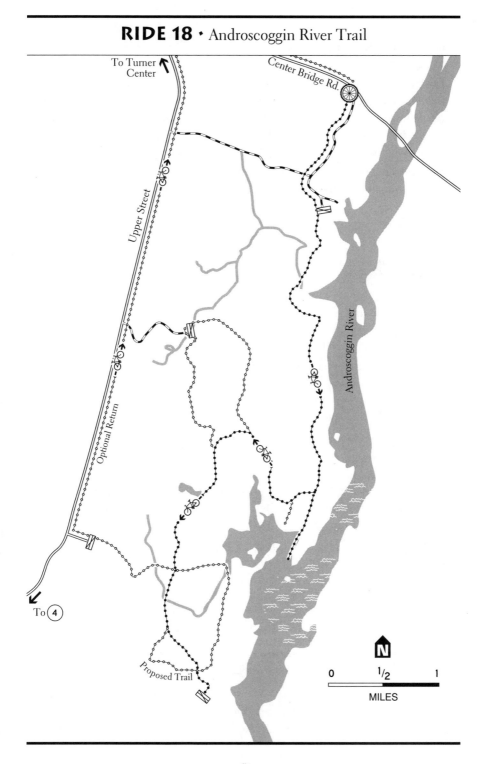

To Turner Center

Center Bridge Rd.

Upper Street

Androscoggin River

Optional Return

To 4

Proposed Trail

N

0   1/2   1
MILES

General location: Just east of Turner Center, this ride follows the Androscoggin River toward Lewiston-Auburn.

Elevation change: The trailhead for this ride is located at about 300'. Although there are a few short, steep climbs and descents on the trail along the river, most of the elevation gain for the ride is accounted for in one fairly tough climb up to Upper Street. This climb features a gain of about 300' and the overall elevation gain for the ride is close to 400'.

Season: This ride is at its best from June through October, though packed snowmobile trails in the winter suggest excellent off-season riding as well.

Services: All services are available in Lewiston-Auburn. There are places to eat all the way from Turner to the twin cities. Bicycle service and parts, as well as additional information on mountain biking in the area, are available at Rainbow Cycles on ME 4. Located at 1225 Center Street in Auburn, the folks at Rainbow Cycles can be reached at (207) 784-7576 or by calling toll free at (800) 244-7576.

Hazards: The trail system along the Androscoggin River is open to ATV users as well as mountain bikers and hikers. Particularly along the second portion of the ride, be aware that you may very suddenly encounter other trail users.

Rescue index: At exactly halfway through this ride, you will be 4.5 miles from potential assistance at the residences along either Cobb Road or Upper Street. There is a store in Turner Center where a telephone is available.

Land status: This ride makes use of a trail system managed by the Maine Department of Conservation.

Maps: This trail is quite well marked, and the roads and river that create boundaries around it are clearly marked in DeLorme's *Maine Atlas and Gazetteer.* The USGS quadrangles for the area are Lake Auburn East and Turner Center. However, as of 1997 the trail information on both of these maps was outdated and potentially confusing.

Finding the trail: Drive north on ME 4 from Auburn. Bear right onto Upper Street just 4 miles from the Auburn town line. Follow Upper Street to Turner Center and, at a crossroads, turn right onto Center Bridge Road. After passing Cobb Road on the left, look to the right for a dirt road that leads to a parking area for trail users. You will know that you have missed this turn if you reach the Androscoggin River.

Sources of additional information: Check in with the folks at Rainbow Bicycles for additional information about this ride and others in the Lewiston-Auburn area.

Notes on the trail: As you drive into the parking area on the west side of the Androscoggin River, notice the dirt road off to the left side of the driveway.

Part of the
Androscoggin River
Trail features
rolling, technical
riding through
wooded terrain.

This is the trailhead. Begin pedaling up this unpaved road, avoiding any side trips down less obvious trails branching off the road. At the first true intersection you come to, an open and somewhat sandy area, bear right and follow the trail beyond a gate that is signed with a recreational trail marking.

From the gate, the trail descends, and you will cross a small brook before climbing up the other side. The trail proceeds over a small bridge and swings in quite close to the river. Almost 4 miles into the ride, you will come to a trail branching off to the right, creating a **T** intersection with the main trail. The ride continues down this trail to the right. However, continuing straight will lead you to the river's edge after just 0.4 mile, and it is a worthwhile trip whether you return to embark on the second stage of the ride or decide to complete the ride by returning the way you came. Remember, if you ride down to the river, the turn to continue the ride will be on your left as you return.

From the **T** intersection, the ride follows a rough road that eventually turns sharply to the right. Follow the road through this turn, which is signed to West Buckfield, Youly's, and Minot. The trail that appears to continue straight at this point is signed to the River and Twitchell's. At a second intersection, the road to the right is signed to, among other places, Upper Street, Lower Street, and Youly's. Continue riding straight, following signs for the Big Apple on Route 4, Twitchell's Airport, and the Chickadee Restaurant. It is at this point that the trail narrows to a single-track path traversing rocky and rooted terrain, up steep hills and down equally challenging grades. The trail splits in two at a location near a bog, but both trails reconnect, so either one is an option.

Arriving at a **T** intersection, turn right and continue riding straight past a trail that descends to the left. You will begin climbing up a moderate grade to reach a fence that, like the one spanning the trail at the beginning of the ride, is signed by the Department of Conservation. To make this a purely off-road ride, turn around here and retrace your route back to the trailhead. If a less challenging return trip is more to your taste, follow a dirt road that bisects corn fields out to the paved Upper Road. Turn right and enjoy the smooth, undulating terrain and gorgeous views to Turner Center. Turn right on Center Bridge Road and then right again into the parking area at the trailhead.

RIDE 19 · Bear Mountain

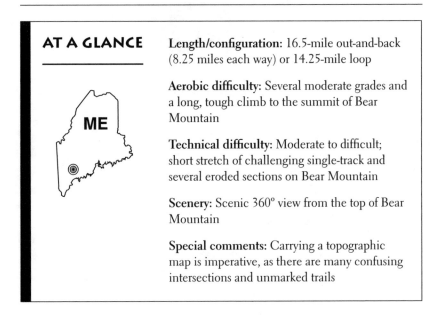

AT A GLANCE

Length/configuration: 16.5-mile out-and-back (8.25 miles each way) or 14.25-mile loop

Aerobic difficulty: Several moderate grades and a long, tough climb to the summit of Bear Mountain

Technical difficulty: Moderate to difficult; short stretch of challenging single-track and several eroded sections on Bear Mountain

Scenery: Scenic 360° view from the top of Bear Mountain

Special comments: Carrying a topographic map is imperative, as there are many confusing intersections and unmarked trails

The trip to the summit of Bear Mountain covers a distance of 8.25 miles, creating an out-and-back ride that amounts to a total distance of 16.5 miles. The terrain is tremendously varied and includes an abandoned railroad bed, a combination of single- and double-track trails, old roads, and some pavement. The ride is moderately difficult, featuring an aerobically challenging climb to the summit of Bear Mountain that also requires good technical skills. This ride also includes the option of returning to the trailhead by means of a different route. Although this alternative creates a loop that is slightly shorter than the out-and-back option, it features a technically challenging descent of 810 feet down the steep southern slope of the mountain and does require some riding on pavement and a little extra climbing.

You will pedal from the low-lying wetlands around Bunganock Pond through woods that were once cleared for pasture and agricultural purposes. As you approach Bear Mountain, you will ride up out of a heavily shaded forest. Vegetation becomes more sparse as you approach the summit, where exposed rock provides a clear view of the surrounding countryside. Bear Pond, situated at the foot of Bear Mountain, is visible from the summit and is often bustling with the activity of seaplanes making use of the base on the pond.

General location: Bear Mountain lies west of the town of Livermore.

Elevation change: From where you begin this ride, just south of Bunganock Pond, your elevation is a mere 465' above sea level. You will climb to the summit of Bear Mountain at approximately 1,210', with only 2 brief downhills for relief. Total elevation gain is 945' for the out-and-back option and 1,255' for the loop.

Season: Trail conditions should be at their best from June through October.

Services: All services are available in Lewiston-Auburn, about 25 miles south. Food and water can also be purchased at any of the general stores in Livermore, Canton, or East Sumner.

Hazards: If you choose to complete the ride by returning to your car by pavement, the steep and eroded descent from Bear Mountain can be dangerous.

Rescue index: There are places throughout this ride where you will come across homes or cross secondary roads. It is advisable to carry a detailed map of the area due to all the unmarked side trails along the way.

Land status: This ride begins on an abandoned railroad bed that is now used as a recreational trail. The remainder of the ride follows a combination of snowmobile trails, old town roads, and logging roads.

Maps: The USGS 7.5 minute quads are Canton and Buckfield.

Finding the trail: This ride begins at the intersection of an abandoned railway bed and ME 140, approximately half a mile north of Hartford Center. From Lewiston-Auburn, travel north up ME 4 through Turner. In North

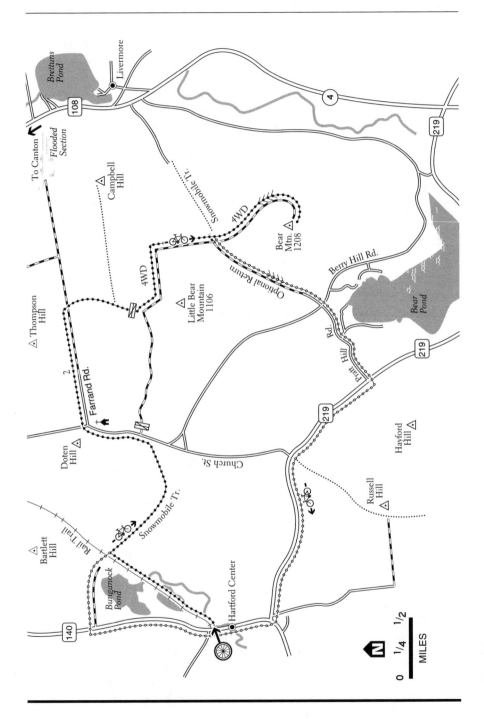

Turner, turn left onto ME 219. After approximately 8 miles, turn right onto ME 140. You will see a sandy lot on the right after just half a mile. Park here and begin riding north up the abandoned railroad bed.

Sources of additional information: None.

Notes on the trail: Begin riding up the railroad bed, which is often covered by water in the spring and early summer. The ground beneath these puddles is nevertheless firm and, when we rode this trail, free of obstacles. You will ride past Bunganock Pond on the left. Beyond the pond, continue along the railroad bed until you reach a trail on the right. This trail is marked for snowmobile travel, and there should be a sign posted to a tree that reads: "Bear Mountain, 5 miles: scenic view." Although you do want to follow this sign, and although there is a scenic view from the summit of Bear Mountain, be warned that the summer route to the summit of the mountain is slightly longer than the winter snowmobile trail! Turn right here and begin down a grassy trail.

Beyond a small clearing, this trail descends into the woods again and crosses a stream where there may or may not be some sort of bridge to facilitate your crossing. The next section of trail is much more technical. You will ride along a narrow stretch of single-track scattered with rocks. Bear left at the first fork you come to, which leads into a more open grassy area. Follow the widest of the trail options through this clearing, bearing right and climbing a sandy little gully. The next trail junction is signed, and you will want to follow a single-track trail on the left in the direction of Bear Mountain. If you happen to miss this turn and you continue straight instead, you will reach a **T** intersection with Church Street. Turning left down the single-track trail, you will also reach Church Street, only slightly farther up the street.

Whichever way you come to Church Street, turn left and begin pedaling up Doten Hill. You will pass a gravel road on the right that, though open to winter snowmobile traffic, is gated in the summer. Continue past this road and climb until you reach the Hartford Community Church on the right. Just past the church, turn right onto Farrand Road. This is a two-wheel-drive road. Ride along the road until you crest a moderate hill. If you continue straight, the road begins to descend and, at the bottom of the hill, is completely flooded by a beaver pond. To continue the ride, be sure to turn right down a grassy trail that branches off from the road before it begins to descend. As you make this right turn, you will notice a stone foundation on your left. Follow the trail as it descends through an open clearing before entering the woods. At a fork in the trail, bear right. This section of the trail crosses a small wet area that looks like a peat bog, and then continues along a path strewn with pine needles.

Upon reaching a **T** junction, turn right. Ride past a metal rope stretched across the road, keeping to the main trail, which is paralleled by stone fences on either side. You will reach a junction with a dirt road. Turn left. Continuing straight through a cleared area, you will begin climbing. Follow the road as it swings sharply to the right. A short distance farther, the road swings around to the left and a trail branches off to the right. Bear left and continue to follow the road. You will pass a snowmobile trail that branches off to the left and, as you approach the summit, the road condition deteriorates.

From the summit of Bear Mountain, you can retrace your route back to the trailhead. Alternatively, you can choose to ride this trail as a loop. To do so, ride back down the road from the summit. As the road swings to the right, continue straight instead and start down an extremely rocky and eroded gully. This gully is, in fact, the Bear Mountain hiking trail. Follow it down to a crossroad, and then continue straight onto Pratt Hill Road. At a T intersection, turn right onto ME 219. Continue on ME 219 until you reach the junction of ME 140. Turn right and return to the parking area.

RIDE 20 · Waterford

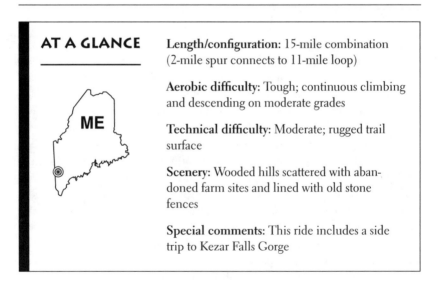

AT A GLANCE

Length/configuration: 15-mile combination (2-mile spur connects to 11-mile loop)

Aerobic difficulty: Tough; continuous climbing and descending on moderate grades

Technical difficulty: Moderate; rugged trail surface

Scenery: Wooded hills scattered with abandoned farm sites and lined with old stone fences

Special comments: This ride includes a side trip to Kezar Falls Gorge

Waterford's agricultural heritage is exemplified throughout this 15-mile loop. The trail rambles past overgrown orchards, abandoned farms, and old mill sites, following a network of discontinued old roads that now provide excellent double- and single-track riding. Riders should possess at least intermediate-level riding skills and good cardiovascular endurance. This ride features plenty of climbing and descending along trails that wander well off the beaten track.

As you ride by the old foundations of abandoned farms, try to imagine the thriving communities that were at one time linked solely by the roads over which you pass. Wagons and ox carts once lumbered along these roads carrying apples, hay, and livestock. Forests now engulf the remnants of the old farms. The great stone fences that still crisscross this now remote and relatively wild place provide the only clue to the activities of many years go.

You have the option of taking a scenic excursion to Kezar Falls Gorge on this ride. The gorge is located off an improved two-wheel-drive road that parallels Kezar River and can be reached by a short trail that descends through woods from the road. You will probably hear the falls before you reach them, especially during periods of high water. The gorge is approximately 30 feet deep and 120 feet long, and has been carved by water that cascades through a series of 3-foot drops before collecting in a deep pool. The falls are a great place to stop and enjoy any snacks you may have brought with you. In addition to Kezar Falls Gorge, this ride offers a host of side trips along single-track trails that will take the intrepid rider, possessing a topographical map, to the top of one of the many surrounding hills. Views of distant Mount Washington are possible from many of the hilltops.

Upon the completion of the ride, carnivores should be sure to stop at Tut's General Store in North Waterford to try one of Tut's famous bison burgers. The bison are locally raised and provide a tasty alternative to beef. Tut's General Store dates back to the Civil War and is a quintessential New England general store, stocking everything from bug dope to homemade pies and cookies.

General location: This ride passes through parts of the towns of Waterford, Sweden, and Lovell in western Oxford County.

Elevation change: You will begin pedaling from approximately 1,100'. You will gain 300' and lose 820' over a series of short climbs and long descents, to reach an elevation of 480'. The trail then climbs a long grade to return to the trailhead. Total elevation gain is approximately 1,200'.

Season: Mid-May through October are ideal times to ride this trail.

Services: Food, groceries, and accommodations are available in Waterford, North Waterford, and Lovell. Bike-related services are some distance away, so it is best to come prepared with extra tubes and cables. The closest source for such items is in Norway.

Hazards: There are several rutted and eroded sections along the trail. Watch out for motor vehicle traffic along Irving Green Road and Five Kezars Road. If it is hot, be sure to carry plenty of water. There may be logging operations under way along some areas of the trail. Stay clear of the equipment and always pull completely off the road if a logging truck approaches.

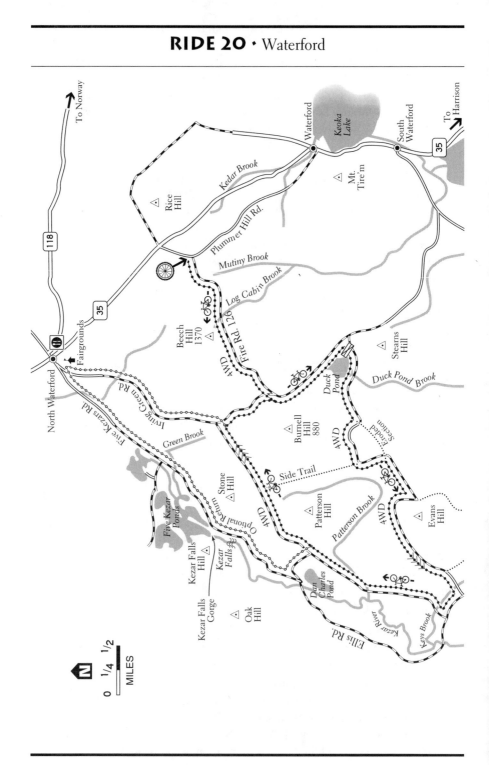

Rescue index: You are never more than 4 miles from assistance.

Land status: This trail follows a combination of discontinued and active town roads and snowmobile trails.

Maps: All of the roads and trails are shown in the DeLorme Mapping Company's *Maine Atlas and Gazetteer* (map 10, sections D-3, D-4, and E-3). The USGS quad for the area is North Waterford.

Finding the trail: From Waterford Village take ME 35 toward North Waterford. At 2.2 miles, turn left at a four-way intersection with Plummer Hill Road. Drive for approximately 0.6 mile and look for Fire Road 126. It will be on the right at the point where Plummer Hill Road curves to the left. There is room to pull off the road; be sure to park without blocking either road.

Source of additional information: Tut's General Store in North Waterford can provide general information about the area.

Notes on the trail: Begin the ride by pedaling up Fire Road 126. You will be following a double-track trail through the woods. Be sure to stay straight at all trail intersections as you climb part-way up Beech Hill and then descend over approximately the same distance. There are beautiful stone fences on either side of this trail. As you climb into a large old pasture, look for an old foundation on the left. Ride straight across the pasture to a smaller clearing in the upper left corner. Stay left where the trail forks immediately after leaving the pasture. At the next fork, only 0.1 mile beyond, bear right and begin climbing a steep, moderately technical incline. At this point in the ride, you will be following a rough, muddy, single-track trail that descends after passing some boulders that have been placed to keep vehicles out. After passing through a couple of grassy, open areas and past the wreckage of an old farmhouse, you will begin a long descent. Watch for rocks lurking in the grass of this four-wheel-drive trail. At a **T** junction with a two-wheel-drive dirt road, turn left.

You will climb for a short distance before beginning a long descent to Duck Pond. Keep your eyes peeled for Duck Pond, which will appear on the right after the road levels out. You will be looking for the first road on the right after passing Duck Pond. The road is grassy and slightly rutted, and will probably have a cable across it with an attached sign prohibiting all-terrain vehicles. According to the landowner, the cable was placed there to keep motor vehicles from damaging the trail. He indicated that he did not mind mountain bikers using the trail. Turn right onto this trail.

Although the trail is rough, it is also very scenic, offering views of Duck Pond to the right. Old stone fences line the sides of the trail as it passes through an area that was once pasture but has since ceded to forest. Continue along the trail for approximately 1 mile, and begin looking for a small grass and dirt trail on the right. This narrow trail bypasses a badly eroded and

An old road
upon which oxen
once trod.

impassible section of the main trail. Follow it until you come to a **T** intersection. This intersection will be signed as ITS 80, indicating Bridgton and Lovell to the left and North Waterford to the right. Turn left toward Bridgton and Lovell, and descend for a short distance. Bear right at the next intersection, following the signs for ITS 80.

You will be riding along a wider two-wheel-drive road that descends gradually. Stay right on ITS 80 where the main road turns sharply left. This rutted, muddy, four-wheel-drive road climbs slowly through a mixed stand of pine and birch trees, past an old farm site. The road gradually improves, and after reaching the top of Evan's Hill, you will descend quickly. After passing several structures on the left, the road swings sharply to the left. Look for a narrow single-track trail that continues straight. Follow this trail, which is also the route the snowmobile trail follows. After crossing an old stone bridge, you will come to an improved two-wheel-drive dirt road (Ellis Road). Turn right.

After pedaling approximately one-half mile, turn right onto a grassy, double-track road. This will be the first road that you come to on the right. Continue straight through several intersections along this road, which gradually climbs, passing through a logged-over area. Although the road gradually becomes less developed, it remains in good condition with a sand and gravel surface. At the top of the hill, after passing through an area that has recently been logged, you will descend on a moderately technical section of the road. When you reach a **T** intersection with an improved two-wheel-drive road, turn right and pedal another mile to the intersection of a snowmobile trail and four-wheel-drive road on the left. This is the first section of the ride. Retrace the route back to your car.

The optional route past Kezar Falls Gorge adds approximately 2.5 miles to the total distance of the ride but compensates for the increased mileage by offering more gradual climbs on better road surfaces. To reach the Kezar Falls Gorge, turn right on Ellis Road, onto the grassy double-track road as described for the main route. Approximately 2.1 miles after making the turn, look for an improved dirt road on the left. This will, in fact, appear to be the more heavily traveled road. Turn left on this road, and then turn right about half a mile later onto a well-traveled two-wheel-drive road. This is the Old Waterford Road. Continue along the Old Waterford Road for approximately 1 mile. The gorge will be at the end of a short trail that turns off the main road on the left.

After visiting the gorge, continue riding along the Old Waterford Road, which eventually changes from dirt to a paved surface. Just before the road comes to a **T** intersection with ME 35, turn right and follow a road up past the North Waterford Fairground. Follow this road, which climbs the northwest slope of Beech Hill, for several miles. The road surface gradually deteriorates as you pedal away from North Waterford. Ride all the way to the intersection of the loop portion of this ride and the spur on which you began the ride. Turn left, back down the spur, to return to the trailhead.

RIDE 21 · Cold River Valley

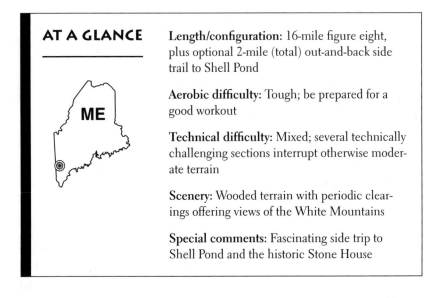

AT A GLANCE	Length/configuration: 16-mile figure eight, plus optional 2-mile (total) out-and-back side trail to Shell Pond
ME	Aerobic difficulty: Tough; be prepared for a good workout
	Technical difficulty: Mixed; several technically challenging sections interrupt otherwise moderate terrain
	Scenery: Wooded terrain with periodic clearings offering views of the White Mountains
	Special comments: Fascinating side trip to Shell Pond and the historic Stone House

This 16-mile ride goes through the heart of the Cold River Valley, one of the most beautiful valleys in Maine. The ride incorporates single- and double-track trails, improved dirt roads, and two short links on pavement to form a figure eight. Several rigorous climbs and fairly technical terrain make this ride suitable for intermediate and advanced riders in good physical condition.

An optional side trail to Shell Pond provides an interesting diversion. The route passes the site of the historic Stone House, one of the original houses constructed in the valley. The story of the construction of the Stone House illustrates the rigors of settling what was then wilderness. It was built by one Abel Andrews, sometime in the early 1800s. D. B. Wight, in his book *Wild River Wilderness* (Littleton, NH: Courier Printing Company, 1971), describes the method by which Abel assembled his house:

> Abel was a large, husky man six feet two inches tall. He quarried huge blocks of granite out of the mountainside for the walls of his house, and during the winter months used oxen to haul them to the site. In order to lift these heavy blocks into position, he built a log bridge from the rising ground in back of the house, up over the layers of stone, making it an easy matter for the oxen to draw the blocks into place. After laying each row of blocks the bridge was raised so as to put the next layer in place. Holes were drilled into the upper and lower sides of the stone and iron rods inserted to [e]nsure the walls remained in place.

The Stone House can be viewed from the Shell Pond trail, which runs along a grassy airstrip in front of the house. The airstrip also provides spectacular views of the Baldface Range, which looms 3,500 feet over the valley floor.

General location: This ride is located in the town of Stow.

Elevation change: From where you begin this ride at the parking area on Forest Road 9, the elevation is 720'. You will climb to approximately 940' on Deer Hill before enjoying a steady descent to Stone House Road at 550'. The trail descends slightly to 460' at the junction of FR 9 and ME 113. You will climb to 560' on FR 9 before descending to 500' at Colton Brook. You will climb Colton Hill to reach an elevation of 800'. The trail descends to its junction with Union Hill Road at 480' and then climbs to 900' on Wiley Mountain. You will descend slightly and then climb back up to FR 9. You will gain another 160' before returning to the trailhead. Total elevation gain for the ride is approximately 1,200'.

Season: This route lies within a mountain valley that may hold snow until mid-May. The best riding conditions will be in the summer and fall.

Services: There are several general stores in the area, including one in the town of Stow that includes a fantastic bakery. Camping is permitted at several sites in the White Mountain National Forest. The closest campground is the Cold River Campground, several miles north of the trailhead on ME/NH 113. Bicycle service and repair is much farther afield but can be found in Bethel and Norway.

Hazards: Use care when riding on FR 9 and ME/NH 113, where you may encounter vehicles.

Rescue index: You will be 3 miles from assistance at the farthest point on this trail.

Land status: This ride uses both private and public (national forest) land. The Stone House property is private, and trail users must stay on the marked trail. Continued access is dependent upon this. The Appalachian Mountain Club Cold River Camp is also private. The camp manager with whom we spoke asks that riders walk their bicycles through the camp to avoid collisions with campers.

Finally, a portion of the Link Trail that used to connect Stone House Road with Deer Hill Road (FR 9), has been closed by the landowner. This necessitates riding along paved ME 113. The landowner is adamant about this closure. As tempting as it might be to ride this single-track trail the whole way through, don't try it!

Maps: Much of this ride can be traced in DeLorme's *Maine Atlas and Gazetteer* (map 10, section D-1). The USGS quads for the area are Center Lovell, Speckled Mountain, Wild River, and Chatham.

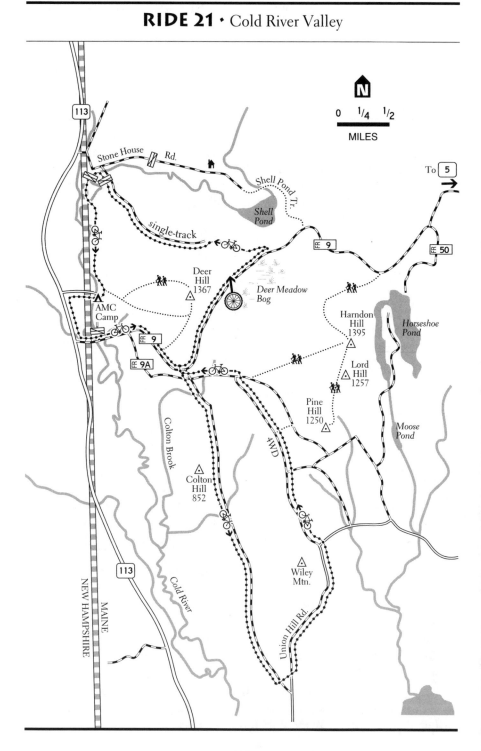

Speckled Mountain rises above the Cold River Valley.

Finding the trail: From Fryeburg, drive north on ME/NH 113. Drive through the towns of North Fryeburg and Stow, and continue traveling north on ME/NH 113. Just before the road crosses Chandler Brook, look for a dirt road on the right. This road, FR 9, is most easily identified by a large sign that reads: "Windagan." Turn right onto this road, and drive 2.8 miles to reach a parking area on the left side of the road. Deer Meadow Bog is opposite the parking area and can be reached by a short trail leading out to an observation blind overlooking the water.

Source of additional information: For descriptions of many of the trails and hiking paths in this area, consult the most recent edition of the hiking guide published by the Appalachian Mountain Club: *AMC Maine Mountain Guide.*

Notes on the trail: From the parking area, continue traveling east on FR 9. The road turns away from Deer Meadow Bog and descends slightly. Only 0.2 mile from the parking area, turn left up an old woods road. The road climbs steeply at first and is quite severely eroded and muddy in places. It is worth persevering up this hill, however, because the road gradually narrows to a single-track trail that follows a blissfully long descent. This trail is rooty and winds between cut-over forest with views of Speckled Mountain through the trees. You will descend on this trail, which gradually widens into FR 355, an old woods road. You will follow it across a bridge over Shell Pond Brook and then you will come to a T junction with Stone House Road (FR 16). The ride continues to the left, and, almost immediately, you must turn left again onto the Leach Link Trail that leads to the AMC Cold River Camp. However, you can also turn right on Stone House Road and complete a 2-mile out-and-back side trip (1 mile each way) to the Stone House and Shell Pond.

The Link Trail to the AMC camp will take you to a small stream that you will have to ford. Beyond the stream, you will continue riding for a short distance before reaching the Cold River. Follow the river until you reach a dam. Turn right and portage over the dam, following signs to the camp. The AMC caretaker has requested that riders walk through the camp, which is often crowded with campers. Follow the camp road out to ME/NH 113. Turn left on ME/NH 113 and ride on pavement until the road crosses Chandler Brook. Just beyond the brook, turn left onto FR 9, a dirt road most easily identified by a large wooden sign that reads: "Windagan."

Pedal up FR 9, crossing the Cold River and passing the trailhead for the Deer Hill Spring trail on the left. Shortly beyond this trail junction, turn right on a four-wheel-drive road that is marked with a small "CTA" (Chatham Trails Association) sign on a nearby telephone pole. This road forks almost immediately; follow the grassy, less traveled route straight ahead. This intersection begins the lower loop of the ride, which you will complete by returning on the road on the left.

You will cross a snowmobile bridge over Colton Brook before climbing steeply up an eroded section of the trail that ascends Colton Hill. The trail descends the other side of Colton Hill, and its condition gradually improves. After several miles, look for a snowmobile trail that branches off to the left and ends at a T junction with Union Hill Road. Turn left on Union Hill Road, a wide, two-wheel-drive road with sections of pavement on some of the steeper grades. You will descend on pavement until the road makes a sharp right turn. At this point, continue straight and up a driveway, following a well-maintained stone wall on the left. Head straight past several houses, beyond which you will begin to climb steadily through the woods on a grassy jeep trail.

You will continue up a long, steady grade, and as you approach the crest of this hill, the road forks. Bear left and climb a grassy knoll, beyond which you will begin to descend. As you approach a logged-over area, the trail drops very steeply. This section of the trail is severely eroded, and most riders will want to portage across it. At the bottom of this steep, deteriorated section, continue straight past a logging road branching off on the left. At this point, the road is a double-track trail with a vegetated center median. You will descend very quickly past a stone foundation and a hiking trail on the right, and across an expanded steel bridge. When you reach a T intersection with another dirt road, turn left and follow the road out to FR 9. Turn right on FR 9 and follow it all the way back to the parking area.

RIDE 22 · Evergreen Valley

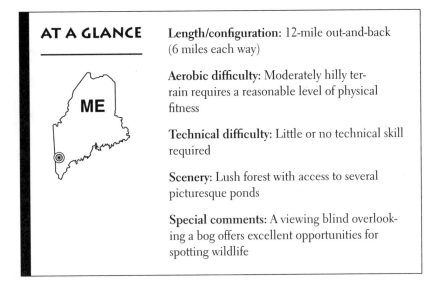

AT A GLANCE

Length/configuration: 12-mile out-and-back (6 miles each way)

Aerobic difficulty: Moderately hilly terrain requires a reasonable level of physical fitness

Technical difficulty: Little or no technical skill required

Scenery: Lush forest with access to several picturesque ponds

Special comments: A viewing blind overlooking a bog offers excellent opportunities for spotting wildlife

The Evergreen Valley ride is a 12-mile (total) out-and-back on an unpaved Forest Service road named Deer Hill Road. Several short, scenic side trips are possible along the way. Beginning from what was once a resort that offered skiing in the winter, and golf, swimming, and tennis in the summer, Deer Hill Road passes through the southernmost portion of the White Mountain National Forest. Although the road surface lends itself to easy cruising, this ride includes steady climbs and descents along its entire length. Very little technical skill is needed, but riders should be prepared for some hill climbing.

Although the resort at Evergreen Valley closed several years ago, it is easy to see why the location was originally selected. Evergreen Valley is beautiful year-round: lush in the spring and summer when leaves create welcome shade from the sun; brilliant with color during the fall; and breathtaking beneath the cover of winter snow. This ride also provides access to both Horseshoe Pond and Shell Pond, two scenic locations nestled between wooded hillsides. In addition, a moose blind has been constructed on the edge of Deer Meadow Bog, offering patient viewers the opportunity to watch moose, beaver, and a variety of waterfowl. Farther up the road, a trail to Deer Hill Spring rewards anyone willing to make the short 0.7-mile trip with cold, clear water. Deer Hill Spring is a fascinating shallow pool with air bubbles rising up through the water from a small sandy area on the bottom. The spring has also been called "Bubbling Spring."

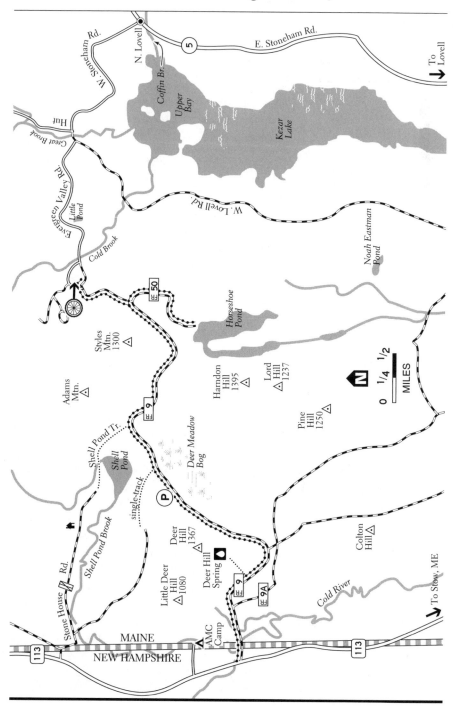

General location: Deer Hill Road extends west from Kezar Lake to the New Hampshire border.

Elevation change: The ride begins and ends at 500' and climbs to about 1,000' at the junction of the Shell Pond trail. Total elevation for the ride is about 1,200'.

Season: Excellent conditions exist from May through October. Winter riding is also possible once snowmobile traffic has packed the snow.

Services: Water is available at Deer Hill Spring, which is located along a small path at a distance of 0.7 mile from Deer Hill Road. Camping is available in the White Mountain National Forest. There are a few sites at Crocker Pond, just west of ME 35, and more available at a site in Hastings, on ME 113. Basic supplies can be purchased in Center Lovell or North Waterford. For any bicycle-related needs, the bike shop at Sunday River just north of Bethel is the closest available resource.

Hazards: Some vehicles travel quickly along Deer Hill Road.

Rescue index: There are seasonal camps at either end of Deer Hill Road, where assistance could be sought. Due to the many hiking trails in this area, other people are quite likely to be nearby.

Land status: A forest road in the White Mountain National Forest.

Maps: This trail is clearly marked in *The Maine Atlas and Gazetteer* published by the DeLorme Mapping Company (map 10, section D-1).

Finding the trail: From points south and east, travel to Fryeburg on US 302. In Fryeburg, turn north on ME 5 and drive through Lovell and Center Lovell. As you come to the north shore of Kezar Lake, in the town of North Lovell, turn left on West Stoneham Road. Continue past an intersection with Hut Road on the right and cross Beaver Brook. Bear right at the fork in the road and continue to follow signs to Evergreen Valley. Pass a golf course on the left, and just past some old tennis courts also on the left, park in an unpaved lot. The ride begins by turning left down the unpaved road beyond this parking area.

Source of additional information:

Evans Notch Ranger District
RFD 2, Box 2270
Bethel, ME 04217
(207) 834-2134

Notes on the trail: Begin riding along the unpaved Deer Hill Road heading west. After slightly more than 1 mile, you will come to Forest Road 50, branching off on the left. The ride continues to the right, following Deer Hill Road. However, FR 50 descends part of the way to Horseshoe Pond,

Deer Meadow Bog is located just off Evergreen Valley Road.

connecting to a footpath that continues to the water's edge. This short side trip is a great way to end the ride.

Continuing along Deer Hill Road, you will climb steadily at first and then descend to Deer Meadow Bog, where a small parking area provides an alternative starting point and access to a wooden blind that overlooks the water. From this point, you will climb a short distance up Deer Hill before descending to a bridge across the Cold River (notice a trail sign on your right as you descend that marks the path to Deer Hill Spring). Deer Hill Road continues just a short distance past the Cold River, to a junction with ME 113. Turn around and retrace your route back to Evergreen Valley. Remember to turn right onto FR 50 if you want to finish the ride with a trip down to Horseshoe Pond.

The side trip to Shell Pond is a more difficult detour and follows the Shell Pond Trail, which branches off Deer Hill Road halfway between FR 50 and the parking area at Deer Meadow Bog. The trail is rough and quite narrow. When you reach Shell Pond, you can continue to follow the trail over a small stream and onto an airstrip that opens up great views of the Baldface Range. From the airstrip, you can also make out the historic Stone House, set back from the trail at the edge of the woods. Turn around to retrace your tracks back to Deer Hill Road.

RIDE 23 · Albany Mountain

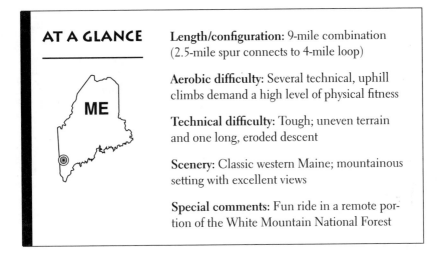

AT A GLANCE

Length/configuration: 9-mile combination (2.5-mile spur connects to 4-mile loop)

Aerobic difficulty: Several technical, uphill climbs demand a high level of physical fitness

Technical difficulty: Tough; uneven terrain and one long, eroded descent

Scenery: Classic western Maine; mountainous setting with excellent views

Special comments: Fun ride in a remote portion of the White Mountain National Forest

The Albany Mountain trail will challenge the most skilled riders. It is a beautiful, rugged, combination ride that covers a total distance of nine miles. The predominantly single-track trail challenges riders with short, steep climbs and descents over rocky and often eroded terrain. The result is a trail suited to riders with a substantial level of both fitness and skill.

The Albany Mountain ride starts from a picturesque pond in the heart of the Evans Notch region of the White Mountain National Forest, and winds its way around the base of Albany Mountain. The trail rewards the rider with gorgeous mountain scenery in an area of western Maine often bypassed by visitors on their way to the loftier peaks to the west. The remoteness of this trail increases the likelihood of viewing deer, moose, and possibly black bears. Riders should be well versed in their route-finding skills, as the trail tends to be quite overgrown in mid- to late summer.

The section of this trail that descends to Keewaydin Lake is a rewarding yet challenging downhill that offers glorious views of the Baldface Mountains in the distance. It is rutted, rough, and technically challenging at the top, but gradually improves until you reach a dirt camp road that runs along the lake. The return climb begins up a grassy four-wheel-drive road that narrows into a sweet run of single-track trail before reconnecting with the initial spur.

There is a small campground at the trailhead, which overlooks Crocker Pond. Drinking water, rest rooms, and a number of beautiful tent sites are available. We discovered that this trail offers excellent winter riding; in the right conditions, snowmobiles pack snow into a hard, smooth surface. As a result, the trail becomes free of the technical challenges present during the summer and fall.

General location: This ride is located in Stoneham, about halfway between Kezar Lake to the south and Bethel to the north.

Elevation change: At Crocker Pond, you will begin pedaling from 825'. You will climb to 900' before dropping to 680'. A 320-foot climb follows. Dropping down to Keewaydin Lake, you will reach a low elevation of 675' before climbing steadily to 1,180'. From here, you will descend to 680', climb to 900', and finally cruise back to Crocker Pond. The total elevation change for this ride is 1,120'.

Season: Avoid this trail in the spring and early summer, when the ground is liable to be wet from spring runoff.

Services: The closest supply of food and water is the general store in North Waterford. These and all other services can be found in Bethel, about 8 miles north. The trail passes several small streams that may provide sources of water in an emergency. All water should be filtered and treated before drinking.

Hazards: Be observant of the condition of the snowmobile bridges along this ride. Also, there is a metal chain crossing the dirt road that begins the climb back to the spur from Crocker Pond. If you were to ride the loop in the opposite direction to that which we have suggested, the chain would appear quite suddenly at the end of the old logging road. Watch out for snowmobiles if you attempt this ride in the winter.

Rescue index: The primary attribute of this ride is its remoteness, and it is important to recognize this and ride accordingly. As you get closer to Keewaydin Lake, there are numerous seasonal homes where you may be able to summon assistance.

Land status: Other than a short distance along a dirt camp road, most of this ride covers land that is part of the White Mountain National Forest.

Maps: Consider purchasing the USGS map for this area, which is East Stoneham. DeLorme's *Maine Atlas and Gazetteer* shows only certain sections of the trail (map 10, sections C-3 and C-2).

Finding the trail: The campground at Crocker Pond can be accessed from the north by following the road that runs south from US 2 opposite the West Bethel post office. This road becomes Forest Road 7 when it enters the White Mountain National Forest at 4.5 miles. At 5.8 miles, turn right on FR 18, following signs for 1.5 miles to the campground, where there is parking available for day use.

If you are traveling from the south, follow ME 35 north from North Waterford. Bear right in Lynchville to continue on ME 35, and then fork left onto ME 5. After approximately 1.25 miles, bear left onto an unsigned paved road

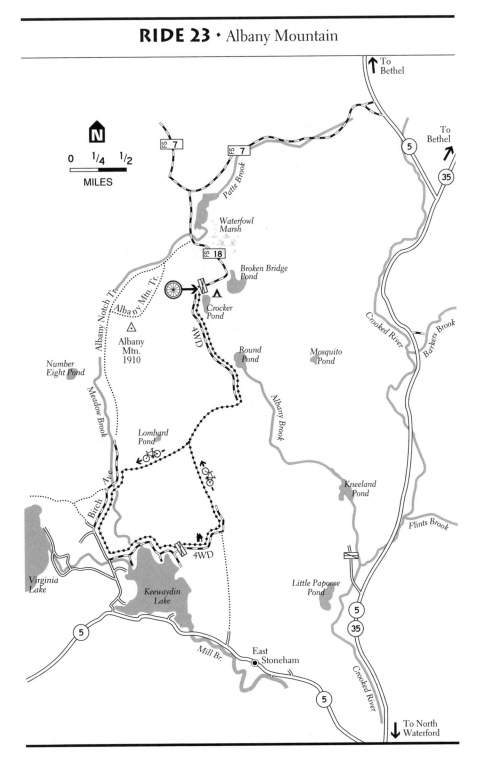

One of the easier
sections of the
Albany Mountain
Trail.

and follow it to a **T** junction. Turn left; this road becomes FR 7. After 3 miles, turn left onto FR 18 and follow signs to the campground 1.5 miles away.

Sources of additional information:

Evans Notch Ranger District
RFD 2, Box 2270
Bethel, ME 04217
(207) 834-2134

A ranger station for this district is located on US 2 east of Bethel Village. The station is open only during regular business hours.

Notes on the trail: From the parking area, ride back down FR 18 for a short distance. Turn left up a logging road and ride past a gate. This road climbs to a cleared logging yard, and then narrows but continues in the same direction. You will pass a beaver flowage on the right before beginning a steep climb. As the grade lessens, you will cross a flat saddle that may be rather wet. From this section of the trail, you will reach a small clearing and the junction with the loop portion of the ride. If snowmobile signs remain, the left-hand trail will be signed to Keewaydin Lake and North Waterford. This is the trail you will ride up to complete the loop. To begin it, continue straight at this junction and then make a quick turn to the right back into the woods.

This portion of the ride descends to Lombard Pond along a path that becomes more rutted and eroded the closer you get to the pond. You will cross a small brook by means of a snowmobile bridge and then run into a rocky, rutted, and overgrown stretch of trail. This is the most technically challenging section of the ride, but it also offers the best views: you will be able to catch glimpses of the White Mountains, specifically the Baldfaces and Carter Dome. After passing Lombard Pond on the right, the trail begins to improve again.

A second snowmobile bridge takes you over another stream, beyond which you will ride into a small clearing. Bear left through the clearing and continue riding to a T intersection. Turn left (the path to the right is the hiking trail to the top of Albany Mountain). Cross Meadow Brook over another bridge. (This bridge was out when we pedaled the route in the summer.) You will soon reach another trail junction. Continue straight (the trail that climbs to the right is a snowmobile trail that continues to Virginia Lake and Evergreen Valley). The road will gradually improve from this point on, and you will pass a number of camps and houses.

Continue straight when the road becomes paved, and then take the first left down a dirt and partially paved camp road that runs along the northern shore of Keewaydin Lake. You will continue along this road for exactly 1 mile, crossing a wooden plank bridge and the inlet of Meadow Brook by means of a large culvert. Beyond this point, look for the first road on your left; it will come just before a huge boulder. This road is grassy, and there is a metal chain across it to prevent vehicles from driving up. Turning left up this road, you will be riding up and away from the lake. You will pass through a wide, clear area that may once have been pasture. You will also pass a small camp on the left.

Beyond this camp, the road climbs more steeply. There will be a logging road off to the right beyond the steepest portion of this climb; bear left despite the fact that this trail is less worn and less distinct. You will crest this hill and see large rock formations on the left. The trail then begins to descend, and you'll enjoy a beautiful run along single-track all the way back to the junction of the loop and spur. Bear right to return to Crocker Pond.

RIDE 24 · Virginia Lake

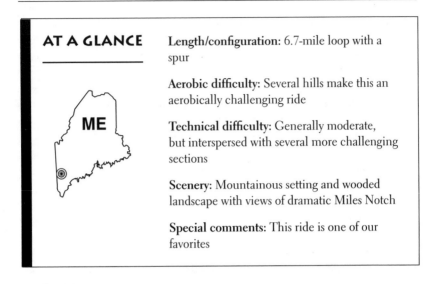

AT A GLANCE

Length/configuration: 6.7-mile loop with a spur

Aerobic difficulty: Several hills make this an aerobically challenging ride

Technical difficulty: Generally moderate, but interspersed with several more challenging sections

Scenery: Mountainous setting and wooded landscape with views of dramatic Miles Notch

Special comments: This ride is one of our favorites

Virginia Lake is tucked into the foothills of the White Mountains and lies just south of a network of old roads, logging trails, and snowmobile routes. This ride begins up a trail that connects to a long loop through a portion of White Mountain National Forest north of Virginia Lake. The ride covers a total of 6.7 miles and features a number of challenging climbs on moderately technical terrain. Because of the relatively remote setting and the need for good navigational skills, this ride is appropriate for intermediate and advanced riders in good physical condition.

General location: This ride is located in the town of Stoneham, within the boundaries of the White Mountain National Forest.

Elevation change: Along with several short climbs, this ride features one major 450-foot climb over the flank of Cecil Mountain. The total elevation gain is more than 800'.

Season: This ride should not be attempted until mid-June, when the trails have dried out enough to sustain bicycle traffic.

Services: Groceries are available in Lovell and North Waterford. The nearest bike shop is located in Norway. Camping facilities exist throughout White Mountain National Forest.

Hazards: Beware of waterbars placed along some sections of the trail—some of them are quite deep. There are also a couple of eroded sections covered by loose rock.

Rescue index: You are never more than 4 miles from assistance.

RIDE 24 · Virginia Lake

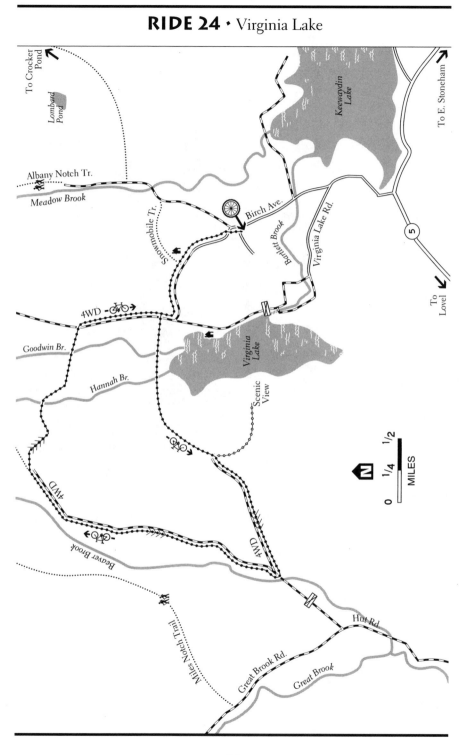

To Crocker Pond

Lombard Pond

Keewaydin Lake

To E. Stoneham

Albany Notch Tr.

Meadow Brook

Birch Ave.

Snowmobile Tr.

Bartlett Brook

Virginia Lake Rd.

5

4WD

To Lovel

Goodwin Br.

Virginia Lake

Hannah Br.

Scenic View

N

0   1/4   1/2

MILES

4WD

4WD

Beaver Brook

Miles Notch Trail

Hut Rd.

Great Brook Rd.

Great Brook

Virginia Lake.

Land status: White Mountain National Forest, Evans Notch District.

Maps: This trail is shown on the USGS quads for Speckled Mountain and East Stoneham.

Finding the trail: From East Stoneham Village head west on ME 5. After passing Keewaydin Lake on the right, turn onto the first road on the right. After half a mile, bear right at a fork in the road and continue on Birch Avenue. Continue to the end of Birch Avenue, where several driveways branch off to the left and an unpaved camp road continues straight. Pull off to the side of the road to park, taking care not to block any driveways or impede vehicular passage along the road.

Sources of additional information: None.

Notes on the trail: Begin pedaling down the unpaved camp road, following signs directing you to the Albany Notch Trail. Proceed until you come to a two-wheel-drive road that immediately veers uphill to the left. This road can easily be mistaken for a driveway. Turn left and climb steadily past several seasonal homes. The road gradually deteriorates into a four-wheel-drive trail. The trail levels out at the crest of the hill, and you will pass a small camp on the right. Bear left just beyond this camp, following the snowmobile trail signs along a trail that branches off from the old woods road. The trail is rolling and rooty at this point.

After a short, moderately steep descent, follow the trail as it swings around to the right—passing a trail on the left that leads to a private camp on Virginia Lake. This section of the trail can be quite muddy, depending on the amount of recent rainfall and the time of year. A short distance beyond this intersection, the trail forks. This is the start of the loop. We suggest turning left to take advantage of the easier grade up the hill you will have to climb on the return. The trail skirts the north end of Virginia Lake, crosses a small stream, and starts to climb. The trail is fairly well worn and therefore quite easy to follow. You will climb up the flank of Cecil Mountain along a wide single-track trail. As you crest the hill, look for a trail on the left. This is a 0.75-mile out-and-back (1.5-mile total) side trip to the heights overlooking Virginia Lake. This trail can be ridden most of the way, although most riders will opt to walk the last section, which climbs steeply.

Continuing the ride past the side trail, you will want to hang on tightly and be ready to use your brakes! The trail descends very quickly and crosses several eroded sections. Gradually, the trail levels out and you will come to a **Y** intersection. Turn right up an old logging road that starts to climb slowly and then, beyond an area that has been washed out, continues up a more severe grade. This is a long 450-foot climb, but the views of Miles Notch from the top are worth the effort. You will crest the hill, beyond which the trail descends gradually and crosses a series of waterbars. When you come to a snowmobile trail branching off on the right, turn right.

You will ride down to a stream, passing an old farm site on the right. There is a bridge across the stream, and the trail continues up to a **T** intersection. Turn right onto a wide, grassy trail, which will take you back to the intersection that marked the beginning of the loop. Retrace your tracks back to the trailhead and your car.

RIDE 25 · Highwater Trail

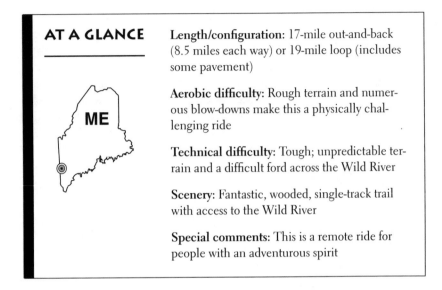

AT A GLANCE

Length/configuration: 17-mile out-and-back (8.5 miles each way) or 19-mile loop (includes some pavement)

Aerobic difficulty: Rough terrain and numerous blow-downs make this a physically challenging ride

Technical difficulty: Tough; unpredictable terrain and a difficult ford across the Wild River

Scenery: Fantastic, wooded, single-track trail with access to the Wild River

Special comments: This is a remote ride for people with an adventurous spirit

The Highwater Trail follows the northwestern bank of the Wild River in the White Mountain National Forest. The terrain is rugged and fairly remote, requiring endurance and determination along with good technical skills. The riding surface includes a combination of hard-packed single-track trails and logging roads. There is a good chance that you'll be portaging over blow-downs with your bike, and depending on how you choose to ride the trail, you may need to ford the Wild River.

The Wild River is appropriately named. In several places, bridges that once spanned the river have been torn down by raging high waters. In a dry summer season, it is hard to imagine that the shallow, beautifully clear water could cause such damage. Because the Highwater Trail follows the Wild River for much of the ride, there are many scenic viewing opportunities from the riverbank. The Wild River provides excellent fly fishing opportunities and attracts many visitors, particularly in the fall when the leaves are at their brightest.

There are several options along this ride. You can turn back at any time to retrace the route back to the parking area. Unless the water is too high for a safe crossing, you can also cross the Wild River and make your way to the Wild River Campground to refill your water bottles. From the campground, you can cross the river again to return the way you came, for a 17-mile out-and-back journey. Alternatively, you can ride down the campground access road to the Hastings Plantation and return to the trailhead by way of paved

RIDE 25 · Highwater Trail

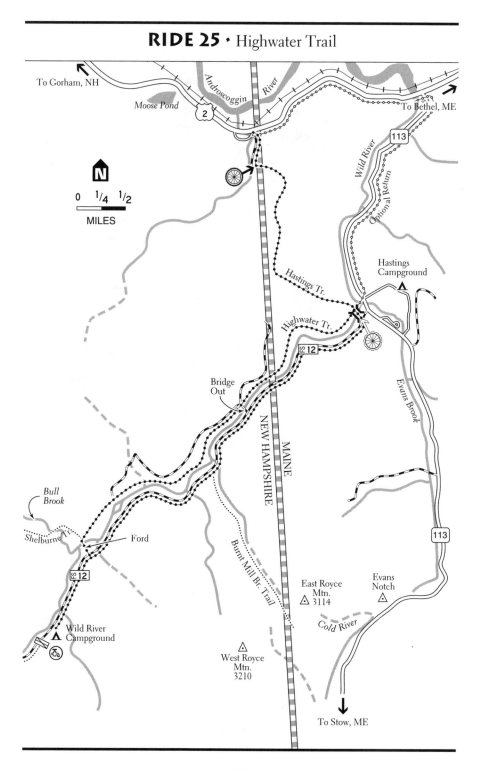

The Highwater Trail features several miles of gorgeous single-track in the White Mountain National Forest.

ME 113 and US 2. This option, though slightly longer, is the more moderate ride and traces a loop of 19 miles. There is also an alternative parking area available near the site of Hastings Plantation and the intersection of the Wild River Campground access road and ME 113. A new bridge (rebuilt in 1997) spans the Wild River close to this site and provides direct access to the trail, eliminating the need to ride the first part of the ride.

General location: On the Maine–New Hampshire border, south of Bethel, in the White Mountain National Forest.

Elevation change: The trailhead is located at approximately 700'. You will climb to 1000' and then descend to 840'. A long, gradual climb ends at 1,060'. Total elevation gain for the out-and-back ride is approximately 840'. The loop option, though longer, features a lesser gain of 580'.

Season: This trail can be ridden from late June into the fall. Fall foliage season is the most spectacular time of year to ride.

Services: Water and campsites are available at the Wild River Campground. There is a small store on US 2, just north of its junction with ME 113. All services are also available in Bethel, several miles to the north, including a bike shop at the Sunday River Mountain Bike Park.

Hazards: It is possible that you will encounter many blow-downs along this ride, as well as several severely eroded sections of the trail. Crossing the Wild River can often be extremely difficult, as the water level fluctuates greatly depending on the time of year and the amount of rainfall. Follow the guidelines in the Preface for tips on fording rivers.

Rescue index: This trail is fairly remote, and the availability of assistance will depend on the number of hikers or other riders in the area. The closest source of assistance is the Wild River Campground, which also serves as the trailhead for several hiking trails. However, during high water it may not be possible to cross the Wild River, and your closest source of assistance will be at the trailhead, on US 2. On weekends and holidays, the river is a popular fishing destination, and you may therefore encounter other people. Most people, though, stay to the more accessible southeast bank of the river. Since the bridge across Wild River near the site of Hastings Plantation has been rebuilt, access to assistance has been significantly improved. The parking area near this site is popular, and traffic along nearby ME 113 is frequent.

Land status: White Mountain National Forest.

Maps: The USGS quads for this area are Shelburne, Gilead, Speckled Mountain, and Wild River.

Finding the trail: From Bethel, follow US 2 heading west. Pass the intersection with ME 113 on the left, and travel 2 miles before looking for a dirt road on the left. Turn in here, and follow the road to a small clearing that serves as a parking lot. Alternatively, turn left up ME 113 and drive to the site of Hastings Plantation (at the intersection of ME 113 and the access road to Wild River Campground). There is a parking area on the right and a small trail that leads to a bridge across the Wild River. If you choose this option, your ride will begin to the left after you cross the bridge and will be several miles shorter in distance.

Source of additional information:

Evans Notch Ranger District
RFD 2, Box 2270
Bethel, ME 04217
(207) 834-2134

This ranger district is on US 2 east of Bethel Village.

Notes on the trail: From the parking area, look for a dirt road that is marked with a sign that reads: "corridor 12 & 19 to points south and east, Chatham

Sarah enjoys a pensive moment along the Wild River. White Mountain National Forest.

and Maine." Begin pedaling up this road, which twists and winds through woods. You may notice the sound of Connor Brook off to the right. At the first intersection, bear left, following signs to the Wild River (the road on the right is a private drive). At this point the road turns into a grassy double-track trail. At the next intersection, you will see an old trail on the right, intentionally blocked with a pile of brush. Keep to the left here, following the newer trail up a steep and very rough climb still littered with slash. The trail then flattens out and narrows into a fantastic single-track run through the woods. Continue riding until you reach the Wild River, at the site of a new bridge (rebuilt in 1997 after the previous one was destroyed by high water).

At the Wild River, turn to the right and follow a single-track trail upriver. You will cross several small ravines and may also find the trail littered with blow-downs. The trail continues to follow the river, at times coming quite close to the bank. You will reach an intersection with a grassy road at what was once another bridge site. Cross this road (which continues to your right) and continue to follow the Highwater Trail along the river. Some sections of the trail are rather eroded along this portion of the ride. At the next junction with another grassy road, you have the option of turning around and retracing your route back to the parking area, or crossing the river and returning by way of the road. If you are in need of water, you may also want to cross the river and ride up to the campground to fill up your water bottles before choosing your return route.

To cross the river, turn left down to the water. The trail here is rather washed-out and extremely rocky. You will need to cross first a small stream and then the Wild River, picking up the trail again on the other side. Though there may not be any clear signs marking the way, the trail is not difficult to find after you've crossed the river. Once on that trail, you will very quickly reach a dirt road. Turn right to reach the campground, and enjoy cold water from the pump.

If you choose to return to the trailhead via the campground access road (the longer though easier loop option for the ride), turn back down the road and continue past the trail you followed up from the river. Ride to the Hastings Plantation, at the junction of the camp road and ME 113. Turn left on ME 113 and follow the road to a **T** junction with US 2. Turn left on US 2 and ride for 2 more miles on pavement to return to the trailhead.

RIDE 26 · Mount Abram Valley

AT A GLANCE

ME

Length/configuration: 11.5-mile point-to-point (11.5 miles one way, then vehicle shuttle to return)

Aerobic difficulty: A series of long climbs and quick descents requires at least a moderate level of fitness

Technical difficulty: Moderate; several areas of rocky, eroded terrain

Scenery: A picturesque, wooded valley with several opportunities to view the surrounding mountains

Special comments: Interesting side trips to old quarries and an ice cave make this a fantastic, full-day excursion

The Mount Abram Valley ride is a scenic, 11.5-mile point-to-point trip that can also be ridden as a 21.5-mile out-and-back (10.75 hilly miles each way). The trail follows rugged four-wheel-drive roads through the remote, seldom-visited valley that follows the rolling foothills of Mount Abram and Tibbetts, Elwell, Long, Uncle Tom, and Oversett Mountains. Thrilling downhills are combined with long, moderate grades that climb to great views of the surrounding mountains. Although most of the route is not technically difficult, riders should be in good physical condition for this ride.

For most of the ride, you will be following the old county road that was once the most direct connection between the towns of Bethel and Norway. The severe grades along this old route have since been bypassed by the construction of modern highways. There is plenty of evidence along the way to show that this was once an important transportation corridor for farmers and travelers. The route is lined with stone fences, old foundations, and the occasional cemetery. There are also several trails branching off from the main trail, offering side trips to the site of an old quarry, an ice cave, and spectacular Oversett Pond. The first option is a steep climb to an abandoned quarry. This is a great place to picnic or just hang out on a sunny summer afternoon.

The ice cave is found by following a technical single-track trail that branches off the west side of the trail. Most people will prefer to walk this trail, and even those who ride it will have to dismount for the final climb up to the caves. The ice cave, the largest of a series of caves, was formed when retreating glaciers left a jumble of boulders on the hillside. Due to its sheltered location on the northeast side of Uncle Tom Mountain, the cave is protected from direct sunlight. Some years the cave contains ice year-round. Even if you don't find ice in the cave, the view from the ledges is worth the trip.

Although we did not make the trip, others have said that Oversett Pond offers spectacular scenery, as the cliffs on the southwest side of Oversett Mountain rise up directly behind the pond. Oversett Pond can be accessed by taking a two-mile side trip from the main trail.

General location: This trail is located in the town of Greenwood.

Elevation change: The trailhead is located at approximately 920'. You will climb slowly to 1,360', descend 110', and then climb to 1,375' over the shoulder of Elwell Mountain. From there, you will enjoy a steep 300-foot descent. The trail to the ice caves climbs a quick 100', after which you will descend to Willis Mill. From Willis Mill you will climb 400' up Patch Mountain. The trail concludes with a gradual descent toward Hutchinson Pond. Total elevation gain is approximately 1,120'.

Season: The best time to ride this trail is between June and October, as snow lingers in the valley late into the spring.

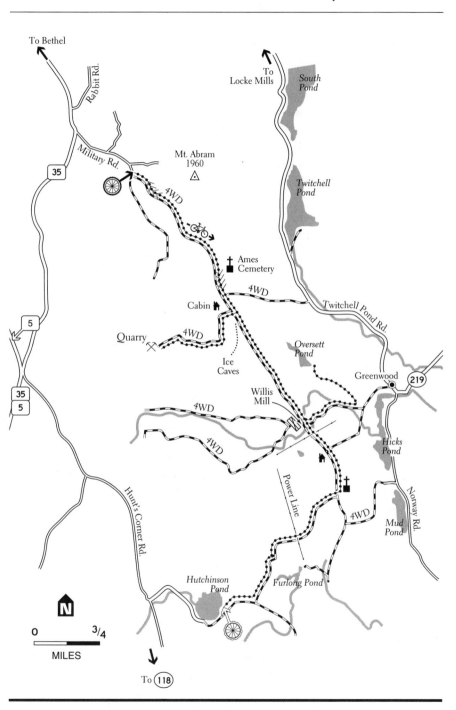

To Bethel

Rabbit Rd.

To
Locke Mills

*South
Pond*

Military Rd.

35

Mt. Abram
1960

4WD

*Twitchell
Pond*

5

Ames
Cemetery

4WD

Twitchell Pond Rd.

Cabin

4WD

Quarry

Ice
Caves

*Oversett
Pond*

Greenwood

219

35
5

4WD

Willis
Mill

4WD

*Hicks
Pond*

Power Line

Hunt's Corner Rd.

4WD

*Mud
Pond*

Norway Rd.

N

0   3/4

MILES

*Hutchinson
Pond*

Furlong Pond

To 118

Services: All services are available in Bethel. The nearest bike shop is located at the Sunday River Mountain Bike Park.

Hazards: The trail can be very rutted, with many sections of loose rock and sand. There are also several washouts, particularly where culverts have been displaced. Be aware that such obstacles often occur at the bottom of long downhill sections. All-terrain vehicles also frequent these trails, and there may be vehicular traffic on the sections of the trail that cross two-wheel-drive roads.

Cleated cycling shoes make scrambling around the ice-cave rocks quite hazardous—be careful in your explorations!

Rescue index: There are residences located at the trailhead, the endpoint, and the small settlement of Willis Mill. You may at times be as far as 4 miles from assistance. Rescue will take a long time.

Land status: The trail follows discontinued town roads. Side trips to the quarries and the ice caves require that you cross private land.

Maps: All of the trails are shown on the USGS Greenwood quadrangle. The trails are also shown in the DeLorme Mapping Company's *Maine Atlas and Gazetteer* (map 10, sections B-4 and C-4).

Finding the trail: From Bethel Village, head south on ME 35 for approximately 3 miles. Turn left at the second road you encounter after leaving the village (the first is Rabbit Road). This paved road may be called Old Irish Neighborhood Road or the Military Road and heads toward the western base of Mount Abram. Drive approximately 1 mile to where the main road veers to the left and a smaller one heads right. There is a kennel surrounded by a large brown fence at this spot. Bear right onto the smaller road. This is the start of the trail. There is a pulloff on the right, just after you make the turn, where you can park.

If you plan on riding the trail as a one-way point-to-point, you will want to leave a vehicle at the endpoint as well. To reach the endpoint near Hutchinson Pond, drive back out to ME 35 and turn left. After 3.75 miles, turn left onto Hunts Hill Road, which is located just before the junction of ME 35 and ME 5. Drive for 4.25 miles on Hunts Hill Road, and then turn left onto Hutchinson Pond Road. The road becomes gravel, and at 1.5 miles you will pass Hutchinson Pond on your left. Park at any of the many pulloffs located on the side of the road, being careful not to block any logging roads.

Sources of additional information: None.

Notes on the trail: From the parking area near the base of Mount Abram, begin pedaling southeast along an old road. Bear left at the first fork in the trail, a short distance beyond the parking area. After crossing two small bridges, you will begin a long, relatively steep climb with several severely eroded sections. At one point, the road bends to the left and a snowmobile trail continues straight, following a stone fence on the right. The road and the snowmobile trail reconnect a short distance farther along, so it does not matter which one you take. You will continue to climb to another fork in the trail. Continue straight, keeping the stone fence to your right. When you come to a crossroad marked with a sign indicating food and fuel in 11 miles, continue straight.

You will reach the top of a hill, beyond which you will descend quickly. If you are interested in old cemeteries, keep your eyes open for a narrow trail on the left that leads to Ames Cemetery, barely visible from the road. At the bottom of the hill the road forks. Bear right and cross an old, dislodged culvert. You will begin to climb, passing a small cabin on the right. As the trail levels off a short distance from the cabin, a road branches off on the right. This side trail climbs steeply to an open clearing and a small quarry pit. If you choose to ride to the quarry, turn right. At a three-way fork in the road, follow the middle trail up to the quarry.

Back on the main trail, you will climb a bit farther before reaching the crest of the hill at a small clearing. Branching off the right side of this clearing is a narrow single-track trail that climbs up to the ice caves. It is possible to ride to the base of the caves, where you can scramble on foot to the open ledges or the deep, cold interiors of the caves. Return to the main trail and turn right, continuing southeast.

At the next fork in the trail, at the end of a short descent, bear left and cross a snowmobile bridge. Continue riding straight past a road that branches off to the right at an acute angle. When you come to a junction with an improved dirt road, bear left. A short distance farther, you will cross a small bridge and ride up to a major snowmobile trail intersection. Continue straight, passing a road and a cabin on the right and a house on the left. The road bears left, and a jeep trail continues straight. The ride continues straight, following the jeep trail. However, for a short excursion to Oversett Pond, follow the road around to the left. Pedal down the road for approximately 1 mile, looking for a jeep trail on the left. The jeep trail approaches the pond from the south. Retrace your tracks back to the previous intersection to continue the main trail.

Riding down the jeep trail, you will cross Sanborn River by way of a bridge at Willis Mill. There are many homes and camps at Willis Mill. As you continue straight, the road becomes a rough jeep trail, crossing under power lines and climbing to a large white farmhouse on the right. The views are outstanding from this point. Continue straight past a road coming in on the left until you reach Patch Mountain Cemetery. Turn right onto a trail located directly across from the cemetery.

From here it is helpful to follow the snowmobile trail signs back to Hutchinson Pond. Bear left at the first fork in the trail. There is a cabin a little farther down the trail to the right. Shortly beyond this point, ride past another trail that branches off to the left. The trail is grassy at this point and crosses beneath power lines a short distance farther. You will come to a short descent that is marked with a sign reading: "Warning: narrow crooked trail for two miles." Bear left after this descent. The trail becomes an improved dirt road. Continue to follow the main trail, avoiding any side roads. You will reach a **T** junction with Hutchinson Pond Road. Turn right and continue riding until you come to where you parked your vehicle shuttle.

RIDE 27 · Sunday River Mountain Bike Park

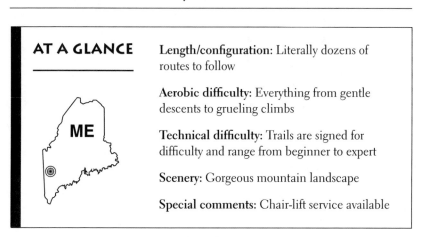

AT A GLANCE

Length/configuration: Literally dozens of routes to follow

Aerobic difficulty: Everything from gentle descents to grueling climbs

Technical difficulty: Trails are signed for difficulty and range from beginner to expert

Scenery: Gorgeous mountain landscape

Special comments: Chair-lift service available

ME

At New England's leading mountain chain, the action doesn't end when the snow melts; it just shifts gears! As skis and snowboards are put into storage, the Sunday River Mountain Bike Park prepares for summer. Rivaling the skiing and snowboarding in winter, the Mountain Bike Park offers another exhilarating way to experience the thrill and beauty of the western Maine mountains.

The Sunday River Mountain Bike Park offers 60 miles of marked and patrolled trails. Varying in difficulty from beginner to expert, these trails offer invigorating mountain terrain for riders of all skill levels. Access to the park is at the White Cap Base Lodge, where trail and lift passes can be purchased. The park is serviced by two chair lifts. From the top of either lift, you can either coast down or test yourself with grueling uphill climbs and single-track descents. Wherever you choose to ride, you will discover panoramic views, sparkling mountain streams, and more than 100 different types of wildflowers. Hawks, ravens, grouse, deer, fox, and moose may also be seen at any time.

Special events at the Sunday River Mountain Bike Park include the annual River Rage Mountain Bike Racing Festival, part of the Trail 66 Mountain Bike Race Series. A NORBA-sanctioned event, River Rage has racers competing in cross country, dual slalom, and the dirt criterium (a short-track lap race that includes hills, bumps, and one "big air" jump). In addition to

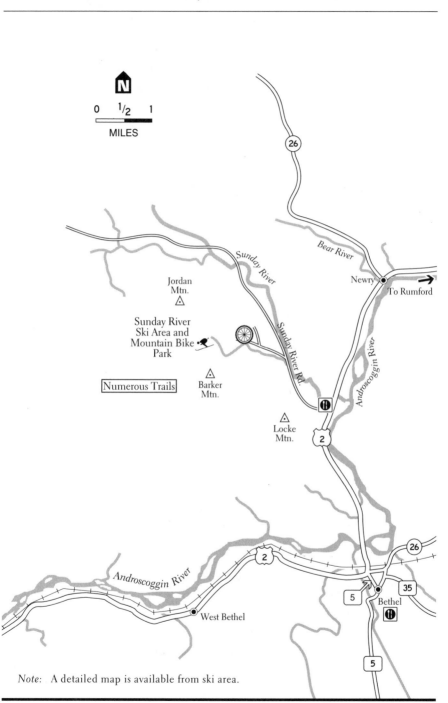

Note: A detailed map is available from ski area.

the races, the festival offers music, mountain bike clinics with Gary Fisher pros, kids' races and games, moonlight rides, and a free bonfire pasta feast.

General location: Newry, 4 miles northwest of Bethel.

Elevation change: Sunday River boasts a vertical drop of 2,340'.

Season: The Sunday River Mountain Bike Park is open daily from the end of June to the beginning of September. In addition, the park is open on weekends beginning at the end of May. The hours of operation are weekends from 9 A.M. to 4 P.M., and weekdays from 9 A.M. to 3 P.M.

Services: There is a bike shop at the White Cap Base Lodge, which offers a full-service rental and repair shop as well as light snacks and nutritional and energy supplements. Clinics and tours are available by appointment. Lodging and a variety of dining opportunities are available in nearby Bethel.

Hazards: None.

Rescue index: The trails at the Sunday River Mountain Bike Park are patrolled, so assistance should never be far away.

Land status: Sunday River is a privately owned and operated resort.

Maps: Trail maps are available at the bike shop located in the White Cap Base Lodge. In addition, many bike stores throughout the state also carry a good supply of trail maps.

Finding the trail: From Bethel, take US 2 east toward Rumford. Just 3 miles outside Bethel, turn left onto the Sunday River Road and follow signs to the mountain.

Source of additional information:

> Sunday River
> P.O. Box 450
> Bethel, ME 04217
> (207) 824-3000

Notes on the trail: The Sunday River Mountain Bike Park features trails divided into four categories of difficulty: beginner, intermediate, advanced, and expert. Beginners' trails, of which there are 10, are characterized by relatively flat terrain or rolling grades. The 15 intermediate trails range from short, rocky climbs to long, curvy downhills. Everything from steeps to bumpy uphills to technical single-track can be found along the 11 advanced trails, and for the most accomplished riders, one expert trail requires not only excellent fitness and skill levels, but extra caution as well.

Details for the Sunday River ride were provided by Michael Bertie of Sunday River, Maine.

RIDE 28 · Sawyer Notch

AT A GLANCE	**Length/configuration:** 9-mile out-and-back (4.5 miles each way)
	Aerobic difficulty: Moderate
ME	**Technical difficulty:** Multiple stream crossings require agility and determination!
	Scenery: Glacially-carved, U-shaped valley in wooded, mountainous setting
	Special comments: This ride is a rugged back-country adventure

Sawyer Notch is a remote, nine-mile out-and-back ride that shadows Sawyer Brook from Andover to C Pond. It follows a wide single-track trail that is rocky in sections and often obstructed by deadfall. Three of the four stream crossings on this ride are without bridges of any kind. The route crosses the Appalachian Trail and cuts through a wooded, almost parklike landscape with spectacular, tall trees. This ride is moderately difficult for riders with intermediate-to-advanced riding skills in good physical condition.

Western Maine is characterized by spectacular U-shaped valleys, like Sawyer Notch, which were deepened by the flow of melting glacier ice some 20,000 years ago. Sawyer Brook was the low point for the drainage of glacial Lake Cambridge. After the ice retreated, the elevation difference between the valley floor and the surrounding mountains was significantly increased. Sawyer Brook, at an elevation of 1,070 feet at the start of this ride, is dramatically situated at the base of 2,440-foot Moody Mountain on its northern shore, and 2,800-foot Hall Mountain to the south. The brook is highly responsive to heavy rain and spring runoff.

The trail up Sawyer Notch was originally developed by farmers, who would band together and head up to C Meadows, where they would camp and cut hay. The hay was stacked in huge bundles to be retrieved in the winter when the farmers were able to haul it down in sleds pulled by oxen. There was also much lumbering done along this section of trail. Unlike hay, wood was cut in the winter, and many men spent the winter at lumber camps erected in the woods. Logs were cut and hauled to landings on Sawyer Brook by oxen. With the coming of high water in the spring, the logs were then

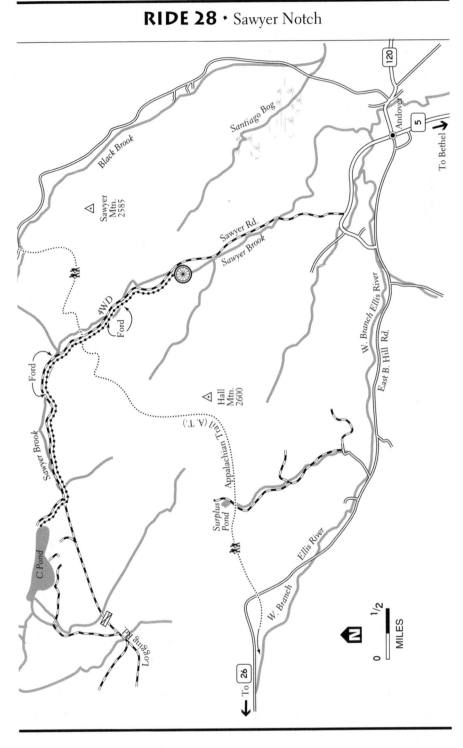

floated down the brook, guided by crews of river drivers, to Ellis River and on to the sawmills in Andover.

General location: This ride begins just north of the town of Andover, and continues through Sawyer Notch to C Pond.

Elevation change: Although the Sawyer Notch ride is overlooked by peaks more than 2,500' high, the trail follows Sawyer Brook along the lowest elevation through the notch and gains a modest 380' in elevation.

Season: Because this trail crosses Sawyer Brook a total of 4 times, it is best to save this ride until spring runoff from the surrounding mountains has subsided. In the fall, colorful foliage adds to the beauty of the valley.

Services: Basic needs can be met in Andover, where there is a small grocery store. For bicycle parts and service, however, you will have to travel toward Bethel or Rumford. In Newry, just north of Bethel, there is a bike shop located at the Sunday River Mountain Bike Park. In Rumford, find your way to Wallace's Wheels, located on US 2. The staff at Wallace's Wheels are a good source of information about riding in the area and can be reached at (207) 364-7946 or (800) 834-7946.

Hazards: The stream crossings on this ride are the most difficult sections of the trail and require much caution. In the spring and early summer, Sawyer Brook is quite deep in places and the water runs quickly. It is advisable to pack an extra pair of socks on days that might turn cool. At any time of year, carry plenty of water and extra food.

Rescue index: This trail is in a remote location. Rescue will take several hours at best. At the farthest point along this ride, you will be 9 miles from assistance. The closest sources of help are the few houses at the beginning of Sawyer Notch Road.

Land status: This land is privately owned, with the exception of the Appalachian National Scenic Trail Corridor.

Maps: The USGS quadrangle for Sawyer Notch is Andover.

Finding the trail: From the south, drive into Andover on ME 5. As you come into town, the road turns sharply to the right, onto ME 120. Continue straight through this intersection. After crossing the Ellis River, continue for about 1 mile before looking for Sawyer Notch Road on the right. Turn right and continue straight until the road ends in a logging yard.

Sources of additional information: None.

Notes on the trail: From the parking area, begin riding in a northwesterly direction and follow a wide trail to Sawyer Brook. At the time we rode here there was no bridge across the brook, although evidence seemed to point to there once having been one. Beyond the brook, the trail continues on the

Riding deep into the woods of Sawyer Notch near Andover.

other side. You must cross Sawyer Brook again, a short distance farther. Here, the remains of a snowmobile bridge were enough to prevent our feet from getting wet a second time.

Beyond the second stream crossing, the trail cuts an obvious path through the woods. You will cross the Appalachian Trail before crossing the stream for the third time. The day we rode along Sawyer Notch, a rather blustery and drizzly one, we met a solitary chef in the middle of the trail at this point, preparing lobsters over a camp stove for a crew of hikers doing trail maintenance. Sadly, we were not invited to supper and were forced to continue on to the third and deepest portage across Sawyer Brook! Although there are several options for tackling this particular crossing, there is no way you will stay dry doing it.

From the stream crossing, the trail climbs quickly, forcing you around several eroded sections. At the next fork, stay on the well-worn section to the right. This will take you past a privately owned cabin. After passing the cabin, the trail drops back down to the stream for the final crossing you will have to make. Keeping to the main trail, you will eventually come to an area of recent logging activity. The trail descends to a logging yard, with a road going down to the left and a lesser road heading right. To get to C Pond, take the road on the right and follow it until you reach the pond. Retrace your route to return to the trailhead.

RIDE 29 · Little Blue Mountain

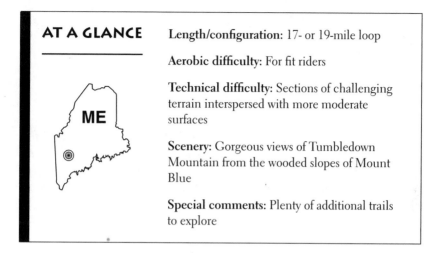

AT A GLANCE

Length/configuration: 17- or 19-mile loop

Aerobic difficulty: For fit riders

Technical difficulty: Sections of challenging terrain interspersed with more moderate surfaces

Scenery: Gorgeous views of Tumbledown Mountain from the wooded slopes of Mount Blue

Special comments: Plenty of additional trails to explore

This ride is a 17- or 19-mile loop, depending on the route you choose once you reach a lookout and shelter on the western slope of Mount Blue. You will be riding over single- and double-track trails through the beautiful, forested hills of Mount Blue State Park. The route is technically varied and challenging: a combination of hard-packed trails over rocks and roots, and overgrown old carriage trails that are rocky and extremely wet in places. The shorter of the two loop options also makes use of the unpaved Mt. Blue Road for an easier return trip. Either option is suitable for riders of intermediate to advanced ability with a high level of physical fitness.

Mount Blue State Park features approximately 25 miles of multi-use trails. In addition, the Mt. Blue Road offers less technical riding along a dirt road that climbs to a scenic lookout and shelter. The two loop options we have described below highlight the best terrain and most dramatic features the park has to offer. However, there are rides for everyone but the unadventurous at this park. With the use of the trails and the unpaved road, any number of rides can be created, depending upon your skill level and the amount of time you have. The trail system features a striking combination of wooded single-track trails, and a number of wide fields and hilltops that open out onto fantastic views of Mount Blue as well as Jackson, Little Jackson, and Tumbledown mountains to the west. The beauty of riding at Mount Blue State Park is further enhanced by the fact that the trails have been designed with riders in mind; not only are they well maintained, well signed, and able to support use by a great number of riders, but they have been laid out to highlight the natural beauty of the park.

General location: Mount Blue State Park is located just north of the town of Weld, above the northeast shore of Webb Lake. Rumford is just 20 miles to the south, and Farmington about the same distance to the east.

Elevation change: From the trailhead at approximately 1,040' above sea level, you will face undulating terrain and a number of steep climbs on your way up to 1,700' on Little Blue Mountain. From here, the ride descends to the Mount Blue shelter at 1,400' before returning to the trailhead. The side trip up Hedgehog Hill will take you to an elevation of 1,298'. Total elevation gain is approximately 710'.

Season: The trail system at Mount Blue State Park is open for year-round use. It is best to avoid using the trails in the early spring, however, when riding in wet conditions can severely damage them. Autumn is spectacular in this part of the state, and the views of the Tumbledown Range become colored by the glorious red, gold, and orange hues of changing fall foliage.

Services: Basic services are available in Weld, where there are several general stores. There is a privy in the parking area at the trailhead but no water. However, there is a spring farther along Center Hill Road, and a short ride along the road will enable you to fill your water bottles with fresh, cold water. Camping is available at a beachside tenting area on the western shore of Lake Webb, where swimming and picnicking facilities are located as well.

For bicycle-related needs, you will have to travel to either Farmington or Rumford. Farmington is home to Northern Lights Hearth and Sports, located downtown at 2 Front Street (phone (207) 778-6566 or (800) 789-6566). Wallace's Wheels in Rumford is another full-service bike store, located just south of downtown on US 2. To contact Wallace's Wheels, call (207) 364-7946 or (800) 834-7946.

Hazards: The trails at Mount Blue State Park are open to hikers, horses, and all-terrain vehicles, so be prepared to yield to other trail users. Any other potential hazards are usually marked in advance, including bridges, dips, and road crossings.

Rescue index: The trail system is numbered at approximately 1-mile intervals, so it is easy to explain where an injury or accident has left someone awaiting help. There is a park ranger station located at the trailhead, and the trail system intersects the Mt. Blue Road at several points.

Land status: State park.

Maps: Trail maps are available at the information board at the trailhead. In addition, the *Maine ATV Trail Map* published by the Department of Conservation includes a map of the trails at Mount Blue State Park. To obtain one of these maps, contact the ORV Division/ATV Program of the Bureau of Parks and Lands, 22 State House Station, Augusta, ME 04333, (207) 287-4958.

Finding the trail: From US 2, travel north up ME 142 until you reach Weld, at the intersection of ME 142 and ME 156. Continue straight up Center Hill Road and follow it around to the left. As the hill reaches a plateau, you will pass a parking and lookout area on the left. Continue just past this area, and turn right into a parking lot reserved for trail users.

Source of additional information: For additional information about the park, or to make camping reservations, call (207) 585-2347.

Notes on the trail: The trailhead is marked by an information board located at the edge of the woods. From here the trail is signed, so look for the ATV signs to direct you. In most cases, the ride we have described follows the cross-country ski trail signs as well. It is worth noting that despite all these signs, not all of the logging roads that exist in the park are actually noted on the map, and as a result, some trail junctions can be confusing.

From the trailhead, you will follow the treeline for a short distance before turning right into the woods and onto a section of the trail that may be quite wet and muddy even in the summer months. You will begin a short, steep, and potentially slippery climb to the first intersection. Turn right onto a stretch of fast, newly cut single-track. This trail eventually opens onto a wider, grassy trail that offers a clear view of Mount Blue in the distance. The next intersection is in another clearing. It is to this clearing that you will return if you opt for the longer return trip from the Mount Blue shelter. For now, you need to make a hairpin turn to the left onto a two-wheel-drive road. After a short distance, and at the crest of a small hill, look for a large boulder on the left and follow the ATV and cross-country ski trail heading back into the woods. If you miss this turn, you will continue along the road to a logging yard.

The ride continues through the woods on a single-track trail. The next trail junction marks the turnoff for Hedgehog Hill, a side trip well worth taking for spectacular views of Jackson Mountain and the surrounding foothills. Turn left for this short side trip, and be prepared to leave your bike and walk up the final climb to the top. This secluded hilltop is a wonderfully peaceful spot at which to stop for lunch or a snack, and there is even a picnic bench at the top.

Enjoy the quick descent from Hedgehog Hill back to the trail. You will continue along a more open, grassy trail before returning to more rugged single-track through the woods. The trail then turns left down a rocky old road, which descends over very rough terrain before improving slightly up a short incline to Mt. Blue Road. Because the next section of the ATV trail is often torturously wet and muddy, turn right and continue up the road instead.

After about 1 mile, and at the point where the road turns slightly to the right, continue straight ahead in order to pick up the ATV trail again. You will immediately begin a long, steady climb up and around Little Blue Mountain.

RIDE 29 · Little Blue Mountain
RIDE 30 · Center Hill

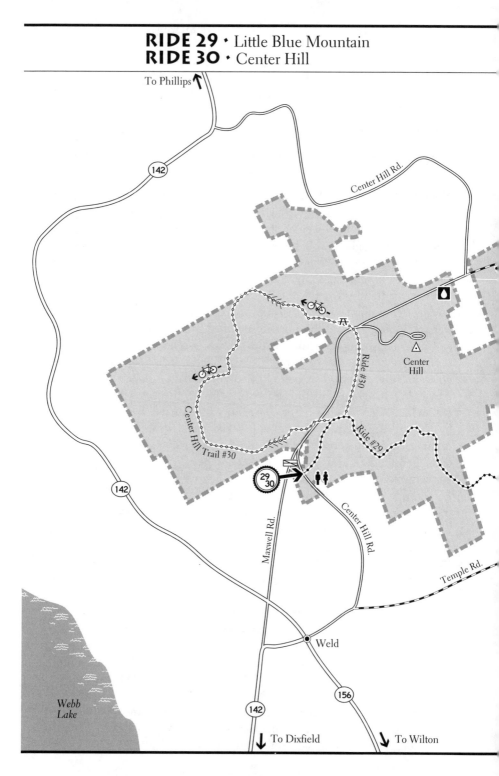

To Phillips

142

Center Hill Rd.

Ride #30

Center Hill Trail #30

Ride #29

Center
Hill

29
30

Center Hill Rd.

Maxwell Rd.

Temple Rd.

Weld

142

156

Webb
Lake

142

To Dixfield

To Wilton

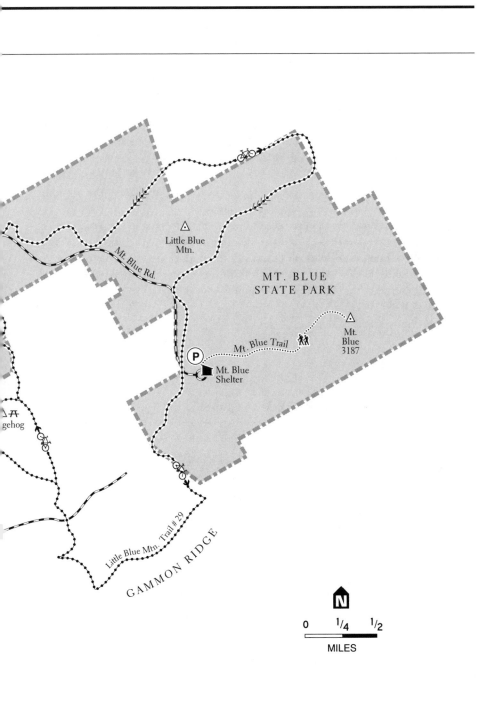

Little Blue
Mtn.

Mt. Blue Rd.

MT. BLUE
STATE PARK

Mt. Blue Trail

Mt.
Blue
3187

P

Mt. Blue
Shelter

gehog

Little Blue Mtn. Trail # 29

GAMMON RIDGE

N

0   1/4   1/2
MILES

At a clearing, follow the trail around to the right. You will eventually come around to the eastern side of Little Blue Mountain and enjoy a well-earned descent back toward Mt. Blue Road. Bear left just before the road to continue riding along the ATV trail, which essentially parallels Mt. Blue Road to its end at the small parking area, the shelter, and the trailhead for the foot trail that leads up to the summit of Mount Blue. When we rode this particular section of the trail it was newly cut and still extremely rough. As an alternative, it is possible to follow the road instead. Whichever way you choose, turn left after a short distance and follow the road up to a small parking area. The Mount Blue shelter is located at one end of the parking lot, at the top of a small pasture, and makes for another scenic rest stop.

From the shelter, you have several options for returning to the parking area and trailhead. The less difficult route simply follows Mt. Blue Road back down to Center Hill Road, all the way to the parking area. Alternatively, and for a slightly longer loop, ride down from the shelter and turn left onto the continuation of the ATV trail. The trail swings down to Houghton Brook at the base of Gammon Ridge and then crosses Temple Road to reconnect you with the first part of the trail at the site of the second clearing. At this point you can retrace your route back to the trailhead and parking area.

RIDE 30 · Center Hill

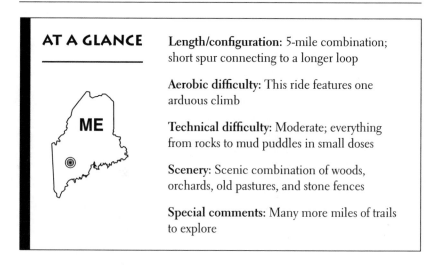

AT A GLANCE

ME

Length/configuration: 5-mile combination; short spur connecting to a longer loop

Aerobic difficulty: This ride features one arduous climb

Technical difficulty: Moderate; everything from rocks to mud puddles in small doses

Scenery: Scenic combination of woods, orchards, old pastures, and stone fences

Special comments: Many more miles of trails to explore

This short, five-mile loop is a beautiful escape through parklike scenery that includes a grassy orchard, an old cut in which raspberry bushes run wild, and a stand of tall pines interrupted only by the lines of old stone fences.

Though the ride includes a steep descent over a muddy, rocky trail and a diffi-cult climb back to Center Hill Road, the short length of the loop makes this a route that beginning riders will relish for its challenge, and intermediate riders will enjoy for its scenery. A side trip up the park road to Center Hill provides views of surrounding countryside. Furthermore, it is possible to combine this loop with a combination of trail options available at Mount Blue State Park.

General location: Mount Blue State Park is located just north of the town of Weld, above the northeast shore of Webb Lake. Rumford is just 20 miles to the south, and Farmington about the same distance to the east.

Elevation change: From the trailhead at 1,040', you will drop down the west-ern slope of Center Hill and then climb back up to Center Hill Road for a modest elevation gain of 200'.

Season: Mount Blue State Park is open year-round. It is best to avoid riding in the spring and early summer, in order to allow the ground to dry out. Au-tumn is a particularly beautiful time of year in this part of the state, and the views of Jackson Mountain to the northwest and Spencer Mountain to the southwest are superb.

Services: Basic services are available in Weld, where there are several general stores. There is a privy in the parking area at the trailhead as well. The closest bike shop is probably Wallace's Wheels in Rumford or Northern Lights Hearth and Sports in Farmington. Water is available at a spring located along Center Hill Road. There is a beachside tent-camping area on the southwest shore of Webb Lake.

Hazards: The trails at Mount Blue State Park are open to hikers, horses, and all-terrain vehicles. Any other potential hazards are usually marked in ad-vance, so you will be alerted as to bridges, dips, and road crossings.

Rescue index: You will not venture farther than 2 miles from Center Hill Road. Furthermore, the trail system at Mount Blue State Park is numbered at approximately 1-mile intervals, so it is easy to explain where an injury or acci-dent has left someone awaiting help. There is a park ranger station located at the trailhead.

Land status: State park.

Maps: There are maps of the Mount Blue State Park trail system available at the trailhead. In addition, the *Maine ATV Trail Map* published by the De-partment of Conservation outlines the trails. To obtain one of these maps, contact the ORV Division/ATV Program of the Bureau of Parks and Lands, 22 State House Station, Augusta, ME 04333, (207) 287-4958.

Finding the trail: From US 2, travel north up ME 142 until you reach Weld, at the intersection of ME 142 and ME 156. Continue straight up Center Hill Road and follow it around to the left. As the hill reaches a plateau, you will

Cruising down through the meadow below Center Hill.

pass a parking and observation area on the left. Continue just past this, and turn into a parking area for trail users on the right.

Sources of additional information: You can obtain information about Mount Blue State Park by calling (207) 585-2347. For additional insight about riding in the area, you may want to contact Northern Lights Hearth and Sports in Farmington at (207) 778-6566 or (800) 789-6566, or Wallace's Wheels in Rumford at (207) 364-7946 or (800) 834-7946.

Notes on the trail: The trailhead is at the information board located at the edge of the parking area, at the perimeter of the woods. From here the trail is signed, so look for the ATV signs to direct you. In most cases, the trails follow the cross-country ski trail signs as well.

From the trailhead, you will skirt the woods for a short distance before turning right onto a trail that may be quite wet and muddy even during the summer. You will begin a short, steep, and potentially slippery climb to a four-way intersection. Continue straight through this intersection, noting that the trail on the left is where you will complete the loop. Cross the paved Center Hill Road and descend along a grassy trail through an old apple orchard. The trail will gradually close in, and you will begin to descend a rather steep trail that, despite a series of culverts, usually boasts plenty of mud and rocks. Entering an old clear-cut, the trail will once again open up, and you will be riding along an old road into the valley. Rounding a sharp corner will find you in a more heavily lumbered area, where raspberries have emerged in abundance. Reentering the woods, tall pines surround the trail. At trail marker #2, the trail follows the path of an old road clearly visible between two old stone fences. You will descend to a swampy area traversed via two wooden platforms, and then begin to climb. Although this road continues straight ahead, the trail actually turns to the left through a stone fence. This turnoff is clearly signed.

Through this section of the ride, you will be zigzagging through stone fences and climbing steadily back to Center Hill Road. Cross the road, where the trail continues, and you will quickly find yourself back at the first four-way intersection. Turn right to return to the parking area, and enjoy the much easier descent of the first hill you climbed!

RIDE 31 · West Farmington–to-Jay Rail Trail

AT A GLANCE

Length/configuration: 28-mile out-and-back (14 miles each way)

Aerobic difficulty: Moderate; endurance and conditioning are required to complete the entire ride

Technical difficulty: Modest; a few sandy areas require strength and good bike handling skills

Scenery: Woods, wetlands, and several small communities

Special comments: Easy access to Troll Valley from the northern portion of the trail (see Ride 32)

ME

An abandoned railroad bed between the towns of West Farmington and Jay now serves as a multi-use recreational trail and offers bikers a flat alternative to riding in this rather hilly region of the state. Access to the trail exists at many points and facilitates any number of rides of varying distances along different sections of the trail. Many local riders can actually hop on the trail from their own backyards! As an out-and-back excursion from one end of the trail to the other and back again, the ride covers a total of 28 miles. Riders of intermediate ability in good physical condition will have no trouble with this distance. For less experienced riders, the best option is to leave a vehicle at either end of the trail and pedal it as a point-to-point ride of 14 miles.

For the most part, the riding is easy and follows a flat, graded, gravel surface. The only difficult parts of the ride are those where deep, soft sand covers the trail. With practice, by lightening up on your handlebars, riding through this is actually more frustrating than difficult, as your progress will be slowed considerably. Along other sections of the trail, the surface is hard-packed and smooth, allowing for some great cruising.

The railroad bed that this ride follows creates a narrow corridor among the communities of West Farmington, Wilton, and Jay. Among these three towns, you will be riding through woods and meadows, past several wetland areas, and across a number of streams. However, as the ride passes through each town, you will also ride through the backyards of these communities: past the sites of old stations and behind homes that once saw the regular passage of trains. Train service began along this line in 1859, and when service was discontinued in 1956, a tradition of almost 100 years ended. There remains, nevertheless, something tangible about the history of the railroad in this trail and the vital role it played in the history of the towns through which it passed. As you ride, you may find yourself pedaling to the rhythm of the trains that once ran here.

General location: Southern Franklin County, between the towns of Jay and West Farmington.

Elevation change: Railway beds were rarely constructed to include grades of more than 4 percent. As a result, this ride is relatively flat.

Season: Trail conditions are good throughout the year. This is a particularly beautiful ride in the fall, when the surrounding hillsides are painted in the red, orange, yellow, and gold hues of fall foliage. Once snowmobiles have packed the snow, a pair of studded tires and some warm clothing make this a spectacular winter outing.

Services: All services are available in Jay and Farmington. In Jay, TNS Cyclery is a good resource for bicycle needs and can be reached at (207) 987-6834. You can't miss the store; it is the converted red train depot located at the intersection of the rail trail and ME 4. In Farmington, Northern Lights

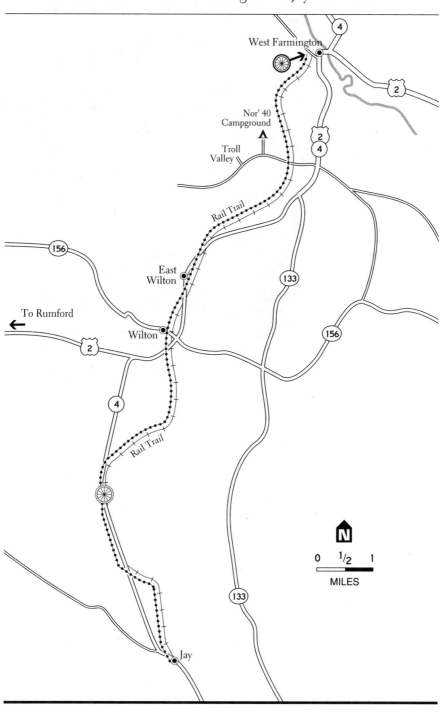

A leisurely ride along the recreational trail between West Farmington and Jay.

Hearth and Sports on Front Street is another excellent resource. The staff at Northern Lights can be reached at (207) 778-6566 or (800) 789-6566.

Hazards: Soft sand along some stretches of this trail can be difficult to handle. Other trail users may include equestrians, so consult the guidelines outlined in the Preface for tips and suggestions on how to handle horse and rider encounters on the trail.

Rescue index: From beginning to end, this ride never strays far from assistance. Besides passing through several small towns, the trail crosses many roads and runs behind a number of homes and businesses.

Land status: State recreational trail.

Maps: This ride is illustrated in the *Maine ATV Trail Map,* which is available from the Department of Conservation, Bureau of Parks and Lands, ORV Division/ATV Program, 22 State House Station, Augusta, ME 04333. Phone (207) 287-4958.

Finding the trail: This ride can be begun at any point along the trail, although parking is easiest at either end. In Jay, begin the ride at TNS Cyclery, just south of downtown Jay. You will have to cross ME 4 and pick up the railroad bed as it heads north toward Farmington. Alternatively, from Farmington, cross the Sandy River into West Farmington and take the first right after the bridge. Bear left at the next intersection and look for parking on the right in an area that was once part of a rail yard. From here, the ride heads south across a snowmobile bridge.

Sources of additional information:

TNS Cyclery
Route 4
Jay, ME 04239
(207) 897-6834

Troll Valley Cross Country Ski and Fitness Center
Red Schoolhouse Road
RR 4, Box 5215
Farmington, ME 04938
(207) 778-3656

Troll Valley is a private facility that offers its own mountain biking trails and direct access to the rail trail.

Notes on the trail: Once you begin this ride, it is almost impossible to get lost. The railway bed runs like a corridor through West Farmington, Wilton, and Jay. You will be riding in the woods, through wetlands and bogs, alongside meadows, over streams, and across several impressive snowmobile bridges. Just south of Old Jay Road, picnic tables have been set up in what was once quite a large rail yard. This is a great place to stop for lunch or a snack, and to enjoy the view.

RIDE 32 · Troll Valley

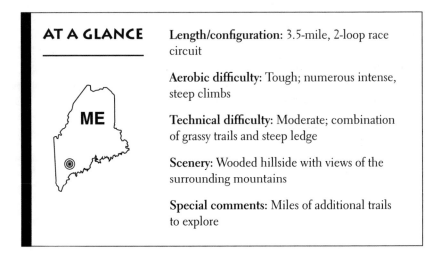

AT A GLANCE

Length/configuration: 3.5-mile, 2-loop race circuit

Aerobic difficulty: Tough; numerous intense, steep climbs

Technical difficulty: Moderate; combination of grassy trails and steep ledge

Scenery: Wooded hillside with views of the surrounding mountains

Special comments: Miles of additional trails to explore

Though there are several riding options available to those who find their way to Troll Valley, we most enjoyed the 3.5-mile race circuit. Suitable for anyone, from the beginner to the really advanced or adventurous, the circuit is made up of two loops that can be ridden alone or in quick succession. The first is directed over grassy, mowed trails. The second and more rigorous loop features a series of short climbs and descents over less refined and more technically challenging terrain. Together, they create a loop that can be ridden as many times as your body permits!

In addition to the race circuit, Troll Valley opens ten miles of cross-country ski trails to mountain bikers in the summer months. Trails are opened as conditions allow. Finally, Troll Valley also has direct access to the rail trail that runs between Farmington and Jay.

Throughout the summer, several races and events are held at Troll Valley. In August, the Tom Sayward Memorial Fat-Tire Festival features cross-country races for all classes and categories. These races are on the NORBA circuit and are part of the Maine Mountain Bike Association State Championship Series.

General location: Troll Valley is located 3 miles outside Farmington.

Elevation change: The race circuit at Troll Valley is characterized by a series of short, steep climbs and descents.

Season: Troll Valley is open to mountain bikers from Memorial Day weekend through Columbus Day from 9:00 A.M. to dusk, Wednesday through Sunday.

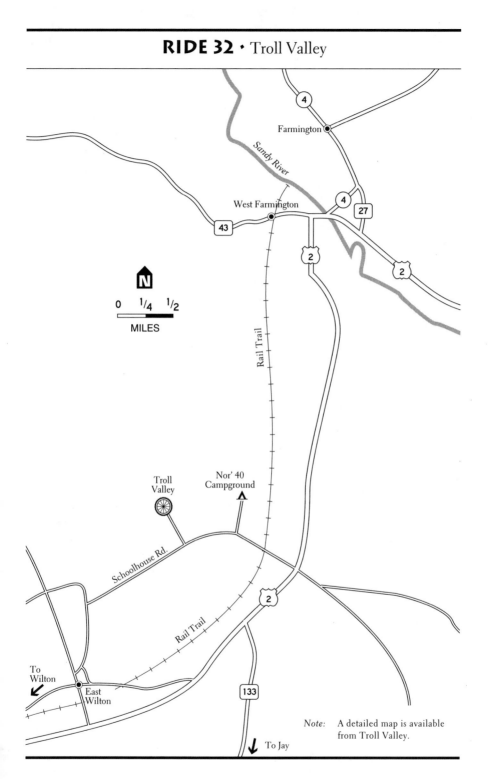

Note: A detailed map is available from Troll Valley.

Services: All the services you need are right at Troll Valley. In addition to great mountain biking, there are organized trail rides, a fitness center and sauna, a lunch counter, a rental facility, and tent-camping facilities. Minor bike repairs can be made at the lodge, and bike sales and major repairs can be sought in Farmington.

Hazards: None.

Rescue index: At the farthest point on the circuit you will not be more than a mile from the main lodge.

Land status: Troll Valley is a private facility open to mountain bikers for a nominal fee that goes toward trail maintenance.

Maps: Trail maps are available at the lodge.

Finding the trail: From Interstate 95, take Exit 12 and travel north on ME 4 toward Farmington. Five miles beyond the intersection of US 2 with ME 4, turn left onto Schoolhouse Road. Troll Valley is located just 1 mile up the road on the right.

Sources of additional information:

Troll Valley Cross Country Ski and Fitness Center
Red Schoolhouse Road
RR 4, Box 5215
Farmington, ME 04938
(207) 778-3656

Or, check out Troll Valley's home page at www.maine.com/tst/tvalley/welcome.html

Notes on the trail: The race circuit begins and ends at the announcer's box over a wide, grassy field. The circuit is clearly marked, and you will begin along the wide, mowed trails of the lower loop. Back at the announcer's box, you'll cross a stone fence and begin the second loop, which curls up the hill behind the lodge. A series of steep climbs and descents will afford views of the Longfellow Mountains, the western Maine foothills, and the flatlands of the Sandy River basin to the east. This section of the circuit is awesome; the trail has been designed to highlight the ledge cliffs and rolling steeps of the hillside. There is also a picnic table perched on a ledge if you want to take some time out to really enjoy the view. You will complete the circuit back at the announcer's box, where you can call it a day or continue for another round.

RIDE 33 · Wire Bridge

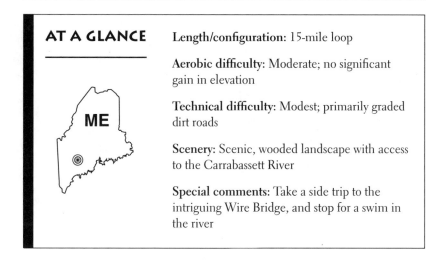

AT A GLANCE

Length/configuration: 15-mile loop

Aerobic difficulty: Moderate; no significant gain in elevation

Technical difficulty: Modest; primarily graded dirt roads

Scenery: Scenic, wooded landscape with access to the Carrabassett River

Special comments: Take a side trip to the intriguing Wire Bridge, and stop for a swim in the river

This moderately challenging 15-mile loop rolls along scenic two-wheel-drive dirt roads for about ten miles, a wooded double-track trail for four miles, and finally a rural highway for a mile. First, you will pedal past handsome farms and open fields. After this warm-up, the ride passes by a small airport in a field and heads into secluded woods on a jeep road that turns into a trail.

Along the first section of the ride there is a fun side trip to an unusual architectural structure — a 145-year-old suspension bridge made out of wire cables, wooden slats, and shingled towers. It is called (not surprisingly) Wire Bridge and is recognized by both the National Register of Historic Places and the American Society of Civil Engineers as the only bridge of its kind still in use in New England. The bridge was successfully designed to withstand torrents of water and ice during the spring flooding of the Carrabassett River. In the summer, the river is the picture of serenity, and you will find many people taking advantage of a swimming hole not far from the bridge.

General location: Just south of Kingfield on ME 16.

Elevation change: This is rolling terrain with regular, not-too-steep climbs on dirt roads and trails.

Season: Any time between late June and fall is good for riding. Snowmobilers pack down the trails during winter.

Services: All services are available in Kingfield.

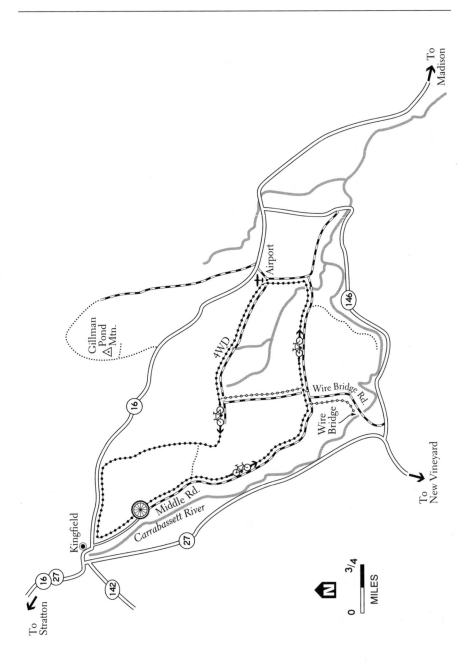

The Wire Bridge has spanned the Carrabassett River since 1846.

Hazards: Watch out for occasional obstructions on the trail (ruts, logs, rocks) that can be obscured by vegetation in late summer. There is some traffic on ME 16 for the last 1.5 miles.

Rescue index: You are about 1 mile from assistance at the farthest.

Land status: Active town roads and abandoned county roads. *Note:* This ride closely passes several secluded homes. Be considerate and friendly.

Maps: The USGS quad for this ride is New Portland. Also, *The Maine Atlas and Gazetteer* published by the DeLorme Mapping Company will guide you through this trail (map 30, sections E-1 and E-2; map 20, sections A-1 and A-2).

Finding the trail: From the south on ME 16, take a sharp left turn just before crossing the bridge into Kingfield, at a large barn on the left. From the north, the turnoff is a half mile east of the junction of ME 16 and ME 27 in Kingfield. Head south on Middle Road for a mile, until it becomes gravel. Park on either side of the road.

Source of additional information:

Holden Cyclery
317 Madison Avenue
Skowhegan, ME 04976
(207) 474-3732

This shop can also give you information about other rides in this area.

Notes on the trail: Head south on Middle Road for about 4.5 miles. To do a scenic side trip, turn right after 5 miles onto Wire Bridge Road. (A sign at the junction reads: "One Lane Bridge.") After 1 mile, you reach the historic bridge and a swimming hole. Return to Middle Road, turn right, and ride for another 2 miles. (To do a shorter loop, just after Wire Bridge Road on the right turn left onto another dirt road that climbs. At a **T** junction turn left onto the four-wheel-drive road that becomes a trail.) Turn left onto Millay Hill Road just after a brick house on the left. After about a mile, you will reach a fork at an island. Turn left and pass a private airport on the right. The road becomes four-wheel-drive, passes a junction on the left (the shortcut from Middle Road), and becomes a trail. The trail veers to the right and, after about 2 miles, while going downhill, forks left and comes out on ME 16. Turn left and ride on the gravel shoulder for 1.4 miles, until you reach the left turn onto Middle Road. Alternatively, veer right across a bridge and visit attractive Kingfield.

Information on the Wire Bridge ride was provided by Paul Angiolillo, author of Mountain Biking Northern New England *and* The Mountain Biker's Guide to Southern New England.

RIDE 34 · Rangeley Lake

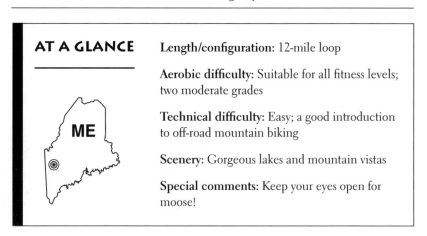

AT A GLANCE

Length/configuration: 12-mile loop

Aerobic difficulty: Suitable for all fitness levels; two moderate grades

Technical difficulty: Easy; a good introduction to off-road mountain biking

Scenery: Gorgeous lakes and mountain vistas

Special comments: Keep your eyes open for moose!

This beautiful 12-mile loop uses a combination of rail trails and two- and four-wheel-drive roads to create a ride suitable for novice mountain bikers. The route was developed through the efforts of Rangeley-area residents and businesses and the Trails for Rangeley Area Coalition (TRAC). Highlights of this ride include scenic vistas of the mountainous terrain that surrounds the region's extensive system of lakes.

For part of this ride, you will be riding along a section of the now-abandoned narrow-gauge railway that at one time served the Rangeley area. This railway was once part of the most extensive system of narrow-gauge railways in North America, a system that connected most of the major towns in Franklin County. The railroad gradually lost favor to trucks and automobiles and was abandoned in the 1930s. Nevertheless, in places you will experience the rhythm of the old tracks as your wheels cross 60-year-old ties that were left in place when the steel rails were gathered up and sold as scrap.

The rest of the trail follows logging roads and two-wheel-drive roads. There are breathtaking views of Rangeley Lake and Saddleback Mountain from the top of Dallas Hill, which makes the long climb to the top of the hill worth the effort. Enjoy!

General location: The town of Rangeley, situated on Rangeley Lake in western Maine.

Elevation change: You will encounter only 2 moderate grades on this ride. The first is a 200-foot climb on a logging road after you leave the railroad grade, and the second is a steep climb on pavement to the top of Dallas Hill.

Season: Riding in the Rangeley area can begin in June and continue well into the fall. The best conditions for this ride are in late summer and early fall.

Services: All services are available in Rangeley. Camping is available at Rangeley Lake State Park, located on the southern shore of Rangeley Lake. The park is open from May 15 through September 30. For additional information, call (207) 864-3858.

Hazards: This trail crosses ME 16 twice, and care should be used at these junctions. Be aware that logging trucks may also use some of the roads on this ride, particularly on the section between the rail trail and Saddleback Lake.

Rescue index: You will remain within a few miles of ME 16 or ME 4. This area is also a popular destination for outdoor enthusiasts, and you will be likely to encounter other trail users.

Land status: This ride follows an abandoned railroad and private trails secured for public use by the Trails for Rangeley Area Coalition (TRAC).

Maps: Maps of this route are available through the Rangeley Mountain Bike Touring Center, located on Main Street (ME 4) in Rangeley. The DeLorme Mapping Company's *Maine Atlas and Gazetteer* depicts most of the loop as well (map 28, section E-5; map 29, section E-1).

Finding the trail: From points south, the town of Rangeley is most easily accessed via Farmington on ME 4. From points north and east, ME 16 from Stratton provides an alternative route. Once you have reached Rangeley, make your way to the parking area that services the town cove on Rangeley

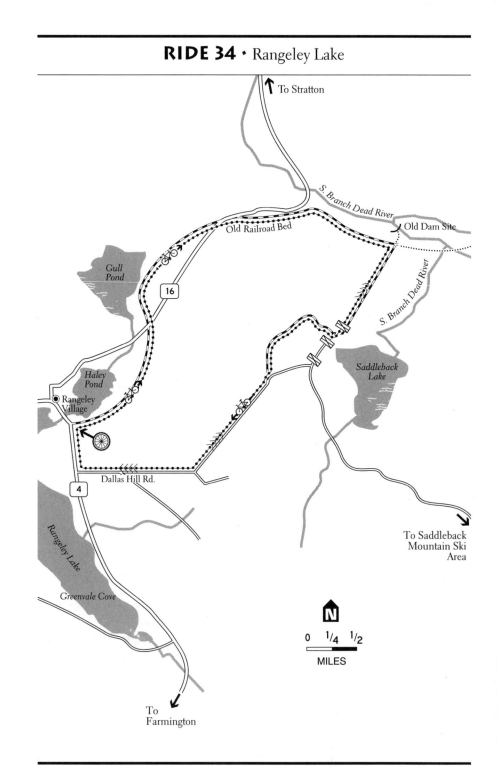

To Stratton

S. Branch Dead River

Old Railroad Bed

Old Dam Site

Gull Pond

16

S. Branch Dead River

Haley Pond

Saddleback Lake

Rangeley Village

Dallas Hill Rd.

4

To Saddleback Mountain Ski Area

Rangeley Lake

Greenvale Cove

N

0   1/4   1/2

MILES

To Farmington

The spectacular Rangeley Lake region is one of Maine's best known recreation destinations.

Lake by following signs for both the Chamber of Commerce and the boat landing. The parking lot is located on ME 4 south of the junction of ME 4 and ME 16.

Sources of additional information:

Rangeley Mountain Bike Touring Center
53 Main Street
Rangeley, ME 04970
(207) 864-5799

Rangeley Recreation Department
(207) 864-3327

Rangeley Lakes Chamber of Commerce
(207) 864-5364

Notes on the trail: From the parking area overlooking Rangeley Lake, turn right onto Main Street (ME 4) and pedal a short distance through the bustling town of Rangeley, looking for the Mountain Bike Touring Center on your left. At the touring center you will be able to pick up a map of the trail and receive any additional instructions or information that you might need. The trailhead can be found just beyond the touring center, on the same side of the street.

The trail begins in front of an electrical substation. You may see signs

Old ties still mark
the path of a narrow
gauge railway 60
years after its
abandonment.

posting the trail with the following greeting: "Welcome to the Rangeley Lakes
Multi-Use Trail System." You will begin riding along a rail trail beneath a power
line, skirting the southern shore of Haley Pond. You will come to ME 16, which
you must cross to reconnect with the trail that enters the woods on the other
side. After a short but nevertheless beautiful ramble through the woods, the trail
suddenly opens out into a clear-cut. To your left, gorgeous views of the mountains to the northwest almost make up for the lack of trees. Continue riding
straight as the trail merges with a logging road through this area.

The road eventually swings to the right, toward ME 16, but it is possible to
continue riding straight for a short distance and delay your arrival at ME 16.
Turn left when you reach ME 16, and ride on the pavement until you spot a
yellow road sign indicating a sharp curve in the road to the left. Turn right,
before the curve in the road, onto a logging road. Ride to a T junction and
turn right. You will begin the first climb of the ride from this point, traveling
past a few logging yards before coming to another T intersection. Turn right
again and ride to Saddleback Lake Lodge, overlooking Saddleback Lake.

From the lodge, the ride continues along a dirt road that eventually changes to a paved surface. You will traverse the second hill of the ride on pavement, climbing Dallas Hill. From the top of Dallas Hill, the ride descends quickly toward Rangeley Lake. Be prepared to stop at a T junction with ME 4. Turn right to return to the downtown area and your vehicle.

RIDE 35 · Sugarloaf/USA

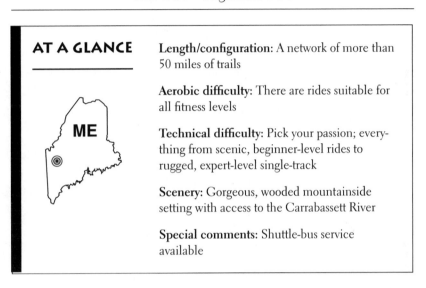

AT A GLANCE

Length/configuration: A network of more than 50 miles of trails

Aerobic difficulty: There are rides suitable for all fitness levels

Technical difficulty: Pick your passion; everything from scenic, beginner-level rides to rugged, expert-level single-track

Scenery: Gorgeous, wooded mountainside setting with access to the Carrabassett River

Special comments: Shuttle-bus service available

Sugarloaf/USA is rapidly becoming known as the place to be for mountain biking. The four-season resort uses a combination of areas throughout its 7,000 acres to create a mountain bike park that is truly unique. There are more than 50 miles of trails at your handlebars when you arrive, ranging in difficulty from beginner to expert and covering an awesome variety of terrain. There are paved roads, dirt roads, ski trails, and old logging roads, as well as more technically challenging single- and double-track trails. There really is something for everyone.

The Sugarloaf/USA Bike Park is nestled amongst the Longfellow Mountains of Maine, where three of the four largest mountains in the state are located. The park is at the hub of mountain biking activity in the Carrabassett Valley; many other trails and roads in the area provide excellent riding and are seeing more use each year from mountain bikers. In addition, Sugarloaf/USA is the home of the Widowmaker Challenge Mountain Bike Race: an annual three-day event that is part of the Trail 66 Mountain Bike Race Series.

Trail 66 is the new standard in bike festivals. It is the biggest NORBA-sanctioned mountain bike race and festival series in the East.

The Widowmaker Challenge consists of a cross-country race, dual slalom, short-track derby, and a Krazy Kids Circuit race. Novice to pro classes compete for more than $15,000 in cash and prizes and accumulate points in the seven-race Trail 66 series. But the Widowmaker Challenge is more than just racing; it shines through with family and spectator events like world champion trials' riders, Krazy Kids races, bike throws, a bonfire and pasta feast, night rides, inflatable climbing mountains, and clinics with pro riders from Gary Fisher.

General location: Sugarloaf/USA is located in the Carrabassett Valley on ME 27 north of Kingfield.

Elevation change: Situated on the northern slopes of Sugarloaf Mountain and descending to the Carrabassett River, the rides at the park range in elevation from 1,000' to 2,000'.

Season: The bike park at Sugarloaf/USA opens in June and offers services through August.

Services: Sugarloaf/USA is a full-service resort offering everything in the way of accommodations, dining opportunities, and outdoor experiences. There are two centers to the bike park: the Sugarloaf Bike Shop, located on Main Street in the Village Center, and the Outdoor Center, located farther down the mountain near Moose Bog. The bike shop is open five days a week during the month of June and every day after July 1. As well as a full-service repair facility, the bike shop sells and rents mountain bikes. To contact the folks at the bike shop, call (207) 237-6986. The Outdoor Center also includes a full-service bike shop, complete with accessories and a fleet of rental bikes. In addition, outdoor accessories such as hiking boots, packs, and other assorted necessities are available here.

Hazards: Beyond the usual variations in terrain that characterize most rides, potential hazards on the trails at Sugarloaf/USA include permanent snow-making equipment, towers, and utility lines and their components. Mowing and trail-maintenance procedures may be under way at any time, making it imperative that you read and heed all posted signs.

In addition, due to the park's location amongst the Longfellow Mountains, lightning and thunderstorms can strike suddenly. If you get caught in such a storm, make your way to lower elevations and be sure to avoid taking shelter under isolated trees and lift towers, and in lift buildings.

Rescue index: Depending upon the route you choose, you may be several miles from assistance. Accidents and injuries should be reported to Sugarloaf Mountain Security.

RIDE 35 • Sugarloaf/USA

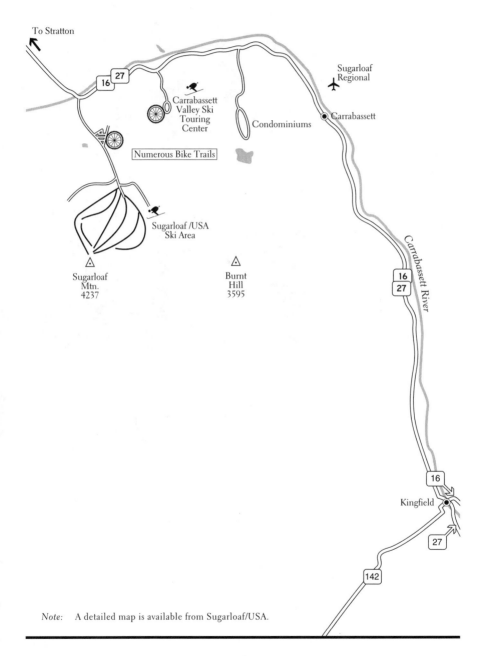

To Stratton

16 27

Carrabassett
Valley Ski
Touring
Center

Numerous Bike Trails

Sugarloaf /USA
Ski Area

Sugarloaf
Mtn.
4237

Burnt
Hill
3595

Sugarloaf
Regional

Carrabassett

Condominiums

Carrabassett River

16
27

16

Kingfield

27

142

Note: A detailed map is available from Sugarloaf/USA.

Views abound
from the trails at
Sugarloaf/USA.

Land status: Sugarloaf/USA is a privately owned and operated resort.

Maps: A mountain bike guide is available at the Sugarloaf/USA Outdoor Center or the Sugarloaf/USA Bike Shop located in the Village Center. All trails are marked and rated for difficulty, and range from graded dirt roads to expert single-track trails.

Finding the trail: From points south, travel north on Interstate 95 to Augusta and exit onto ME 27 North. Drive through Farmington and Kingfield. Sugarloaf/USA is located approximately 10 miles north of Kingfield.

Source of additional information:

Sugarloaf/USA
Resort Activities & Information Center
Main Street, Village Center
Carrabassett Valley, ME 04947-9979
(207) 237-2000
http://www.sugarloaf.com or e-mail: info@sugarloaf.com

Notes on the trail: The Sugarloaf Bike Park has more than 50 miles of fun waiting for you. There is a wide selection of trails that intersect the resort. We have picked out three rides representing different levels of difficulty to give all riders an insider's view of the mountain bike park.

Difficult: Leaving from the Sugarloaf base area, you begin the ride with a steep climb up the Whiffletree lift line. After passing two lift towers, a gradual traverse to the east helps ease the burn you will feel after Whiffletree. The traverse brings you to Mountainside Road, the main access road to many of Sugarloaf's condominiums. Straight across the road, easy entry is gained to the Condo Cross Cut alpine ski trail. Proceed down the trail about 15 feet and make a quick right turn.

Dropping into some of the Sugarloaf/USA's premier single-track trails, you had better make sure your brakes work and get ready to grab a handful when necessary. This roller coaster of tight turns and technical riding dumps you out onto Sugarloaf/USA Outdoor Center trail #21. Trail #21 is a mix of rolling hills, ending with a nice downhill to the intersection of trail #7. Take a right onto trail #7 and enjoy more of the same wide-open riding on the Sugarloaf/USA Outdoor Center's double-track trail. Follow this trail directly into the Outdoor Center, and skirt around Moose Bog. There is a good possibility of a moose sighting on this section, where Sugarloaf Mountain towers in the background. Continue on trail #7 to the intersection of trail #1. Bank right and get ready for a mellow climb out of the Outdoor Center area and back to the base.

Intermediate: Starting from the Village Center area, proceed west past the SuperQuad® lift and down trail #20 (known as the carriage road). Trail #20, a nice gradual downhill, intersects with West Mountain Road. A short hop on West Mountain Road puts you at the head of trail #26. Follow trail #26, and take in the beautiful sights of the Sugarloaf/USA golf course and continue down to ME 27.

Cross ME 27 to Bigelow Station and pick up trail #9 (known as the Narrow Gauge). Be on the lookout for picture-perfect picnic sights along the Carrabassett River. There will be a trail intersection on trail #9—take the right turn to trail #25. Be sure not to miss this because it is the only river crossing for the next 6 miles. Cross ME 27 and begin the climb to the Sugarloaf/USA Outdoor Center. At the Outdoor Center, pick up trail #1 for the last push back to the Sugarloaf/USA base area.

Moderate: From the Sugarloaf/USA Village Center, proceed down the Snubber lift line past the Sugarloaf Inn, the Sugarloaf Sports & Fitness Club, and many of the condominium complexes. Pick up trail #1, and enjoy a nice, easy downhill ride to the Outdoor Center. Once at the Outdoor Center, relax for a while and take a look at the outstanding scenery provided by mother nature. For the last half of the ride, take trail #4 out of the Outdoor Center around Moose Bog. At the intersection of trails #4 and #1, take a right onto trail #1 and begin the return trip on the same trail that led to the Outdoor Center.

Pick up the Snubber lift line and head up to the Sugarloaf/USA base area. Don't hesitate to stop for a breather or a drink at either of the Sugarloaf Sports & Fitness Club or the Sugarloaf Inn!

Details for the Sugarloaf/USA chapter were provided by Mark Latti of Sugarloaf/USA, Maine.

RIDE 36 · Poplar Stream

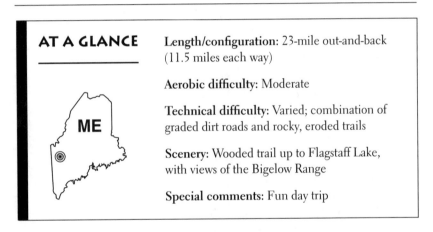

AT A GLANCE

Length/configuration: 23-mile out-and-back (11.5 miles each way)

Aerobic difficulty: Moderate

Technical difficulty: Varied; combination of graded dirt roads and rocky, eroded trails

Scenery: Wooded trail up to Flagstaff Lake, with views of the Bigelow Range

Special comments: Fun day trip

This 23-mile out-and-back ride follows Poplar Stream upriver, from the town of Carrabassett Valley to the easternmost point of Flagstaff Lake. The route begins along a rough old road that presents a technical challenge on the way up, and a rattling descent on the return trip. This road eventually links up with a graded dirt road that runs along the southern shore of Flagstaff Lake. The result is a trail suited for riders of intermediate to advanced ability, and a great blend of tricky, technical rock-picking and easy cruising through forest wilderness.

Following Poplar Stream for much of the way, this ride can include a short side trip to Poplar Stream Falls. Here, a bridge crosses the stream, and it is possible to pick your way down the falls a short distance to reach a perfect little swimming hole. Farther up the trail, and as you draw closer to Flagstaff Lake, there are great views of the Bigelow Mountain Range. In fact, the ride crosses the Appalachian Trail just before it heads upward toward the summit of Bigelow Mountain. Blazed by foresters in the 1920s, the A.T. (as it is known) connects Mount Katahdin in central Maine to Springer Mountain in northern Georgia. During our ride to Flagstaff Lake, we chanced upon a through-hiker who had begun walking several weeks earlier from Mount Katahdin. Katahdin is the traditional finish to the trail, which most people hike from south to north. The hiker we encountered, traveling the trail from north to south instead, still had more than 1,900 miles to walk before reaching the other end of the trail in Georgia.

Flagstaff Lake has a story of its own. Notice, as you make your way down to the water, that the road you're on continues straight into the water. More than just a convenient boat ramp, this road once led to the now-submerged villages of Flagstaff and Dead River. These two farming communities were flooded after 1949, when the gates on the Long Falls Dam were closed. The construction of this dam transformed the Dead River valley into a huge reservoir, now counted as Maine's fourth largest lake. This ride, at its halfway point, drops down to the water's edge at a campground and day-use area. On hot summer days this is an excellent place to stop for a break, to swim, or just to enjoy the breeze coming off the lake.

General location: Poplar Stream runs down to the Carrabassett River from the easternmost tip of Flagstaff Lake. At the trailhead, you will be just 8 miles north of Kingfield.

Elevation change: From the town of Carrabassett Valley at 840', this ride climbs steadily to Flagstaff Lake for a total elevation gain of approximately 420'.

Season: This route is best ridden from late June through the fall. In the spring and early summer, the trail is likely to be extremely wet and washed-out in several places. Mosquitos are also to be found in vast numbers along this route in the spring.

Services: Food, gas, and essentials are available in Kingfield. Any bike-related needs are best met at the bike shop located in the base lodge area of Sugarloaf/USA. Water and a pay telephone are available at the trailhead outside the Carrabassett Valley Town Office.

Hazards: The first few miles of this trail may be washed-out in early spring or after an extreme rainfall.

Rescue index: Your best source of assistance is at the trailhead, where there are likely to be people at the Carrabassett Valley Town Office, the fire station, or the recreation center. Once you reach Flagstaff Lake, it is quite likely that

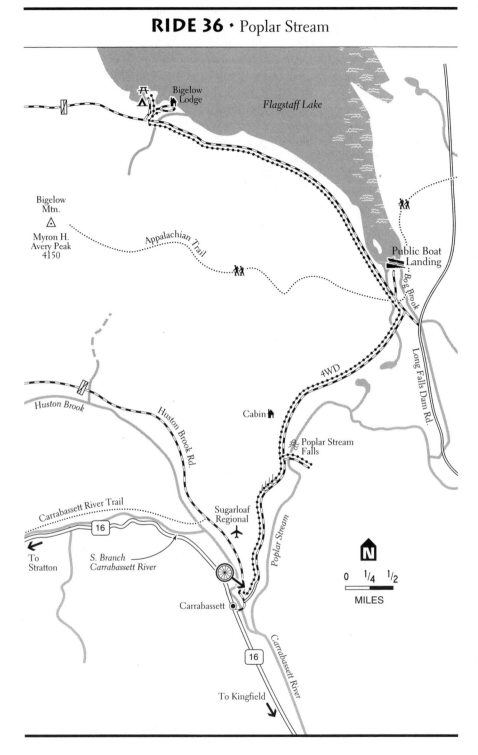

Flagstaff Lake

Bigelow Lodge

Bigelow Mtn.

Myron H.
Avery Peak
4150

Appalachian Trail

Public Boat Landing

Bog Brook

4WD

Long Falls Dam Rd.

Huston Brook

Huston Brook Rd.

Cabin

Poplar Stream Falls

Carrabassett River Trail

16

To Stratton

S. Branch Carrabassett River

Sugarloaf Regional

Poplar Stream

N

0   1/4   1/2

MILES

Carrabassett

Carrabassett River

16

To Kingfield

WESTERN MAINE MOUNTAINS AND LAKES *167*

you will encounter other visitors, and even vehicles traveling to the lake from the access road. There are several seasonal camps along the lake and a campground at the ride's halfway mark.

Land status: You will be riding up an old road, alongside private property. Once you reach Flagstaff Lake, you will be riding on Maine public reserve land through a portion of the Bigelow Preserve.

Maps: The 7.5 minute quads for this ride are Poplar Mountain and Little Bigelow Mountain. The ride can also be picked out in *The Maine Atlas and Gazetteer* (map 29, section C-5), published by the DeLorme Mapping Company.

Finding the trail: The town of Carrabassett Valley is located on ME 27, about 8 miles north of Kingfield and south of Sugarloaf/USA. Coming from the south on ME 27, look for a modest sign on the right for the Carrabassett Valley Town Office. Turn right at a junction known as Valley Crossing and pass over the Carrabassett River. Immediately after crossing the river, turn left into the parking lot for the town office, fire station, and recreation center. Plenty of parking is available here.

Sources of additional information:

Sugarloaf Area Chamber of Commerce
RR 1, Box 2151
Carrabassett Valley, ME 04947
(207) 235-2100

A chamber of commerce information center is located on ME 27, just north of Valley Crossing and the Carrabassett Valley Town Office.

Notes on the trail: Turn left out of the parking area and begin riding north up Valley Crossing. Ride straight through the intersection with Huston Brook Road, and continue straight as the road deteriorates into the unimproved Poplar Stream Trail. You will notice Poplar Stream on your right. Although there is a trail along this road maintained by a snowmobile club in the winter, its summertime condition is rough and extremely rocky.

At a fork in the trail, bear left to continue riding or follow the trail to the right for a short side trip to Poplar Stream Falls. This intersection may be marked with snowmobile trail signs that indicate Flagstaff and Bigelow to the left, and Claybrook Lodge and Lexington Highland to the right. Whether or not you opt to ride to the falls, the ride continues up the trail to the left. You will pedal over a bridge before passing a small brown hunting camp on the left, beyond which you will cross another stream. Over all of these waterways, the bridges used and maintained by the snowmobile club may be in varying states of disrepair, and in some cases you will have to gingerly make your way over piles of logs, rocks, and deadfall.

The rugged Poplar Stream Trail provides access to Flagstaff Lake.

Continue straight up the road. At a power line, follow the trail up to the graded access road to the eastern part of Bigelow Preserve. Turn left on this road, and enjoy the views of Bigelow Mountain to your left. Bear right at the first intersection you come to. You will cross the Appalachian Trail and ride past a cluster of cabins before the road ends abruptly at Flagstaff Lake. To continue the ride, backtrack up to the last intersection and bear right, following a well-maintained dirt road toward Bigelow Lodge. This road will give you the sensation of riding a roller coaster and, with many short dips and hills, offers many opportunities for spotting wildlife. You will pass the signed entrance to Bigelow Lodge on the right. Bigelow Mountain soars high into the sky directly opposite this intersection. Just a short distance beyond, there is another road on the right that will take you down to the campground and day-use area.

You will need to retrace your route to return to the parking area in

Carrabassett Valley. Ride back up the campground access road, and turn left at the top, back onto the main road. At the fork in the road, bear right, and then look for the Poplar Stream Trail turnoff. It will be on your right, just past the Bigelow Preserve sign and just before the power lines.

RIDE 37 · Carrabassett River Trail

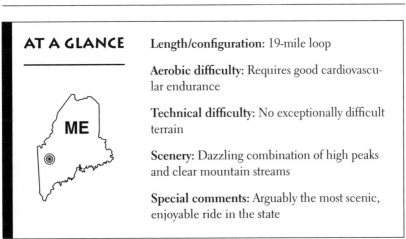

AT A GLANCE

Length/configuration: 19-mile loop

Aerobic difficulty: Requires good cardiovascular endurance

Technical difficulty: No exceptionally difficult terrain

Scenery: Dazzling combination of high peaks and clear mountain streams

Special comments: Arguably the most scenic, enjoyable ride in the state

Tucked between the Carrabassett River and the Bigelow Mountain Range, this 19-mile loop is virtually unmatched in scenic beauty. The terrain is not technically difficult but offers an excellent cross-section of trail conditions for riders of intermediate to advanced ability. The ride begins up a little-used two-wheel drive road, and branches off onto a stretch of fantastic single-track. This trail eventually merges with the unpaved access road from Stratton Brook Pond to ME 27. A short climb and descent on ME 27 provides a link to the rugged, narrow-gauge rail trail that parallels the Carrabassett River and completes the ride.

General location: Carrabassett Valley, south of Flagstaff Lake.

Elevation change: You will begin riding from approximately 840' at Valley Crossing. The first leg of this ride covers rolling terrain with a gradual gain of 600'. You will descend a modest 80' before gaining another 220' up a paved, 1-mile hill. From this high point at 1,580', you will gradually descend back to the trailhead. Total elevation gain for the ride is roughly 820'.

Season: This trail is at its best from late June through October.

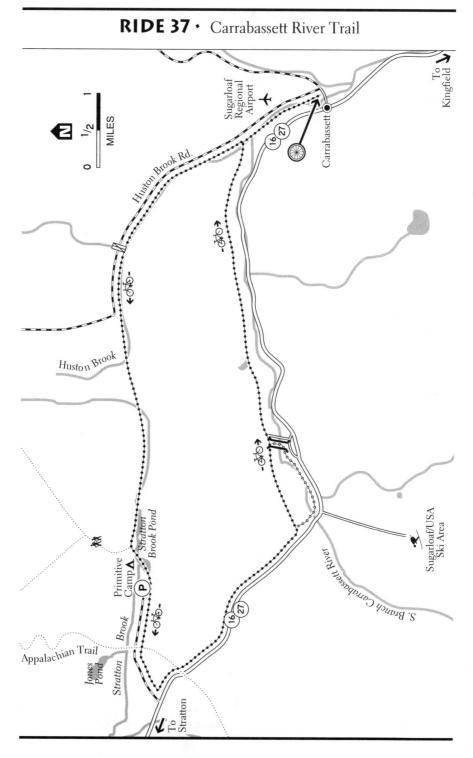

N

0   1/2   1
MILES

Sugarloaf Regional Airport

To Kingfield

16 27

Carrabassett

Huston Brook Rd.

Huston Brook

Stratton Brook Pond

Primitive Camp

P

Appalachian Trail

Jones Pond

Stratton Brook

To Stratton

16 27

S. Branch Carrabassett River

Sugarloaf/USA Ski Area

Services: Food, gas, and essentials are available in Kingfield. Any bike needs are best met at the shop located in the base lodge area of Sugarloaf/USA. Water and a pay telephone are available at the trailhead outside the Carrabassett Valley Town Office, although we strongly recommend you bring your own water in case the spigot has been turned off.

Hazards: Be aware of other trail users, particularly hikers. Also, some areas of the trail along the Carrabassett River are prone to washing out.

Rescue index: The most remote part of this trail is along Stratton Brook, at the base of the Bigelow Mountain Range. Even here, you will be only 3 miles from ME 27. The trail itself is popular and appears to be well traveled. There is a rescue squad located at the trailhead in Carrabassett Valley.

Land status: You will be riding along an overgrown old town road along the Stratton Brook portion of the trail. An access road and a short stretch on paved ME 27 will hook you up to the abandoned narrow-gauge railroad bed that completes the loop.

Maps: Consult *The Maine Atlas and Gazetteer,* published by the DeLorme Mapping Company (map 29, sections C-5, C-4, and C-3). You will need two USGS 7.5 minute quads to examine the trail in detail: Poplar Mountain and Sugarloaf Mountain.

Finding the trail: The town of Carrabassett Valley is located on ME 27, about 8 miles north of Kingfield and just south of Sugarloaf/USA, a popular ski area and resort. Coming from the south on ME 27, look for a sign on the right for the Carrabassett Valley Town Office and a junction known as Valley Crossing. Turn right on Valley Crossing and cross the bridge over the Carrabassett River. Turn left immediately past the bridge and into the parking lot for the town office, fire station, and recreation center. Plenty of parking is available.

Sources of additional information:

Sugarloaf Area Chamber of Commerce
RR 1, Box 2151
Carrabassett Valley, ME 04947
(207) 235-2100

An information center is located on ME 27, just north of the Carrabassett Valley Town Office.

Notes on the trail: From the parking lot, turn left onto Valley Crossing and then turn left again onto Huston Brook Road. Follow this gravel road through a cluster of small ski camps and continue as it meets and parallels the Carrabassett River. After a short distance, the road swings to the right, away from the river. At this point, look for the rough and rocky beginning to a trail

A gorgeous ride along the Carrabassett River.

that continues straight, following the river. This is the narrow-gauge rail trail on which you will eventually complete the loop. To begin the ride, however, continue pedaling up Huston Brook Road.

After riding over a small bridge, bear right at a fork (the trail to the left will probably be posted with a number of snowmobile signs). You will cross a second and third bridge before bearing left at another fork. Follow the road beneath a power line, beyond which an information board marks the boundary of Maine public reserve land. After two more bridges, you will pass through a gate into posted "backcountry." A short distance beyond this gate, bear left at a fork. Continue to follow the road for another 1.5 miles, and then look for a narrow trail on the left that may be somewhat obscured by foliage. Turn left onto this trail, which branches off the main road just before the road swings to the right. You will quickly come to a small clearing before crossing Stratton Brook.

For the next 2 miles, you will be riding along an excellent trail that basically follows Stratton Brook to Stratton Brook Pond. The trail opens up slightly as you approach the pond, and you will be able to see Sugarloaf Mountain off to your left. When we rode this trail in June, Sugarloaf was still capped with snow! In the foreground, the area of marsh around Stratton Brook Pond is also a great place to watch for moose. As you continue along the trail, the view will also open up on the right, and you will be able to catch glimpses of the Bigelow Mountain Range. Continue over a bridge that spans a small waterway, beyond which is a primitive campsite and the trailhead for the Bigelow hiking trails. Cross the stream ahead of you and continue straight out to the parking area provided for the Bigelow Mountain trails. Ride down the gravel access road. Bear right at the first split in the road, and then fork left up a road that may look like a driveway. You will ride past a few camps before reaching a T intersection with ME 27. Turn left and begin pedaling uphill.

Despite the fact that you are now on pavement, and climbing, this section of the ride can be quite interesting. It was, in fact, one of the highlights of our trip. As we were grinding uphill at what felt like a torturously slow pace, a slight, rustling sound in the trees off to the right alerted us to the presence of a young bull moose. Stopping traffic in both directions, he took his time crossing the road and gave us an "up close and personal" view of his very long, thin legs, seemingly too-large body, oddly shaped head, and flickering ears.

You will eventually crest the hill you have been climbing and begin a well-earned descent. Keep your eyes open, though; before you reach the south branch of the Carrabassett River, you need to turn left into the remains of the Bigelow railway station. Ride past a cluster buildings, and pick up the beginning of the narrow-gauge rail trail. After a short distance you will come to an intersection. Turning right will take you to the Carrabassett River, where you can enjoy the view over the water from a bridge that connects its banks. Crossing this bridge will bring you out on a dirt road from which ME 27 is accessible in either direction. To complete the ride, however, continue straight through the intersection.

The trail at this point descends almost imperceptibly through the woods, and occasionally opens out at the site of small wetland areas. You will ride beneath tall, shading trees before reaching the last stretch of the trail. It provides the best opportunities for enjoying the river along an easy-to-follow single-track trail that never veers far from the bank. Watch for several particularly rocky sections where water seeps down to the river from the bank above. The last stretch of the ride is fast, as you will be enjoying a slight descent. Bear right at the intersection of Huston Brook Road and retrace your tracks back to the parking area, where access to the river from the parking lot at the town office will give you the opportunity to clean off and cool off after the ride.

RIDE 38 · Bigelow Preserve

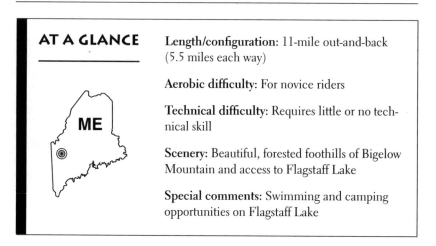

AT A GLANCE

Length/configuration: 11-mile out-and-back (5.5 miles each way)

Aerobic difficulty: For novice riders

Technical difficulty: Requires little or no technical skill

Scenery: Beautiful, forested foothills of Bigelow Mountain and access to Flagstaff Lake

Special comments: Swimming and camping opportunities on Flagstaff Lake

Following the West Flagstaff Road into the heart of the Bigelow Preserve, this 11-mile out-and-back ride is an easy cruise along a dirt two-wheel-drive road. The preserve is an exceptionally beautiful area that highlights the dramatic contrast between Flagstaff Lake and the series of high mountain peaks that make up the Bigelow Range. The forest that covers most of the Bigelow Preserve is composed primarily of hardwoods, which in the autumn become a blaze of reds and yellows. On this ride, you will periodically catch a glimpse of Bigelow Mountain, which rises steeply from the shore of Flagstaff Lake. Several side trails provide access to Flagstaff Lake, where small, sandy beaches invite swimming and primitive campsites encourage an overnight stay.

The creation of the Bigelow Preserve is an inspiring story about one of the first grass-roots environmental battles in the state of Maine. At one time, the north slope of Bigelow Mountain was proposed as a site for a major downhill skiing resort, billed as "the Aspen of the East." Opposition to this proposal resulted in the creation of a grass-roots organization that lobbied for the preservation of the wilderness area. As a result, an act to create the preserve was passed by public referendum in June, 1976. The acquisition of up to 40,000 acres of land was authorized by this act, with the purpose of setting aside land "to be retained in its natural state for the use and enjoyment of the public." As a result of this effort, Flagstaff Lake and the Bigelow Mountains offer a diversity of recreational opportunities, including camping, boating, hiking, and, of course, mountain biking.

General location: Bigelow Preserve is located on the south shore of Flagstaff Lake, just west of the town of Stratton.

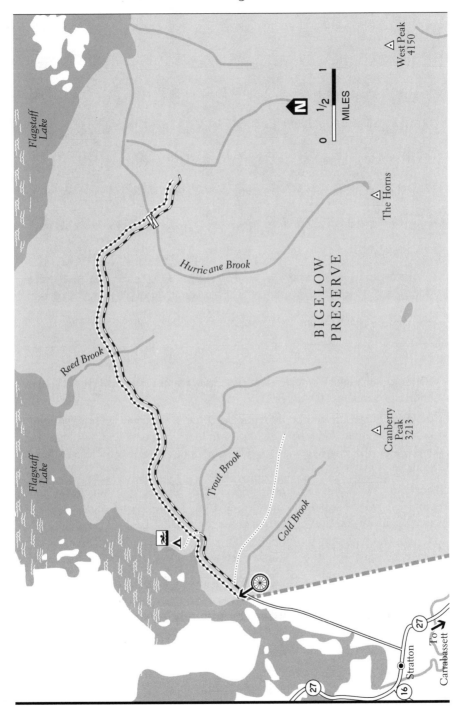

Swimming is possible at one of the many beaches located on the shore of Flagstaff Lake.

Elevation change: This ride stays close to the south shore of Flagstaff Lake and gains a modest 100' in elevation.

Season: This route can be ridden at any time of year with the exception of spring, when the road is best left to dry out to prevent permanent damage. In the winter, the road becomes a snowmobile trail connecting to several other trails open for wintertime use.

Services: Water and supplies are available in Stratton or at a convenience store located at the base of Sugarloaf/USA. For bicycle parts and/or repairs, make your way up the access road to the Sugarloaf/USA Bike Shop, located among the buildings surrounding the base lodge. If your trip includes an overnight stay, primitive campsites are dotted along the shore of Flagstaff Lake.

Hazards: None.

Rescue index: At the end of West Flagstaff Road you will be 7 miles from Stratton, the closest source of any kind of assistance.

Land status: Maine public reserve land.

Maps: There may be pamphlets available at the bulletin board located in the preserve. These provide a lot of information about the preserve as well as a detailed map. They are also available at the Sugarloaf Area Chamber of Commerce on ME 27, just north of the Carrabassett Valley Town Office. Or, consult *The Maine Atlas and Gazetteer* (published by the DeLorme Mapping Co., Yarmouth, ME).

Finding the trail: Take ME 27 north to Stratton. As you enter town, look for the Stratton post office on the right and turn right onto School Street, the road immediately beyond it. School Street leads directly to the preserve. You will pass a sign for the preserve on the left. Continue driving, crossing a large culvert, until you reach an information bulletin board on the left of the road. There is an area on the left beyond this board where you can park.

Source of additional information:

Maine Bureau of Public Lands
P.O. Box 327
Farmington, ME 04938
(207) 778-4111

Notes on the trail: You will begin riding east from the Bigelow Preserve information sign. After crossing Trout Brook, there is a road on the left that will take you to the lake, where there is a small beach and several campsites. This is a great place to stop on your way back. West Flagstaff Road turns away from the lakeshore beyond this point, until it reaches a dead end beyond Hurricane Brook. At this point, turn around to retrace your route.

For riders seeking more of a challenge and a little adventure, there are several side trails to explore that involve riding on rough single- and double-track trails. Many of these trails are used by snowmobiles in the winter.

KENNEBEC VALLEY

The Kennebec River rises at Moosehead Lake and flows 150 miles to the Atlantic Ocean. It was here, at present-day Phippsburg, that one of the first attempts at settlement on the East Coast took place. The year was 1607, the same year that settlement was attempted at Jamestown in Virginia. Led by Sir George Popham, a group of Englishmen landed at the mouth of the river. Their stay was to be short-lived, however. The harsh Maine winter proved to be too much, or too unexpected, for the colonists, and many of them perished. The few men who survived until spring built a small ship, which they called the Virginia, and returned to England.

Although the Popham colony was unsuccessful, the Virginia proved her worth in several transatlantic voyages. In the history of the region, she is known as the first in a long line of well-built ships that were constructed on the Kennebec River. The river was one of the first to be explored by European settlers, and many trading routes were established along its length. One of the most famous marches in military history followed, in part, the Kennebec River. Benedict Arnold led an army of men upriver, using wooden bateaux, on his way to Quebec City.

The river also plays a prominent role in Maine's logging history. Stone pilings still remain in some places along the river, remnants of the days of river drives. These pilings were the supports that once anchored log booms and created holding areas for logs. Activity on the Kennebec did not stop during the winter: ice harvesting, a major business before refrigeration, began as soon as the water froze. Huge blocks of ice were cut with large saws and stored in sawdust until the river opened up and they could be transported.

Despite its significant role in the commerce of the region in the nineteenth century, the Kennebec River remains one of the most beautiful, unspoiled rivers in Maine. The river valley is rich in wildlife as well as history, and the rides in this region of the state are scenic excursions. The towns of Greenville and Jackman are both old lumbering communities that have recently pursued recreation in an effort to diversify their economy. In addition to promoting trails for mountain bikers, they are popular destinations for snowmobilers in the winter.

LOGGING ROADS

Many of the rides in the Kennebec Valley region utilize logging roads. Approximately ten million acres of forest lie within the unorganized townships of the state. (Unorganized townships have no form of organized government and are therefore governed by the state.) Maine's network of logging roads are a mountain bicyclist's dream. They range from wide, two-wheel-drive roads to overgrown wet tracks. Adventurous riders can set out on multi-day expeditions and travel for literally hundreds of miles. The logging roads provide access to scenic ponds and some of the remote high mountains in the northwestern part of the state.

The fact that bicycling is allowed on these privately owned roads reflects a shift in policy by a number of paper companies, the largest landowners in the state. Recognizing that it is nearly impossible to control all forms of access to their lands, they have begun to allow nearly unlimited access for recreationalists. Nevertheless, riders must remember that the roads exist primarily to enable companies to cut and remove trees. Therefore, all logging activities take precedence over the interests of bicyclists.

There are a few simple rules to keep in mind when riding on logging roads. First of all, be sure to avoid all areas where active logging is taking place. Second, use extreme caution when riding on any logging road. Logging trucks barrel along the roads at high speeds. They are large, heavy vehicles and cannot stop quickly. The narrow, curvy roads provide little room for a truck to pass, even if the driver sees you. Keep in mind that you are far more likely to hear an approaching truck than you are to see one. If you do, stop and get off the road immediately. It is not appropriate to discuss the finer points of road-use etiquette with an enraged truck driver in the middle of the woods. They have the right of way in all cases.

Logging roads can change annually, and the only maps that keep up with the changes are owned by the paper companies. These maps are not usually available to the public. It is therefore very easy to get lost. Intersections often look alike, and roads that appear on more general maps of the region may have long since disappeared or been rerouted. Also, many of the roads extend for miles, making it easy not only to get lost, but to venture considerable distances into the woods before realizing it. We suggest that, when venturing out onto any of the systems of logging roads, you carry a supply of food and plenty of water. Many riders also stop at the intersections of logging roads in order to mark their route with a cairn, branch, or flagging tape. If you get lost, it is better to retrace your route than to attempt any route that appears to be a shortcut.

For persons interested in exploring some of Maine's logging roads, there are several companies in the Greenville, Rockwood, and Rangeley areas that will lead bicyclists on guided trips.

RIDE 39 · Summerhaven Use Area

AT A GLANCE

ME

Length/configuration: 7-mile loop, with several side trails branching off the main trail

Aerobic difficulty: Moderate; rolling terrain

Technical difficulty: Suitable for beginning and intermediate riders

Scenery: Wooded trails around Tyler Pond and several gravel pits

Special comments: Tyler Pond is a great place to end the ride

The Summerhaven Use Area around Tyler Pond features a seven-mile loop signed for ATV users. The ride follows a combination of single- and double-track trails that weave through the woods and across two gravel pits. Intermediate and beginning riders will enjoy this ride, which features some technical riding over sandy sections and numerous side trails off the southeast side of the circuit.

Tyler Pond is a popular fishing spot at the heart of the Summerhaven Use Area. Access to the water exists in two places, and provides picturesque views of the pond and a number of places to stretch out and relax after the ride. Though we have described the ride as we rode it (in a clockwise direction), there is no reason not to vary your rides here, and to try riding the loop in a counterclockwise direction as well.

General location: Summerhaven lies just 5 miles north of Augusta.

RIDE 39 · Summerhaven Use Area

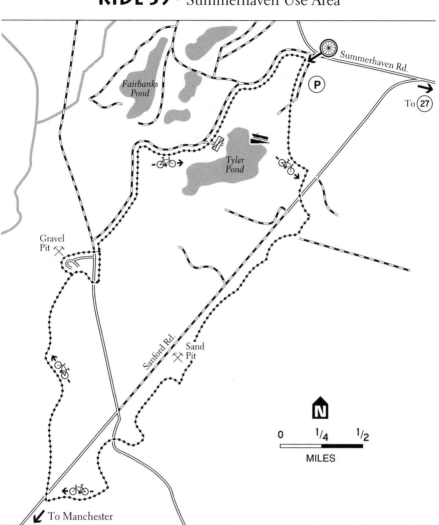

Elevation change: Other than a few short hills, this ride features no dramatic change in elevation.

Season: Riding conditions should be good from late May through October and in the winter, when adequate snow cover has given snowmobiles the opportunity to pack down the trail.

Services: All services are available in Augusta. If your bike is in need of parts or service, make your way to Auclair Cycle & Ski on ME 9. The staff at Auclair are familiar with other biking areas in and around Augusta. Their address is 64-66 Bangor Street (ME 9), Augusta, ME 04330, or they can be reached by phone at (207) 623-4351.

Hazards: There is at least one active gravel pit located off Sanford Road. Because this ride crosses Sanford Road twice, it is important to pay attention to the signs signaling a road crossing because there may be a lot of heavy traffic using the road. It is possible, in the course of riding this loop, to get sidetracked along one of several trails that branch off into the woods from the gravel pit on the east side of Sanford Road. While it is not really possible to get lost on these trails, be aware of keeping your bearings, and also watch out for walkers and other cyclists.

Rescue index: Throughout the length of this ride you will remain within fairly close proximity to several well-traveled roads. In addition to passing traffic, there are many homes along Summerhaven Road, from which the boat access road to Tyler Pond branches off.

Land status: The Summerhaven Use Area is just one of several trail systems for which the state has agreements with private landowners for the public use of the trails.

Maps: The *Maine ATV Trail Map*, published by the Department of Conservation, outlines this loop around Tyler Pond. To obtain one of these maps, contact the ORV Division/ATV Program of the Bureau of Parks and Lands, 22 State House Station, Augusta, ME 04333, (207) 287-4958.

Finding the trail: From Augusta, travel north on ME 27. As you approach the Wicked Good Family Restaurant on the right-hand side of ME 27, prepare to turn left on Summerhaven Road. Continue past Sanford Road on the left and past Parkview Terrace. At about 0.8 mile, turn left onto the access road for the boat launch area on Tyler Pond. There is a cleared area at the top of the road for parking.

Source of additional information:

Department of Conservation
Bureau of Parks and Lands
ORV Division/ATV Program
22 State House Station
Augusta, ME 04333
(207) 287-4958

Notes on the trail: From the parking area, begin riding down the access road for the boat ramp. At a fork in the road, bear left (to the right is an area designated for parking for boaters and anglers). You will be riding through a section of scrubby trees, including white pine and birch. The trail approaches a small gravel pit, traces the perimeter of the pit, and then climbs up to Sanford Road. Cross the road and follow the trail on the other side, passing another

The wide, sandy trails of Summerhaven Use Area are perfect for an afternoon cruise.

sandy gravel pit on the left. At an intersection in the trail, turn right sharply and ride over a sandy and root-infested section of trail as you pass another gravel pit on the right. The next intersection comes just 1.5 miles into the ride. The signed ATV trail bears right down a short hill, swings to the left at the bottom of the hill, and opens onto a huge, sandy pit. From here, skirt the left side of the pit, eventually coming to an old access road. Beyond this road, and at the end of the pit, the ATV trail signs reappear, and the trail climbs to firmer ground before dropping down to a paved road and continuing into the woods on the other side.

There is, however, an alternate route that bypasses the deep sand of the gravel pit. At the intersection at the 1.5-mile point, stay straight instead of dropping down to the gravel pit, and ride up a small rise that will afford a view of the gravel pit on the right. As you approach the edge of the pit, stay to the left and follow a trail into the woods. You will ride down a steep hill, at the bottom of which you will want to keep to the left. At a four-way intersection of trails, turn right and make your way to a three-way intersection. Continue riding on the middle trail, which passes a rusted-out car on the right. This trail ends at a road, quite close to the intersection of the old access road to the pit. Drop down to the road and turn right. You will quickly reconnect with the ATV trail, which crosses this road; turn left onto the trail as it heads into the woods.

At the edge of another sandy gravel-pit area, drop down the bank of the gravel pit and look for the trail to continue up a bank on the other side, just slightly off to the right. Continue riding and follow the trail across another road. The next section of the ride is somewhat narrower, and very well signed. Cross another road and continue straight. You will reach another gravel pit, where you will make a sharp right turn and ride along the edge of the pit before bearing left and back into the woods (be sure not to follow the gravel road that leads up and out of the pit). After crossing through a sandy area, the trail stretches out over a straightaway until reaching a small pond on the right. Bear right just beyond the pond at a three-way intersection, and begin the last leg of this ride over a fun double-track trail that crosses gently rolling terrain through the woods.

At a trail branching off to the left and signed for Fairbanks and Gould Ponds, bear right and continue following the main trail. You will come across an open area on the right, with a trail heading downhill. This side trail descends to Tyler Pond and, being just .75 mile from the trailhead and parking area, makes a great place to relax after almost completing the ride!

RIDE 40 · Vienna Mountain

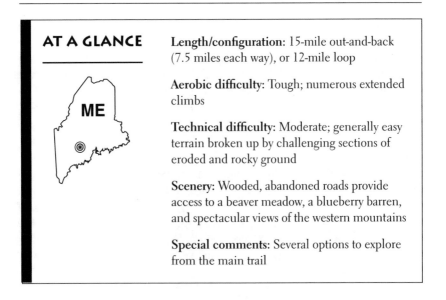

AT A GLANCE

Length/configuration: 15-mile out-and-back (7.5 miles each way), or 12-mile loop

Aerobic difficulty: Tough; numerous extended climbs

Technical difficulty: Moderate; generally easy terrain broken up by challenging sections of eroded and rocky ground

Scenery: Wooded, abandoned roads provide access to a beaver meadow, a blueberry barren, and spectacular views of the western mountains

Special comments: Several options to explore from the main trail

There are at least two ways to enjoy this scenic ride located to the west of the Belgrade Lakes region. The longer option is to tackle it as a 15-mile out-and-back. Alternatively, the ride can be completed as a 12-mile loop. The difference is five miles of pavement: the road between Mount Vernon and Vienna that connects one end of the ride with the other to create a loop. For those who prefer to keep their knobby tires off-road, the out-and-back ride is the best and most strenuous option. For others, speeding back to the trailhead on smooth pavement is a welcome break. No matter which option you choose, this ride is for intermediate and advanced riders in good physical condition. The route follows rough logging roads and rugged four-wheel-drive trails over hill after hill after hill. Several sections of the trail are also technically challenging due to severe erosion and the haphazard placement of boulders and large rocks in the trail.

The town of Vienna is a tiny community that overlooks Flying Pond and enjoys a backdrop of medium-sized mountains and hills. This ride begins up Berry Hill, circles John Brown Mountain, and then climbs to the top of Vienna Mountain. Crossing a saddle to McGaffey Mountain, the ride then descends almost to Mount Vernon. For riders following the out-and-back option, this descent is followed by a quick turnaround and a long climb back up McGaffey and Vienna Mountains. The rigorous ride does enjoy its rewards, however. The view from the blueberry barren atop Vienna Mountain is spectacular at any time of year. Looking west, the view begins across several lakes and ponds before stretching up to the White Mountains in New Hampshire. Another convenient option exists for riders who dawdle through the sunset on summer evenings: there is an access road up to Vienna Mountain that can be followed back into town for an easier return to the trailhead.

General location: The town of Vienna is located just west of the Belgrade Lakes region, approximately 12 miles southeast of Farmington.

Elevation change: The trailhead at the spring just outside the town of Vienna is at 400'. You will begin the ride with a climb up Berry Hill to 930'. You will then descend to 840' before climbing to the top of Vienna Mountain at 1,177'. A second descent, down the southeast slope of Vienna Mountain, drops you to an elevation of 890'. Pedaling part-way up McGaffey Mountain, you will gain another 160' in elevation before dropping to 700'. If you ride this trail as an out-and-back ride, you will turn around at this point and retrace your route to the trailhead for a total elevation gain of about 1,864'. If you opt to complete the ride as a loop, your trip will add up to a lesser, yet still impressive 1,137'.

Season: The months between June and October are good ones in which to ride here. The blueberry barrens at the top of Vienna Mountain burst into a blaze of red in the fall. A tremendous view of the Mount Blue area to the west can also be enjoyed at the top of Vienna Mountain.

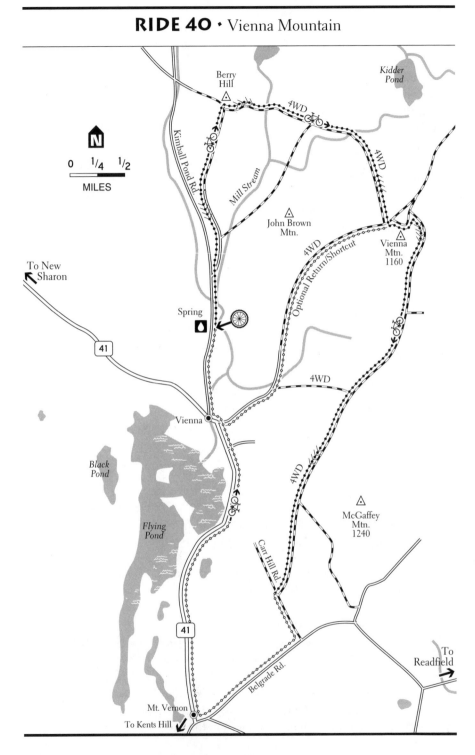

Services: Farmington and Waterville are the closest source of bike-related services in the area. In Farmington, find your way to Northern Lights Hearth and Sports at 2 Front Street, or call them at (207) 778-6566 or (800) 789-6566. If Waterville is a more convenient direction, check out CM Cycle at (207) 872-8681, or Mathieu's Cycle & Sport in Oakland at (207) 465-7564.

Hazards: The trail off the southern slope of Vienna Mountain is strewn with large boulders. Although this section of the trail is short, most riders will need to dismount and walk their bicycles over the rocks.

Rescue index: Although this ride covers trails that feel fairly remote, you will never actually venture more than 2 or 3 miles from secondary roads on which scattered residences may be a source of assistance.

Land status: Over a combination of four-wheel-drive tracks and logging roads, this ride crosses private property and makes use of old right-of-ways. The Vienna community cherishes the access they enjoy to the breathtaking views atop Vienna Mountain and works to preserve that privilege. Those of us who visit from out-of-town need to respect the rights of property owners and the work that the Vienna community has put into maintaining the area for hiking and biking. Of particular note is the blueberry barren atop Vienna Mountain. When riding, be sure to remain on the road that bisects the barren, and leave all the plants and berries undisturbed.

Maps: The USGS quadrangle for this area is Belgrade Lakes. The ride is also depicted in *The Maine Atlas and Gazetteer*, published by the DeLorme Mapping Company (map 20, section E-3).

Finding the trail: Vienna is an easy trip from Farmington: drive east on US 2 and bear right onto ME 41 about 4 miles out of town. ME 41 will take you straight into Vienna, where you need to turn left up Kimball Pond Road just before the bridge that crosses Mill Stream. The Vienna post office is on Kimball Pond Road, and you will pass it on the left as you continue driving. Over a small rise, you will be able to park in a small clearing and turnaround on the right side of the road, directly opposite a spring that is a perfectly convenient place to fill up your water bottles.

From points south, ME 41 branches off US 202 in Winthrop (approximately 8 miles west of Augusta and 13 miles northeast of Lewiston-Auburn). Following ME 41 through Readfield, West Mount Vernon, and Mount Vernon, you will enter Vienna from the south end of town, cross Mill Stream, and take the first right, which is Kimball Pond Road.

Sources of additional information: None.

Notes on the trail: From the parking area and spring, continue north up the paved Kimball Pond Road. At 0.3 mile you will cross a small stream. Just 0.1 mile beyond this, bear right onto Berry Hill Road, also Fire Road 151. Berry

Blueberry barrens
cover the top of
Vienna Mountain.

Hill Road is unpaved, and it is the first road on the right that you will come
to. You will be riding through woods that have grown up inside pastures and
cleared land, evidenced by the old stone fences that remain. As you approach
a steep climb up Berry Hill itself, notice a trail off to the right. This trail is a
possible option that will shorten the ride and eliminate both the climb up and
the descent from Berry Hill.

Continuing straight, you will crest a significant hill at the site of a clearing
and an old road branching off on the left. Continue straight here, following a
hard-packed, grassy jeep trail bordered by an old stone fence. Brief views off
to the right suggest the shape of outlying hills. At an intersection, turn right to
descend the eastern side of Berry Hill, along a rocky and somewhat eroded
trail. At the bottom of this hill is a cleared area with a marsh on the left. Follow the trail over a small bridge that crosses Mill Stream. At a second clearing, the site of a logging yard, notice the road that comes into the clearing
from the right. This is the alternative route mentioned above, and does offer a

quick return to the trailhead if you need to cut the ride short. To continue the ride, proceed straight ahead.

The next intersection is a T junction distinguished by an old apple tree on the left corner. Bear right here, crossing a small stream before beginning the climb up Vienna Mountain. This road is wide and rocky, with several washed-out and eroded sections that provide some technical challenge. After climbing for half a mile, you will come to another T intersection. Turn right and then left almost immediately, through a gap in a stone fence that follows the perimeter of a blueberry barren. The ride continues up through the barren to the summit of Vienna Mountain, along a double-track jeep trail. There is, however, another shortcut available to you at this point. If you continue past the left turnoff up through the barren, you will continue riding down a double-track trail that eventually connects to Vienna Mountain Road and leads back to town and ME 41. Turning right will take you over Mill Stream, and then turning right again, up Kimball Pond Road, will return you to the trailhead. If you choose to continue the ride instead of taking this option, it will be another possible route back to the trailhead if you opt to ride this trail in an out-and-back configuration.

To continue the ride to the top of Vienna Mountain, follow the jeep trail around to the right, avoiding the route that swings left down to a house and barn. You will ride over some exposed rock and down a small bank, skirting the woods that encircle the barren and keeping them on your right. You will find yourself descending along a rough four-wheel-drive road that presents some technical challenge. At an intersection with another road (which climbs up to the barren on the left), turn right and negotiate a short stretch of road literally strewn with large boulders. Shortly beyond this obstacle, a T intersection will connect you to a beautiful old road that stretches out beneath a canopy of leaves and branches. Turn right here, and enjoy some moderate hill climbs along the northwest side of McGaffey Mountain. You will ride past a side trail on the left that is signed for Round Top, and then past 2 more trails on the left.

Six miles into the ride, continue straight along a recently logged ridge, passing a gravel road that turns right down the hill. Passing several logging roads that shoot off the main trail in all directions, continue straight along what is obviously the main trail. As you continue, you will pass rows of old maple trees, old foundations, stone fences, and clusters of apple trees—all of which tell of a time when this road was settled and the land around it farmed.

At a clearing, keep to the right and continue down the road. You will come to a place where, off to the right, Flying Pond is visible from the trail. Continue descending, eventually coming to a gravel road with a house on the right. Though the road to the right once continued all the way to Vienna, it is no longer possible to travel this route. Instead, at this point you must either turn around and retrace your route to return to the trailhead, or turn left and complete the ride on pavement. If you choose the latter option, turn left (onto Carr Hill Road) and follow it to its intersection with the paved Elizabeth Arden Road. Turn right and ride into Mount Vernon, bearing right again to ride up ME 41 to Vienna. Cross Mill Stream and turn right up Kimball Pond Road to return to the parking area.

RIDE 41 · Waterville Ridge Loops

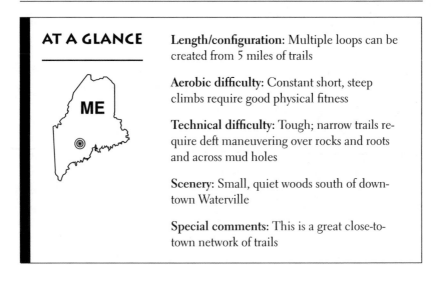

AT A GLANCE

ME

Length/configuration: Multiple loops can be created from 5 miles of trails

Aerobic difficulty: Constant short, steep climbs require good physical fitness

Technical difficulty: Tough; narrow trails require deft maneuvering over rocks and roots and across mud holes

Scenery: Small, quiet woods south of downtown Waterville

Special comments: This is a great close-to-town network of trails

Riders can design their own circuit using the five miles of trails available at this small, wooded mountain bike paradise. Because of the relatively short distances covered by these trails, the riding is suitable for any riders interested in tackling hilly single-track terrain. The trails are rough, with plenty of rocks and roots, and potentially quite wet, with several small stream crossings. For skilled riders, the terrain offers several steep climbs and an equal number of rough descents.

The Waterville Ridge loops are a fine example of single-track mountain bike trails located close to a downtown area. If you live in Waterville, you can probably ride to the trailhead. Once on the trails, you will be riding in the woods: a perfectly sweet getaway from hot city streets. The ride we have described here traces the perimeter of the trail system. In doing this, you will quickly learn how each of the trails intersect and can then create your own loops and circuits through the woods and fields.

RIDE 41 · Waterville Ridge Loops

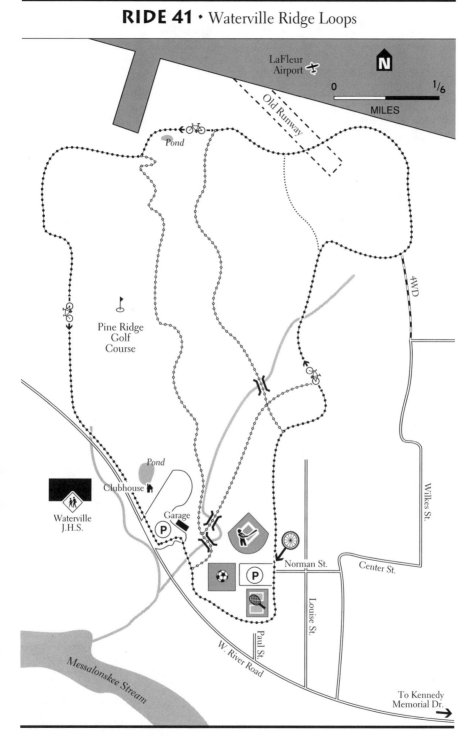

General location: The trailhead is located at a town recreational park, located at the southern edge of downtown Waterville.

Elevation change: These trails are characterized by short, steep climbs and descents.

Season: In the early spring and after any rainfall, damage and erosion to these trails will rapidly deteriorate the quality of the riding available. It is best to ride here well after the spring thaw. Riding can continue until late fall.

Services: All services are available in Waterville.

Hazards: There are no particular hazards along these trails, but do keep a look out for other riders and also for hikers.

Rescue index: These trails are bordered on all sides by roads and residential areas. You will never be very far from assistance.

Land status: Town park.

Maps: There is a map and detailed trail description for this ride in a small booklet published by Evergreen Publications for the Kennebec Valley Tourism Council. The booklet can be purchased at some bike stores, at L.L. Bean in Freeport, or by contacting the Kennebec Valley Tourism Council at the following address or phone number:

> 179 Main Street
> Waterville, ME 04901
> (800) 778-9898

Finding the trail: From Interstate 95, take Exit 33 in Waterville and turn onto Kennedy Drive (ME 137), heading east toward the Kennebec River. Just before ME 137 crosses Messalonskee Stream, turn right onto West River Drive (ME 104). After less than 1 mile, turn right on Louise Street. Turn left on Norman Street and into the parking area for the park.

Source of additional information:

> Mid-Maine Chamber of Commerce
> P.O. Box 142
> Waterville, ME 04901
> (207) 873-3315

Notes on the trail: From the parking area, ride up along the right side of the ballfield, between the field and the tree line. Beyond the ballfield and up a short, steep bank, the trail enters the woods. Keep to the right at the next two junctions, crossing a stream before beginning an uphill climb. At the next trail junction, turn sharply to the right and follow the trail around to the left.

If you find yourself descending to a grassy pipeline, you will know you have missed this curve to the left and you will find yourself coming out on or near Wilkes Street in a residential area. If this happens, continue down Wilkes

A labyrinth of
single-track trails
makes Waterville
Ridge an urban
rider's playground.

Street and turn right onto Center Street. This should return you to Norman
Street and the parking area where you started.

If you stay on track, you will come to a grassy field and old airport runway.
Bear left across the field and runway, and head back toward the trees. The
first trail you see coming out of these woods will return you to the parking
lot. Continue along the perimeter of the woods, keeping the field on your
right. Pass a second intersection, which also bisects the wooded area and will
return you to the park. At the third intersection, follow the trail back into the
woods.

At a four-way intersection, turn right. You will ride through an overgrown
field before reentering the woods. Turn left at the intersection and begin riding downhill. You will come to another field, at which point you will bear left
and ride toward the tree line. You will be able to see a golf course ahead of
you at this point. Follow the tree line out to the paved West River Road. Turn
left, and then left again into the golf-course parking lot. Keep to the right of

the garage and cross a small stream. Ride around the back side of the soccer field, keeping the field on your left, and behind the tennis courts to reach the parking area where you started. Having completed this "boundary" ride, exploring all the other trails will be fairly straightforward.

RIDE 42 · Solon-to-Bingham Rail Trail

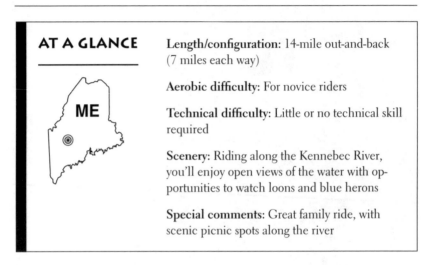

AT A GLANCE	Length/configuration: 14-mile out-and-back (7 miles each way)
ME	**Aerobic difficulty:** For novice riders
	Technical difficulty: Little or no technical skill required
	Scenery: Riding along the Kennebec River, you'll enjoy open views of the water with opportunities to watch loons and blue herons
	Special comments: Great family ride, with scenic picnic spots along the river

This ride closely follows the eastern bank of the Kennebec River along a well-maintained sand and gravel path that once formed part of the Somerset Railroad. Vacationers used to travel this line up to Moosehead Lake and the resort on Mount Kineo. Today, all the rails and ties have been removed, and the seven-mile stretch between the towns of Solon and Bingham makes for a gorgeous 14-mile out-and-back ride. For beginning-level riders, this is an easy cruise over relatively flat terrain that provides access to any number of scenic rest areas along the river.

Although the towns of Solon and Bingham offer little more than a few places to get a bite to eat, the natural corridor that connects them is rich in history. The Kennebec River rises at Moosehead Lake and flows 150 miles to the Atlantic Ocean. In 1775, when the war for independence was in its early stages, Benedict Arnold led an army of 1,100 men north along an old Indian trail along the Kennebec. Their destination was Quebec City, and their goal was to capture the city and eventually force Canada to be annexed as the 14th colony. The Caratunk Falls, near the trailhead of this ride, was just one of the obstacles that the army encountered on its march. Just north of Bingham, the

RIDE 42 · Solon-to-Bingham Rail Trail

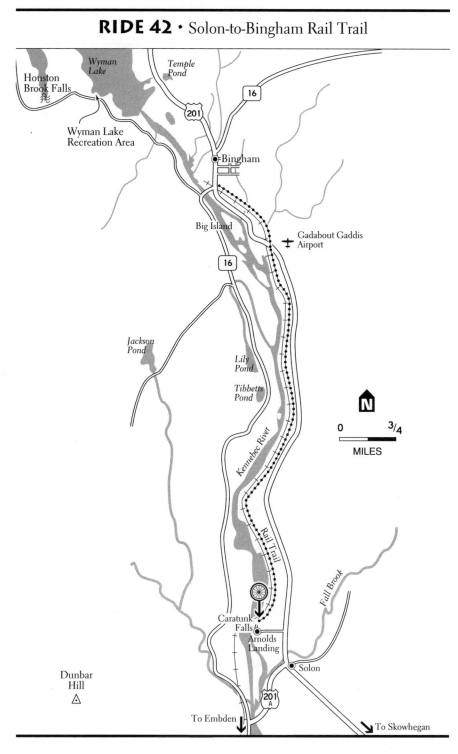

Houston
Brook Falls

*Wyman
Lake*

*Temple
Pond*

16

201

Wyman Lake
Recreation Area

●Bingham

Big Island

Gadabout Gaddis
Airport

16

*Jackson
Pond*

*Lily
Pond*

*Tibbetts
Pond*

Kennebec River

N

0   3/4

MILES

Rail Trail

Fall Brook

Caratunk
Falls
Arnolds
Landing

●Solon

Dunbar
Hill
⚠

201
A

To Embden ↓

↘To Skowhegan

Arnold expedition turned westward and followed the Carrying Place Stream to the Carry Ponds and on to the Dead River.

The army did eventually make it to Quebec, although they surrendered in battle and many of the soldiers were taken as prisoners. The expedition, nevertheless, is famous for successfully completing the journey to Quebec through almost unexplored wilderness. Later on, many mill towns were established along the length of the Kennebec River, and it became famous for the log drives that used to take place in the spring.

General location: This ride follows the Kennebec River Valley between the towns of Solon and Bingham, just 15 miles north of Skowhegan.

Elevation change: Because you will be following the relatively level route of a former railroad bed, there is virtually no change in elevation.

Season: This ride can be enjoyed year-round.

Services: The towns of Solon and Bingham will adequately satisfy any food and water needs. However, Skowhegan is the closest city for bike service and repair. Holden Cyclery can be found at 317 Madison Avenue, Skowhegan, ME 04976, or at (207) 474-3732.

Hazards: Although this trail appears to drain fairly well in the spring, keep your eyes open for washouts early in the season. Erosion is a concern along sections of the trail that hug the bank of the Kennebec. Because this ride follows a multi-purpose trail, be on the lookout for other trail users.

Rescue index: You will never be far from one of the many houses and roads that come quite close to the trail.

Land status: This former railroad right-of-way is now a public multi-use recreational trail.

Maps: Although the route of this abandoned railroad bed no longer appears on most maps, US 201 between Solon and Bingham is clearly marked on any state highway map. The trail is tucked between US 201 and the Kennebec River, and it extends between Solon and Bingham.

Finding the trail: From Skowhegan, travel north on US 201 to the town of Solon. Drive through downtown Solon to the northern outskirts of town. Follow a sign to the Williams Boat Launch, and turn left off US 201 down Falls Road. The road will turn to the right and open into a large gravel parking area. To the left is the Caratunk Falls Hydro Station. The road continues to the right, where a few more parking spaces can be found near the boat launch.

Sources of additional information: This trail is included in a small booklet published by Evergreen Publications for the Kennebec Valley Tourism Council. A guide to road and mountain biking in Maine's Kennebec Valley and Moose River Region, the booklet can be purchased at some bike stores,

Following in Benedict Arnold's footsteps along the Solon-to-Bingham Rail Trail.

at L.L. Bean in Freeport, or by contacting the Kennebec Valley Tourism Council at 179 Main Street, Waterville, ME 04901 or (800) 778-9898.

Notes on the trail: From the boat launch, the trail proceeds north toward Bingham by following the eastern bank of the Kennebec upriver. Notice the worn and weathered piers that were once used to direct logs as they were brought downriver from the northern woods. Farther up, the river narrows and, if you're lucky, you'll have the opportunity to watch great blue herons fish or to listen to the eerie calls of a loon. As you approach Bingham, you may notice people picking fiddleheads in the early spring.

The trail ends at its junction with US 201. Turn around to complete the ride, or if you feel like exploring Bingham, cross US 201 and continue along the trail for a short distance. You will discover an old railroad junction and a somewhat overgrown spur shooting off to the right. This spur was once the main line of the Somerset Railroad, which continued north to Moosehead Lake and the town of Rockwood. There, many passengers would board a ferry to Mount Kineo.

Or detour to a popular swimming area at Wyman Lake. The ride is paved and hilly, but well worth the trip on a warm day. Ride up US 201 to the bridge that crosses the Kennebec. Bear right after crossing the river and ride to Wyman Lake for a swim, or continue up to scenic Houston Brook Falls.

RIDE 43 · Greenville Junction–to–Shirley Mills Rail Trail

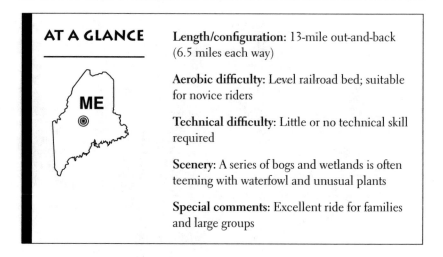

AT A GLANCE

ME

Length/configuration: 13-mile out-and-back (6.5 miles each way)

Aerobic difficulty: Level railroad bed; suitable for novice riders

Technical difficulty: Little or no technical skill required

Scenery: A series of bogs and wetlands is often teeming with waterfowl and unusual plants

Special comments: Excellent ride for families and large groups

Just west of Greenville's town center, an abandoned railbed extends south from Greenville Junction to Shirley Mills and beyond. This family or beginning-level ride is a scenic introduction to fat-tire touring. The trail is wide enough for vehicles to travel along, and the hard-packed gravel surface is easy to ride on. Riders can choose to ride the trail as an out-and-back affair for a total of 13 miles or, leaving a car at either end, as a point-to-point excursion of 6.5 miles.

The first few miles of this ride pass through an area of Maine public reserve land that has been designated for special protection. Wiggins Brook Bog, which covers roughly 283 acres of raised peatland, is classified as a "domed" or "convex raised" bog. Because this area harbors the potential for containing certain rare plants, and provides habitat diversity within the context of the reserve, it has received considerable attention from the Department of Conservation and is being maintained for wildlife and research purposes. The latter half of the ride parallels the east branch of the Piscataquis River and terminates at Shirley Pond, where benches overlooking the pond provide a scenic resting place.

General location: Greenville.

Elevation change: You will be following an abandoned railroad bed that sees very little change in elevation along its entire length.

Season: This ride is feasible year-round, with the best riding conditions most likely to occur from July through September.

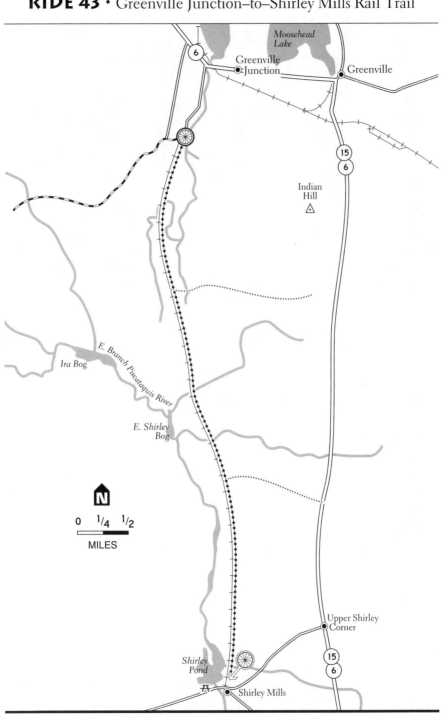

Shirley Pond.

Services: All services are available in Greenville.

Hazards: Apart from possible vehicular traffic, there are a few sections of the trail that may be wet, and there is an occasional washout.

Rescue index: The best sources of assistance are in the area of the trailhead, where traffic along ME 15/6 is regular and access to Greenville town center is quick and easy.

Land status: International Paper Company owns the right-of-way along this abandoned railroad bed.

Maps: This route is adequately represented in the DeLorme Mapping Company's *Maine Atlas and Gazetteer* (map 41, sections D-2 and D-3).

Finding the trail: From Greenville town center, drive west on ME 15/6 toward Greenville Junction. Immediately after passing under the railroad trestle, turn left and begin driving south. Parking is available off the side of the road.

Source of additional information:

North Woods Outfitters
Main Street
Greenville, ME 04441
(207) 695-3288

North Woods Outfitters not only offers bicycle sales and service, but a staff of knowledgeable riders who can provide you with trail information and a coffee shop that serves java in all its delectable forms. Kayaks, canoes, and camping equipment are also available at this excellent resource for outdoor explorers.

Notes on the trail: The rail bed runs in a southerly direction all the way to a T intersection with Upper Shirley Corner Road. The route is easy to follow and runs in almost a straight, north–south line between Greenville Junction and Shirley Mills.

RIDE 44 · Little Squaw Mountain

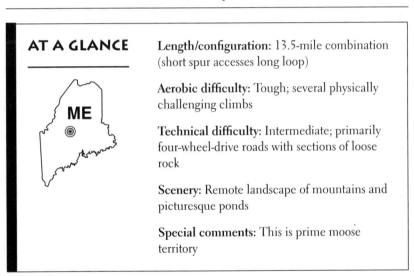

AT A GLANCE

ME

Length/configuration: 13.5-mile combination (short spur accesses long loop)

Aerobic difficulty: Tough; several physically challenging climbs

Technical difficulty: Intermediate; primarily four-wheel-drive roads with sections of loose rock

Scenery: Remote landscape of mountains and picturesque ponds

Special comments: This is prime moose territory

This rugged, 13.5-mile loop features physically challenging climbs in a remote mountain setting. Although steep grades require that riders be in good physical condition, most of the ride covers terrain that requires only intermediate riding skills. A few exceptions to this rule exist along several steep, severely eroded sections of the trail that may require all but the most skilled riders to dismount. The ride follows the route of the Tour de Moose, a mountain biking event that takes place every year in conjunction with "Moose Mainea": a month-long festival celebrating the Maine moose. True to the name of this event, there are plenty of moose to be found near the many ponds that are located in the area. Early morning and dusk are the best time to catch a glimpse of these awkward-looking but interesting beasts. The quiet and observant rider may also catch a glimpse of a black bear, deer, and many bird species such as ducks, grouse, and hawks.

This ride is located entirely within the Little Squaw Management Unit of the Maine Public Reserved Lands System. The reserve extends over approximately 13,544 acres and encompasses land just west of the southern tip of Moosehead Lake, including most of the Little Squaw Mountain Range. The land was acquired in two pieces: the first from Great Northern Nekoosa Paper Company in 1975, and the second from Scott Paper Company in 1984. The history of this previous ownership is evidenced in the old logging roads that still traverse the area. These roads, rather than detracting from the scenic, semi-remote character of the area, actually facilitate access to some of the most beautiful spots within the reserve. Most of this ride follows some of these logging roads, though in places their condition has deteriorated to the point that they are hardly recognizable as roads.

Of the five ponds located within this unit of Maine public reserve land, two of them, Big Indian Pond and Trout Pond, are accessible from the trail. Big Squaw Pond, located approximately one mile from the trail at the end of a hiking path, is another beautiful location that is well worth the side trip.

General location: Big Squaw and Little Squaw townships, approximately 5 miles from the town of Greenville.

Elevation change: From the trailhead at 1,080', you will climb to an elevation of 1,770'. From there, you will descend to 1,680' before climbing again to 1,980'. You will then descend quickly toward Big Indian Pond and drop to an elevation of 1,260'. From there, you will begin a long, 750-foot climb past Trout Pond and into the saddle of Big Squaw Mountain at an elevation of 2,010'. From the saddle, you will descend all the way to the trailhead. Total elevation gain is approximately 1,740'.

Season: This ride may be snow-covered and wet well into May. Summer and early fall are the best times to ride.

Services: All services, including grocery stores, a full-service bike shop, and a variety of lodging opportunities, are available in Greenville. Be sure to carry adequate food with you on this ride. Water is available from many of the streams and ponds along the ride but should be filtered and treated prior to drinking.

Hazards: There are several severely eroded sections on this trail along which all but the most accomplished riders should consider walking. Good brakes are essential: the descents are long and steep, with hazards requiring careful negotiation by all riders. The last 4 miles of this ride follow a graded two-wheel-drive gravel road that is entirely downhill.

The road is characterized by numerous sharp turns. Gonzo riders should consider the possibility of meeting a logging truck, gravel truck, camper, or

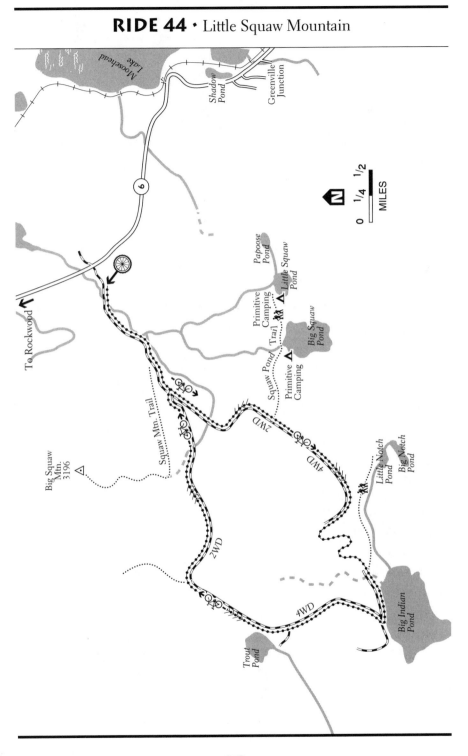

other vehicle laboring up the hill. The road is narrow and there may not be enough room to get by easily. We must stress the need to ride in a controlled manner on this ride. Getting help will require a long hike down to the highway to flag a passing motorist.

Rescue index: This is remote country. Rescue, if needed, will take a while. Your best bet is to try to make it to ME 15 and flag down a vehicle. This may require a 7- or 8-mile hike to the highway. There is a hospital located in Greenville. Please ride in a careful, restrained manner.

Land status: State of Maine public reserved land. Several of the ponds in the reserve still have seasonal camps located on the shore. These are leases that were held over when the land was acquired by the state. These camps are privately owned, and visitors should respect the privacy of the owners.

Maps: DeLorme's *Maine Atlas and Gazetteer* (map 41, section D-1) shows the entire route. The USGS topographical map, which provides further detail of the area, is Big Squaw Pond.

Finding the trail: If you are coming from the south, take ME 15 through Greenville and Greenville Junction. You will be on the west side of Moosehead Lake. The trailhead will be 3.7 miles after you pass beneath the railroad trestle in Greenville Junction. Look for the Maine Public Reserved Lands sign and entrance on the left.

From Rockwood, or points north, drive on ME 15 toward Greenville. Look for the entrance to the Big Squaw Mountain Ski Area. The entrance to the public reserved land is 0.8 mile beyond the entrance to the ski area. Turn right onto the two-wheel-drive dirt road and park near the information sign. The ride begins up the dirt road.

Source of additional information:

North Woods Outfitters
Main Street
Greenville, ME 04441
(207) 695-3288

Notes on the trail: From the parking area at the road entrance, begin pedaling up the unpaved access road into the reserve. You will ride approximately 1.5 miles before coming to a fork in the road; bear left. There may be a sign here with the initials "T.D.M." (Tour de Moose) and an arrow pointing to the left. The road climbs gradually at first, and then more steeply as you approach the trailhead for the hiking trails to Big Squaw Pond and Little Squaw Pond. Just beyond these trails, you will come to the end of the maintained dirt road. Continue straight on an overgrown old logging road, climbing gradually. After descending suddenly about 100', bear right past an overgrown road branching off to the left. You will begin to climb again, and you will pass a gravel pit. At

An early autumn snowfall covers the trail at Little Squaw Mountain.

the crest of this hill, the trail widens, becomes grassy, and begins the long descent toward Big Indian Pond. Use caution on this descent; there are several rocky, eroded sections that should be carefully evaluated. After a badly eroded section that will require most people to dismount, the road levels and a trail branches off to the left.

Look for the initials "T.D.M." painted on a rock at the bottom of the hill, and keep to the right. You will see a large pond in a beautiful bowl as you start to descend again. This is Big Indian Pond. Another old logging road branches off to the left. Again, stay right. Pedal past another logging road, this time on the right, and continue straight until you reach a four-way intersection. The road at this point is fairly rough, with washed-out sections and flooded culverts. From the four-way intersection, turning left will take you to a private camp; continuing straight will lead you to the public campsite on Big Indian Pond; and turning right will continue the ride toward Trout Pond. The road becomes less eroded as you head toward Trout Pond. The pond can be accessed by a trail that is located just beyond a logging road on the left. You must look carefully for this trail, which may be obscured by foliage.

Beyond Trout Pond, the road once again becomes severely eroded and climbs steeply. Continue straight, passing a four-wheel-drive track on the left. At a T intersection with an improved dirt road, turn right and continue climbing until you reach the height of land in the saddle of Big Squaw Mountain. From this point on, it is all downhill to the parking area. Resist the urge to blast out-of-control down this hill, or you may become a hood ornament for one of the large vehicles that frequent this section of road.

RIDE 45 · Mount Kineo

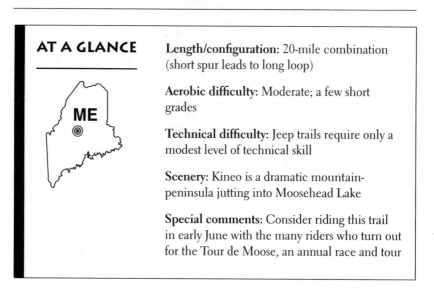

AT A GLANCE

Length/configuration: 20-mile combination (short spur leads to long loop)

Aerobic difficulty: Moderate; a few short grades

Technical difficulty: Jeep trails require only a modest level of technical skill

Scenery: Kineo is a dramatic mountain-peninsula jutting into Moosehead Lake

Special comments: Consider riding this trail in early June with the many riders who turn out for the Tour de Moose, an annual race and tour

This 20-mile loop follows hard-packed logging roads as they meander around the base of Mount Kineo and along the shores of Moosehead Lake, Maine's largest body of water. The trail follows the route of the Tour de Moose, a local race and tour held in conjunction with "Moose Mainea," the Moosehead Lake–area celebration of the largest member of the deer family. The elevation gain is slight, limited to a couple of short, easy climbs, and the technically challenging obstacles are confined to a few washed-out sections that can be crossed with a minimum of risk. This ride is well suited for beginning riders in moderate physical condition. Cyclists who attempt this ride should be equipped with a reliable map and familiar with basic map-reading skills.

Mount Kineo appears to burst from the depths of Moosehead Lake, towering 800 feet over the lake surface. Volcanic in origin, the dramatic cliffs still display the scars of the forces that have acted upon it: from the bubbling lava boiling up from beneath the earth's crust to the grinding action and compression of the glaciers that have passed over it. It was against this backdrop of rugged beauty that the Kineo House was constructed. Built during a time characterized by luxury and opulence, the hotel boasted accommodations for 800. Wealthy patrons from Boston, New York, and Philadelphia favored the area's clean, crisp air and excellent fishing. Vacations usually entailed a stay for the whole summer, so the resort had to be capable of supporting and holding the large numbers of visitors. There was a yacht club, golf course, and riding stable attached to the resort. In fact, the first part of the ride follows some of the old carriage paths that meandered through the area. Around the turn of the century, visitors could board the train in New York City and ride straight through to Moosehead Lake, where a steamer transported people to Mount Kineo. There is nothing left of the old hotel, which was consumed by fire many years ago. A few of the old outbuildings once associated with the inn complex are still standing. They are rather dilapidated, with peeling paint and rotten boards, but nevertheless manage to retain the dignity of this fine resort. There remains a small inn at the site, which provides overnight accommodations, meals, and excellent access to the hiking and mountain biking trails nearby.

We highly recommend completing this ride during the Tour de Moose. The modest entry fee includes a ferry ride to the Kineo House, a T-shirt, and a chance to mix it up with the local mountain bike talent. This is an excellent first mountain bike race for anyone feeling so inclined.

General location: Mount Kineo is located in the center of Moosehead Lake in Piscataquis County.

Elevation change: There is no significant change in elevation throughout this ride, which is characterized by short, moderate hills.

Season: This ride is usually initiated in early June with a race that is organized in conjunction with "Moose Mainea": an annual month-long festival and celebration. Riding conditions remain good well into the fall.

Services: At the base of Mount Kineo, there is a casual inn called the Kineo House. The Kineo House offers lodging, lunch and dinner, and access to a variety of outdoor adventures. Information is available from the Kineo House by calling (207) 534-8812, or can be requested in writing at P.O. Box 397, Rockwood, ME 04478. All other services are available in Greenville.

Hazards: At some points along this ride, culverts have been washed out and water flows freely across the road. Be aware that some of these areas may at times be characterized by soft ground and deep water.

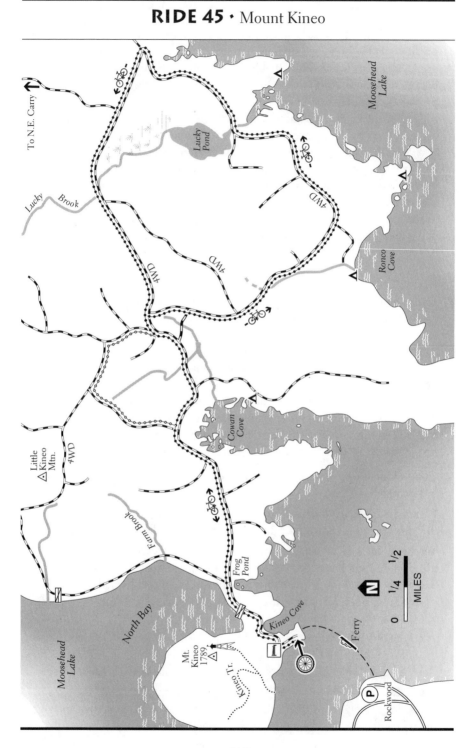

Mount Kineo rises abruptly from the depths of Moosehead Lake.

Rescue index: The most realistic source of assistance on this ride is the Kineo House at the base of Mount Kineo. At the farthest point on the ride, this means that you will be approximately 10 miles from assistance.

Land status: Private logging roads open for recreational use.

Maps: This ride is clearly depicted in the DeLorme Mapping Company's *Maine Atlas and Gazetteer* (map 41, sections A-1 and A-2). Try to use the most recent edition of the *Gazetteer*, as the road system can change from one year to the next. The USGS quad for the area is Mount Kineo.

Finding the trail: This ride begins on Mount Kineo, which is accessible from Rockwood by means of a boat shuttle across Moosehead Lake. Parking for the shuttle is located at the dock in Rockwood.

Source of additional information:

North Woods Outfitters
Main Street
Greenville, ME 04441
(207) 695-3288

North Woods Outfitters not only offers bicycle sales and service, but a staff of knowledgeable riders who can provide you with trail information and a coffee shop that serves java in all its delectable forms. Kayaks, canoes, and camping equipment are also available at this excellent resource for outdoor explorers.

Notes on the trail: From the Kineo House at the base of Mount Kineo, begin pedaling toward the peninsula that connects Mount Kineo with the mainland. Immediately after crossing the peninsula, bear right at the fork in the road. You will be riding toward Cowan Cove. Stay on the main road and avoid several side roads off to the left and right. As the road loops up around Cowan Cove, bear right at the first fork you come to and then bear left at the second fork. After crossing a small stream, bear left. Turn right at the next junction and cross Cowan Brook. Immediately past the brook, turn right. At this point you will begin riding south toward Ronco Cove. Ride past a road branching off on the left and continue along the main road all the way to Lucky Pond. Cross the outlet for Lucky Pond and then pass a road on the right and a road on the left before crossing a small stream. Turn left immediately after this stream. Ride past a road on the right that leads up to Spencer Pond and continue following the road over Lucky Brook. Bear right at an intersection immediately past the brook and return to the junction at Cowan Brook. From here, retrace your route back to Mount Kineo.

RIDE 46 · Attean Township Logging Roads

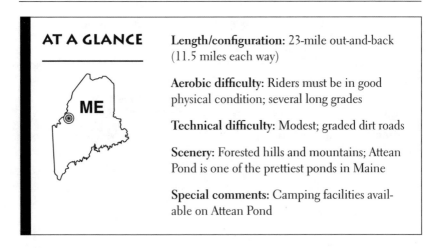

AT A GLANCE

Length/configuration: 23-mile out-and-back (11.5 miles each way)

Aerobic difficulty: Riders must be in good physical condition; several long grades

Technical difficulty: Modest; graded dirt roads

Scenery: Forested hills and mountains; Attean Pond is one of the prettiest ponds in Maine

Special comments: Camping facilities available on Attean Pond

The Attean Township logging roads gently twist and wind around Burnt Jacket, Sally, and Attean Mountains before reaching Hodgeman's Beach on Attean Pond. This ride is an easy-to-moderate, 23-mile out-and-back over hilly terrain on unpaved logging roads. Riders of all levels can enjoy this ride in its entirety or, with less time or energy, can shorten the trip by turning around at any point. The relatively even riding surface along the entire length of this ride also lends itself to self-contained, overnight camping trips. Campsites are conveniently located around Attean Pond.

The opportunities for spotting wildlife along this ride are excellent, and views of the surrounding mountains are beautiful. It is nevertheless the destination that really distinguishes this ride from any other in the area. Attean Pond is tucked in between Sally Mountain to the north and Attean Mountain to the southwest. A popular fishing spot, Attean Pond is a tranquil location and the perfect refueling site for tired, hungry cyclists. Hodgeman's Beach is a large, sandy beach with picnic tables, fire rings, and a privy.

Several other options exist for this ride. About halfway to the pond, the Burnt Jacket Mountain hiking trails intersect the route. These trails are well marked and well worth exploring. In addition, it is possible to lengthen the ride by following the road that swings around to the right at the top of the climb just beyond the railroad tracks. This road can be followed for another six to seven miles and continues through some beautiful hills, offering views of No. 5 Mountain (distinct because of the fire tower at its summit) and No. 6 Mountain. The road eventually deteriorates as you approach the Canadian Atlantic Railway tracks at a point approximately four miles to the west of your first crossing.

General location: Attean Township is a few miles southwest of the town of Jackman, in Somerset County.

Elevation change: At Wood Stream, where this ride begins, you will be at about 1,200' above sea level. When you cross the Canadian Atlantic Railway, you will be at 1,255', and at Attean Lake you will be at the lowest elevation at 1,180'. Moderate hills between these three points account for approximately 250' in elevation gain.

Season: The months between June and October usually offer the best conditions for this ride. Weekends and holidays are the best days to ride because you will avoid the logging trucks that still use these roads.

Services: All services are available in Jackman. A snack trip to Granny's Cap Bakery and Guide Service is an absolute must for hungry cyclists; you can't miss it on Main Street in Jackman. For bicycle service and parts, check out the Bent Spoke Bicycle Shop. Located just 3.5 miles from ME 201 on ME 6 and 15, the Bent Spoke offers service for all bikes, as well as sales of new and used bikes. Contact the folks at Bent Spoke at (207) 688-7655.

Hazards: The roadways you will be traveling on this ride are maintained for logging operations. Large trucks may be using these roads at any time and often travel at high speeds. It is important to recognize and respect the fact that these trucks have the right-of-way. Furthermore, because these logging

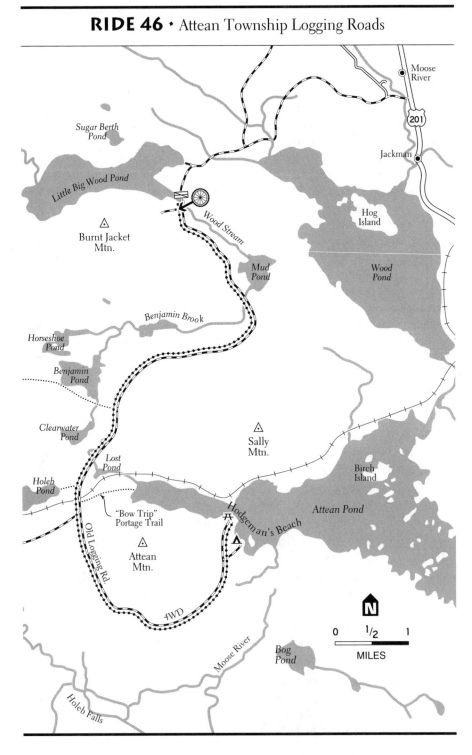

Moose
River

201

Jackman

Sugar Berth
Pond

Little Big Wood Pond

Hog
Island

Wood Stream

Burnt Jacket
Mtn.

Mud
Pond

Wood
Pond

Benjamin Brook

Horseshoe
Pond

Benjamin
Pond

Sally
Mtn.

Clearwater
Pond

Lost
Pond

Birch
Island

Holeb
Pond

Attean Pond

"Bow Trip"
Portage Trail

Hodgeman's Beach

Old Logging Rd

Attean
Mtn.

4WD

N

0   1/2   1

MILES

Moose River

Bog
Pond

Holeb Falls

roads are wide, little protection exists from the hot summer sun. Bring plenty of water whenever you ride this route.

Rescue index: At Hodgeman's Beach on Attean Pond, you will be almost 12 miles from the trailhead, and even farther from assistance. Though many people use these roads for recreational purposes, the number of people you encounter along the trail will lessen as you get farther from the trailhead.

Land status: The Attean Township logging roads are on privately owned land, including land owned by paper companies. Attean Pond is part of the Holeb unit of Maine public reserve land.

Maps: The USGS quadrangle for Attean Township is Attean Pond. There is also a small map for this ride included in a small booklet published by Evergreen Publications for the Kennebec Valley Tourism Council. The booklet can be purchased at some bike stores, at L.L. Bean in Freeport, or by contacting the Kennebec Valley Tourism Council at:

> 179 Main Street
> Waterville, ME 04901
> (800) 778-9898

Finding the trail: From Jackman, travel north on US 201 and turn left onto Sandy Stream Road after crossing the Moose River. Bear left at the first fork, and continue to bear left along an unpaved road until you reach a gated bridge over Wood Stream (you will have traveled about 4 miles on the unpaved road). There is a small parking area just before the bridge.

Sources of additional information:

> Jackman–Moose River Chamber of Commerce
> P.O. Box 368
> Jackman, ME 04945
> (207) 668-4171

For additional information about the Holeb unit of Maine public reserve land, which includes Attean Pond, contact the Western Region Office of the Bureau of Parks and Lands at (207) 778-4111.

Notes on the trail: Cross the gated bridge over Wood Stream and follow the road as it curves around to the left. After crossing Benjamin Brook, the road begins to climb. Bear right and cross another small bridge. Five miles into the ride, you will pass the Attean Pond foot trail on the left. A large boulder on the right side of the road signals this trail intersection. Just a short distance farther, a hiking trail on the right is signed for Burnt Jacket Mountain via Benjamin Valley. Continuing on the road, you will come to the tracks of the Canadian Atlantic Railway. Just beyond the tracks and on the left side of the road, a narrow footpath leads to the western tip of Attean Pond about 1 mile

Attean Pond is the highlight and halfway point of the Attean Township ride.

away. Continue up the road and, as you reach the top of a moderate climb, continue straight onto a somewhat indistinct gravel road.

At this point, the road you have been traveling on continues around to the right and Attean Mountain appears on the left. Be sure to stay straight at this intersection if your goal is to reach Attean Pond. Keeping Attean Mountain on your left, follow the road through several ups and downs and keep bearing left all the way to the pond. As you approach the pond, you will catch a good view of Sally Mountain directly in front of you. Bear left at a fork before the beach, and follow the road until its end. At this point, pick up a path and follow it down to Hodgeman's Beach, about 600 feet beyond.

RIDE 47 · Rancourt Pond

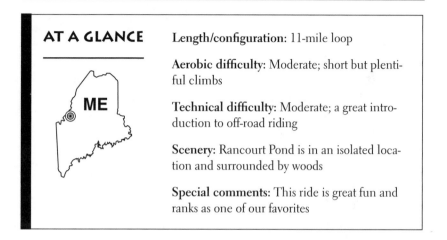

AT A GLANCE

Length/configuration: 11-mile loop

Aerobic difficulty: Moderate; short but plentiful climbs

Technical difficulty: Moderate; a great introduction to off-road riding

Scenery: Rancourt Pond is in an isolated location and surrounded by woods

Special comments: This ride is great fun and ranks as one of our favorites

Just a few miles outside Jackman, the 11-mile Rancourt Pond loop follows a jeep trail over moderately technical terrain. If you are visiting Jackman and only have time for one ride, this is the one to pick. Rancourt Pond is a startlingly beautiful body of water fringed by trees and tall grasses. Access to the pond is possible at two different points, where short footpaths lead to open vistas along the water's edge. Early risers will enjoy misty mornings at the pond, when the possibility of seeing moose is at its highest.

Primarily hard-packed double-track, this trail includes some riding over rough, eroded areas, a stream crossing, some wet terrain at the perimeter of a beaver bog, and a few tricky technical spots. All skill levels will enjoy this ride, provided that they are in reasonable physical condition and don't mind a little mud and water. There are several ways to ride the Rancourt Pond loop: you can pedal it clockwise or counterclockwise, and, in either direction, you can begin the loop from its southernmost point or its northernmost point. If you start the ride from its northern tip, from Holeb Road, you will begin and end the ride by crossing Sandy Stream. Although the streambed is rocky and firm, it is also fairly wide and water levels vary tremendously throughout the year. During high water, or if you just prefer not to soak yourself at the beginning of a ride, begin the ride from the south along Sandy Stream Road, where a small bridge will take you across the stream.

General location: Rancourt Pond is located just a few miles north of Jackman, on the west side of US 201.

Elevation change: This ride is characterized by both short, steep climbs and more moderate grades.

RIDE 47 · Rancourt Pond

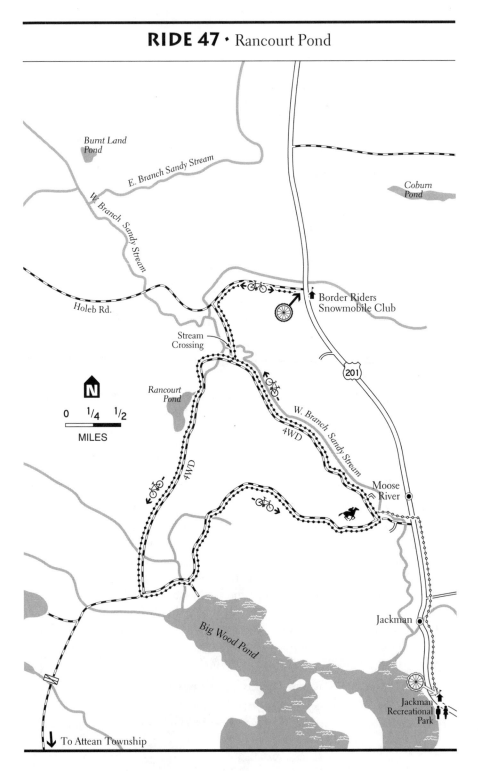

Season: Summer and autumn are the best seasons in which to ride this trail. Wet conditions in the spring and after any rainfall make the trail more vulnerable to damage and erosion.

Services: All services are available in nearby Jackman. If your bike needs attention, contact the Bent Spoke Bicycle Shop at (207) 688-7655.

Hazards: There is a horseback riding stable located on Sandy Stream Road. During one of our rides along this loop, we encountered a large group of equestrians setting out on a trail ride. We were able to pull to the side of the road and talk to both the riders and their horses as they rode by. Because some horses are nervous around bikes, it is preferable to give them the right-of-way.

Rescue index: You will remain within 4 miles of US 201 on this ride, and downtown Jackman will never be more than 6 miles away.

Land status: The Rancourt Pond ride follows a jeep trail across privately owned land. Riding is permitted, but it is extremely important to remember that we are guests on somebody else's property. Have respect for the land and the neighborhoods this ride passes through, and hopefully we will all be enjoying this ride for many years to come.

Maps: Although this route is fairly simple to follow, a USGS 7.5 minute series topographic map for Jackman will guide you through some of the intersections and direct you to several possible side trips along the way. There is also a small map for this ride in a road and mountain biking guide put together by the Kennebec Valley Tourism Council. Look for a copy at your local bike store, at L.L. Bean in Freeport, or by contacting the Kennebec Valley Tourism Council at:

179 Main Street
Waterville, ME 04901
(800) 778-9898

Finding the trail: To begin the ride from its northernmost point, ride or drive north out of Jackman on US 201. If you need to park a vehicle, park off the road at the Border Riders Snowmobile Club. Your ride will begin and end on Holeb Road, where a rough trail will connect you to the Rancourt Pond loop by way of a wet crossing of Sandy Stream.

If you prefer to avoid wet feet, especially on cold autumn mornings, you can begin this ride from its southernmost point and complete the loop without having to ride through Sandy Stream. To do this, park at Jackman Recreational Park, located just behind the information booth on Main Street (US 201). There are tennis and basketball courts, rest rooms, and a pay telephone here, as well as access to Big Wood Pond. From the park, begin by riding north up US 201. You will cross a bridge over the Moose River and then look for the first road on the left: Sandy Stream Road. Turning left, you will cross a

Crossing Rancourt
Stream in
Jackman, Maine.

bridge over Sandy Stream and quite quickly reach a fork in the road. Bear left
to begin the loop; the road on the right is the one on which you will return.

Source of additional information:

Jackman–Moose River Chamber of Commerce
P.O. Box 368
Jackman, ME 04945
(207) 668-4171

Notes on the trail: From the Border Riders Snowmobile Club, turn left
down Holeb Road, a wide dirt road with power lines along its edge. Begin
looking for a small jeep trail on the left as Holeb Road evens out. At the time
we rode here, a pile of slash (limbs and other logging debris) marked the
entrance to the trail. You will know if you have missed this trail if you come
to a bridge, where Holeb Road continues across Sandy Stream. Turning left
onto the jeep trail, you will ride a stretch of trail that includes a few deep dips

that may or may not be filled with water. Cross Sandy Stream and continue following the trail on the other side as it climbs uphill.

At the first intersection, turn right. There is also a trail descending to the left. This is the route on which you will return to complete the loop. After turning right, the trail skirts a beaver bog on the right. Upon crossing an exposed culvert, the trail swings left and climbs steeply for a short distance. Continue straight at an intersection with a trail that branches off to the right, and you will find yourself at Rancourt Pond. There is a narrow foot trail that leads to some great rest spots that offer an excellent vantage point for viewing the pond.

The trail continues to the left, over the outlet to the pond. You will climb gradually before the trail evens out and follows the eastern shore of the pond high up on the bank. Just before the trail begins to descend, there is a footpath on the right that leads down the steep bank to the edge of the pond. Concealed by the trees, this path offers moose and waterfowl seekers excellent coverage for a discreet descent to the water's edge. Back on the main trail, you will begin to descend, rounding a sharp curve to the right as the trail passes an open clearing on the left. You will ride over a small bridge and past a road branching off on the right before coming to the end of the jeep trail at a gravel road. Turn left onto this road.

Cross a plank bridge that spans Gander Brook, and you will come to another intersection. Turn left here unless you want to follow the road out to US 201 and make a side trip into Jackman. If you turn left to continue the ride, you will pass a horse stable on the right. The road gradually narrows into a double-track trail over grassy terrain. Sandy Stream parallels the trail on the right. As the road becomes more rutted, you will come to the intersection that marks the beginning and end of the loop. To complete the ride, turn right and ride down to Sandy Stream for another trip through its sparkling waters. Ride back out to Holeb Road, and turn right to return to US 201 and your vehicle.

RIDE 48 · Sandy Bay Loop

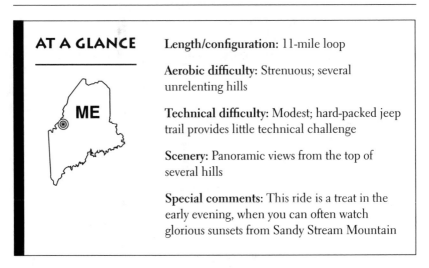

AT A GLANCE

ME

Length/configuration: 11-mile loop

Aerobic difficulty: Strenuous; several unrelenting hills

Technical difficulty: Modest; hard-packed jeep trail provides little technical challenge

Scenery: Panoramic views from the top of several hills

Special comments: This ride is a treat in the early evening, when you can often watch glorious sunsets from Sandy Stream Mountain

This ride is an 11-mile loop around Sandy Stream Mountain. The terrain is technically easy: seven miles along the double-track jeep trail named Dumas Road, and four miles along the paved US 201. However, the ride begins with a long, extended climb around the southern base of Sandy Stream Mountain and continues across hilly terrain. There is also a bit of a climb up US 201, though this is more than made up for by the exhilarating descent that follows and completes the ride. Riders of any level will be able to complete this ride with little difficulty, provided that they enjoy a reasonable level of physical fitness.

In spring and summer, the border of this trail is filled with wildflowers. The landscape is one typical of many in which the logging industry has been active. There are some benefits to riders as a result of this activity, however: First of all, the logging roads provide access to some scenic and remote areas that would otherwise be inaccessible by mountain bike. Second, the thinning and clearing of trees has resulted in some tremendous views that would not otherwise exist. This ride is an excellent late-afternoon jaunt because it offers fantastic views of the sun setting over Slidedown Mountain. As you complete the ride on US 201, be sure to notice the well-trodden paths of moose and deer on the side of the road. In places, the presence of these animals makes the roadside look like a pasture where cows and bulls have congregated in their favorite places.

General location: The Sandy Bay ride begins 7 miles north of the Moose River Bridge in Jackman.

RIDE 48 · Sandy Bay Loop

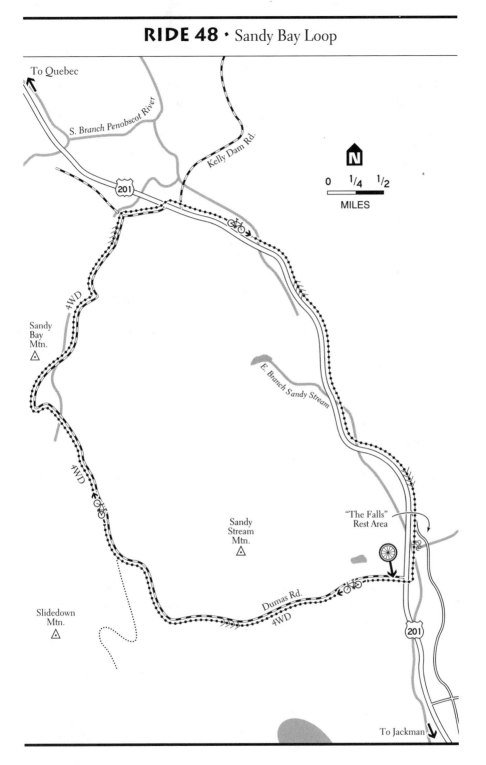

To Quebec

S. Branch Penobscot River

Kelly Dam Rd.

201

N

0   1/4   1/2

MILES

4WD

Sandy
Bay
Mtn.
△

E. Branch Sandy Stream

4WD

Sandy
Stream
Mtn.
△

"The Falls"
Rest Area

Slidedown
Mtn.
△

Dumas Rd.
4WD

201

To Jackman

Elevation change: The parking area at the falls on US 201 is at 1,680'. The ride begins with a short descent to Dumas Road at approximately 1,580'. On Dumas Road, you will climb to 1,815' and then drop to 1,710'. From there, you will pedal along moderately hilly terrain before climbing still farther to reach a high elevation of about 2,000'. You will then descend a substantial grade to US 201 at about 1,760'. On US 201 you will gain about 160' before descending back to the falls. Total elevation gain for the ride is approximately 790'.

Season: Because this ride uses roads built for logging vehicles, it is less susceptible to damage during wet and rainy seasons. Good conditions exist from spring through fall.

Services: All services are available in Jackman. Basic bike needs can be met at the Bent Spoke Bicycle Shop on ME 15, just 3.5 miles from US 201. You can contact the folks at Bent Spoke at (207) 688-7655.

Hazards: There is a wide shoulder along US 201, but cyclists should use caution along this road because vehicles travel at high speeds.

Rescue index: At the farthest point, you will be just 3.5 miles from US 201, where it is likely that you could flag down a vehicle in the event that you required assistance. Jackman is 7 miles south on US 201.

Land status: The trail around Sandy Stream Mountain is a private logging road that is nevertheless open to recreationalists.

Maps: The USGS quadrangles for Sandy Bay Township are Jackman and Campbell Brook. There is also a diagram of this ride in a booklet put together by the Kennebec Valley Tourism Council. The booklet can be purchased at some bike stores, at L.L. Bean in Freeport, or by contacting the Kennebec Valley Tourism Council at the following address or phone number:

179 Main Street
Waterville, ME 04901
(800) 778-9898

Finding the trail: From Jackman, drive north on US 201 for about 7 miles. The trailhead will be on the left, at Dumas Road, but parking is available just beyond this on the right. Here, a scenic stop-off features "The Falls": a 15-yard drop in Sandy Stream that has warranted the creation of a small picnic area. From this parking area, turn left back down US 201 until you reach Dumas Road on the right.

Source of additional information:

Jackman–Moose River Chamber of Commerce
P.O. Box 368
Jackman, ME 04945
(207) 668-4171

An old logging road near Sandy Stream Mountain rewards riders with spectacular mountain scenery.

Notes on the trail: Begin riding up the unpaved Dumas Road. You will climb for several miles, crossing a series of bridges and keeping Sandy Stream Mountain on your right. After this initial climb, the trail continues over undulating terrain that opens every now and again to give views of Slidedown Mountain to the west and Sandy Bay Mountain to the north. You will reach a wide, cleared area that opens up the view to the north. Bear right here, and start a fast, steep descent. At a **T** intersection, turn right on what was once the paved Canada Road. This road will take you back to US 201. Turn right, or south, on US 201 and return to the falls, enjoying the swift, paved descent that concludes the ride.

MIDCOAST MAINE

Midcoast Maine is tucked between the mouths of the Kennebec River and the Penobscot River. The region is characterized by a series of long, jagged peninsulas that jut out into the ocean, creating a mesmerizing series of harbors, coves, and bays. Farther inland, the landscape is dominated by a series of rocky hills and long ridges. The area was once extensively farmed, as evidenced by numerous old mill sites and cemeteries. Many of the rides in this portion of the state follow the routes of old, abandoned roads. These roads tend to follow the valleys or meander along the high ridges.

One of the most prominent towns in the Midcoast region is Camden. A town that developed from the business of building and sailing ships, Camden is now home to a great many avid off-road riders. It is largely because of the efforts of this local community of riders that many of the trails we have described in this guidebook even exist. The town itself was one of the earliest resort communities on the coast of Maine and is still graced with many grand summer "cottages." A local saying describes the town as resting "where the mountains meet the sea." Indeed, the size and extent of the nearby Camden Hills are impressive. Sharing many characteristics with the mountains of Mount Desert Island farther north, the Camden Hills are a compact group of mountains that rise dramatically above the western shore of Penobscot Bay. Camden Hills State Park encompasses most of the range and includes an extensive network of hiking trails and one bike trail.

Lupine is just one of the many treasures awaiting riders in midcoast Maine.

ISLE AU HAUT

The French navigator Samuel Champlain is responsible for the name of this distinct island at the edge of Penobscot Bay. The English translation reads "high island," an apt description of the small but mountainous island that prominently rises from the water. Shell heaps along the shore of Isle au Haut give clues to the wanderings and lifestyle of some of the indigenous people that camped here. It was not until the end of the Revolutionary War that a permanent settlement of fishermen, boat builders, and farmers was established on the island.

About one half of Isle au Haut is federal park land, part of Acadia National Park. Mountain biking is indirectly recommended in the brochure offered to visitors by the park service, which advises people against biking because of the rough, unpaved conditions of roads on the island. These roads actually offer mountain bikers the unique experience of exploring the breathtaking beauty of one of Maine's coastal islands.

RIDE 49 · Pleasant Mountain

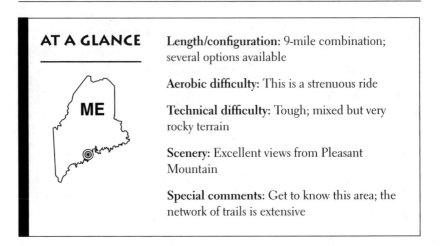

AT A GLANCE

Length/configuration: 9-mile combination; several options available

Aerobic difficulty: This is a strenuous ride

Technical difficulty: Tough; mixed but very rocky terrain

Scenery: Excellent views from Pleasant Mountain

Special comments: Get to know this area; the network of trails is extensive

This ride is characterized by a diversity of terrain and a rather untidy configuration. Covering a possible total of nine miles, it follows a rough, unpaved old road up the natural corridor that runs between Meadow Mountain to the west and Pleasant Mountain to the east. A network of single- and double-track trails branches off the east side of this road and offers some excellent and technically challenging riding up and along the south side of Pleasant Mountain. A side trip to the summit of Pleasant Mountain features a breathtaking view of West Penobscot Bay. There is also the option of riding out through the Meadow Mountain Preserve and across Quiggle Brook to the site of what was once Wattons Mills.

The route that we have described features what we felt to be some of the highlights of the trail system around Pleasant Mountain. The terrain is rugged and requires at least intermediate-level riding skills. Furthermore, despite the effort we have made to clearly map the trails, good route-finding skills are extremely helpful. There are many ways to ride these trails, and we suggest you utilize the map we have provided to create alternatives to the route we have described. As you become familiar with the area and the specific terrain of each trail, you will be able to design rides that best meet your style and ability.

General location: This ride climbs to the top of Pleasant Mountain, located to the west of West Rockport.

Elevation change: If you follow the route we have described, you will begin riding at 400' and first drop down to 300'. From this point, you will gain 740' to reach the summit of Pleasant Mountain at 1,040'. From the summit, you

RIDE 49 · Pleasant Mountain

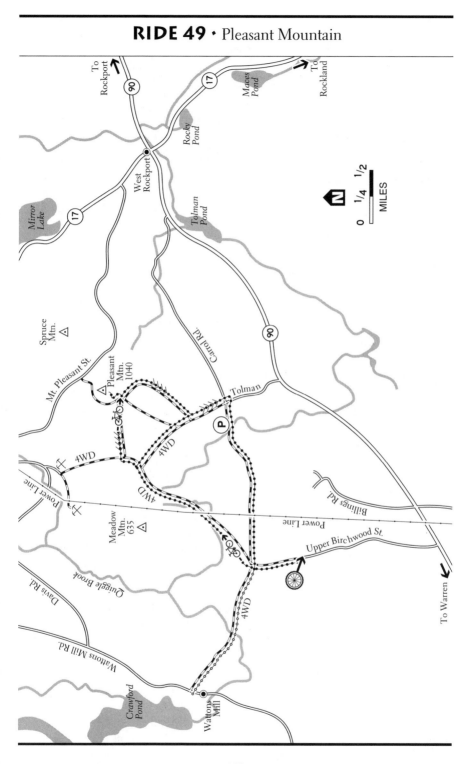

N

0 1/4 1/2

MILES

To Rockport

To Rockland

Maces Pond

Rocky Pond

West Rockport

Tolman Pond

Mirror Lake

Spruce Mtn.

Pleasant Mtn. 1040

Mt. Pleasant St.

Carroll Rd.

Tolman

P

4WD

4WD

4WD

Power Line

Meadow Mtn. 635

Power Line

Billings Rd.

Upper Birchwood St.

Davis Rd.

Quiggle Brook

Wattons Mill Rd.

4WD

Crawford Pond

Wattons Mill

To Warren

227

will drop to 380' before climbing back to 500'. If you ride out to Wattons Mills, you will descend to 160' before returning to the trailhead at 400'. Total elevation gain for the ride is approximately 1,100'.

Season: Riding on the Pleasant Mountain trails can begin in June and continue through the fall. Because snowmobiles pack down the trails in the winter, there is also the opportunity to ride through the winter.

Services: All services are available in Rockport and Camden.

Hazards: Certain sections of the trail network around Pleasant Mountain are severely eroded. In particular, the short trip to the summit of the mountain may require most riders to dismount for a quick hike to the top.

Rescue index: You will not venture more than 2 miles from assistance on this ride.

Land status: This route follows the pathways of old county roads and snowmobile trails, and includes the possibility of a 4-mile, out-and-back side trip on an unimproved dirt road through Meadow Mountain Preserve.

Maps: Certain portions of this ride are mapped out in the DeLorme Mapping Company's *Maine Atlas and Gazetteer* (map 14, section D-2). Although the USGS quadrangle for this area (West Rockport) offers more detail, it provides no more information about the network of trails on which you will be riding.

Finding the trail: From Rockport, travel west on ME 90. Continue straight through the intersection with ME 17 in West Rockport. Just over 4 miles farther on ME 90, the road crosses a power line. Turn right onto the next road you come to, which may be signed as Upper Beechwood Street. Continue driving until the road deteriorates into an unpaved jeep trail, and look for a suitable place to pull over and park.

Sources of additional information: Maine Sport Outfitters is a large sporting goods store with a full-service bicycle department staffed with riders who can give you suggestions for mountain biking in the area. You will find Maine Sport on US 1 just south of Camden. Call them at (207) 236-8797 or (800) 722-0826.

Notes on the trail: From your parking place on Upper Beechwood Street, begin riding north. You will come to a crossroad with Carrol Road. To the left is the 4-mile, out-and-back trip to Wattons Mills. The road straight ahead begins the ride to the summit of Pleasant Mountain. You will pass an area that has been flooded due to beaver activity. Just 0.25 mile farther, the road bears right and crosses beneath power lines. Continue riding along what is a rough and rocky old road. Continue past two trails branching off on the right (the second of which is the route by which you will return). As the road crests, begin to look for a rough little trail on the right. This turnoff is a tricky one, but you will know you have missed it if you begin to descend the old road, which eventually reaches a gravel pit. The trail you are looking for branches off from the road at a rather acute angle and begins to climb the steep slope of Pleasant Mountain through an area cleared for blueberry bushes.

As you reach what feels like the top of Pleasant Mountain, the grassy jeep trail you have been climbing continues into the woods. A short distance farther, you will come to a crossroads: to the left is an extremely rough and eroded trail up to the true summit of Pleasant Mountain (an optional side trip); to the right is a section of slickrock that drops down the mountain; and ahead of you is the continuation of the ride. This route traverses the southern slope of Pleasant Mountain before descending. You will reach a grassy clearing at a T junction. Turn right and ride down a grassy jeep trail through a partially cleared area in which blueberry bushes and young oak trees have emerged. In just 0.3 mile, you will come to another T intersection. Turning left here will connect you to Carrol Road, and if you turn right on Carrol Road, you will enjoy a relatively smooth and flat ride back to the very first four-way intersection encountered on the ride (turning left would return you to your car, and continuing straight would take you down to Wattons Mill).

Alternatively, if you turn right at this junction, you will continue the ride along a more rigorous route that involves a little more climbing and traverses more difficult terrain. Ride past a trail branching off the right side of the road and continue on to where a snowmobile trail cuts left into a field overgrown with sumacs. This grassy double-track trail will quickly land you at a clearing easily identified by an old stone foundation to the right. Bear left past this foundation and descend through the woods until you rejoin the extension of Upper Beechwood Street at a T intersection. Turn left and backtrack to the four-way intersection with Carrol Road and the jeep trail down to Wattons Mill. To continue riding, turn right for the 4-mile round-trip to Wattons Mill, or continue straight to complete your ride and return to the trailhead.

RIDE 50 · Camden Snow Bowl

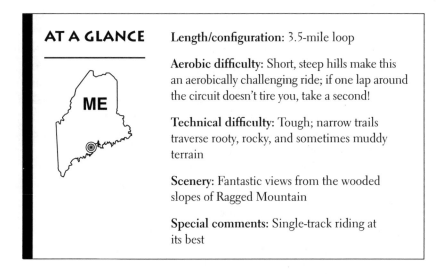

AT A GLANCE

Length/configuration: 3.5-mile loop

Aerobic difficulty: Short, steep hills make this an aerobically challenging ride; if one lap around the circuit doesn't tire you, take a second!

Technical difficulty: Tough; narrow trails traverse rooty, rocky, and sometimes muddy terrain

Scenery: Fantastic views from the wooded slopes of Ragged Mountain

Special comments: Single-track riding at its best

Just four miles from the town of Camden, Ragged Mountain features a ski area called the "Snow Bowl," which is operated by Camden's department of parks and recreation. Though the mountain is not promoted for summertime use, mountain biking is permitted in the area. This 3.5-mile loop begins at the foot of Ragged Mountain and follows a race circuit often referred to as the Spring Runoff Course. Despite its relatively short distance, this ride is for the technically proficient and aerobically fit rider. Beginning with a climb up a grassy ski slope, the trail traverses the mountain before ducking into the woods for a rugged single-track loop through the woods. Several steep drops and a swampy area studded with large boulders will present a challenge to all riders.

Ragged Mountain rises to an elevation of 1,300 feet and, even from its lower slopes, offers expansive views of Bald Mountain to the north. In the fall, Bald Mountain virtually dances in a brilliant splash of autumn colors. In addition to the race circuit described here, it is possible to ride to the summit of Ragged Mountain. Some riders dare to choose the most direct route straight up one of the ski slopes, although there is a slightly more gradual climb beginning from the single-track loop in the woods.

General location: The Snow Bowl, or Ragged Mountain Recreation Area, lies just 4 miles west of Camden.

Elevation change: The Spring Runoff Course is characterized by a series of short, steep climbs and descents.

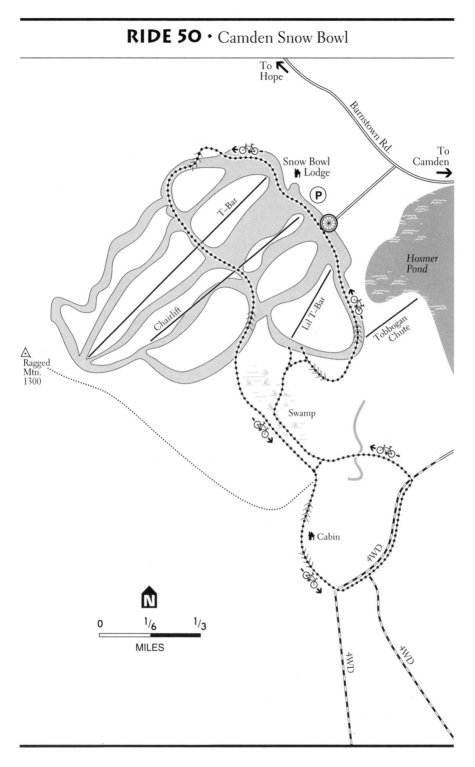

To Hope

Barnstown Rd.

To Camden

Snow Bowl Lodge

P

T-Bar

Chairlift

Lil T-Bar

Hosmer Pond

Tobbogan Chute

Ragged Mtn. 1300

Swamp

Cabin

4WD

4WD

4WD

N

0   1/6   1/3

MILES

Season: This trail should be in fairly good condition from late June until well into the fall.

Services: All services are available in Camden, where there are two bike shops: Fred's Bikes, located at 53 Chestnut Street, (207) 236-6664; and Oggibike, at 29 Mountain Street, (207) 236-3631. Bike services and lots of helpful information about area riding are also available at Maine Sport Outfitters, located on US 1 just south of Camden. Phone (207) 236-8797 or (800) 722-0826. There is a camping area at Camden Hills State Park, located just outside the north side of town.

Hazards: There are a few sections along this ride covered with large boulders, and one or two short but extremely steep descents. These areas are posted for races, and the signs often remain hanging long after these events are over.

Rescue index: Though the length of this loop ensures that you will never be far from assistance, the technical nature of the trail may mean that help is some time away. The Camden summer recreation program is based at the Snow Bowl, so there will often be people at the trailhead. There are also residences near the trailhead and close to the single-track loop at its farthest point from the ski slopes.

Land status: The Camden Snow Bowl is owned by the town of Camden. The race circuit may cross over some private property along trails that are accessed by snowmobiles in the winter.

Maps: We picked up a photocopy of the Spring Runoff Course at Maine Sport Outfitters, located on US 1 just south of Camden. The circuit is a popular riding route among local riders. It is usually possible to identify the route by means of well-worn trails.

Finding the trail: From US 1, turn up John Street, which is about 1 mile south of the center of town. Go straight through the first four-way intersection and then bear left at a fork in the road, following the signs for the Snow Bowl. You will come to Hosmer Pond on the left, beyond which you will turn left into a large parking area.

Source of additional information:

Camden Parks & Recreation
P.O. Box 1207
Camden, ME 04843
(207) 236-3438

Notes on the trail: From the parking area, ride away from the pond and in front of the ski lodge. Stay behind the T-bar hut and begin riding up the farthest slope, named Lower Spinnaker. As you pass the first island of trees on the left, look for a single-track trail on the right, which enters the woods,

A stone wall channels Sarah around a corner at the Camden Snow Bowl.

crosses an old stone fence, and then quickly rejoins the ski slope. Continue climbing up the slope and then bear left at the first split in the ski trail. Cross the next run (Northeaster), and then drop slightly and bear right to cross beneath a **T** bar. Continue traversing the main ski slope (Windjammer), descending slightly toward the chair lift. You will ride under the chair lift and then cross the Halfhitch trail, before turning uphill to the right when you reach the ski slope with lights (Lookout). You will begin climbing up this ski run until the slope increases dramatically; at this point look for a narrow single-track trail entering the woods on the left. There may be flagging tape marking this trail.

This first stretch of single-track terrain is rocky and wet in some areas, and involves a fair bit of climbing. At a **T** junction, turn right. Alternatively, and for a shorter ride, look to the left and see another trail that, if you bear left onto it, will take you back to the ski area. This is also the last section of the ride if you choose the longer loop. After turning right for the longer loop, continue riding to a fork in the trail and bear left. At a second fork in the trail, bear left again. (The trails up to the right will take you on a steep climb to the summit of Ragged Mountain.) Continue riding until a small lodge becomes visible ahead. Bear right as you approach this building. Beyond this point, you will encounter a technical section of the trail that requires the crossing of a small stream over fairly large boulders. At the next intersection, bear left onto a smoother, downhill trail. Bear left again at the next fork. This trail will connect you to a logging road onto which you want to turn right. Stay straight on this road, passing a trail coming in on the right.

You will soon be able to see houses ahead of you through the trees. Bear left at this point, back onto a less improved trail that leads into the woods, and then left again past an indistinct single-track trail that heads downward and to the right. You will be riding with more mature forest to the right, and a recent cut to the left of the trail. Cross a stream (there was a dilapidated old snowmobile bridge here when we rode through). At the next intersection, bear right (the left option would return you to the first part of the trail). You will ride through a somewhat treacherous section here, making your way over numerous boulders and then bearing right across a rocky swamp.

Crossing a gap in a stone fence, you will descend steeply. The trail almost reconnects with the ski slope beyond this point, but then veers around to the right and descends steeply again. The trail then runs along a stone fence before leaving the woods and reconnecting with the ski slope. Turn right down this slope and return to the parking area. This circuit would be ridden several times during a race. It is well worth tackling the ride a second time, as even a basic knowledge of the trails will improve your riding dramatically!

RIDE 51 · Camden Hills State Park

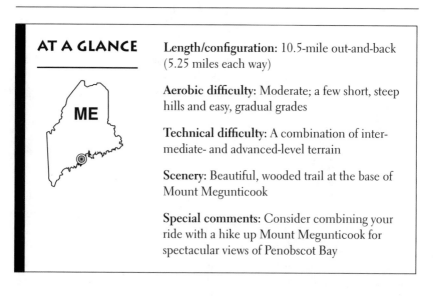

AT A GLANCE

ME

Length/configuration: 10.5-mile out-and-back (5.25 miles each way)

Aerobic difficulty: Moderate; a few short, steep hills and easy, gradual grades

Technical difficulty: A combination of inter-mediate- and advanced-level terrain

Scenery: Beautiful, wooded trail at the base of Mount Megunticook

Special comments: Consider combining your ride with a hike up Mount Megunticook for spectacular views of Penobscot Bay

This out-and-back ride covers 5.25 miles (in each direction) along an old road that is used as a snowmobile trail in the winter. From the park entrance on US 1, the trail begins along undulating terrain, through the wooded slopes of Mount Megunticook. Because water is a problem along one particular stretch of the road, a narrow single-track trail has been cut to bypass this area. This trail, appropriately named the "summer bypass," is technically challenging and requires good bike handling skills. This section of the ride will be great fun for riders of advanced ability, and a rewarding challenge for intermediate riders interested in improving their skills. Once this bypass reconnects with the main trail, the terrain becomes more smooth and suitable for even novice riders.

The Camden Hills rise dramatically from the western shore of Penobscot Bay, creating a stunning backdrop to the town of Camden. In fact, a local saying describes the town as resting "where the mountains meet the sea." Camden Hills State Park includes Mount Battie, Cameron Mountain, Bald Rock Mountain, and Mount Megunticook. Reaching a height of 1,380 feet above sea level, Mount Megunticook is the second highest point along the Atlantic seaboard in the United States (Cadillac Mountain, farther up the coast, is the highest point, at 1,530 feet). Although riders cannot use the trails that climb these mountains, it is possible to ride up the toll road to the summit of Mount Battie, where you will be rewarded with a panoramic view of Penobscot Bay from a charming stone lookout tower. If you plan on spending the day in Camden, it is well worth combining your ride with a hike along any of the many trails open to hikers.

General location: Camden Hills State Park lies just a few miles north of Camden on US 1.

Elevation change: Despite the fact that there are so many mountains within the park, this ride features only gradual changes in elevation. There are short climbs along undulating terrain, and a gradual slope from the site of the ski shelter to Youngtown Road.

Season: This trail is open from late spring through fall, or as conditions permit. Be sure to check with park personnel, or consult the sign at the trailhead to determine whether the trail is open.

Services: All services are available in Camden, where there are two bike shops: Fred's Bikes, located at 53 Chestnut Street, (207) 236-6664; and Oggi-bike, at 29 Mountain Street, (207) 236-3631. There is a camping area at Camden Hills State Park.

Hazards: This trail may be heavily used by hikers, particularly from the northern trailhead off Youngtown Road.

Rescue index: Halfway through this ride, you will be at the farthest point from assistance: 2.5 miles from park headquarters or Youngtown Road.

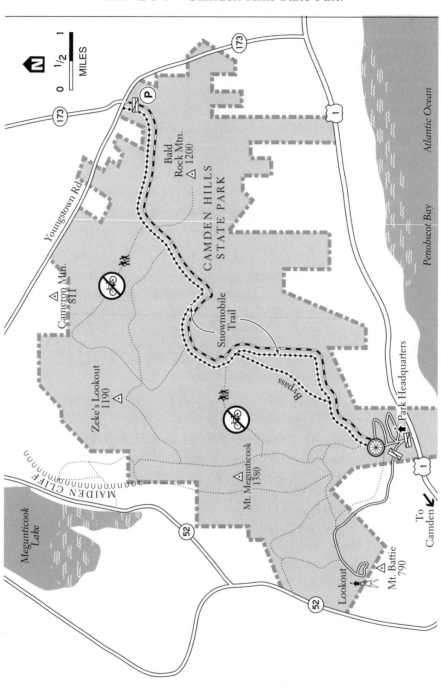

Rocks and ruts lurking beneath the leaves demand the complete attention of the mountain biker at Camden Hills State Park.

Land status: State park.

Maps: A map of the trail system is available at the information booth at the entrance to the park. The snowmobile trail, including the summer bypass, is the only trail open to mountain bikes.

Finding the trail: The park entrance is on US 1, just north of Camden.

Source of additional information:

Camden Hills State Park
Route 1
Camden, ME 04843
(207) 236-3109 or 236-0849

Notes on the trail: From the park entrance, begin pedaling up the paved road toward the camping area, following signs for the Mount Megunticook foot trail. Continue straight onto a gravel road. The trailhead is a short distance up this road, on the left. Be sure to read the sign at the trailhead, which will indicate whether or not the trail is open. A short distance from the trail-head, the snowmobile trail heads to the right toward a green water tower, splitting off from the Mount Megunticook foot trail, which is closed to bikes. The trail is fairly well maintained, following a distinct path through the woods. You will just be able to make out the ocean on the right, especially in the fall when leaves no longer obscure the view. After a little more than 1 mile, the summer bypass trail cuts off to the left. This trail will take you far-ther up the east slope of Mount Megunticook and is characterized by numer-ous dips and tight turns over more rocky and rooty terrain. When the trail re-joins the old road, turn left. You will cross a stream and pass the site of an old ski shelter.

The remainder of the ride, down to Youngtown Road, is less technical, and you will easily be able to take in the beauty of the surrounding woods. To return, merely retrace your route back to the park headquarters. Alterna-tively, it is possible to create a loop back to the parking area by turning left on Youngtown Road. At its intersection with ME 52, turn left again and then, as you enter Camden, turn left back onto US 1. Though this option requires riding on paved roads, the ride is quite scenic and offers a dramatic view of the sheer, 800-foot drop of Maiden Cliff from the eastern shore of Lake Megunticook.

RIDE 52 · Hope

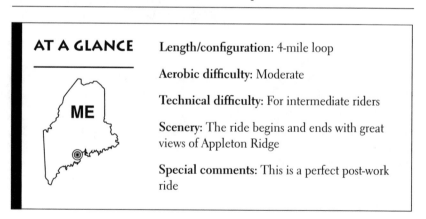

AT A GLANCE	
	Length/configuration: 4-mile loop
	Aerobic difficulty: Moderate
	Technical difficulty: For intermediate riders
	Scenery: The ride begins and ends with great views of Appleton Ridge
	Special comments: This is a perfect post-work ride

This ride is a short four-mile loop that circles Philbrick Mountain in the town of Hope. The ride begins along an unpaved road, turns onto a grassy, abandoned road, and then climbs along more rugged double-track terrain around the southern slope of Philbrick Mountain. Despite its short distance, this ride ascends some rocky and rutted slopes that require at least an intermediate level of technical skill and a moderate level of physical fitness.

You will be traversing the wooded slopes of Philbrick Mountain for most of the ride. There is, however, a fantastic view at the trailhead; you will be able to look across a pasture toward Moody Mountain to the northeast. To the west, Appleton Ridge is visible, and the Appleton Ridge ride is not more than five miles away. Toward the end of the ride, you will come to a clearing that looks like an old logging yard. Blueberries grow in abundance here and provide excellent snacking when they ripen in August.

General location: This ride forms a loop around Philbrick Mountain, located in the town of Hope.

Elevation change: The trailhead is situated at 600', and the ride begins with a descent to 400'. From there, you will gain 300' to reach the western slope of Philbrick Mountain at 700'. Descending to 500', you will gain 350' riding up the steep eastern slope of Philbrick. The total elevation gain for the ride is 650'.

Season: Riding here is feasible from June through late fall. There is snowmobile traffic on the trails in the winter, and with studded tires, the trails make for superb winter riding.

Services: All services are available in Camden. In addition, there is a general store in Hope that will more than adequately satisfy any need for refreshments.

Hazards: Apart from a little rough terrain, there are no specific hazards on this ride.

Rescue index: You will remain within 2 miles of the homes and farms located on Pleasant Street, where assistance may be available.

Land status: Most of this ride makes use of old roads with continued public access. The final portion of the loop uses a farm road that passes through private property. At the time we rode, permission to use this trail was being granted to mountain bikers. As with all private ways, however, be respectful of the land you are riding on and be aware of any changes that may restrict access at certain times.

Maps: The route for this ride is shown in DeLorme's *Maine Atlas and Gazetteer* (map 14, section C-2). For further detail, consult the USGS quadrangle for the area, which is Searsmont.

Finding the trail: The town of Hope lies about 5 miles northwest of Camden, at the intersection of ME 105 and ME 235. At this intersection, continue driving west on ME 105 for 2.3 miles and turn left, after a hill, up Peasetown Road. Park at the top of the road, where the unpaved continuation of Peasetown Road continues to the right, and Pleasant Street, which is

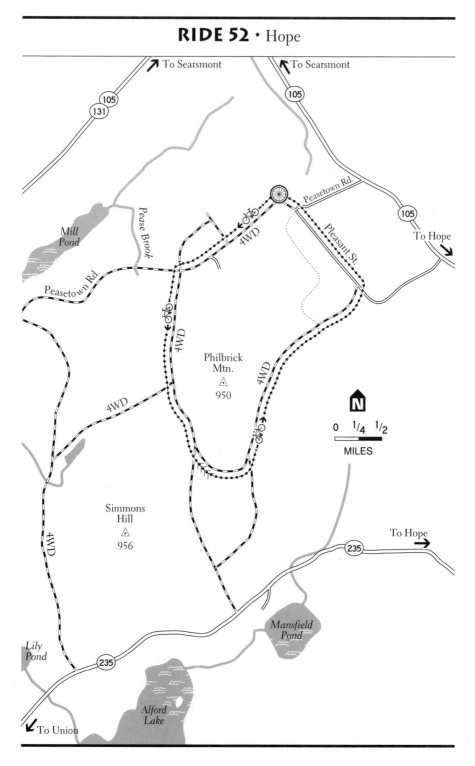

To Searsmont

To Searsmont

105
131

105

Mill
Pond

Pease Brook

Peasetown Rd.

Peasetown Rd.

4WD

4WD

4WD

4WD

4WD

4WD

Pleasant St.

105

To Hope

Philbrick
Mtn.
△
950

N

0   1/4   1/2

MILES

Simmons
Hill
△
956

To Hope

235

Mansfield
Pond

Lily
Pond

235

Alford
Lake

To Union

Rolling farmland and blueberry barrens surround the old, wooded roads of this ride in Hope.

paved, continues to the left. Take care not to block access to a gated field located at the edge of the road.

Sources of additional information: For information on riding in the area, contact one of three area bike and outfitting stores: Fred's Bikes, at 53 Chestnut Street, (207) 236-6664; Oggibike, at 29 Mountain Street, (207) 236-3631; and Maine Sport Outfitters, located on US 1 just south of Camden, (207) 236-8797 or (800) 722-0826.

Notes on the trail: From the trailhead at the corner of Peasetown Road and Pleasant Street, begin riding west along the unpaved portion of Peasetown Road. You will descend on this road, passing a road branching off to the left and another one branching off to the right. Beyond a small rise, the trail continues to descend; at this point begin looking for a wide trail on the left that will probably be marked with snowmobile signs. Turning left onto this trail, you will cross Pease Brook and continue along a trail that follows the route of an old road still marked by the steadfast line of a stone fence on the right. Pass a snowmobile trail that branches off to the right in the direction of Appleton, Union, and Sennebec Pond. You will be following signs for Hope, Camden, and Rockport.

Turn left onto a grassy trail at the next trail intersection. There are snow-mobile signs here indicating that you are entering the Hatchet Mountain Snowmobile Trail System. The grassy trail deteriorates quickly; you will cross several brooks and climb up a series of rutted and rocky inclines. As you reach the high point of the trail, you will once again be traveling on a grassy double-track trail that will be quite overgrown in the summer. This trail descends into an old logging yard. Follow the trail through this cleared area and then bear right into a field. Follow a farm track out to Pleasant Street, and turn left to re-turn to your vehicle.

RIDE 53 · Appleton Ridge

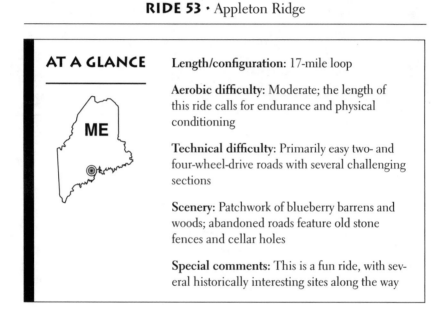

AT A GLANCE

Length/configuration: 17-mile loop

Aerobic difficulty: Moderate; the length of this ride calls for endurance and physical conditioning

Technical difficulty: Primarily easy two- and four-wheel-drive roads with several challenging sections

Scenery: Patchwork of blueberry barrens and woods; abandoned roads feature old stone fences and cellar holes

Special comments: This is a fun ride, with sev-eral historically interesting sites along the way

This 17-mile loop features a fantastic combination of startling views and woodsy trail riding. Beginning from the top of Appleton Ridge, the ride descends to the St. George River, offers a scenic side trip down to Newbert Pond, and returns past Pettengill Stream to the ridgetop. There is a stream crossing at the beginning of the ride, and the trail continues over a combina-tion of dirt roads and double- and single-track trails. Riders of intermediate ability will enjoy this ride, which includes enough technical challenges and covers enough distance to appeal to advanced-level riders as well.

The top of Appleton Ridge is covered with blueberry barrens. After the harvest in August, the bushes turn a brilliant scarlet and virtually light up the top of the ridge. The view from the ridgetop is stunning, overlooking Sennebec Pond on the southeast side and rolling hillsides in all directions. This ride follows the path of abandoned roads that once connected old farms and pastures with mills and town centers. Though many of these old roads were developed, widened, and eventually paved, some were merely abandoned and replaced by alternative routes. On this ride, you will have the opportunity to explore old mill sites; the hollow foundations of farms long since abandoned; and old roads that, though overgrown, worn, and rutted, still trace paths between stone fences.

General location: This ride traverses the northwest side of Appleton Ridge, just a few miles southwest of the town of Searsmont.

Elevation change: A series of short, moderate climbs and descents accumulates to a total of 930' in elevation gain.

Season: Due to the possibility of flooding along several sections of this trail, save this ride for late June through October. During hunting season, Sunday is the best day to ride unless you are willing to deck yourself out in bright colors. As well as the usual reflective vests, it is possible to purchase a blaze-orange cover for your helmet, which should clearly distinguish you from other wildlife.

Services: All services are available in Camden.

Hazards: You will have to ford the St. George River at the beginning of this ride. Follow the safety tips for river crossings outlined in the Preface. It is also quite likely that you will encounter equestrians at some point along this trail. Remember to yield to oncoming riders, and to alert horses and riders ahead of you that you are approaching.

Rescue index: Due to the number of secondary roads you will either cross or travel along during this ride, you will never be more than a few miles from a road or home.

Land status: For the most part, you will be riding along public throughways during this ride; be mindful of the fact that most of the adjoining land is private property. The side trip to Newbert Pond passes through land owned by the Nature Conservancy. It is extremely important that you stay on the trail we have described through this portion of the ride. The area around Newbert Pond, Appleton Bog, is a national natural landmark. It encompasses an area containing one of the northernmost stands of Atlantic white cedar in North America, a species that has become quite rare due to timber harvesting.

Maps: The USGS topographic maps for this ride are Searsmont and Washington. Most of the ride is also depicted in the DeLorme Mapping Company's *Maine Atlas and Gazetteer* (map 14, sections B-1, B-2, C-1, and C-2).

RIDE 53 · Appleton Ridge

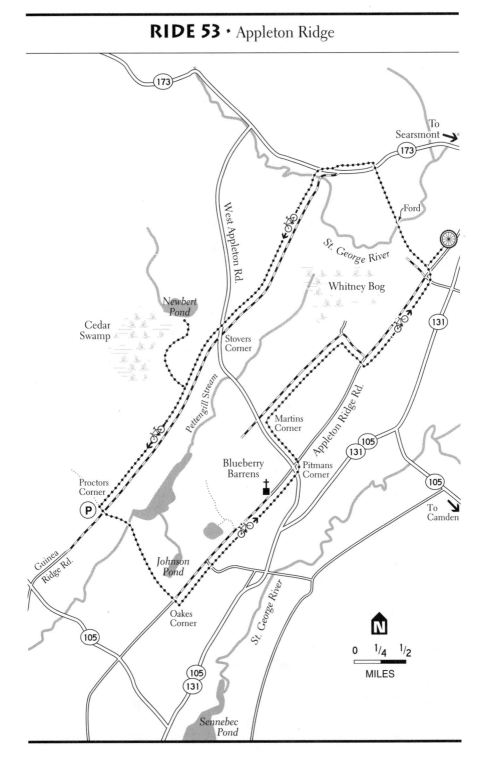

173

To
Searsmont

173

Ford

West Appleton Rd.

St. George River

Whitney Bog

Newbert
Pond

Cedar
Swamp

Stovers
Corner

131

Pettengill Stream

Martins
Corner

Appleton Ridge Rd.

105

Blueberry
Barrens

131

Pitmans
Corner

105

Proctors
Corner

P

105

To
Camden

Guinea
Ridge Rd.

Johnson
Pond

Oakes
Corner

St. George River

105

N

0   1/4   1/2

MILES

105

131

Sennebec
Pond

Despite recent development, a network of abandoned roads still provides access to the St. George River, Newbert Pond, and Pettengill Stream at the base of Appleton Ridge.

Finding the trail: Appleton Ridge and Appleton Ridge Road parallel ME 131 between Union and Searsmont. From Searsmont, drive south on ME 131. After just 1 mile, bear right onto Appleton Ridge Road. The road climbs, descends just slightly, and reaches the crest of a hill that, to your right, has been cleared for the cultivation of blueberries. Look for a tiny pull-in on the right side of the road, which offers just enough space for parking several vehicles.

Sources of additional information: None.

Notes on the trail: From the small parking area at the top of the blueberry barren, begin your ride by continuing to travel south on Appleton Ridge Road. You will descend, passing a tree farm on the right, before reaching the base of the hill. You will notice a road on the left and a small trail on the right. This trail, blocked against vehicular traffic by several large boulders, marks the trailhead. Turn right onto this trail, which is in fact an overgrown old road alongside which old stone fences are still standing. The beginning of this trail includes some wet areas, which diminish as the trail descends slightly and enters a fairly dense forest.

As the trail appears to make a sharp turn to the left, look to the right and see a much narrower trail continuing through the trees. Take this trail on the right, and after just 0.1 mile, you will find yourself on the banks of the St. George River. Tall oaks, maples, and firs grace the banks of this river, which flows south, unhurried, toward Thomaston and St. George into Muscongus Bay. It is well worth exploring the riverbank because upriver just a short distance is the site of an old bridge. A short walk downriver is equally interesting, as there is an old dam and mill site. The trail continues straight across the river on the other side, and there is no way to continue the ride without getting wet feet.

Once across the river, the trail continues up a short bank and quickly re-connects with what used to be the main road. Bear right here, although you may want first to turn left to explore the old bridge site from this side of the river. The terrain from this point on becomes quite overgrown. You will have to wrestle your way through alders that have grown up in the old road because of wet conditions brought on by flooding due to beaver activity. Beyond this area, the trail opens up again, and you will pass an abandoned school bus. The apple trees nearby betray this spot as an old house site, and if you walk into the woods for just a short distance, you will come to a clearing and the re-mains of a foundation to what once was a large barn.

Beyond the abandoned school bus, the trail widens into an improved dirt road. At an intersection with a paved road (ME 173), turn left and proceed no more than 0.25 mile, until you see a rough paved road branching off to the left. Turn down this road, which soon deteriorates into a jeep trail and crosses the St. George River by way of a plank bridge with metal railings. Continue straight on this jeep trail, past a cabin on the left and a grassy trail bearing off to the right and following the riverbank. Recent logging operations along this road have left it rutted, wet, and washboarded. You will, however, ride beyond this area and continue to follow the road as it narrows. You will pass a snow-mobile trail on the left and a spruce plantation on the right. Several woods roads also branch off either side of this road, but the route remains clear as long as you stay straight.

About 3.5 miles into the ride, this road improves and you will pass a blue-berry barren on the left. At a four-way intersection with the paved West Apple-ton Road, you are at Stovers Corner. Cross the road and continue on the other side, riding up a dirt road riddled with hollows and dips that are usually filled with water. After only 0.25 mile, keep your eyes open for a grassy trail that branches off the right side of the main road. This trail may be signed for snowmobiles, and it leads into land protected by the Nature Conservancy. Al-though the trip is an out-and-back affair, it is well worth bearing right down this trail and making your way to Newbert Pond. You will ride over rugged double- and single-track trails through the woods, descending to the pond and toward an area referred to as Cedar Swamp, the natural area protected by the Nature Conservancy.

As you begin the ride to Newbert Pond, you will descend gradually to a **T** intersection that resembles a hairpin turn. Bear left here (you will notice a gated way on the right). The trail descends before rising again and crossing a small clearing and an old stone fence. Bear left just beyond this stone fence, noticing another trail that proceeds downhill on the right. As you come to a small bog on the left, bear right down the hill (though the trail also continues straight ahead along a small ridge). This trail continues to descend all the way to the pond. In the winter, snowmobile traffic crosses the frozen water over the pond, but in the summer months, the trail stops at the water's edge. Newbert Pond makes a good rest or lunch spot, and chances are good that you won't encounter anyone else at the water's edge. Return to the main trail by retracing your route.

Back at the dirt road, turn right to continue in the direction you were traveling. Almost immediately, bear right at a fork in the road. You will continue riding straight along this road until you reach what is called Proctors Corner, a four-way intersection that now marks the point where the improved Rowel Road meets the jeep trail. There is a narrow, rough, old road on the right that leads to Sawpit Corner, but the ride continues along the road to the left. You will pass a house on the left, and another one on the right, before the road once again deteriorates into a rough jeep trail. Ride past a rough trail on the right that will probably be chained or gated. You will then reach a rickety snowmobile bridge that crosses Pettengill Stream at the site of a dam and an old mill. To your left, across the water, you will be treated to a fine view of one of the blueberry barrens on the northeast slope of Appleton Ridge. Crossing the snowmobile bridge, you will quickly encounter a rough trail heading up Johnson Hill. This stretch of the ride is much narrower than the previous jeep trail and is considerably more difficult in terms of the technical skill required to negotiate the rather steep, rocky climb. In the late autumn, many of the rocks, roots, hollows, and dips will be artfully obscured by fallen leaves. Take some time, nevertheless, to notice the stone fences and old foundations along this trail.

Continuing up this old road, you will pass a snowmobile trail cutting into the woods on the right just before reaching the southern shore of Johnson Pond. As you come to the end of the pond, a footpath will be visible on the left. This path offers access to some rocks and ledges that afford a good view of the pond and make good resting and snacking spots. Just 0.25 mile farther up the road, you will come to Appleton Ridge Road, at a junction called Oakes Corner. On your left will be a blueberry barren, and across the road will be a great big old house that looks down on Sennebec Pond. Turn left here and enjoy the views as you ride along Appleton Ridge Road. Pass Sprague Cemetery on the left and enjoy a swift descent to Pitmans Corner, a four-way intersection with Town Hill Road on the right and West Appleton Road on the left. Turn left up West Appleton Road. You will climb and crest a hill on the top of which there are several chicken houses on the right. Begin the descent, but keep your eyes open for Pettengill Lane on the left.

Very soon after passing Pettengill Lane, turn right onto another rough jeep trail that is bordered by old stone fences. This intersection is known as Martins Corner. Ride along the jeep trail, which becomes a more improved road, and follow it around a sharp turn to the right. Shortly after, you will come to a T intersection with Appleton Ridge Road. Turn left and you will reach the trailhead and parking area in just under 2 miles.

RIDE 54 · Frye Mountain

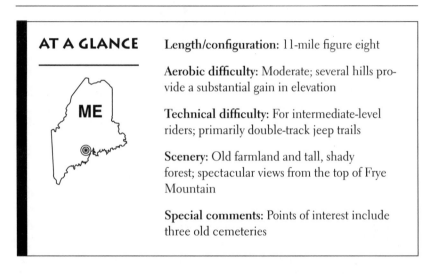

AT A GLANCE

Length/configuration: 11-mile figure eight

Aerobic difficulty: Moderate; several hills provide a substantial gain in elevation

Technical difficulty: For intermediate-level riders; primarily double-track jeep trails

Scenery: Old farmland and tall, shady forest; spectacular views from the top of Frye Mountain

Special comments: Points of interest include three old cemeteries

This interesting 11-mile ride through Frye Mountain State Game Management Area follows a combination of dirt roads and double-track trails in what is almost a figure eight configuration. There is only one stretch of technically difficult riding down an eroded, rock-strewn, old road. This short portion of the ride can be walked by less experienced riders. Several hills, while featuring relatively even surfaces, require a reasonable level of cardiovascular fitness. Overall, the ride can be rated for intermediate riders.

The 5,111 acres that make up the management area around Frye Mountain include upland forests and abandoned farm fields—a combination that creates an excellent habitat for deer and small mammals. Evidence that much of this land was once used for farming can be seen in the old stone fences, apple orchards, and remains of old foundations.

You will ride past several cemeteries, one of which is at least 200 years old. Named Pierce Hill Cemetery, it is elevated slightly from the trail and heavily shaded by old trees. If you don't stop anywhere else along this ride, take a minute or two to wander the footpaths that still meander through this cemetery. You will be able to decipher worn names on weathered, gray stones and move just a bit closer to the lives of people who once farmed the land nearby.

Farther along, you will pedal up a rugged forest service road that climbs southeast to the summit of Frye Mountain at 1,139 feet. At the summit, you can climb the ladder to the top of a Maine Forest Service fire tower and enjoy a 360° view of the surrounding countryside, including Penobscot Bay to the southeast. The ledge summit of the mountain is also a perfect place to take a break and stretch out on sun-warmed rocks.

General location: Frye Mountain is located in the Waldo County town of Montville, 12 miles west of Belfast.

Elevation change: At the parking area on Walker Ridge Road, your elevation will be 550'. You will climb to Carter Cemetery at 842'. Turning right on Tower Lois Lane, continue climbing to 900'. From there, you will descend to 770' before climbing Pierce Hill to reach an elevation of 860'. Riding downhill, past Pierce Hill Cemetery, you will drop to 500'. From this point, you will gain 438' in 5.5 miles to reach the trail to the fire tower. The fire tower is located at the summit of the mountain, at 1,139' above sea level. From the fire tower, only a few slight grades interrupt the descent to the trailhead. Including the trip to the fire tower, total possible elevation gain is approximately 1,080'.

Season: Good riding conditions generally begin in late May and continue through the fall. Because hunting is permitted in the management area, Sunday is the best day to ride during hunting season.

Services: There are no services available within the management area. Restaurants and general stores are scattered throughout small, nearby towns, but all bicycling needs will have to be met in Waterville, Augusta, or Camden.

Hazards: Approximately 3 miles into the ride, the trail descends along an old road that is severely eroded in some places. Caution should be used by all riders negotiating this descent.

Rescue index: You will remain within 2 miles of the few homes and camps that lie along this route.

Land status: Frye Mountain Game Management Area is state land managed by the Fish and Wildlife Department.

Maps: This ride is mapped in its entirety in the DeLorme Mapping Company's *Maine Atlas and Gazetteer* (map 14, sections A-1 and A-2). The USGS quad is Morrill.

Finding the trail: From Interstate 95 in Augusta, take Exit 30 and travel east on ME 100. Crossing the Kennebec River and continuing north along the east bank, you will come to the junction with ME 3. Turn east onto ME 3

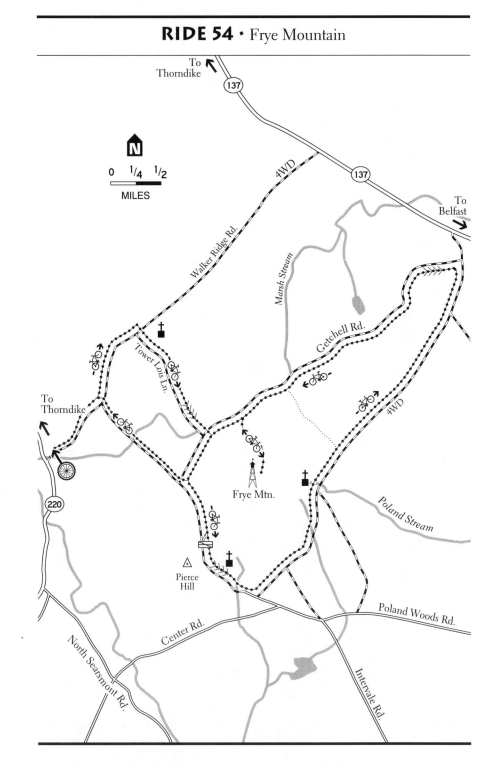

To
Thorndike

137

137

To
Belfast

N

0   1/4   1/2

MILES

4WD

Walker Ridge Rd.

Marsh Stream

Getchell Rd.

Tower Lois Ln.

To
Thorndike

220

4WD

Frye Mtn.

Poland Stream

Pierce
Hill

Poland Woods Rd.

Center Rd.

North Searsmont Rd.

Intervale Rd.

One of several old cemeteries that provide a fascinating glimpse into the past of Frye Mountain.

and travel through South China and Palmero toward Lake St. George. Beyond the lake, turn north on ME 220, following the road as it swings to the right at Whites Corner and then to the left at Beans Corner. The entrance to Frye Mountain Management Area will be on the right just a mile past Beans Corner. Turn onto a dirt road (Walker Ridge Road) and pull into a cleared area on the left that is marked by a clubhouse and an outhouse.

Source of additional information:

Department of Inland Fisheries and Wildlife
284 State Street
41 State House Station
Augusta, ME 04333-0041
(207) 287-8000

Notes on the trail: The ride begins from the parking area off ME 220 and commences up unpaved Walker Ridge Road. Ride to Carter Cemetery and turn right on Tower Lois Lane, just before the cemetery and across from a stand of beautiful locust trees. After climbing a short distance, you will cruise down Tower Lois Lane to a T intersection. Turn right. At the next intersection, turn uphill to the left. You will pedal up a gradual grade to a small, grassy clearing at the top of Pierce Hill. An orange-colored gate restricts vehicular access down the next portion of the trail, which descends on a severely eroded old road. Ride around the gate and follow the road as it descends past a meadow and then enters the woods. After crossing a rocky stream bed, you will reach the site of Pierce Hill Cemetery on the left. Beyond the cemetery, the road improves and you will ride past Stone Wall Farm Antiques.

After passing the farm, look for a rough trail on the left that comes just before a small house (also on the left). Turn left onto this trail and ride through a rather damp and watery area created by beaver activity. The advantage of the clearing created by this water is that you will get a view of Frye Mountain on the left. Beyond the beaver flowage, the trail is a beautiful, hard-packed double-track through the woods. Continue straight at an intersection with Rowe Mill Road (on your right) and Sunnyside Cemetery (on your left). The next intersection you reach will be with the main access road into the management area: Getchell Road. Turn left onto this road and prepare yourself for a little hill-climbing. After covering 2 miles on Getchell Road, watch for a trail on the left that is signed as the access road to the fire tower. The trail to the fire tower climbs quite steeply and requires some technical skill. You will, in fact, reach the side of a cliff where you will have to leave your bike and continue following a footpath to the summit.

Descending from the fire tower, turn left back onto Getchell Road. Continue past the intersection with Tower Lois Lane on the right and then turn right at the next T-intersection. You should recognize this intersection; at the beginning of the ride, you turned left at this intersection to climb Pierce Hill. In roughly 1 mile, you will be back at Walker Ridge Road; turn left and return to the parking area.

RIDE 55 · Isle au Haut

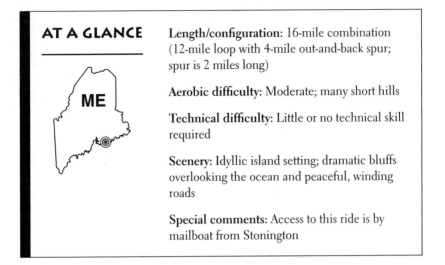

AT A GLANCE

ME

Length/configuration: 16-mile combination (12-mile loop with 4-mile out-and-back spur; spur is 2 miles long)

Aerobic difficulty: Moderate; many short hills

Technical difficulty: Little or no technical skill required

Scenery: Idyllic island setting; dramatic bluffs overlooking the ocean and peaceful, winding roads

Special comments: Access to this ride is by mailboat from Stonington

It is possible to ride completely around Isle au Haut using a combination of paved and dirt roads. This loop around the island, including a side trip down Western Head Road at the southern tip of the island, makes for a 16-mile ride. Just five miles of the loop are ridden on paved roads, while the remainder follows an improved dirt road and a few miles on a more rugged jeep trail. The route is not difficult to follow and is characterized by short, moderate hills. Riders of all abilities will be able to manage the terrain on Isle au Haut, though it is important to be able to carry extra clothing, food, and water for the trip.

Mountain biking on Isle au Haut is an adventure that begins from the Atlantic Avenue Hardware Dock in Stonington. Because parking is limited, it is best to arrive early and enjoy the sight of early morning mist rising from the shore as the quiet harbor comes alive. The trip to Isle au Haut is made by mailboat. Be sure to arrange your passage on the boat that disembarks at the town landing on Isle au Haut. In the summer, direct service to Duck Harbor, the main entrance of Acadia National Park, is also offered. Although this service is designed to accommodate day trippers and overnight campers to the park, bicycles are not permitted on these runs.

The mailboat leaves from the dock in Stonington without much fanfare. Beyond the small harbor, the bay is dotted with tree-covered islands with names like Potato Island, Devil Island, Ram Island, and No Man's Island. As you head out across the water, the first island you pass on the right is Crotch Island. Clearly visible from the boat are the granite facilities on this island, where some of the best granite in the world is quarried. Granite from Crotch Island built the Brooklyn Bridge, Rockefeller Center Plaza, and the Kennedy Memorial. Crotch Island is the only commercial quarry left in Maine.

The trip from Stonington to the town landing on Isle au Haut takes about 45 minutes. From the mailboat run over potentially choppy waters, to the rugged island coastline and the solitude of the southern park area, a trip to Isle au Haut is an exhilarating experience. For some, the intrigue and appeal of the island have been lasting, and, as a result, a year-round fishing community is joined in the summer months by numbers of part-time residents. In 1943, heirs of the founder of the original summer community donated land in the southern portion of the island to the federal government as part of Acadia National Park. During the summer season, you may be surprised that you are met at the town landing by a ranger from the park. Rangers will be able to answer most questions you may have about the island and are generally available to guide visitors to the park.

If you have planned to spend the day on Isle au Haut, consider leaving your bike at any one of the trailheads to the hiking trails. One option that we highly recommend is to ride out to the end of Western Head Road, park your bike, and begin hiking on the Cliff Trail. For a loop of two to three miles, continue on the Western Head Trail, which eventually turns inland and reconnects with Western Head Road—which you would then want to follow to the right in order to return to your bike. This loop will take you along the southern cliffs of Isle au Haut and offers breathtaking views of the Gulf of Maine. To those of you who usually ride with clipless pedals, consider switching back to toe clips so that you can wear a pair of light hiking boots that will serve you well on the trails.

General location: Isle au Haut is located in East Penobscot Bay, several miles south of the town of Stonington on Deer Isle.

Elevation change: Isle au Haut, when translated from the French, literally means "high island." The island can indeed be seen across the water for great distances, and the road that loops around it climbs and descends numerous hills.

Season: There is year-round mailboat service to Isle au Haut from Stonington. Although reduced rates from the middle of October through the middle of April offer an excellent incentive for off-season riding, both your boat trip and your tour of the island will be more enjoyable in warmer weather. Because access to Isle au Haut is limited to the mailboat, there is no service to the island on postal holidays. In addition, there is very limited Sunday service.

Unless you plan on camping and have secured a reservation, it is best to plan your trip to Isle au Haut for a whole day, arriving on one of the earliest boats and departing on one of the latest.

RIDE 55 · Isle au Haut

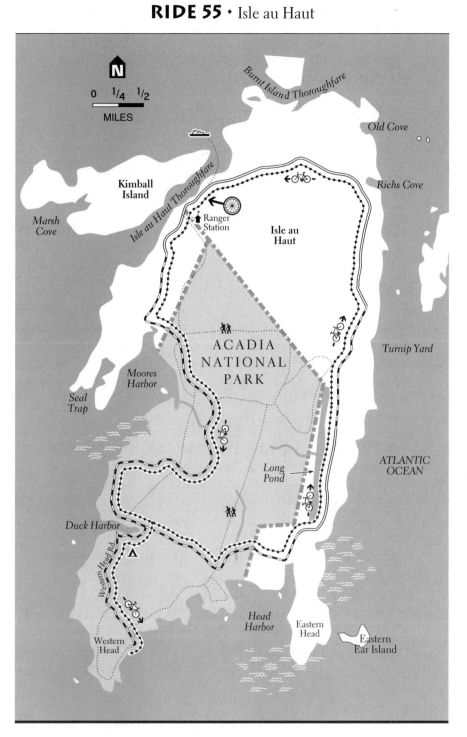

N

0   1/4   1/2
MILES

Burnt Island Thoroughfare

Old Cove

Kimball Island

Richs Cove

Marsh Cove

Isle au Haut Thoroughfare

Ranger Station

Isle au Haut

ACADIA NATIONAL PARK

Moores Harbor

Seal Trap

Turnip Yard

Long Pond

ATLANTIC OCEAN

Duck Harbor

Western Head Rd.

Western Head

Head Harbor

Eastern Head

Eastern Ear Island

Services: Other than a small store on the island, a ranger station for directions, and the opportunity to camp at Duck Harbor, there are no other services available on the island. For information on camping, contact Acadia National Park at P.O. Box 177, Bar Harbor, ME 04609, or by calling (207) 288-3338.

Hazards: It is important to carefully plan your trip to Isle au Haut. Not only are there very few services available on the island, but weather conditions can change quickly. Keep in mind, also, that you need to allow enough space in your schedule to return to the town landing in time to catch the boat back to Stonington. Be sure you have a current boat timetable.

Rescue index: Although the park maintains a ranger station and there are summer cottages and year-round residences on the island, some sections of this ride, particularly in the southern park area, are quite remote.

Land status: Almost half of Isle au Haut is federal park land; the other half is privately owed. Public access is permitted along the road that loops around the island.

Maps: Visitors to Isle au Haut are very obvious to the captains of the mailboat; you will most likely be handed a map of the island on the boat. Maps are also available at the ranger station, or may be obtained by contacting Acadia National Park at the address and phone number listed below.

Finding the trail: Stonington is located on the southern tip of Deer Isle, at the end of ME 15. To get to Stonington, head south on ME 15 from US 1, just a few miles east of Bucksport. Follow ME 15 through Blue Hill, across a bridge over Eggemoggin Reach to Little Deer Isle, across the causeway to Deer Isle, and down to the southernmost tip of the island. The mailboat leaves from the Atlantic Avenue Hardware Dock.

Sources of additional information:

Acadia National Park
P.O. Box 177
Bar Harbor, ME 04609
(207) 288-3338

Isle au Haut Ferry Company
Stonington, ME 04681
(207) 367-5193

Notes on the trail: From the town landing on Isle au Haut, pedal up to the main road and turn right to begin your ride. You will pass the ranger station on the left. Shortly after the ranger station, the road becomes unpaved. Stay to the main road, keeping off private drives and all hiking trails in the park portion of the island. To make the out-and-back trip to Western Head, bear right on Western Head Road just past Duck Harbor (you will be able to see a

Quintessential Maine coastline.

large concrete landing in Duck Harbor). This road will take you right down to the shore, where several hiking trails lead to dramatic cliffs along the rugged coastline.

Re-trace your way back up Western Head Road and turn right at the junction with the main road. You will ride along a short stretch of paved road at the southern tip of Long Pond, and then return to gravel. About three quarters of the way up the east side of the island, the road becomes paved again, and you will complete your ride back to the town landing on pavement.

PENOBSCOT VALLEY

The watershed of the Penobscot River drains the heart of Maine. From where it draws its first drops, just northwest of Jackman on the South Branch and near the St. John River on the North Branch, the river threads its way between two other great rivers, the St. John and the Kennebec, passing within five miles of each. All three rivers claim their headwaters within a roughly 30-mile radius around Seboomook Lake. The Penobscot starts out as two branches, simply named North and South, which cascade through a series of rips, gorges, and falls, before linking together and pooling in a series of large lakes. The lakes are man-made, created at a time when the river was the mode by which logs were moved from the stump to the mill. They were constructed to capture the spring runoff, storing it to ensure there was adequate water to float the logs to the saw mills located downriver.

After passing in the shadow of Mount Katahdin, the river winds through the paper mill towns of Millinocket and East Millinocket. Just past East Millinocket the river joins with the East Branch, so named because it drains the eastern part of the Penobscot watershed. It is now a significant river, the calm surface concealing the swift current running beneath it. Passing by the river towns of Medway, Mattawamkeag, the great mill at Lincoln, and Howland, the river continues on to Old Town, where it splits. Along with parts of Old Town and Orono, the University of Maine is situated on the island at the middle of this split.

Beyond the island, it is a quick eight miles to Bangor, where ships were once moored, gunwale to gunwale, while lumber and other wood products were loaded. It was said that so many ships used to assemble in Bangor that it was possible to walk from one side of the river to the other by hopping from deck to deck. It is also in Bangor that the river first feels the effect of the tide. Beyond Bangor, the river widens, passing the former shipbuilding, fishing, and farming communities of Orrington, Hampden, and Winterport. The homes of former sea captains dot the high bluffs overlooking the river, attesting to the area's maritime heritage. Penobscot Bay, one of the finest along the coast, is where the river finally terminates.

For mountain bikers, the Penobscot River Valley offers moderately sized hills and mostly wooded trails. The long history of settlement in the area has left an extensive network of old farm roads crisscrossing the area. These roads, now excellent mountain biking trails, traverse challenging and undulating terrain. The surface of these old roads is very similar now to what it was when they were first constructed. Plagued by mud in the spring and snow and ice in the winter, travel was limited to the dryer seasons of summer and fall. One can only speculate how mountain bikes might have facilitated travel at the turn of the century! As you ride, try to visualize what the low hills must have looked like at that time, when they were completely devoid of trees.

Bangor is the major urban center in the area. A relatively small city by U.S. standards, it boasts a population of approximately 33,000. It is considered Maine's third largest city. Most amenities can be found in Bangor. It is home to a number of decent restaurants, a brew pub, and several bicycle shops. Eight miles north of Bangor, in the town of Orono, is the flagship campus of the University of Maine system.

LOGGING ON THE PENOBSCOT

This part of Maine is considered by many to be untrammeled wilderness. It has, in fact, been altered greatly since the first Europeans arrived in the area. Logging started in the early 1800s and progressed up the river as the great pines that grew along its sandy banks were harvested. At one time, Maine boasted immense trees some five or six feet in diameter. The labor cycle of the region provided continuous employment for men. In the summer and fall they would work their farms. After harvest, the farmers would travel by foot and buckboard into the woods. There they would construct the camp where they were to live throughout the winter.

Life in the camps provided much of the lore from this era. Conditions were harsh, with food lacking in variety (mostly beans!) though rarely in quantity. Throughout the winter, the men cut trees and used oxen and horses to drag the logs to the riverbank. In the spring, as soon as the waterways were mostly free of ice, the logs were rolled into the streams and floated to the mills. Both timing and luck were necessary for a successful drive. Low water, log jams, and fast water made this a risky activity for all participants. Many river drivers perished on the log drives. After a fatality, the body would be buried on the riverbank, near where it was recovered. The dead driver's boots, distinctive because of the caulks in the soles, would be nailed to a tree near the grave. It is said that some of the boots were still visible on the trees 20 or more years after being placed there.

Just before the river reached Bangor, a series of booms across it collected the logs. The piers to which the booms were anchored are still visible in the river today. The logs were then sorted and turned over to their owners. Each log had the owner's symbol stamped in each end for identification. It wasn't until the completion of the drives that the men received compensation for their work. Bangor sported a number of establishments that catered to the men coming out of the woods. Bars, brothels, and various other establishments sprang up to try to separate the men from their pay. Many of the men lost everything they had earned and returned penniless to their farms, to start the cycle all over again.

RIDE 56 · Mount Waldo

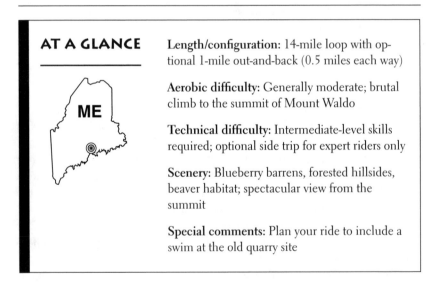

AT A GLANCE

ME

Length/configuration: 14-mile loop with optional 1-mile out-and-back (0.5 miles each way)

Aerobic difficulty: Generally moderate; brutal climb to the summit of Mount Waldo

Technical difficulty: Intermediate-level skills required; optional side trip for expert riders only

Scenery: Blueberry barrens, forested hillsides, beaver habitat; spectacular view from the summit

Special comments: Plan your ride to include a swim at the old quarry site

This 14-mile loop is a pleasant ride along four-wheel-drive roads and single-track trails. From blueberry barrens to deep, shaded forest, the landscape is one of diversity. Intermediate riders in good physical condition will find the ride moderately challenging. There is an optional side trip to the top of Mount Waldo that will challenge even the fittest and most skilled riders.

Although this ascent is only half a mile long, it features a thigh-burning, 560-foot gain in elevation over exposed rock. At an elevation of 1,040 feet, the summit is the highest point in Waldo County and provides spectacular views of the Penobscot River Valley to the north and Penobscot Bay to the south. The trip to the summit, popular among local mountain bikers, is naturally followed by a terrifying descent.

Mount Waldo was the sight of one of the more important granite quarrying operations in Maine. A second side trip up the eastern slope of the mountain leads to an old quarry that now serves as a popular swimming hole. Quarrying commenced at the site in 1851 by Pierce, Rowe and Co., and lasted until 1969, when the final owners, Grenci and Ellis of New York, declared bankruptcy. The story of Mount Waldo granite is replete with unionism and danger and reveals the inevitable tie between granite production and economic conditions. While the economy permitted, Mount Waldo granite was used in many structures, including bridges and buildings in places such as New York, Philadelphia, St. Louis, and Washington. Granite production ended with the introduction of other building materials such as sandstone and concrete, which were less expensive to produce and much easier to transport.

Quarrying was done by workers called "cutters." The granite was removed by drilling a series of holes along a seam. A tapered plug was then hammered into the holes, causing the granite to fracture along the seam. The spoils piles you see near the quarry site are evidence that it was difficult to split the granite exactly, and often mistakes were made when the rock did not fracture as intended. From Mount Waldo, the blocks were transported via railway to a cutting shed located along the banks of Marsh Stream. In the cutting shed, the granite was cut to a desired shape with large saws. The granite was then loaded onto barges and shipped to its destination. The remains of the cutting operation, the partially buried hull of a granite barge, and a wharf can still be seen from US 1A near Mendall Marsh Wildlife Refuge.

General location: This ride is located in the town of Frankfort.

Elevation change: Most of this ride covers only moderately hilly terrain around the base of Mount Waldo. The side trip to the summit features a gain of 560'. If you make the trip up to the old quarry site, you will gain an additional 400'.

Season: You can ride this trail from mid-May to early October.

Services: There are convenience stores located in Frankfort, Prospect, and Winterport. The closest bicycle shop is Birgfeld's in Searsport.

Hazards: The granite on Mount Waldo (known as Maine "slickrock") is completely unforgiving. Ride with caution; many riders have been injured on Mount Waldo. Loose gravel on the granite can act like ball bearings, sending

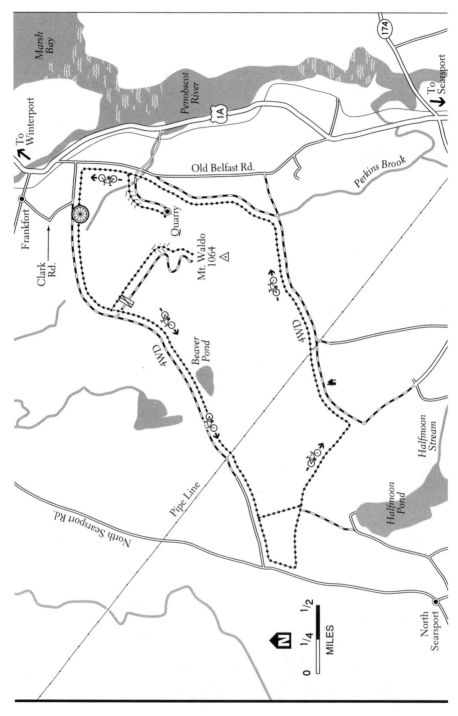

careless riders flying. There are also sudden drop-offs that may not be readily apparent.

If you choose to ascend the road to the top of Mount Waldo, please stick to the well-worn trails that have been established already. The mosses and lichens found at the top cling to the thin layer of organic material and gravel that overlays the granite. Some of the lichens are hundreds of years old and are nearly impossible to reestablish once lost. You will see how vehicular travel has devastated the vegetation on the side of the mountain.

This is a private road and its continued use is contingent on the respect shown by users.

The roads around the mountain have many eroded sections. There may be beaver ponds across some of the roads. If you stop to swim at the old quarry, look out for glass and don't dive in head first (despite what you see the locals doing).

Rescue index: You may be as far as 3 miles from assistance.

Land status: This trail uses a combination of discontinued town roads and a private road to the top of Mount Waldo.

Maps: The DeLorme Mapping Company's *Maine Atlas and Gazetteer* shows this trail (map 22, sections D-5 and E-5; map 23, sections D-1 and E-1). We suggest that you obtain a copy of the USGS quad for the area (Mount Waldo), which shows alternative routes that may be useful in the event that the main trail is blocked by a beaver pond.

Finding the trail: Frankfort Village is located approximately 15 miles south of Bangor on US 1A. After you cross Marsh Stream (where there is a fire station on the left), take the first right onto Loggin Road. Look for an immediate left before you pass beneath the railroad trestle. Go up the steep hill, following the road as it bears sharply to the left.

After only 0.6 mile, turn right onto a paved road. Continue straight onto the unpaved portion of this road as the main throughway bears right. After a short distance you will see a small pulloff on the left where you can park. On the right side of the road there should be a large blueberry barren.

Source of additional information: Birgfeld's Bicycle Shop (phone (207) 548-2916 or (800) 206-2916) has very limited information about this route.

Notes on the trail: From the parking spot, continue up the old road through the blueberry barrens. Resist the temptation to gorge in the field for 2 reasons: This is a commercial operation, and helping yourself will be viewed as theft by the owners. Second, the fields are sprayed with pesticides that may be toxic depending on how soon after the application the berries are consumed.

At just over 1 mile, the road splits. The left road, which is gated, begins the 2-mile out-and-back trip to the top of Mount Waldo. Follow it for just a short distance before the trail heads straight up over the exposed granite. Take some time at the top to enjoy the view, and then return to the main road and turn left. You will continue riding straight on the dirt road, passing through a cross-roads with a pipeline and past a beaver pond on the left. At the next fork in the road, bear right along an obvious descent over steep, rocky terrain into the woods. You will pass beneath a power line, over another washed-out section of the road, and past a road that branches off to the left. Beyond this point, the road improves, and you will come to a **T** intersection with the paved Searsport Road. Turn left.

After traveling only 0.6 mile on Searsport Road, look for an indistinct woods trail on the left. This intersection comes just before the power lines cross from the left to the right side of the road. There are no other good land-marks to indicate this trail, so look carefully. Pedal straight along this woods trail until you come to a four-way intersection congested with the remains of numerous junk cars. Continue straight through this intersection even though the main road bears right. Pedal through the next wooded section of the trail until it joins a slightly improved dirt road. Bear left at this junction and pass an old farmhouse on the right. As you continue riding, you will recross the pipeline you passed over earlier in the ride. Continue straight, following the snowmobile signs for ITS 82N. The left turn along the pipeline will return you to the first leg of the ride, near the base of Mount Waldo.

Beyond the pipeline intersection, there was a beaver pond blocking the trail when we rode here. Although we did manage to cross the pond by means of wading and walking along the dam, it was not without a struggle. Since then, the dam may have been breached. If it hasn't, you can ride back to the pipeline and turn right to reconnect with the road at the base of Mount Waldo or you can get wet! If you choose to wade, carry a stick to gauge the depth of the water and keep your shoes on. The trail is visible, emerging from the water on the other side.

Beyond the site of the beaver dam, there is an intersection. Continue straight along the old road until you pass a house on the left. From this point, the road conditions are greatly improved. Turn left where the road splits and pass by a clearing with great views of Mount Waldo. Shortly after, you will come to an intersection with a paved road. Turn left and descend the hill until you come to a four-way intersection. If you feel inclined to swim in the old quarry, turn left at this intersection and climb the hill. The road will be-come rockier and steeper, and most riders will choose to dismount and walk their bikes. As you ascend the trail, you will see the ties left over from the rail-way that was used to carry the granite blocks from the quarry to the ware-houses located beside the river. Continue along this trail until you reach the quarry. This is a popular place to swim in the summer. Backtrack to the paved road at the four-way intersection, and turn left to continue the ride.

Turn onto the first paved road you come to on the left. Retrace the way you drove in, continuing straight onto the unpaved portion of the road to return to your car.

RIDE 57 · Monroe

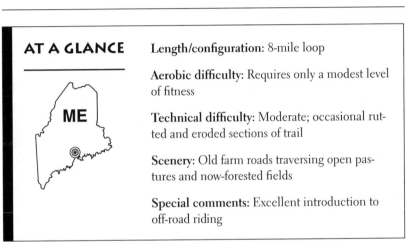

AT A GLANCE

ME

Length/configuration: 8-mile loop

Aerobic difficulty: Requires only a modest level of fitness

Technical difficulty: Moderate; occasional rutted and eroded sections of trail

Scenery: Old farm roads traversing open pastures and now-forested fields

Special comments: Excellent introduction to off-road riding

This 8-mile loop for beginning- and intermediate-level riders is a scenic trip along old farm roads, now-rutted grassy trails, in the town of Monroe. Of historical interest, part of this ride follows the old Brooks-Augusta stagecoach route. The trail passes a small pond and weaves between and around the low hills typical of this part of Waldo County. The route ends at an abandoned farmhouse. This house is situated atop a hill that opens out onto a landscape of rolling hills, woods, and farmland. This ride is a very enjoyable way to spend a Sunday afternoon or weekday evening.

Monroe was typical of the towns that developed in this area, most of which were established along waterfalls or alongside rivers where hydropower could be used to turn mills. Farms were typically located atop the long, low, open ridges, whereas the major roads were located along the valley floors. Agricultural products and wood were moved along these corridors to be milled. It is hard to imagine that Monroe Center, now a heavily wooded area, was once a thriving industrial locale. Only a couple of houses remain from that era. Careful observation as you cross Marsh Stream will disclose the remnants of the old saw and grist mills that once lined its banks. Other mill sites include Stove Pipe Alley and Monroe Mills. What is currently viewed as the town center is, in fact, Monroe Mills.

Alert mountain bikers may glimpse a red fox, white-tailed deer, hare, or grouse, all of which inhabit the area. During our ride in Monroe, we were quite surprised to see a flock of 60 wild turkeys eating corn in a field. Pay particular attention to wildlife as you pass through the old apple orchards that are located near the old farm sites. Grouse and white-tailed deer thrive on the apples these trees produce in the fall.

General location: This ride follows old town roads in the Waldo County town of Monroe.

Elevation change: There is one long climb on this trail and several short ones. Total elevation gain is approximately 500'.

Season: This ride is best from May through mid-November.

Services: There is a general store located in Monroe. The nearest bicycle shops are located in Bangor and Brewer.

Hazards: Be prepared for a few rutted and rocky sections along this trail. Watch for equestrians and other trail users. This area is frequented by hunters from mid-October until the last weekend in November.

Rescue index: You are never more than 1 mile from assistance.

Land status: Two- and four-wheel-drive town roads. There is one short section of single-track that may cross private land.

Maps: For detailed information about this trail, consult the USGS quadrangle for Brooks East. The DeLorme Mapping Company's *Maine Atlas and Gazetteer* shows all of the trail in less detail (map 22, section E-4).

Finding the trail: From Monroe Village, drive south on ME 141 for 2 miles. Turn right at the junction of the first paved road you come to: Back Brooks Road. Cross a stream and follow the road as it turns sharply to the right in front of a farm. Continue straight and then follow the road as it swings sharply to the left.

Beyond this bend in the road, you will pass a dirt road branching off to the left at the top of a small hill. Continue past this road, and begin to descend the hill. The trailhead is located at the bottom of the hill, half a mile beyond the bend in the road. Look for a brushy trail on the left. There is a pulloff at the trailhead. If you miss the trailhead you will come to Thistle Pond on the left. Turn around and look for the trail on the right, just past the pond.

Source of additional information: Area information may be obtained at the Monroe General Store located on ME 139 in Monroe Village (phone (207) 525-9900).

Notes on the trail: From the trailhead, begin riding along a rough old road through the trees. Not far from the trailhead, you will be able to see Thistle Pond to your right. The old camp overlooking the pond is known locally as

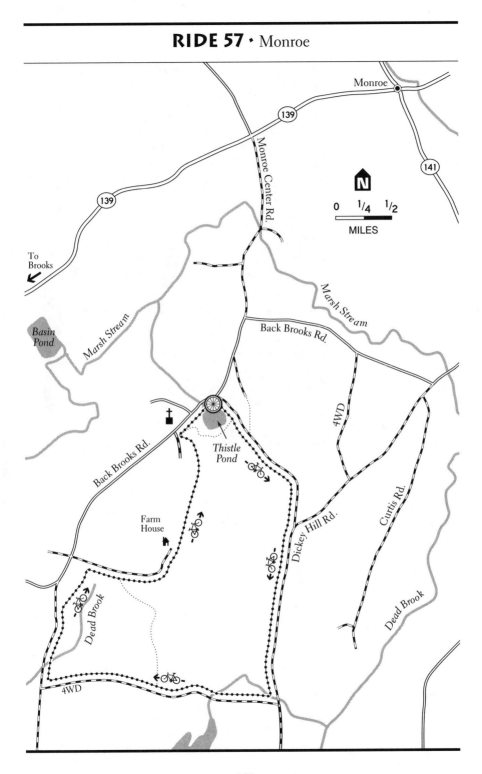

David enjoys a
fall ride in one
of his favorite
places in the
state—Monroe.

the Monroe Hilton! Continue straight along this old road, passing several side trails, until you reach a large pasture. Although the right-of-way technically crosses the field, stay to the right and follow the perimeter of the field out to a two-wheel-drive road (Dickey Hill Road). Turn right. You will follow Dickey Hill Road for approximately 1.4 miles.

As the road descends slightly, look for an improved dirt road on the right. There are really no distinguishing features to this road, and it can easily be mistaken for a driveway. Turn right. After half a mile you will come to a short, steep hill that will take you to a set of farm buildings at the top. Continue past the buildings, which will be on your left, and follow the grassy trail that represents the old right-of-way. This portion of the trail may be mowed for equestrians. It climbs steadily, passing a side trail to the right as it crests. Continue straight, watching for occasional ruts in the trail.

At a **T** junction, turn right (left will take you to Waldo Station Road). The trail descends along a rocky, washed-away section of the old road, and you will pass a beaver pond on the right. After a difficult, eroded section of the trail over which most riders will have to portage, the trail improves and becomes a wide, grassy road. Begin looking for a snowmobile trail that veers off to the right. This trail provides a short section of fun single-track. If you miss this turn, don't sweat it; you will soon come to the paved Back Brooks Road. Turn right on the pavement and pedal several hundred feet to a four-way intersection. Turn right onto a two-wheel-drive dirt road, and you will see the snowmobile trail you missed on the right, shortly after making the turn. If you were able to find the snowmobile trail, follow it to the two-wheel-drive dirt road and turn right.

Begin pedaling up the unpaved two-wheel-drive road, which gradually deteriorates. Bear left as you come upon a trail that diverges to the right. After climbing a short, steep hill the road opens into a large pasture with a beautiful, sweeping view of the surrounding countryside. There is an abandoned farmhouse in the middle of the pasture. The road continues in a straight line through the pasture, although it is not very distinct. At the edge of the pasture, the trail enters the woods through a gap in a stone fence. From here, you will be following a single-track trail. If you look carefully, you can make out the old right-of-way in the woods. You will pass a foundation on your left. (Be careful of the well if you choose to explore the foundation.) Stay on the old road, following snowmobile trail signs. You will then pass through an area that has recently been logged. Beyond this site, the road becomes an improved dirt road and descends quickly to a house and driveway. Do not go through the dooryard of the house; follow the old right-of-way that passes to the right of the driveway and parallels it before joining it farther away from the house. Ride out to the paved Back Brooks Road. Turn right to return to your car.

RIDE 58 · Common Hill

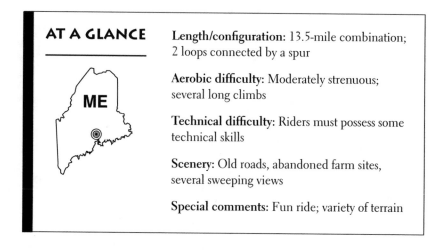

AT A GLANCE

Length/configuration: 13.5-mile combination; 2 loops connected by a spur

Aerobic difficulty: Moderately strenuous; several long climbs

Technical difficulty: Riders must possess some technical skills

Scenery: Old roads, abandoned farm sites, several sweeping views

Special comments: Fun ride; variety of terrain

The Common Hill ride is a rewarding excursion into the heart of the Dixmont Hills. The ride consists of a lower and an upper loop that are joined by means of a connecting trail (ridden twice, once in each direction). The total mileage for the ride is 13.5 miles. Riders of intermediate ability will have no difficulty following the network of rocky double- and single-track trails that traverse rolling terrain through a combination of forest and open pasture.

This area of the state offers prime mountain biking along forested trails that once connected now-abandoned farm sites. Many of these sites are still lined with the stately maples from which the early farmers collected sap to make maple syrup, which they used in place of sugar. Sweeping views of the surrounding hills are provided by the large pastures situated along this ride. Wildlife, such as white-tailed deer, moose, ducks, and grouse, abound in this area, particularly around the many beaver meadows.

General location: This ride passes through the towns of Jackson and Dixmont in the heart of the Dixmont Hills.

Elevation change: You will begin this ride at approximately 470'. The trail climbs steadily to the top of Common Hill at 900'. From there, you will descend to 450' near the junction of Jewel Road and ME 9. You will complete the upper loop of the ride with a gradual climb of 450' back to the top of Common Hill.

Coming down from Common Hill, you will drop 300' along a rolling descent. You will end the ride with a steep, 250-foot descent. Total elevation gain on this trail is approximately 1,000'.

RIDE 58 · Common Hill

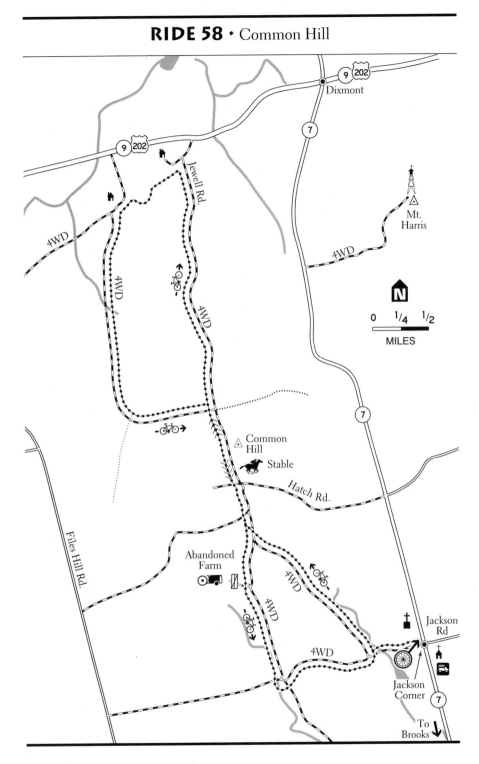

Season: This trail is passable from mid-May to late October.

Services: There is a small grocery store and a hardware store located in Brooks. The nearest bicycle shops are to be found in Bangor.

Hazards: Many sections of this route are covered with loose rock. Watch for deep ruts and rocks hidden by the grass. This part of the state does not see much mountain bicycle traffic, and it is a wonderful area to ride. If you encounter people, please try to take the time to talk to them and explain a little bit about the sport. There are a number of equestrians who frequent these roads, and establishing goodwill between both trail users will help to ensure continued access to the area.

Rescue index: You are never more than 3 miles from assistance on this trail.

Land status: The ride follows discontinued town roads that double as snowmobile trails in the winter.

Maps: All sections of this trail are shown on two USGS quads: Brooks West and Dixmont. The topographical maps also show many of the fascinating side trips that branch off the main trail. In addition, the DeLorme Mapping Company's *Maine Atlas and Gazetteer* depicts this trail (map 22, sections C2, D2, and D3).

Finding the trail: From the town of Brooks, head 4 miles north on ME 7 until you reach Jackson Corners. You will see the Jackson fire station and a church on the right. We suggest you park in the church yard, being careful not to block the doors of the fire station. The trail starts on the other side of ME 7, on a dirt road located opposite the church and fire station.

Sources of additional information: None.

Notes on the trail: From the church and fire station, ride diagonally across the parking lot and cross ME 7. Begin the ride down the dirt road. You will pass a cemetery on the right and a swampy area with a stream passing through it. As you climb to the top of a small rise, begin looking for a moderately wide road heading into the woods on the right. Turn onto this road, which soon deteriorates into a moderately technical jeep trail. Notice the stone fences on either side of the trail, which will be passing through a stand of pretty hardwoods. At approximately 2 miles, you will notice a trail on the left that merges with the main trail at an angle. This will be the trail you take on the return leg of your ride. For now, continue straight. The route narrows to a wide singletrack trail passing a beaver bog on the right. Keep your eyes peeled, as this is a great place to see moose. You will eventually come out onto an improved dirt road.

Turn right onto the improved dirt road. You will pass some buildings on the left. After half a mile, the road veers sharply to the right, with a lesser road

A wet day on the trail to Common Hill.

(Common Hill Road) heading straight. Go straight, passing a farm building on the right. The road, although wide, climbs steeply on an eroded, rocky surface. There will be a stone fence to your left as you make the climb. After cresting Common Hill, the road, now a wide trail, descends quickly through another moderately technical area of loose rock. Near the top of the descent you will come to a four-way intersection. Stay straight. The trail on the left is where you will complete the upper loop of the ride. At the bottom of the descent, you must cross a series of wet areas that may contain deep ruts. Beware, for these ruts can cause you to unexpectedly leave your bike head first in the mud. After the wet areas, the trail gradually improves to a double-track woods road and then to a two-wheel-drive dirt road. You will notice signs along the way that indicate you are following snowmobile route ITS 83. The view from this road (Jewell Road) opens up as you pass through a series of pastures. Beyond the pastures, you will descend once again.

At the bottom of the hill, the road turns sharply to the right. There is also a small road, which looks like a driveway, heading to the left. Turn left here. If you miss this turn, and continue following the road around to the right, you will come to ME 9, which is just around the corner. Backtrack, and take the first road to the right. The road (called Whitaker or Morse Hill Road), passes in front of an old farmhouse on the right and then turns right. Rather than following the road, look instead for a single-track trail that heads straight, past the house. Although this used to be the old town road, it has since been abandoned and has become quite overgrown. The trail, climbing slightly, will take you into a large pasture that offers gorgeous views. Ride along the left side of the field, staying near the stone fence. There will be a cut-in midway through the pasture that leads to an area that has been logged fairly recently. It is possible to explore the top of the ridge by following the logging roads to the left and climbing farther up the hill. The ride continues to the right, following an improved but rutted road down a moderately steep slope. This road will branch off to the right just past a cabin located at the bottom of the hill. Be sure to continue straight here, following the old town road and keeping the stone fence to your left. The road will narrow again, into a double-track trail with a vegetated center median.

A short distance beyond the cabin, turn left on a double-track trail that leaves the old town road. Stay straight on this trail at all the intersections. This is a rough, rocky, and eroded trail with several technically challenging sections. It too was once a town road, and passes through areas where farms once stood. You will climb gradually on this trail, riding through areas alternating between dense plantations and open hardwoods. Stay on the main trail as it turns sharply to the left, and ascend Common Hill. At a T intersection at the top of Common Hill you will have rejoined the section of trail along which you started. Turn right. When you come to the improved dirt road, continue straight and then turn left onto the small side trail on which you came in. After passing by the beaver flowage, climb to the top of a small rise and turn right on a small trail that leaves the main trail at an angle. At a fork in this trail, bear left (the trail on the right heads to a beautiful old farm site, with a huge, rolling pasture). The left fork follows the edge of a pasture and then reenters the woods, alternating between single- and double-track.

Eventually, you will come to a rather confusing junction with an improved dirt road. Take a sharp left to return to Jackson Corners. After an improved section with several houses, this road becomes a rough four-wheel-drive trail. Continue straight, passing a cemetery on the left and ending the ride with a short, white-knuckle descent to an improved dirt road on which you will continue to return to your car.

RIDE 59 · Dixmont Hills

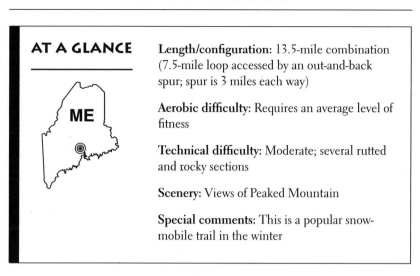

AT A GLANCE

Length/configuration: 13.5-mile combination (7.5-mile loop accessed by an out-and-back spur; spur is 3 miles each way)

Aerobic difficulty: Requires an average level of fitness

Technical difficulty: Moderate; several rutted and rocky sections

Scenery: Views of Peaked Mountain

Special comments: This is a popular snow-mobile trail in the winter

This ride in the Dixmont Hills follows old town roads to create a 13.5-mile excursion suited to riders of intermediate ability. Despite the modest gain in elevation, the ride is characterized by rough and rocky surfaces that require good bike handling skills and some aerobic fitness. In addition, good route-finding skills will come in handy, as several of the trail junctions on this ride can be confusing. The ride begins and ends on a trail that connects to a longer loop, and the many side trails represent a portion of the network of snowmobile trails maintained for winter travel.

Although this trail passes through a primarily wooded landscape, most of the land was once cleared for agriculture. As you ride, you will notice an extensive system of stone fences that once marked property lines and contained livestock. These fences also distinguish old town roads from more recently cut logging roads and snowmobile trails. Other signs of the history of the land include old apple orchards and the foundations of farms long gone. One can only marvel how early farmers scratched a living from the rocky terrain that is found in the area.

General location: The towns of Newburgh and Dixmont.

Elevation change: This ride is characterized by several short climbs and features very little gain in elevation.

Season: The trail passes through several wet areas that may not be passable until late spring. Summer and autumn are probably the best seasons to ride this trail.

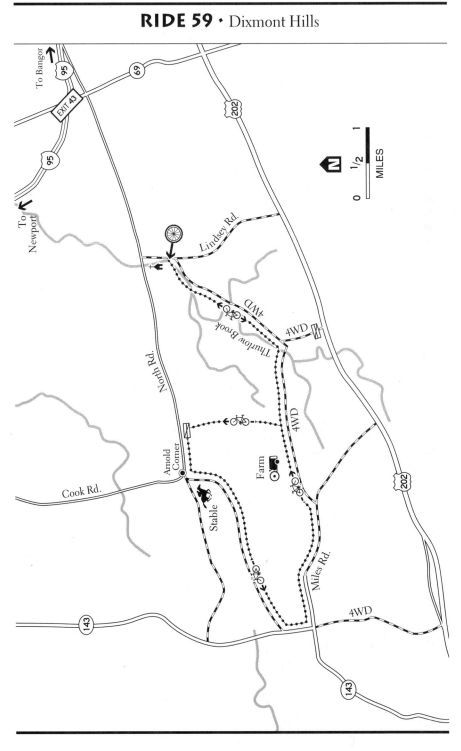

Services: There is a general store on ME 9 in Newburgh Center. All other services, including bike repair, are available in Bangor.

Hazards: Look for rocks, grass-covered ruts, and eroded sections in the trail. After turning off North Road, you will ride along a portion of the trail that goes past a riding stable. Please be on the lookout for equestrians, and be careful not to spook the horses in the pasture as you pass. There may be the odd dog at one of the several farms located along this route. Simply speaking softly and stopping to offer a pat will probably curb any aggressive tendencies held by either the dog or its owner.

Rescue index: You are never more than 3 miles from houses where assistance could be sought.

Land status: This trail follows discontinued town roads. Many of the old roads pass quite closely to homes, and certain sections of the trail may cross private land. Please be courteous and respect the privacy of the owners.

Maps: Consult the DeLorme Mapping Company's *Maine Atlas and Gazetteer* (map 22, sections C-3 and C-4). The USGS topographical map for this trail is East Dixmont.

Finding the trail: From the Bangor area, follow Interstate 95 south to Exit 43 and turn left onto ME 69. Travel approximately 0.1 mile on ME 69 (heading south) and turn right on North Road. After 2 miles you will come to Lindsey Road and a church on the left. Park in the church yard.

Sources of additional information: It may be helpful to try to obtain a snowmobile map of the area. Maps are sometimes available at local general stores.

Notes on the trail: From the church parking lot, turn right onto Lindsey Road. Turn right again, onto the first dirt road you come to. Stay on this road as it changes from an improved dirt road to a jeep trail that eventually crosses Thurlow Brook. Bear right at the next trail junction (the trail on the left crosses a large pasture before entering the woods on the other side and continuing to ME 9). You will come to a snowmobile bridge, beyond which 3 trails branch off in different directions. Follow the center trail, which climbs quickly to the crest of a small hill overlooking the stream. The trail gradually becomes an old woods road, covered with loose rocks, leaves, and needles. Follow this road for less than 1 mile, looking for a snowmobile trail on the right that, if signed, will point to Carmel. This is the beginning of the loop portion of the ride. Turn right down this snowmobile trail and follow it until you come to a T junction with North Road. Turn left on North Road and ride until it turns sharply to the right. Bear left at this point, turning onto a road that leads to a horse stable.

As you ride toward the stable, look carefully for a left turn onto a doubletrack trail that parallels the paddock. Follow this trail through the woods, staying straight until you reach a paved road, which is ME 143. Turn left on ME

143 and then left again onto the paved Miles Road at Simpson's Corner. Miles Road becomes a dirt road after 1 mile. Shortly beyond this point, you must turn left down what appears to be a driveway leading to a farmhouse. The road passes a horse pasture on the left and a pond on the right. You will pass by the house, skirt a fence, and ascend a small rise to a red seasonal cabin on the right. From the cabin, the route descends quickly into the woods, and you will soon pass the snowmobile trail that marked the beginning of the loop. Continue straight and retrace your route from this point back to your car.

RIDE 60 Kenduskeag Stream Park Trail

AT A GLANCE

ME

Length/configuration: 9.5-mile out-and-back (4.75 miles each way)

Aerobic difficulty: Modest; no steep climbs

Technical difficulty: Suitable for novice riders

Scenery: A fascinating contrast of picturesque sites along the stream and the scars of urban development

Special comments: You can hop on this trail from downtown Bangor

From downtown Bangor, this multi-use trail meanders along the Kenduskeag Stream—providing a quick escape from city bustle or an ideal commute into town. Though the maintained pathway ends after 2.25 miles, a narrow, overgrown, single-track trail continues alongside the stream and connects to a rutted jeep trail that winds its way upriver for an additional 2.5 miles. The ride, when ridden as an out-and-back affair, is a 9.5-mile jaunt. For families and riders of beginning ability levels, the first portion of this ride is an excellent outing. The park offers interesting historical diversions and beautiful picnic sites along the river.

General location: The trailhead for the Kenduskeag Stream Park ride is located in downtown Bangor.

Elevation change: This ride crisscrosses over the Kenduskeag Stream several times but, staying close to its bank, remains relatively flat.

RIDE 60 · Kenduskeag Stream Park Trail

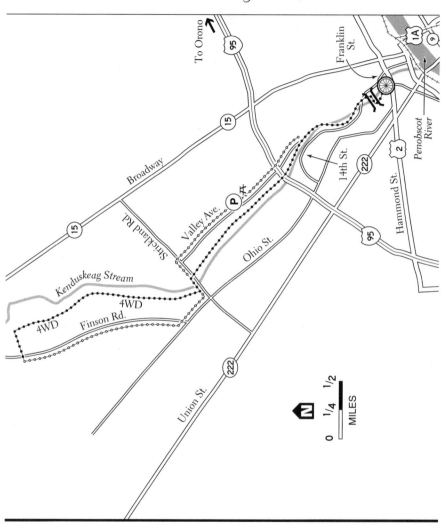

Season: Winter snow cover is really the only restriction to riding this trail.

Services: All services are available in Bangor.

Hazards: There may be many pedestrians on the first part of this trail, the section closest to downtown Bangor. Despite the smooth surface, this is not a trail to go cruising on because of the likelihood of heavy traffic.

Rescue index: It may actually be true to say that you are never more than a shout away from assistance on this ride.

Land status: The trail along the Kenduskeag Stream is part of a public park. Farther up the stream, the ride crosses private land, with informal public access along the river, and then continues on an abandoned public road.

Maps: Although the USGS quadrangle for Bangor does not show the trail alongside the Kenduskeag Stream, it does give a detailed view of the surrounding area.

Finding the trail: In Bangor, you can begin riding from Franklin Street (which crosses the Kenduskeag Stream), or from a parking area located on the east side of Valley Avenue just a few blocks north of US 2 and ME 100.

Source of additional information:

Bangor Recreation Department
(207) 947-1018

Notes on the trail: From Franklin Street, on the west side of the Kenduskeag, begin riding along a narrow trail that is built between a concrete embankment on the left and a wooden fence on the right. Follow the trail as it turns sharply to the right and crosses the stream over a high bridge. This bridge has replaced, but remains on the site of, what was once Morse Covered Bridge. Across the bridge, turn left and continue following the trail as it runs above but alongside the stream.

At a parking lot on the right, you will have to cross Valley Avenue and ride on the road in order to cross the stream and pick up the trail at the other end of the bridge. There is another parking area here as well. Along this stretch of the trail, you will pass the site of an old dam that once provided power for the Maxfield Mill. Just beyond this site, the trail once again makes use of the main road and another bridge that takes you back to the east side of the stream. You will ride under Interstate 95 and pass another old mill site on the left. Beyond this, there is another parking area for the park and a series of picnic benches. At the far end of this recreation area, the maintained portion of the trail ends. However, a single-track trail continues along the stream and ducks into an overgrown stand of sumacs. Watch for a sharp dip as this trail crosses a small stream, just before traversing the bottom of a field.

Beyond the field, the trail reenters the woods for a short distance before veering right and climbing to the paved Strickland Road. Carefully cross Strickland Road and turn left to cross yet another bridge over the Kenduskeag. As you reach the end of the bridge, look on the right for a gravel jeep trail that leads back down to the stream and continues along its western bank. This part of the ride follows this jeep trail over lots of puddles and mud, and stays quite close to the stream; be sure to avoid any of the side roads that branch off on the left. You will reach a wastewater treatment facility and a once-paved **T** junction. At this point you can turn back and retrace your route back to the start, or you can choose to return along the road. To do the latter, go left at the **T** junction (turning away from the stream) and then right to cross a stone barricade. You will find yourself at the end of a dead-end street. Turn left onto what is Pushaw Street and, upon reaching Finson Road, turn left again. Then, upon reaching Ohio Street, turn left and ride to the first set of traffic lights. Turn left at the lights onto Strickland Road and ride across the bridge over the Kenduskeag.

At this point you can choose to descend back to the trail or continue following the road. If you take the road, turn right onto Kenduskeag Avenue. Bear right at a split in the road, and return to the trailhead by way of Valley Avenue.

RIDE 61 · Caribou Bog

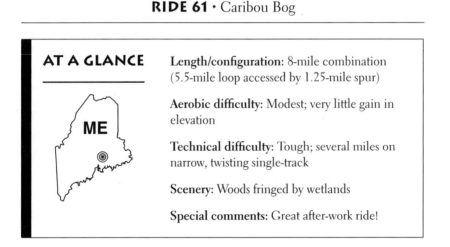

AT A GLANCE

Length/configuration: 8-mile combination (5.5-mile loop accessed by 1.25-mile spur)

Aerobic difficulty: Modest; very little gain in elevation

Technical difficulty: Tough; several miles on narrow, twisting single-track

Scenery: Woods fringed by wetlands

Special comments: Great after-work ride!

From the outskirts of downtown Bangor, this 8-mile loop includes some surprisingly fun single-track riding. The ride features long stretches of single-track trail through wooded and boggy terrain. A dirt road and an abandoned railroad bed serve to connect the trails and facilitate a number of alternative routes. The ride, with such close proximity to downtown, is an excellent after-work escape for intermediate and advanced riders. Beginning-level riders can stick to the dirt road and railroad bed for a shorter and less technical loop.

General location: Just north of the city of Bangor.

Elevation change: There is very little change in elevation on this ride.

Season: Due to the surrounding wetlands in this area, it is best not to ride here until June. Riding can continue late into the fall, until snow cover transforms the trail system into a network of cross-country ski trails and snowmobile trails.

Services: All services are available in Bangor. For bicycle service, check out the Ski Rack located just off Hogan Road at 24 Longview Drive. Not only is the shop very close to the trailhead, but most of the staff has done a lot of riding in the area. Furthermore, the Ski Rack offers evening rides along this trail for all skill levels.

Hazards: If you have never ridden in the area, consider joining the folks at the Ski Rack for one of their evening rides. This will familiarize you with the network of trails that can otherwise be rather confusing.

Rescue index: You will never be more than a mile from assistance.

Land status: City land.

Maps: The USGS quadrangles that depict this area are Bangor, Veazie, and Old Town. However, the trail system is not clearly mapped and all you will be able to do is familiarize yourself with the surrounding area. The abandoned railroad bed is a useful landmark.

Finding the trail: From Interstate 95, take Exit 48 in Bangor and drive south on ME 15. At the junction of ME 15 and Stillwater Avenue, turn left. Drive up Stillwater Avenue to its intersection with Hogan Road. Turn right on Hogan Road and then left almost immediately onto Longview Drive. Turn left again into the parking area for the Ski Rack.

Source of additional information: The Ski Rack, at 24 Longview Drive in Bangor, includes a full-service bike shop. Most of the staff are avid mountain bikers and offer evening rides along this trail. For more information and a schedule of rides, contact the Ski Rack at (207) 945-6474 or (207) 945-6475.

Notes on the trail: From the Ski Rack on Longview Drive, turn right out of the driveway and ride down to Hogan Road. Turn right and ride to the intersection with Stillwater Avenue. Cross Stillwater Avenue and begin riding up Kittredge Road. After riding past an old gate, begin looking for a single-track trail that enters the woods on the right. Descend along this trail to a graded, gravel road. Turn right and ride a short distance before reaching the junction of another trail that branches off at an acute angle to the left. Take this left and begin looking for a small clearing on the right. Turn into this clearing and ride toward the woods. You will find a trail that crosses an old stone fence and continues into the woods. This trail is a narrow single-track studded with exposed rocks, roots, dips, and puddles. At a **T** intersection

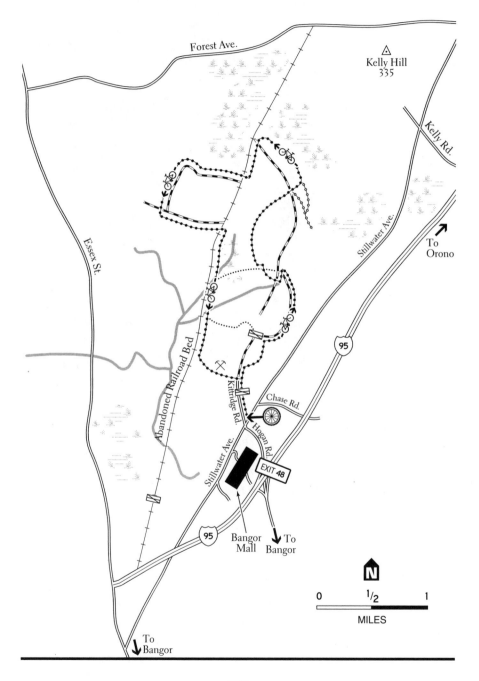

Emerging from
the woods on the
Caribou Bog ride,
not far from down-
town Bangor.

with a yellow-blazed trail, turn left and travel along some more technical, undulating terrain until you see another trail branching off to the right. Although the yellow-blazed trail actually continues straight, it leads to a bog that is impassable in the summer. Turn right onto the single-track trail and follow it along a narrow, twisty, and extremely technical trail through the woods.

After about 1.25 miles, you will reconnect with the main road. From this point, you can cross the dump road and follow another blazed trail that continues straight ahead into the woods, or bear right onto a trail that enters the woods at an angle of approximately 45°. Either trail is an option, as they reconnect at the edge of a large bog and swing around to the west to reach an abandoned railroad bed. Beginning-level riders can also opt to turn left onto the main road, which also connects to the railroad bed.

No matter which route you follow, turn left when you reach the railroad bed. After half a mile of easy cruising, a trail branching off to the right is an option that adds about a mile to the ride. If you take this route, ride to a clearing and look for a side trail on the right. This route swings around and reconnects with a logging road. Turn left onto the logging road to return to the railroad bed. Take a right onto the railroad bed. You will pedal past a trail on the left just before the railroad bed passes through a stand of pines. Farther on, the route becomes wetter because of flooding due to beaver activity. Beyond this section, look for another trail on the left and turn into the woods again. Bear right at a fork and follow the trail up into a sand pit. From the edge of the sand pit, you will see a road rising up on the other side; cross the pit and follow this road back out to Kittredge Road. Turn right on Kittredge Road and return to the Ski Rack.

RIDE 62 · Penobscot Experimental Forest

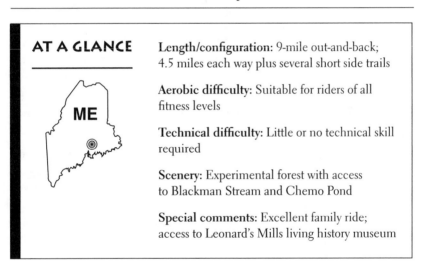

AT A GLANCE

ME

Length/configuration: 9-mile out-and-back; 4.5 miles each way plus several short side trails

Aerobic difficulty: Suitable for riders of all fitness levels

Technical difficulty: Little or no technical skill required

Scenery: Experimental forest with access to Blackman Stream and Chemo Pond

Special comments: Excellent family ride; access to Leonard's Mills living history museum

The Penobscot Experimental Forest is owned by the University of Maine Foundation and serves as an area where an array of silvicultural treatments can be evaluated. More recently, the focus of studies conducted in the forest has been directed toward evaluating the effects of various styles of harvesting on the forest ecosystem. The forest, which covers 3,800 acres, is divided by an access road that provides a fascinating 9-mile out-and-back ride. The access road is graded with a gravel surface and requires little or no technical riding ability. This ride is an excellent family excursion through a scenic and peaceful setting.

The northern portion of the Penobscot Experimental Forest includes access to Leonard's Mills and the Maine Forest & Logging Museum. Leonard's Mills was a village established around a mill site on Blackman Stream in the 1790s. The mill and the village have been reconstructed and now stand as the Maine Forest & Logging Museum. In addition to touring the buildings, walking a nature trail, and learning about Maine's logging past, visitors to Leonard's Mills can plan to attend one of the "Living History Days" organized by the museum. At the very least, the covered bridge over Blackman Stream offers a shady place to relax after the ride.

General location: Towns of Bradley and Eddington, across the Penobscot River from Orono.

Elevation change: There is virtually no change in elevation throughout the ride.

Season: The access road to the Penobscot Experimental Forest is in good condition from May through October.

Services: All services are available in Orono and Bangor.

Hazards: Vehicles, though few, are permitted on the access road. Be sure to stay on the main access road; mountain bikes are not permitted on the network of trails that crisscrosses the forest.

Rescue index: At the farthest point, you will be only 2 miles from assistance.

Land status: University of Maine Foundation.

Maps: The access road through the forest is depicted in *The Maine Atlas and Gazetteer*, published by the DeLorme Mapping Company (map 23, sections A-4 and B-4). In addition, maps may be obtained from the U.S. Forest Service office on Harper Drive.

Finding the trail: From Bangor, cross the Penobscot River into Brewer and head north on ME 9. At Eddington Bend, in Eddington, bear left on ME 178. After crossing the town line into Bradley, look for a road on the right that is signed with a small billboard for Leonard's Mills. This road may or may not be signed as Government Road or Harper Drive. Turn right and follow the road past the U.S. Forest Service office on the left (where you may want to stop and pick up a map). You will follow the road beneath a power line and then bear right at a fork. Bear right again, and follow the signs to the parking area for the museum. The ride continues down the access road, heading southeast.

RIDE 62 · Penobscot Experimental Forest

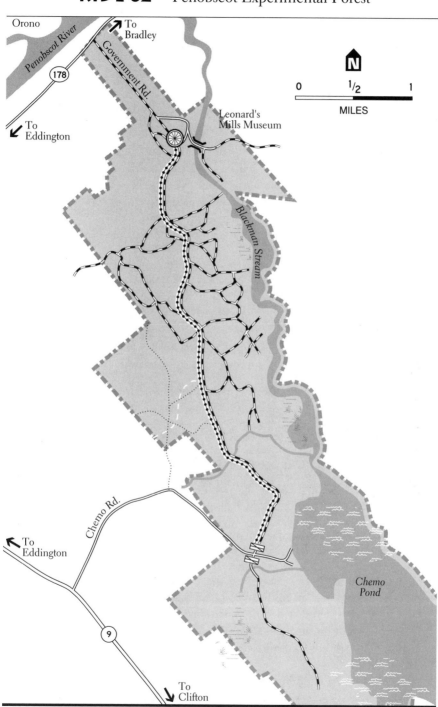

Source of additional information:

Maine Forest & Logging Museum, Inc.
5768 South Annex A
University of Maine
Orono, ME 04469
(207) 581-2871

Notes on the trail: From the parking area, ride down the main access road, passing a gate into the forest. The ride follows the access road all the way to its southern gate, just a short distance from Chemo Pond. A side trail on the left not far from the parking area provides access to Blackman Stream. Throughout the ride you will pass areas of the forest that have been signed with information regarding their management and harvesting.

RIDE 63 · University Woods

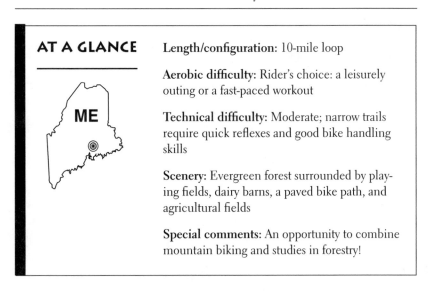

AT A GLANCE

ME

Length/configuration: 10-mile loop

Aerobic difficulty: Rider's choice: a leisurely outing or a fast-paced workout

Technical difficulty: Moderate; narrow trails require quick reflexes and good bike handling skills

Scenery: Evergreen forest surrounded by playing fields, dairy barns, a paved bike path, and agricultural fields

Special comments: An opportunity to combine mountain biking and studies in forestry!

At the heart of the University of Maine in Orono lies the University Forest: a wooded green space that boasts miles of interconnecting trails. The University Forest offers skilled mountain bikers a variety of terrain, featuring steep, rocky climbs and technically challenging sections through muddy, rooty wallows. Riders can link the trails and woods roads together to create a ten-mile loop.

The University Forest has been set aside as an area where the study of forestry and forest practices can take place. Functioning as an outdoor classroom for students in the university's world-renowned School of Forestry, the forest permits firsthand study of tree growth and the effects of harvesting. If you look carefully, you will notice that the area has been gridded into small units called plots. You may encounter signs in the forest that provide information on the species of trees within a particular plot, when the trees were planted, and when the plot was last thinned.

The University Forest features several other interesting sites as well. You may pass by the University Dairy Farm, where visitors are welcome. Visiting hours are posted on the entrance to the barn. It is well worth a stop, although you will be tempted to ride quickly through the farm area when the "honey" wagons are spreading manure on the fields. In another area of the forest, just off the paved bike path, is an unusual concrete structure. This is an old civil defense bunker that was built to serve as a communications center for the area in the event of a nuclear attack. The bunker reportedly boasts a 12-foot-thick roof and was designed to withstand all but a direct hit. The facility has also served as a temporary prison.

General location: Town of Orono and the city of Old Town.

Elevation change: There is generally little elevation gain. There are, however, several short yet steep climbs and quick descents.

Season: The trails should be dry enough to ride by mid-May, and riding can continue into the fall. In the winter, many miles are specially groomed for cross-country skiers; it is best to stay off the trails once these tracks have been laid.

Services: All services are available in Orono and Old Town, including bicycle service and repair.

Hazards: The trails are rooty, rocky, and very muddy. In places, logs have been laid, corduroy-style, across some of the wetter spots. These logs can be treacherous when wet. Avoid areas where logging operations are underway. Please be on the lookout for hikers who also use these trails. Watch carefully for bicycle traffic when entering or crossing the paved bicycle path.

Rescue index: You are never more than 1 mile from assistance. All accidents should be reported to the university police department.

Land status: The trails are located in the University of Maine Experimental Forest.

Maps: The DeLorme Mapping Company's *Maine Atlas and Gazetteer* shows the general area (map 23, sections A-3 and A-4; map 33, sections E-3 and E-4). There is also an excellent trail map available through the Maine Outing Club for a $2 donation. The Outing Club has an office in the Memorial Union.

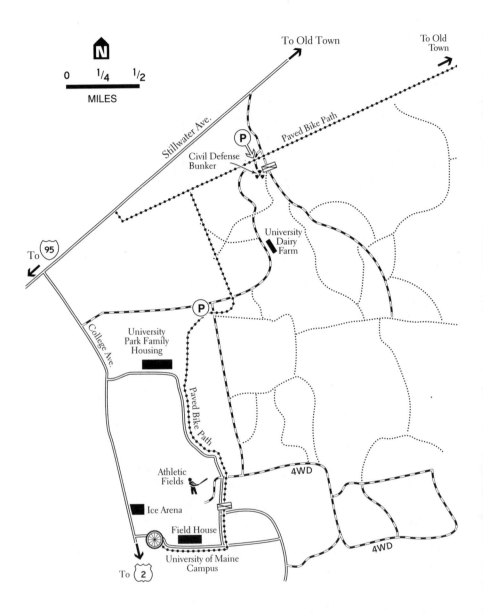

N

0   ¼   ½
MILES

To Old Town

To Old Town

Stillwater Ave.

Paved Bike Path

P

Civil Defense
Bunker

To 95

University
Dairy
Farm

P

College Ave.

University
Park Family
Housing

Paved Bike Path

Athletic
Fields

4WD

Ice Arena

Field House

4WD

To 2

University of Maine
Campus

Note: Ride is any trail or dirt road in the area.

The trails through University Woods provide riders of all levels a chance to sharpen their skills on narrow single-track.

Finding the trail: Take Exit 51 off Interstate 95 and follow the signs to the University of Maine. We suggest obtaining a visitor's parking permit from the University of Maine Public Safety Department, located on College Avenue, especially if you are riding while the university is in session.

Sources of additional information:

The Maine Outing Club
Memorial Union
University of Maine
(207) 581-hike

Rose Bicycle Shop
9 Pine Street
Orono, ME 04473
(207) 866-3525

Any of the folks at the shop will be able to direct you to the trails.

Notes on the trail: The best way to access the network of trails is to follow the paved bike path until you come to one of the many places at which the trails cross the bike path. The bike path is located behind the Stewart housing complex on the north side of campus.

You may also follow the signs to the University Dairy Farm off College Avenue. Drive up the farm road until you meet the bike path. There is a good place to pull off and park there. You can proceed in any direction from there to pick up the trails.

There is no set route, and the area is compact enough for all riders to safely explore. Erosion has been a problem in some areas, so try to avoid skidding on the downhill sections and ride through, rather than around, mud holes to avoid enlarging them.

RIDE 64 · Corinna-to–Dover-Foxcroft Rail Trail

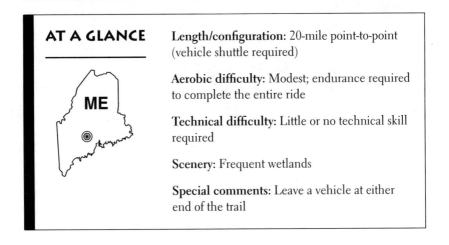

AT A GLANCE	
	Length/configuration: 20-mile point-to-point (vehicle shuttle required)
	Aerobic difficulty: Modest; endurance required to complete the entire ride
	Technical difficulty: Little or no technical skill required
	Scenery: Frequent wetlands
	Special comments: Leave a vehicle at either end of the trail

The abandoned railroad bed between Corinna and Dover-Foxcroft is now occupied by a 20-mile point-to-point recreational trail. The surface of the trail is hard-packed gravel and features virtually no change in elevation. Riders can choose to ride the entire length of the trail one way, leaving a vehicle at either end, or can treat the trail as an out-and-back excursion for a 40-mile round-trip.

From Corinna, the railroad bed follows the east branch of the Sebasticook River to the town of Dexter. The trail enters Dexter over an old railroad trestle, which crosses ME 23. From Dexter, the trail continues up to the bank of the Piscataquis River in Dover-Foxcroft. Although a long, high bridge spans the Piscataquis River, the trail ends at the far bank. Crossing the bridge is therefore entirely optional and will only appeal to courageous and thrill-seeking individuals.

For history buffs, the Dexter Historical Society has converted an old grist

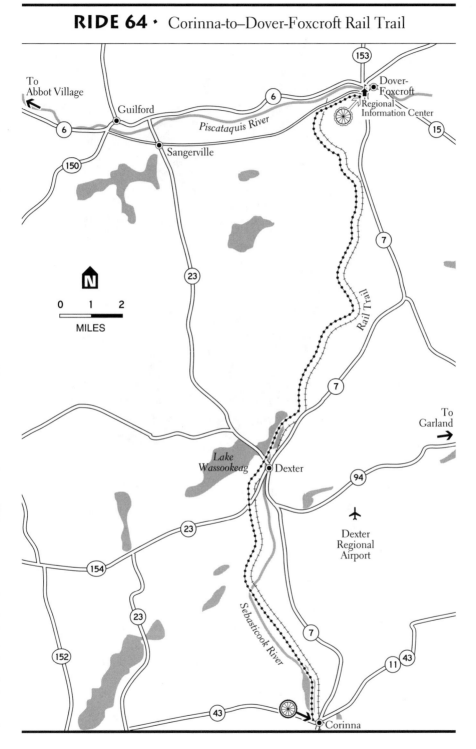

A rider approaches
Dover-Foxcroft
on the rail trail that
begins in Corinna.

mill into a museum of local artifacts. In Dover-Foxcroft, the Blacksmith Shop Museum is another interesting site and features a restored blacksmith shop with much of the original equipment.

General location: An old railroad grade between Corinna and Dover-Foxcroft.

Elevation change: There is virtually no change in elevation along the length of this trail.

Season: This ride can be enjoyed throughout the year. In the winter, riding is best after snowmobiles have packed down the snow on the trail.

Services: Most services are available in Dover-Foxcroft, and there are stores in both Corinna and Dexter as well. For bicycle parts and service, however, the closest sources are in Bangor or Greenville.

Hazards: Other trail users may include all-terrain vehicles in the summer and fall, and snowmobiles in the winter. Care should be used at all of the road crossings and especially at the crossing of Zions Hill Road in Dexter; where there was once a bridge across the road, there are now just steep banks dropping down to the road on both sides. It is extremely important to be prepared to stop at the road, where traffic can be heavy.

Rescue index: Access to ME 7 exists throughout the length of this ride and ensures that you will never be more than a few miles from assistance.

Land status: Old railroad grade.

Maps: Consult DeLorme's *Maine Atlas and Gazetteer* (map 32, sections E-1, D-1, C-2, and B-1).

Finding the trail: This trail can be accessed at many points. We found the best parking spaces to be in Corinna, at the junction of ME 7, ME 43, and ME 222. There is a large gravel lot at the corner of ME 43 and ME 222.

Sources of additional information: None.

Notes on the trail: From the village of Corinna, pick up the trail from ME 43 (called Exeter Road in town) and head north. The first stretch of the ride, between Corinna and Dexter, closely follows the east branch of the Sebasticook River. From Dexter, the trail continues north to the Piscataquis River in Dover-Foxcroft. Throughout the length of this ride, the trail is easy to follow.

RIDE 65 · South Lagrange–to-Medford Rail Trail

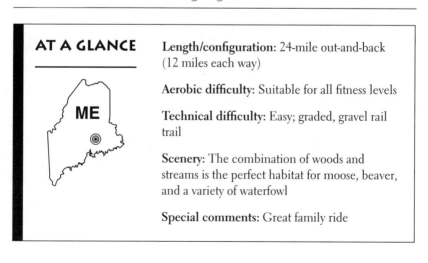

AT A GLANCE

ME

Length/configuration: 24-mile out-and-back (12 miles each way)

Aerobic difficulty: Suitable for all fitness levels

Technical difficulty: Easy; graded, gravel rail trail

Scenery: The combination of woods and streams is the perfect habitat for moose, beaver, and a variety of waterfowl

Special comments: Great family ride

B etween South Lagrange and Medford, south of the Piscataquis River, an abandoned railroad has been converted into a multi-use recreational trail. This trail can be ridden as a 12-mile point-to-point ride, or a 24-mile out-and-back. The hard-packed gravel surface is suitable for riders of all abilities, and because the trail is relatively flat, the ride demands only basic cardiovascular fitness.

As you pedal this trail between South Lagrange and Medford, you will be tracing the old route of the Bangor and Aroostook Railroad. This section of track was constructed in 1906–1907 and extended north from South Lagrange to Packard's Junction. It allowed heavily loaded trains, carrying potatoes from Aroostook County to Boston, to bypass the severe grades near Brownville and make better time. Speed was crucial in transporting potatoes, as they could easily spoil along the way. Over time, improvements were made to the road system, and the potato traffic was slowly absorbed by trucks. Potato tonnage quickly declined during the 1950s, and this route was determined to be redundant by 1979. The rails were removed in 1983.

General location: Northwest of Old Town in Piscataquis County.

Elevation change: This abandoned railroad bed features virtually no change in elevation.

Season: This trail can be ridden at any time of the year. Good drainage from the railroad bed makes this a great ride for early spring, when many other trails remain choked up with mud and water. This ride is also a fun winter outing, when snowmobiles pack down the trail.

Services: Most services are available in Old Town. Closer to the trail, there is a small store and a pay telephone located at the crossroads in Lagrange.

Hazards: The habitat that attracts moose, beaver, and waterfowl to this area also breeds feisty mosquitos and black flies in the spring. A couple of bandanas, a sense of humor, and some dental floss to extract them from between your teeth is all you can do to wage war against these pests—unless, of course, you remember to bring insect repellent.

Rescue index: You can be more than 5 miles from assistance on this ride.

Land status: State recreational trail.

Maps: The *Maine ATV Trail Map*, produced by the Department of Conservation, is available at tourist information centers or by contacting the department at:

Bureau of Parks and Lands
ORV Division/ATV Program
22 State House Station,
Augusta, ME 04333
(207) 287-4958

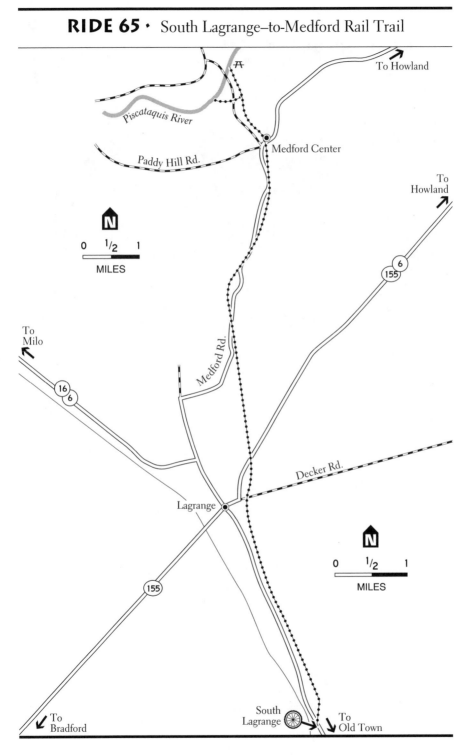

An early November frost brightens the trail between South Lagrange and Medford.

In addition, *The Maine Atlas and Gazetteer*, published by DeLorme, maps this route (map 33, sections A-1, B-1, and C-2).

Finding the trail: Coming from the south on ME 16, look for a sign that directs riders to the Lagrange Rail Trail parking area. You will turn left off the main road and descend slightly to a gravel parking lot. If you plan to ride this trail only one way, you will want to arrange to park a second vehicle in Medford Center. To get to Medford from South Lagrange, continue driving north on ME 16. Drive through Lagrange, and continue toward the town of Milo. As you approach Milo, and before crossing the Piscataquis River, turn right onto Paddy Hill Road. Paddy Hill Road will take you right into Medford Center, where you can pull off to the side of the road to park.

Source of additional information:

Bureau of Parks and Recreation
ORV/ATV Program
(207) 287-4958

Notes on the trail: Begin pedaling north on the rail trail, which passes beneath the highway bridge a short distance from the parking area. The route is obvious and well marked until you approach Medford. Before you reach the village, a trail sign will direct you to leave the railbed and follow a narrow ATV and snowmobile trail. Beyond the village, continue riding north until you come to a place where, to your left, there is a large concrete underpass beneath the old railbed. Turn left, passing through the underpass, and follow a narrow trail down to the southern bank of the Piscataquis River. This spot offers views of the river and is a great place to enjoy a picnic. Retrace your route to return to South Lagrange.

RIDE 66 · Baxter Perimeter Road

AT A GLANCE

ME

Length/configuration: 43 miles from point to point

Aerobic difficulty: Tough; long climbs on loose gravel

Technical difficulty: Modest

Scenery: Splendid; some of the most wild and remote land in Maine

Special comments: We suggest planning your ride in Baxter as a multi-day tour

This ride will take you on a tour through the jewel of the Maine state park system, Baxter State Park. Although the route follows a graded, two-wheel-drive dirt road, this is definitely not a ride for the novice. From gate to gate, the route covers 43 miles of the most remote wildlands in the state. Changeable weather and voracious insects may make this ride an ordeal for the unprepared. Long climbs on loose gravel will tire even the most physically fit riders. We recommend that you plan your visit to Baxter Park as a multi-day tour. This will allow you time for hiking on any of the many trails in the park and for exploring the many sites of historical and natural interest.

Baxter State Park began as a vision in the eyes of Governor Percival Baxter. Over a period of 45 years, Governor Baxter devoted himself to gift-giving, fund-raising, and legislative activity in order to assemble the parcels of land that now make up the more than 201,000 acres of wildlands within the park boundaries. The governor formed the park as a gift to the people of Maine, with the stipulation that the park forever be maintained in its natural state. It was to be used for recreation and experimental forestry and maintained as a game sanctuary for wild beasts and birds. Baxter also established a trust fund to help offset the costs of administering the park.

We think that mountain bikes are one of the best ways to explore Baxter State Park. They are quiet, save for the sound of tires crunching over gravel, and therefore allow riders to hear and see the many beasts that inhabit the area. The cry of a loon, a hooting owl, or perhaps the bellow of a bull moose will allow riders to experience the sensation of wildness that Governor Baxter intended for visitors to this park. With careful planning, this ride can begin and end each day at one of the many campgrounds located in the park. Reservations are essential and must be made well in advance. We suggest riding from the Togue Pond Gate and heading north. With most of the activity of the park focused around Mount Katahdin, which is located in the southeast corner, traffic should lessen as you head north. You have a better chance of securing a campsite at South Branch Pond or Trout Brook Farm, which are located well away from the Mount Katahdin trailheads.

General location: Baxter State Park, which is located 18 miles from Millinocket.

Elevation change: The trailhead at Togue Pond Gate is located at an elevation of 640'. The road features several long grades, some of which climb as much as 700'. The most difficult of these hills is 3 miles from the Togue Pond Gate. The road climbs steeply after Abol Pond, to nearly 1,300' at Abol Campground.

From Abol, the road rises and falls without much net gain in elevation. It reaches its highest point, an elevation of 1,500', over the shoulder of Strickland Mountain and then again at Morse Mountain. After climbing and descending several more times, the end of the road is reached at Matagamon Gate, elevation 660'.

Season: The park is open from May 15 to October 15. However, several of the campgrounds do not open until June 1. We suggest an autumn ride (mid-September) if you can arrange it. Cooler temperatures, fewer insects and people, and the splendors of fall foliage all amount to a fantastic experience.

Services: There are no services available within the park. Water is available at several of the larger campgrounds. Plan on a self-contained expedition if you do the entire perimeter road. Some groceries are available at Pray's Campground, located on Golden Road. All services except bicycle repair are available in Millinocket.

Hazards: There may be heavy traffic on the perimeter road, particularly during summer weekends. If possible, ride either on a weekday or after Labor Day. The loose gravel road can be extremely dusty if there is a lot of traffic. On the other hand, sections of the road can also become quite slippery after heavy rain. Mosquitos and black flies are thick during the summer months.

RIDE 66 • Baxter Perimeter Road

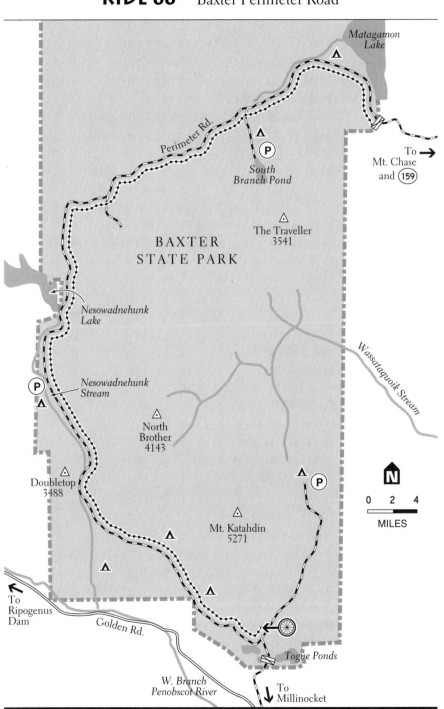

Matagamon
Lake

Perimeter Rd.

South
Branch Pond

To →
Mt. Chase
and 159

BAXTER
STATE PARK

The Traveller
3541

Wassataquoik Stream

Nesowadnehunk
Lake

Nesowadnehunk
Stream

North
Brother
4143

Doubletop
3488

Mt. Katahdin
5271

N

0   2   4
MILES

To
Ripogenus
Dam

Golden Rd.

Togue Ponds

W. Branch
Penobscot River

To
↓ Millinocket

Rescue index: There is enough traffic along the road that you should not have to wait long for assistance. Getting you to a hospital is a different matter, however. The nearest one is located in Millinocket, which can be as much as 50 miles away via rough gravel roads. Ride cautiously! All emergencies should be reported to the Baxter State Park Authority Rangers. Rangers may be found at the gatehouses and at many of the campgrounds.

Land status: The ride is entirely within the confines of Baxter State Park.

Maps: The DeLorme Mapping Company publishes *Baxter State Park and Katahdin,* one of the best maps of the park.

Finding the trail: To reach Togue Pond Gate, follow signs to Baxter State Park from Millinocket. At the gate, out-of-state residents will be required to pay a user's fee in addition to any camping fees. In-state residents must pay for camping only. Ask the gate attendant where you should park.

To reach Matagamon Gate, drive on Interstate 95 to Exit 58. Head north on ME 11 until it intersects with ME 159 in Patten. Turn left on ME 159 and stay on this road until it reaches Matagamon Gate.

The key to doing anything at Baxter is to arrive as early in the morning as possible. Most everything is on a first-come, first-served basis, including parking.

Source of additional information:

Baxter State Park
64 Balsam Drive
Millinocket, ME 04462
(207) 723-5140

Notes on the trail: The rules and regulations are very strict about bicycles being confined to the gravel perimeter road. Please abide by this, no matter how tempting any of the side trails appear to be.

This trip requires that riders be familiar with the rudiments of loaded bicycle touring. You will have to carry everything you will need for the duration of your stay, including food, water, extra clothing, sleeping bag, tent, and stove.

Black bears are present in the vicinity of all the campgrounds. Practice bear-safe camping by removing all edibles and toiletries from your tent and placing them inside a bear-proof container. Alternatively, if no containers are provided, all your food should be placed in a stuff sack and suspended at least 10' above the ground.

DOWN EAST MAINE

Every morning the sun touches the coastal mountains and high bluffs of Washington County before anywhere else in the United States. This easternmost point of the United States is named, appropriately enough, the "Sunrise County." It is quintessential Maine coast: long tongues of granite and basalt jutting into the sea, continuously subjected to the shaping action of the wind and waves; rugged granite cliffs topped with spindly yet hardy spruces, precariously perched with their roots tapping every nook and cranny in the fractured rock for life-supporting nutrients.

The salmon-colored granite cliffs of the Down East coast were formed by lava welling up through fractures in the earth's crust, the result of a cataclysmic collision between roaming continental plates. Approximately 12,000 years ago, the ice crept down from what is now considered northern Canada. Parts of the coast were buried under as much as nine miles of ice and debris, which pulverized the tops of the granite mountains and carried the material far out to sea. Slowly, after a period of warming, the ice retreated. As it withdrew, gravel and till were deposited in the valleys, creating moraines, eskers, and other geologic landmarks. Freed from the compressive weight of the ice, the land sprang back, as it continues to do today.

ACADIA NATIONAL PARK

The coast of Maine has been called a drowned mountain range. Nothing applies to this description better than the dramatic cliffs, the many lakes, and the hills and mountains of Mount Desert Island. This landscape includes

Wild and rugged, the down east coast nurtures the spirit of adventure in every rider.

some of the most interesting glacially sculpted scenery of the east coast. The island is divided into east and west sides by Somes Sound, 168 feet deep and said to be the only true fjord on the east coast. A mountain chain of 17 peaks runs across the island, ranging in elevation from 200 feet to the highest, Cadillac Mountain, at 1,530 feet. Both Jordan Pond and Eagle Lake occupy broad-bottomed glacial valleys, very different from the V-shaped valleys cut by streams and rivers. A disastrous fire in 1947 devastated most of the eastern side of the island. Showing favor to no one, the fire destroyed many structures, including many of the opulent summer "cottages" constructed by some of the wealthiest families in the country. Cadillac and the surrounding mountains, with the topsoil seared from their now-bald summits, testify to the intensity of the fire.

The island began its transformation into a popular resort in the 1850s, when steamboats began to make regular runs to the island. Mount Desert Island became a place for wealthy families to escape from the heat of cities. One individual, George Bucknam Dorr, began working toward saving as much of the island's scenic value as possible. With some of his own money, and with financial assistance from his friends, he began a 27-year struggle to create Acadia National Park. Ultimately, the support of the federal government was needed to see this dream realized. Acadia was created in 1919. John

D. Rockefeller, Jr., another summer visitor to the island, went further and sought to preserve the carriage roads around Seal Harbor by banning automobiles. Acadia National Park has since become the second most popular national park in the United States.

Mountain bike riding in the region is dominated by the extensive system of carriage paths at Acadia National Park on Mount Desert Island. The paths were once traversed by carriages belonging to the Rockefellers and their associates. The paths are architectural marvels, designed to be inconspicuous from the surrounding hills while at the same time maximizing the views for trail users. The drainage system and the many bridges along the paths are equally impressive; the fact that the path infrastructure has been able to withstand the ravages of water and ice and remain in near-perfect condition is testimony to its sound design.

It was not until the early 1990s, after nearly 40 years of neglect and with increasing traffic, that the paths began to wear. A public outcry at the possibility of losing this resource forced the park service to respond. A unique combination of public and private financing, and many hours of volunteer labor, has restored the paths to their former splendor. The work continues to this day.

Many sections of the carriage path system remain under private ownership. Recently, conflicts have erupted between trail users and have resulted in the closure of several of the sections that are privately held. Please respect the closure signs; disregarding them can only result in the closing of additional sections of the carriage path system. Ride prudently and practice proper trail etiquette.

RIDE 67 · Paradise Hill

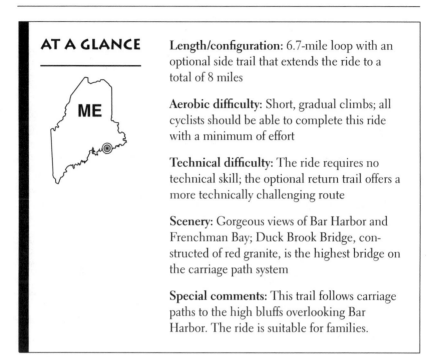

AT A GLANCE

ME

Length/configuration: 6.7-mile loop with an optional side trail that extends the ride to a total of 8 miles

Aerobic difficulty: Short, gradual climbs; all cyclists should be able to complete this ride with a minimum of effort

Technical difficulty: The ride requires no technical skill; the optional return trail offers a more technically challenging route

Scenery: Gorgeous views of Bar Harbor and Frenchman Bay; Duck Brook Bridge, constructed of red granite, is the highest bridge on the carriage path system

Special comments: This trail follows carriage paths to the high bluffs overlooking Bar Harbor. The ride is suitable for families.

This 6.7-mile loop follows the northern section of the carriage path system, past several picturesque ponds to a ridge overlooking Bar Harbor. The smooth surface and relatively easy grades make this ride suitable for riders of all abilities. The route starts at Eagle Lake and climbs gradually, passing first the scenic Breakneck Pond and then massive Duck Brook Bridge, the highest on the carriage path system. Although this portion of the carriage road system tends to be used less than the paths to the south, the views are every bit as rewarding. The high bluffs above Bar Harbor facilitate views of island-dotted Frenchman Bay, Hancock Point, and Sorrento.

In October 1947, the great "Bar Harbor Fire" swept through this area, altering forever the town and surrounding landscape. The fire burned to the sea at Hulls Cove, just below Paradise Hill. Although the town was spared from complete devastation, the great "cottages" that once lined the shore did not fare as well. The fire hastened the transition of Bar Harbor from a summer colony to the vacation destination it is today. Careful observation will disclose evidence of the fire lines that were constructed in a futile attempt to control the spread of the flames. The fire destroyed a residence that was located atop Paradise Hill, leaving only the old driveway and rockwork to mark its location. For a detailed account of the fire of 1947, we highly recommend Joyce Butler's book, *Wildfire Loose: The Week Maine Burned.*

For those seeking a more challenging return to the trailhead, there is an alternative, more technical route that follows Breakneck Road. This option can be ridden to the carriage path near Breakneck Pond, or all the way to Eagle Lake Road (ME 233). Characterized by several eroded and rocky sections, this old road can be quite wet depending on rainfall and the season. This route passes several ponds through a part of the park that is rarely visited. It requires passing through the Visitor Center parking lot and following a short section of extremely busy ME 3.

For those riders who choose to skip the Breakneck side trail, Witch Hole Pond offers a wonderful picnic spot a little more than halfway along the trail. The path gradually descends back toward Breakneck Pond, rejoining the path that will return you to the trailhead at Eagle Lake. For riders with extra energy remaining at the end of their ride, the Eagle Lake loop can provide an additional six miles of easy riding with gorgeous mountain scenery. What a blissful way to spend an afternoon!

General location: Acadia National Park, Mount Desert Island.

Elevation change: The elevation gain is negligible, with no single climb or descent exceeding 100'.

Season: The system of carriage roads at Acadia National Park is open year-round. For cyclists, the best time to ride is after the spring thaw and until the trails have been groomed for cross-country skiers. Because summertime at Acadia is extremely busy, we recommend you ride these trails in the spring and fall.

Because no hunting is permitted at the park, fall is a perfect time to take in the beauty of Acadia. Not only will you enjoy the peace of mind that comes from knowing that there are no hunters around, but you will also be riding on virtually deserted trails.

Services: All services are available in Bar Harbor and include an American Youth Hostel (AYH), open mid-June through August. Contact them at (207) 288-5587. The Pond House, at the southern tip of Jordan Pond, includes a cafe and a gift store where you can purchase cold drinks.

There are two campgrounds within the park. Blackwoods is open all year (phone (207) 288-3274), and Seawall is open from late May to late September (phone (207) 244-3600). No camping is permitted outside designated campgrounds.

Hazards: The carriage roads have many users, including hikers and horses. Mountain bike riders are requested to yield to both. Hiking trails intersect the

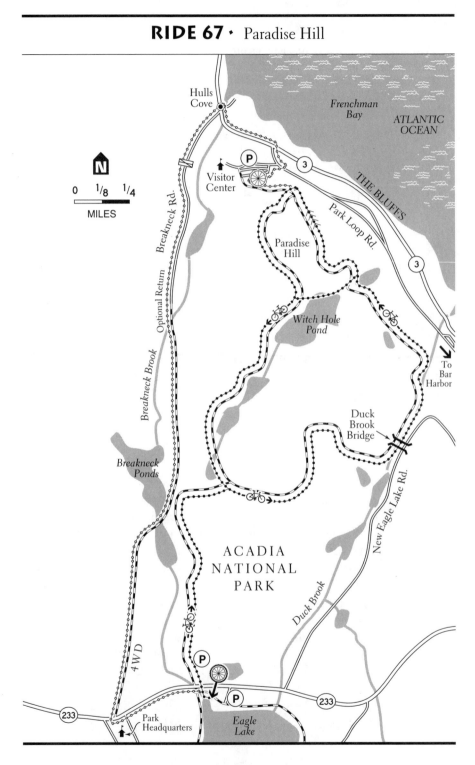

carriage road system at many points, and special care should be taken at these junctions. Also, if you are riding in the same direction as a hiker, be sure to slow down and warn them of your approach with a friendly greeting. Consult the Preface for tips on riding safely past horses.

Finally, the gravel surface of the carriage roads can be loose in places, requiring care around sharp corners and long descents. Hybrids and mountain bikes are best suited to Acadia's carriage paths.

Rescue index: You are never more than 2 miles from assistance. Report all accidents to park headquarters.

Land status: Acadia National Park.

Maps: A map of Mount Desert Island is available at bike shops in Bar Harbor, or by writing to: Superintendent, Acadia National Park, Bar Harbor, ME 04609. Another small book, *Acadia's Biking Guide and Carriage Road Handbook* (from Parkman Publications), includes a handy map and a detailed description of most of the trail system. This pocket-sized guide is available at many bookstores and bike shops.

Finding the trail: Immediately after crossing the bridge onto Mount Desert Island, bear right at a fork onto ME 198/102. Turn left onto ME 198/3 in Somesville. Turn left onto ME 233, following this road for approximately 4 miles, and passing the park headquarters on the right. Just after the park headquarters, look for signs indicating the Eagle Lake parking areas. There are parking lots on both sides of the road.

Sources of additional information:

Superintendent
Acadia National Park
P.O. Box 177
Bar Harbor, ME 04609

Bar Harbor Bicycle Shop
141 Cottage Street
Bar Harbor, ME 04609
(207) 288-3886

Acadia Bike & Canoe Company
48 Cottage Street
Bar Harbor, ME 04609
(207) 288-9605

Notes on the trail: From the trailhead turn right, following the shore of Eagle Lake for a short distance. At the first intersection (signpost 6) turn right, passing beneath ME 233. You will be pedaling north. Turn right at signpost 4 and follow the signs directing you to Witch Hole Pond. At signpost 3, turn right and gradually climb to the top of Paradise Hill. At signpost 1, you have

Mountain bikers will marvel at the intricate stonework of the many bridges along the carriage path system in Acadia National Park.

the option of following an alternate, more challenging trail back. If you wish to take the alternate trail, turn right and begin a long descent to park head-quarters. All others should turn left at signpost 1, right at signpost 2, and then right again at signpost 4 to return to the trailhead at Eagle Lake.

For those interested in following the more challenging route back to the trailhead, the ride continues through the Visitor Information Center parking lot. You must follow the paved road out of the parking lot and follow signs to ME 3 heading toward Hulls Cove. Turn left on ME 3 and pedal the short dis-tance to Hull's Cove, where you will cross a small concrete bridge. Immedi-ately after crossing the bridge, turn left up a somewhat obscure paved road that passes behind several businesses in Hull's Cove. This is Breakneck Road, which you will follow for most of your return trip.

After passing several residences, the road gradually deteriorates into a wide, gravel, four-wheel-drive jeep trail. You will pass a large beaver pond on the left and cross several minor streams. After less than 2 miles, Breakneck Road passes close to the carriage path on which you started. There is a small path linking these trails, and riders who wish to return quickly to their vehicles should take the carriage path back. Turn right upon entering the carriage path to return to the trailhead.

For those riders who wish to continue on Breakneck Road, the old road can be followed as it veers right away from the carriage path and crosses Breakneck Pond. Breakneck Road, much rougher now, continues for another 2.2 miles before coming out onto the paved Eagle Lake Road (ME 233), nearly opposite the park headquarters. Turn left, and coast down the hill to the trailhead.

RIDE 68 · The Heart of Acadia

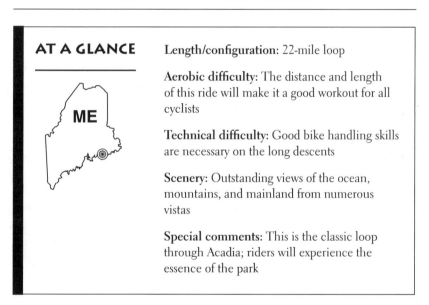

AT A GLANCE

Length/configuration: 22-mile loop

Aerobic difficulty: The distance and length of this ride will make it a good workout for all cyclists

Technical difficulty: Good bike handling skills are necessary on the long descents

Scenery: Outstanding views of the ocean, mountains, and mainland from numerous vistas

Special comments: This is the classic loop through Acadia; riders will experience the essence of the park

This 22-mile loop follows the wide, well-maintained gravel trails that wind through Acadia National Park on Mount Desert Island. Though riding these carriage roads requires very little technical skill, there are several extended climbs along this loop. Cardiovascular fitness will ensure that the views, rather than the climbing, will leave you breathless.

Construction for the carriage road system at Acadia was begun in the early twentieth century by John D. Rockefeller, Jr. The careful layout of these trails highlights the most scenic areas of the park. Along the lower-lying sections of the carriage road system you will be riding along artfully designed roads, through spruce and hemlock woods, and over small wooden bridges. From each pond, however, the trails turn upward, and you will find yourself climbing to tremendous views of Somes Sound, Blue Hill Bay, and the Gulf of Maine. From lush woods you will ride up to the more exposed slopes of Sargent Mountain, across stunning granite bridges, and through the natural amphitheater formed by the south ridges of Penobscot and Sargent Mountains.

The Heart of Acadia ride begins at Eagle Lake and traces a loop through some of the most beautiful areas of the park. From Eagle Lake, you will climb briefly through tall pines and then descend past Aunt Betty Pond to an area of wetland known as Gilmore Meadow. A gradual rise indicates the beginning of an extended yet picturesque climb that crosses Chasm Brook a total of six times. You will continue climbing up the north flank of Sargent Mountain. Here, the woods become more sparse and views begin to open up around you. The tops of many of the mountains at Acadia are devoid of much vegetation as a result of the Great Fire of 1947. Because of this, you will enjoy tremendous views as you ascend to higher elevations. From Sargent Mountain, you will descend to Jordan Pond and then trace a loop around Pemetic Mountain to reach Bubble Pond. Upon reaching the southern tip of Eagle Pond, you can choose to return to the parking area by riding around the west side of the pond, up around Corner Nubble, or along the flatter, eastern-shore trail.

General location: Acadia National Park, Mount Desert Island.

Elevation change: At Eagle Lake, where you begin and end this ride, your elevation is 277'. You will climb just 400' before descending to Aunt Betty Pond at 209'. From Aunt Betty Pond you will climb to the highest point in the carriage road system: 800' above sea level. From this point on Sargent Mountain you will descend more gradually to Jordan Pond at 273'. Skirting the eastern side of Pemetic Mountain to reach Bubble Pond, you will gain only 190'. From Bubble Pond at 336' you will climb to 460' around the western flank of Corners Nubble before returning to Eagle Lake and your starting point at 277'. Total elevation gain is approximately 1,120'.

Season: The system of carriage roads at Acadia National Park is open year-round. For cyclists, the best time to ride is after the spring thaw and until the trails have been groomed for cross-country skiers. Because summertime at Acadia is extremely busy, we recommend you try riding these trails in the spring and fall. Furthermore, because no hunting is permitted at the park, fall is a perfect time to take in the beauty of Acadia. Not only will you enjoy the peace of mind that comes from knowing that there are no hunters around, but you will also be riding on virtually deserted trails.

Services: All services are available in Bar Harbor and include an American Youth Hostel (AYH), open mid-June through August. Contact them at

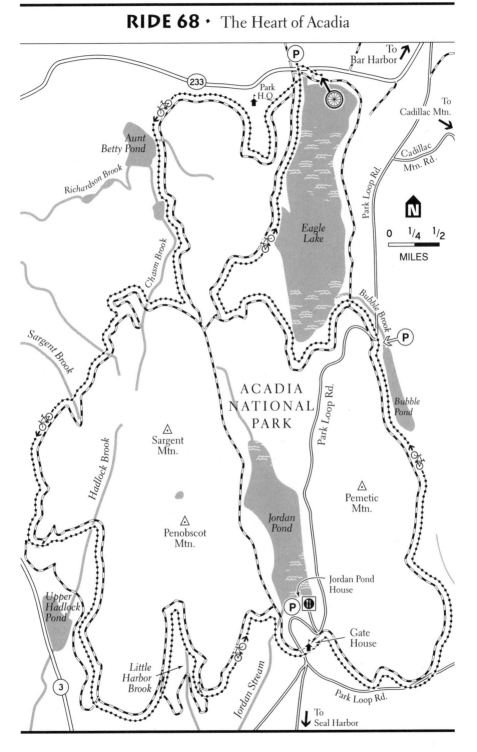

(207) 288-5587. The Pond House, at the southern tip of Jordan Pond, includes a cafe and a gift store where you can purchase cold drinks. There are two campgrounds within the park. Blackwoods is open all year (phone (207) 288-3274), and Seawall is open from late May to late September (phone (207) 244-3600).

Hazards: The carriage roads have many users, including hikers and horses. Mountain bike riders are requested to yield to both. Hiking trails intersect the carriage road system at many points, and special care should be taken at these junctions. Also, if you are riding in the same direction as a hiker, be sure to slow down and warn them of your approach with a friendly greeting. Consult the Preface for tips on riding safely past horses.

Finally, the gravel surface of the carriage roads can be loose in places, requiring care around sharp corners and long descents.

Rescue index: Although the carriage roads are well used and easily accessible, you may be many miles from a trailhead. The trail around Sargent Mountain is particularly exposed; be sure to carry plenty of water and suitable protection from hot summer sun or fierce winter winds.

Land status: National park.

Maps: A map of Mount Desert Island is available at bike shops in Bar Harbor, or by writing to: Superintendent, Acadia National Park, Bar Harbor, ME 04609. Another small book, *Acadia's Biking Guide and Carriage Road Handbook* (from Parkman Publications), includes a handy map and a detailed description of most of the trail system. This pocket-sized guide is available at many bookstores and bike shops.

Finding the trail: You can park and pick up this trail at any of three locations: the parking area connected to the Jordan Pond House off Park Loop Road; the parking area off Park Loop Road at Bubble Pond; and, the point from which we began this loop, the Eagle Lake parking lot or boat launch. To get to the Eagle Lake parking lot, bear right after crossing the bridge to the island and drive south on ME 198/102 until you reach Somesville. Turn left at the junction with ME 198/3 and, after less than 2 miles, turn left on ME 233. Eagle Lake will appear on your right after approximately 4 miles on ME 233. The parking lot is on the left. The boat launch is just a short distance farther along ME 233 on the right-hand side of the road, and provides additional parking spaces.

Sources of additional information:

Superintendent
Acadia National Park
P.O. Box 177
Bar Harbor, ME 04609

Acadia's carriage paths are renowned for their smooth gravel surface and scenic vistas.

Bar Harbor Bicycle Shop
141 Cottage Street
Bar Harbor, ME 04609
(207) 288-3886

Acadia Bike & Canoe Company
48 Cottage Street
Bar Harbor, ME 04609
(207) 288-9605

Notes on the trail: The carriage road system at Acadia is well signed, with numbered posts placed at every trail intersection. Because the Heart of Acadia ride is actually made up of many different trails, the directions below make use of the signpost numbers, as opposed to the trail names.

From the Eagle Lake boat launch, turn right onto the gravel path and then turn left at the first **T** junction (post 6), as though you were going to ride around the lake in a counterclockwise direction. At the first right (post 9), turn up and away from the lake and climb before enjoying the long descent to Aunt Betty Pond. Where the pond merges with Gilmore Meadow (post 11), bear left and, after a gradual rise, begin what is considered to be one of the most challenging climbs of the carriage road system. Crossing Chasm Brook

6 times, this section of the ride highlights the beauty of the park's woods. You will barely have a chance to catch your breath as you approach the intersection with the "Around the Mountain" loop (post 10). Turn right and continue climbing.

This section of the trail takes you up the northern flank of Sargent Mountain; you will be rewarded with stunning views and an exhilarating descent. At the next intersection (post 12) continue straight and come to a deep ravine and waterfall crossed by two granite bridges. The road continues descending, though more gradually. Bear left at post 19 and continue straight at post 20. The trail cuts into the valley between Cedar Swamp Mountain and Penobscot Mountain at this point, tracing the lines of a natural amphitheater and following signs to the Jordan Pond House. Bear left at post 21 and then bear right at post 14, crossing Jordan Stream as you pass the southern tip of Jordan Pond.

Continue straight past the intersection at post 15 (this road is closed to bicycles). Bear left at post 16 and come to Park Loop Road through a beautiful gated entrance directly across from the Jordan Pond Gate Lodge, built in 1932. If you are looking for refreshments at this point in the ride, turn left onto Park Loop Road and ride a short distance past the lodge to the Jordan Pond House, which will be on your left. Otherwise, cross Park Loop Road and pick up the carriage road on the other side.

This part of the ride covers less hilly terrain, and you will enjoy the shade of thick woods. At post 17 continue straight to Bubble Pond, passing a paved road down on your right. You will ride along the western bank of Bubble Pond before crossing a small bridge and coming to a parking area. The trail continues past the parking area and crosses Park Loop Road once again. After just a short distance, you will reach the southern shore of Eagle Lake (post 7). From here, you can choose to turn left and ride away from the lake to follow the trail as it traces a curve around Corners Nubble. You will bear right at post 8 before dropping back down to the western shore of Eagle Lake and returning to the trailhead. Alternatively, you can turn right at post 7 and follow the trail around the eastern shore of Eagle Lake. This latter option is slightly easier, as it eliminates the climb up and around Corners Nubble. Either way, you will quickly find yourself back at the northern tip of Eagle Lake and the parking area from which you began.

RIDE 69 · Schoodic Mountain

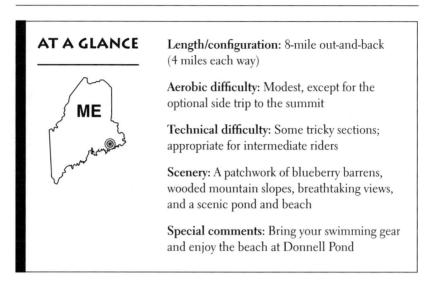

AT A GLANCE

Length/configuration: 8-mile out-and-back (4 miles each way)

Aerobic difficulty: Modest, except for the optional side trip to the summit

Technical difficulty: Some tricky sections; appropriate for intermediate riders

Scenery: A patchwork of blueberry barrens, wooded mountain slopes, breathtaking views, and a scenic pond and beach

Special comments: Bring your swimming gear and enjoy the beach at Donnell Pond

This ride is an eight-mile out-and-back excursion that provides a solution for those seeking more of a challenge than what Acadia's carriage path system offers. The ride uses double-track trails and former woods roads as it passes around the base of one of the most distinctive landmarks along the midcoast: 1,069-foot Schoodic Mountain. This ride is suitable for intermediate riders, although there can be some tricky, washed-out sections that some may elect to walk around.

Glorious 360-degree views of Mount Desert Island to the south, Donnell Pond, and interior Washington and Hancock counties are revealed to riders who make the eight-tenths-of-a-mile (one-way) side trip to the summit of Schoodic Mountain. The side trip should be walked by most people, as it climbs steeply up the solid granite slopes of the mountain. However, it can be ridden by cyclists possessing an advanced level of technical ability. Either walking or riding, the view from the summit should not be missed.

The Schoodic Mountain trail ends at a wonderful sand beach at the southern shore of Schoodic Bay on Donnell Pond. Schoodic Mountain rises sharply from the water's edge, and its wooded slopes and bare summit are mirrored dramatically on the surface of the pond. Swimming is permitted from the beach, and camping and picnicking facilities are available. If you are riding this trail in the summer, be sure to pack swimwear and picnic supplies! Donnell Pond and the surrounding area are extremely beautiful, and apart from the small beach, a boat landing, and a primitive campground at Black Beach, the land has been protected from development since 1988 by the formation of the Donnell Pond Management Unit. Donnell Pond features several sand beaches, small coves, and forested shorelands that form a perfect habitat for deer, bears, eagles, and osprey. Because of its recreational and scenic resource value, Donnell Pond has earned the highest resource class rating in the State of Maine Land Use Regulatory Commission's "Wildlands Lake Assessment."

General location: This ride is located in the town of Franklin and Township T9 SD, Hancock County.

Elevation change: There are several short, steep climbs and descents, but the overall elevation gain is negligible unless you choose to climb to the summit of Schoodic Mountain. From the main trail, this ascent features an elevation gain of approximately 900'.

Season: Good trail conditions begin in June and continue through the fall.

Services: There are primitive camping facilities on Donnell Pond as well as on Tunk Lake, farther east. Apart from a few general stores along US 1, all other facilities are available in Ellsworth, 25 miles to the west.

Hazards: The trailhead is situated at the edge of a blueberry barren. As is the case with many commercially run barrens, this site is sprayed against weeds and pests. Picking blueberries is therefore not only considered stealing but also potentially unsafe.

When we rode this trail at the end of July, we discovered that virtually all the puddles along the trail were inhabited by large bullfrogs. Words to the wise: Be careful not to run these guys over!

Rescue index: In most cases, assistance could be sought both at the trailhead and the active beach area on Donnell Pond, 2 miles away at the farthest. However, during the week, and especially in the spring and late fall, few people are likely to be nearby. In this case, the homes located near the trailhead would be your nearest source of assistance.

Land status: The latter portion of this ride passes through Maine public reserve land. The beginning of the Schoodic Mountain trail and the climb to the summit follow an old jeep trail.

Maps: The Schoodic Mountain trails are depicted in DeLorme's *Maine Atlas and Gazetteer* (map 24, sections E-4 and E-5), and the USGS 7.5 minute quad for the area is Sullivan.

Finding the trail: From US 1 in Sullivan, turn north onto ME 200 and drive 4 miles to East Franklin. At the foot of a steep hill in East Franklin, two bridges cross Carl Mill Stream. In between these bridges is a road that bears east off ME 200. Turn up this road and follow the right fork up a hill. You will come to a clearing at the edge of a blueberry barren where a few parking spaces are available.

RIDE 69 · Schoodic Mountain

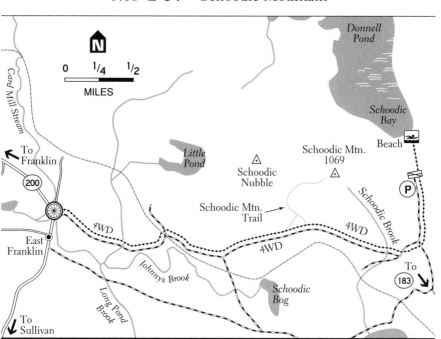

Sources of additional information: For another description of the Schoodic Mountain trail, consult the most recent edition of a hiking guide published by the Appalachian Mountain Club, *AMC Maine Mountain Guide*. For additional information about the Maine public reserve section of this ride, including the facilities on Donnell Pond, contact:

Department of Conservation
Bureau of Parks and Lands
22 State House Station
Augusta, ME 04333
(207) 287-2797

Notes on the trail: The trail begins by traveling east on a gravel jeep trail that runs along the base of the blueberry barren from the parking area. You will ride past a gate and, about 0.1 mile later, bear left at a fork in the trail. The trail then swings left, away from the barren, and ventures into the woods. Through oak, beech, and alder you will head up a short, steep climb over a surface that was once paved and is now quite severely eroded. Follow the trail across a railroad. Turn right after crossing the tracks, and ride alongside the railroad until the trail bears left into the woods. You will pass through an area that looks like an old burn, thick with oak trees, wild blueberries, and grass. At the next fork, bear left toward the mountain

At this point, the road surface changes to loose rock. Descending into a wooded area, you will see the first of the Schoodic Mountain trails on the left, marked by a cairn. Ride past this trail and continue to the crest of a short rise, where a second trail branches off to the left and climbs to the summit. Turn left here for the out-and-back side trip up Schoodic Mountain.

Returning from the side trip to the summit, turn left and continue along the trail that traverses wet, rocky, and moderately technical terrain. Turn left at an intersection with a dirt road and cross into Maine public reserve land. Turn left again onto a wide gravel road, and left one more time on a road that leads to the parking area for the Donnell Pond Recreational Area and Schoodic Beach. The trail down to the beach is at the far end of the parking lot. Take some time to relax at the beach before retracing your route back to your car.

RIDE 70 · Donnell Pond

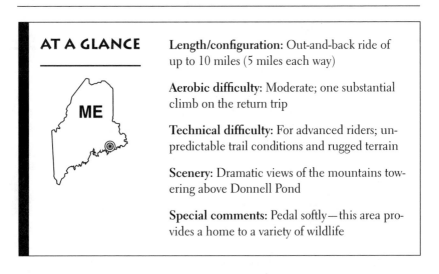

AT A GLANCE

Length/configuration: Out-and-back ride of up to 10 miles (5 miles each way)

Aerobic difficulty: Moderate; one substantial climb on the return trip

Technical difficulty: For advanced riders; unpredictable trail conditions and rugged terrain

Scenery: Dramatic views of the mountains towering above Donnell Pond

Special comments: Pedal softly—this area provides a home to a variety of wildlife

This out-and-back ride begins from Schoodic Beach at the southernmost tip of Donnell Pond. Following a rough and overgrown road up above the eastern shore of the pond, this is a moderately difficult ride suitable for intermediate or advanced riders. The length of the ride depends on where you choose to turn around; Black Beach is 2.5 miles from the starting point, making for a 5-mile out-and-back excursion. Alternatively, it is possible to ride beyond Black Beach and continue pedaling around the western slope of Caribou Mountain and toward Shillalah and Fox Ponds. If you choose to ride out to Fox Pond before turning around, your ride will be a ten-mile trek.

Donnell Pond is nestled at the base of several mountains, which rise dramatically from the water to elevations up to 1,100 feet above sea level. Once targeted for development, the state acquired approximately 7,000 acres around the pond and has, as a consequence, set forth a multiple-use management plan. Along with enhancing the natural resources of the area and overseeing timber management, the Bureau of Public Lands aims to preserve the area for its recreational opportunities. As a result, many people now make use of the pond for summertime boating and swimming. In the fall, however, when we rode this trail, the area was virtually deserted. During the afternoon we spent exploring the trails around the pond, the only creature we came upon was a rather startled black bear.

Donnell Pond is deep and rocky, covering over 1,000 acres. A shoreline of granite boulders and sand beaches frame the pond, which boasts exceptionally clear waters that, when calm, reflect the wooded slopes of Black and Schoodic Mountains. Listen for loons as you reach the water's edge, and take the time to look toward the sky as well, for bald eagles and osprey are often spotted here.

General location: Donnell Pond is located just northeast of the town of Sullivan, and approximately 25 miles to the east of Ellsworth.

Elevation change: The Schoodic Beach parking area lies at 260' above sea level. You will climb 100' before descending to Donnell Pond, at an elevation of approximately 120'. From Black Beach the trail does not climb higher than 300'. The most grueling climb is the trip from Black Beach back to the trailhead, where you gain 220' over 2.5 miles.

Season: Fall is the most spectacular time of year to visit Donnell Pond. However, this trail should be good riding from late June into November.

Services: All services are available in Ellsworth, 25 miles to the west.

Hazards: This ride follows an unpaved old road that has not been maintained for years. The road is severely eroded in places and also obscured by deadfall. In late fall, leaves thickly cover the trail and further obscure rocks, roots, washed-out places, and ruts. Be aware, also, of the potential hazard you present to the area as a rider. There are some unique natural resources in this area, including sensitive wildlife habitats, so it is extremely important to stick to the trail.

RIDE 70 · Donnell Pond

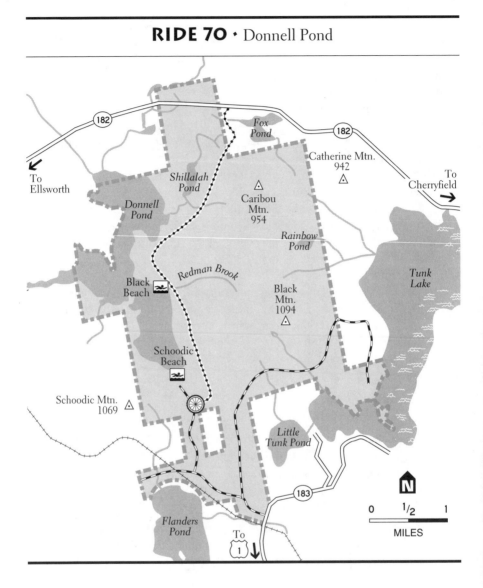

Rescue index: Though activity on the pond may be heavy on certain summer weekends, you will be in remote country throughout this ride. Access to Black Beach, for example, is only possible from the water unless you hike or bike in on the trails. There are homes along Punkinville Road on the way into the reserve, and these would be your closest source of help.

Land status: This ride follows an abandoned management road through Maine public reserve land.

Maps: The USGS quadrangle for this area is Sullivan. However, the topographic map does not show the more recently developed roads that now provide access to the pond. To find the trailhead, it is best to use the more up-to-date maps in *The Maine Atlas and Gazetteer,* published by DeLorme (map 24, section E-5).

Finding the trail: From US 1, turn north up Punkinville Road, which intersects US 1 between the towns of Sullivan and East Sullivan. Drive up Punkinville Road, bearing right at a fork in the road. Cross the railroad and take the first left: an unpaved access road to Donnell Pond. After a short distance, this road takes a sharp left turn and continues all the way to the parking area above Schoodic Beach. Be sure to stay on the main road; there are several turnoffs.

Source of additional information: The Bureau of Public Lands published, in December 1991, a management plan for this area. For further information, contact the bureau at:

Department of Conservation
Bureau of Parks and Lands
22 State House Station
Augusta, ME 04333
(207) 287-2791

Notes on the trail: From the parking area above Schoodic Beach, ride back up the road on which you drove to the top of a short hill. Look for a trail on the left, which is posted as being closed to vehicles. This trail follows the route of an abandoned management road that is still hard-packed but strewn with deadfall and blow-downs. You will cross a footpath that leads hikers to the Black Mountain trails. Continuing straight, the trail runs along a small stream for a short distance. The stream eventually cuts downhill to the left, and the trail continues straight. Shortly beyond this point, the trail crosses the blazed Black Mountain trail and then reaches a severely eroded section of the road. After crossing a small stream, look to the left for views of Schoodic Mountain. The trail will then begin to descend along a narrow stretch of single-track. This descent ends at Black Beach, where you need to cross a double-plank bridge to reach the beach.

Continuing along the beach to the right, you will reach a bulletin board and camping area, complete with an outhouse. The trail cuts away from the water, just to the left of the outhouse, and continues along an old road similar to the one at the beginning of the ride. This road eventually becomes rougher and begins to climb somewhat. Due to a quickly setting sun in late autumn, we turned around at this point (3.5 miles from the trailhead) and retraced our route back to the parking area for a total distance of 7 miles. It is possible,

Negotiating a
rough descent to
Donnell Pond.

however, to continue riding to Fox Pond and lengthen the ride to a total distance of 10 miles.

At whatever point you choose to turn around, retrace your route back to
the trailhead. From the trailhead, it is also possible to ride down the access
road to Schoodic Beach. Use care if you ride in the summer or on a weekend;
there can be quite a bit of pedestrian traffic between the parking area and the
beach.

RIDE 71 · Edmunds Township

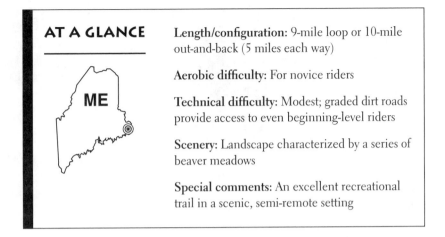

AT A GLANCE

Length/configuration: 9-mile loop or 10-mile out-and-back (5 miles each way)

Aerobic difficulty: For novice riders

Technical difficulty: Modest; graded dirt roads provide access to even beginning-level riders

Scenery: Landscape characterized by a series of beaver meadows

Special comments: An excellent recreational trail in a scenic, semi-remote setting

This ride is a nine-mile loop that traverses the woods roads of the Edmunds unit of Moosehorn National Wildlife Refuge. The loop is completed along Lower Edmunds Road, a paved road that nevertheless passes through beautiful countryside along the shore of Whiting Bay. To eliminate any riding on pavement, you can pedal the woods-road portion of the ride as a ten-mile out-and-back instead. Either way, the ride is rated for cyclists possessing beginning- and intermediate-level riding skills. The combination of semi-remote woods roads and scenic pavement makes this an excellent recreational trail.

The Edmunds unit is the southern section of Moosehorn National Wildlife Refuge. The area it encompasses is a fascinating blend of woods and open areas dominated by a series of flowages. As in the northern unit of the refuge, this area is an excellent one in which to observe a variety of birds and wildlife. In the spring and summer, wildflowers abound in the grassy areas around the flowages. Although the Edmunds unit provides less in the way of accessible mountain biking terrain, it does enjoy the advantage of being situated so close to Cobscook Bay State Park. The park offers campsites overlooking the waters of Whiting Bay, Broad Cove, and Burnt Cove, as well as picnic areas, a boat launch, and nature trails. Cobscook Bay State Park can serve as the trailhead for the Edmunds ride for people taking advantage of the camping or day-use facilities at the park.

General location: Moosehorn National Wildlife Refuge, Edmunds unit, just south of Dennysville.

Elevation change: There are a few moderate grades on this ride but no dramatic changes in elevation.

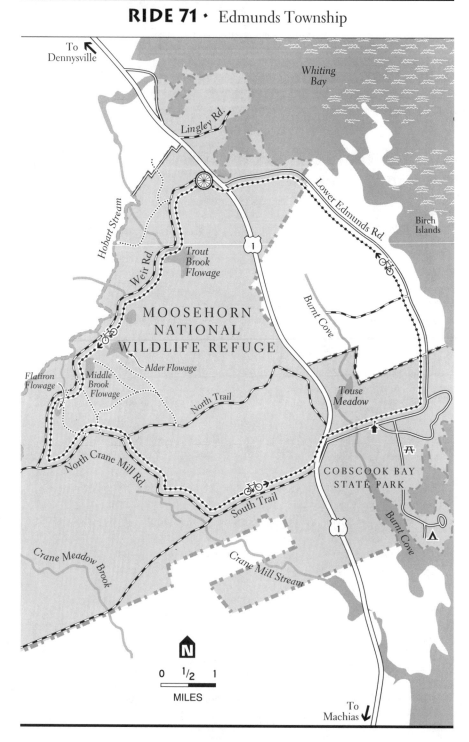

Season: Access to the roads and trails on the refuge is possible throughout the year. For mountain biking, summer and fall offer the best conditions.

Services: Basic services are available in Dennysville. Because bicycle parts and service may be hard to come by, it is advisable to come prepared with your own parts and tools. If you are looking for accommodations, nearby Cobscook Bay State Park is one of Maine's most beautiful campgrounds and one of our personal favorites. Information about camping at Cobscook Bay can be obtained by contacting park headquarters between 9 A.M. and 3 P.M. on weekdays only:

Cobscook Bay State Park
RR 1, Box 127
Dennysville, ME 04628
(207) 726-4412
Instate: (800) 287-3824

Hazards: This ride is accessed from US 1, and caution should be used at all times along this busy stretch of highway.

Rescue index: The Edmunds unit of Moosehorn National Wildlife Refuge is less traveled than the northern Baring unit. Assistance can often be found on US 1 and at the entrance to Cobscook Bay State Park.

Land status: National wildlife refuge.

Maps: Maps of Moosehorn are available at the refuge headquarters in the Baring. The Baring unit is located off US 1, just a few miles southwest of Calais, but can be accessed conveniently from the south by means of Charlotte Road. To reach the refuge headquarters from Dennysville, drive north on US 1 to West Pembrooke. Turn left, heading north on ME 214. Drive through Ayers Junction and then, at Blanchard Corner, turn right onto Charlotte Road. Bear left as the road curves around Round Lake, and continue for approximately 4 miles to Headquarters Road. Turn left and find yourself at the refuge headquarters after just a short distance.

Refuge headquarters are open weekdays only from 7:30 A.M. to 4 P.M.. An outdoor information center may also be stocked with maps if you are visiting the refuge before or after hours, or on the weekend.

Finding the trail: Approaching the ride from the south, drive up US 1 from Machias and toward Dennysville. Drive past the entrance to Cobscook Bay State Park, on the right. Approximately 2 miles past the park entrance, look for Lower Edmunds Road on the right. Just beyond Lower Edmunds Road, there will be a small turn-in on the left side of US 1 that is gated and signed as Weir Road. This is the trailhead. To park, pull off to the side of the road, taking care not to block the gated entrance.

An alternative trailhead is available to riders camping at Cobscook Bay State Park, or for anyone planning to use the day-use facilities at the park.

The quiet woods roads of Moosehorn National Wildlife Refuge offer excellent opportunities to spot white-tailed deer, moose, and black bears.

From the park, ride up to Lower Edmunds Road and turn right. Follow the road to its northern junction with US 1. Turn right onto US 1 and look for Weir Road on the left just a short distance farther.

Source of additional information:

Refuge Manager
Moosehorn National Wildlife Refuge
RR 1, Box 202, Suite 1
Baring, ME 04694-9703
(207) 454-7161

Notes on the trail: From US 1, begin riding along Weir Road. You will pedal past a series of flowages, including Trout Brook, Maple, Alder, Middle Brook, and Flatiron. At a **T** junction with North Trail, turn left. North Trail skirts the perimeter of the wilderness area of the refuge. At a fork in the trail, bear right onto Crane Mill Road. At the intersection with South Trail, bear left and

follow South Trail out to US 1. Turn left on US 1, and after just 500 feet turn
right onto Lower Edmunds Road. The entrance to Cobscook Bay State Park
will be on your right. Follow Lower Edmunds Road all the way back to US 1,
and turn right on US 1 to return to the trailhead.

RIDE 72 · Goodall Heath–to–Barn Meadow

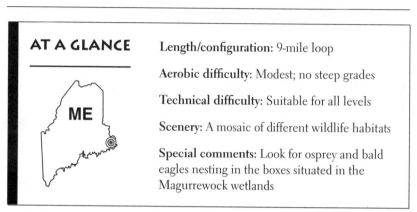

AT A GLANCE

Length/configuration: 9-mile loop

Aerobic difficulty: Modest; no steep grades

Technical difficulty: Suitable for all levels

Scenery: A mosaic of different wildlife habitats

Special comments: Look for osprey and bald
eagles nesting in the boxes situated in the
Magurrewock wetlands

Located in the northernmost portion of the Moosehorn National Wildlife
Refuge, this ride is a nine-mile loop along two-wheel-drive woods roads,
with a short distance on US 1. Riders of any level will enjoy the relatively flat
topography of this area. The terrain is not technically challenging, and it is
quite definitely the scenic beauty of the location and the opportunity to observe wildlife that draws riders to these trails. Though relatively short in distance, the trails through the refuge can, at times, feel quite remote.

Moosehorn National Wildlife Refuge is located in the easternmost corner
of Maine. The refuge consists of two areas: the Baring unit just south of Calais,
and the Edmunds unit, on Cobscook Bay near Dennysville. Between its two
units, Moosehorn features over 50 miles of roads and trails that are closed to
vehicle traffic but open to outdoor enthusiasts for hiking, cross-country skiing,
snowmobiling, and, of course, mountain biking. Wildlife is abundant in the
refuge, and the system of gravel woods roads in both units provides riders with
the opportunity to watch bald eagles and osprey; to catch fleeting glimpses of
timid black bears, deer, and moose; and to observe beavers and otters, geese,
and loons in any of the 50 lakes, marshes, and flowages scattered throughout
the refuge.

This ride, our first at Moosehorn, testifies to the likelihood of spotting
wildlife of many types. We began our ride by startling a black bear as we

rode up Goodall Heath Road. As is usually the case with black bears, this one was even more eager to put some distance between us than we were! At the end of our ride, we took a short side trip down to Two Mile Meadow, where a petulant beaver made it very clear that we were unwelcome visitors. After swimming aggressively toward us in a series of loops, the beaver finally slapped its tail in the water and swam off to a less crowded area. We then encountered some crowds of our own: at the entrance to the refuge, cars were stopped along Charlotte Road as people with binoculars observed a bald eagle in one of the nesting boxes. Mountain bikes, because they are relatively quiet, are the perfect way to explore Moosehorn and benefit from its mission as a refuge and breeding ground for migratory birds and other wildlife.

General location: Moosehorn National Wildlife Refuge, Baring unit, just south of Calais.

Elevation change: There is no significant change in elevation on this ride.

Season: Access to the roads and trails on the refuge is possible throughout the year. For mountain biking, summer and fall offer the best conditions.

Services: Other than bathroom facilities and water fountains at the refuge headquarters, all services must be sought in Calais, a few miles north on US 1. Because bicycle parts and service may be hard to come by, it is advisable to come prepared with your own parts and tools.

If you are looking for accommodations, Cobscook Bay State Park, on US 1 south of Dennysville, is one of Maine's most beautiful campgrounds and one of our personal favorites. Information about camping at Cobscook Bay can be obtained by contacting park headquarters between 9 A.M. and 3 P.M. on weekdays only:

Cobscook Bay State Park
RR 1, Box 127
Dennysville, ME 04628
(207) 726-4412
Instate: (800) 287-3824

Hazards: Moosehorn is open to deer hunting in November, so be sure to dress in bright colors if you are riding at this time of year. Occasionally, refuge vehicles travel on the trails at Moosehorn.

Rescue index: It is possible to ride deep into the refuge, away from any signs of other people. This ride, however, stays in the northern portion of the refuge, within close proximity to the refuge headquarters, Charlotte Road, and US 1.

Land status: National wildlife refuge.

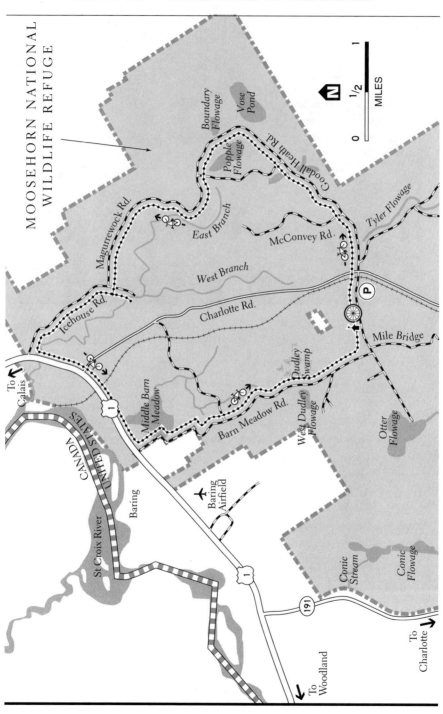

Riding past one of the many flowages that serve as breeding areas and migration stops for a wide variety of waterfowl at Moosehorn National Wildlife Refuge.

Maps: Maps of Moosehorn are available at the refuge headquarters (Monday–Friday, 7:30 A.M. to 4 P.M.), located off Charlotte Road approximately 2 miles south of US 1. An outdoor information center may also be stocked with maps if you are visiting the refuge before or after hours, or on the weekend.

Finding the trail: From Calais, travel south on US 1 for just a few miles. After crossing the east branch of Magurrewock Stream, turn left on Charlotte Road. Drive down Charlotte Road to Headquarters Road and turn right, crossing the tracks of the Maine Central Railroad. Continue on to the refuge headquarters, or park in the area next to the Woodcock Trail, where there are more parking spaces available.

Source of additional information:

Refuge Manager
Moosehorn National Wildlife Refuge
RR 1, Box 202, Suite 1
Baring, ME 04694-9703
(207) 454-7161

Notes on the trail: From the parking lot at the head of the Woodcock Trail, ride back toward Charlotte Road. Cross the road and continue straight, until you reach a fork. Bear left and begin pedaling up Goodall Heath Road. Past Upper Goodall Heath, bear right at the next fork and ride the Vose Pond Road past Vose Pond. Bear right again at the next intersection and ride on Magurrewock Road all the way out to US 1. Turn left onto US 1, watching carefully for traffic.

Ride for about 1 mile on US 1, passing the junction with Charlotte Road and crossing the tracks of the Maine Central Railroad. Once past the railroad crossing, begin looking on the left for Barn Meadow Road, a two-wheel-drive dirt road. Turn left down Barn Meadow Road and follow it to a T intersection. Turning right will take you down to a scenic area around Two Mile Meadow and the Otter Flowage. Turning left will take you to the refuge headquarters, beyond which you will continue along Headquarters Road back to your car.

RIDE 73 · Snare Meadow

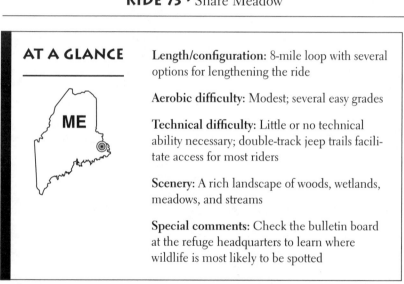

AT A GLANCE

ME

Length/configuration: 8-mile loop with several options for lengthening the ride

Aerobic difficulty: Modest; several easy grades

Technical difficulty: Little or no technical ability necessary; double-track jeep trails facilitate access for most riders

Scenery: A rich landscape of woods, wetlands, meadows, and streams

Special comments: Check the bulletin board at the refuge headquarters to learn where wildlife is most likely to be spotted

Snare Meadow is at least an eight-mile loop that follows a network of access roads through the central portion of Moosehorn National Wildlife Refuge. These access roads are seldom-used jeep trails characterized by a vegetated center median. Beginning- and intermediate-level riders should have no difficulty with the terrain, which includes only moderate hill climbs. For riders looking for a more challenging loop, there are several opportunities to add mileage to this ride and explore deeper into the southern portion of the refuge.

The central portion of Moosehorn National Wildlife Refuge covers an area that was once an active logging region. Horses were used to haul wood to the western bank of the St. Croix River. There, during spring floods, logs were floated to Calais. From the port in Calais, these logs were shipped by schooner and steamship to markets throughout the world. At the beginning of this century, however, the world market for timber declined. At the same time, the forest industry mechanized and the traditional spring river drives were eventually banned. Today, land that was once cleared has now returned to forest. All that remains to tell the story of the industry that once dominated this land are the old stone fences and the cellar holes of farms long-since abandoned.

General location: Moosehorn National Wildlife Refuge, Baring unit.

Elevation change: There are some moderate grades along this trail but no significant change in elevation.

Season: Access to the roads and trails on the refuge is possible throughout the year. For mountain biking, summer and fall offer the best conditions.

Services: Other than rest rooms and water fountains at the refuge headquarters, all services must be sought in Calais, a few miles north on US 1. Because bicycle parts and service may be hard to come by, it is advisable to come prepared with your own spare parts and tools.

If you are looking for accommodations, we strongly recommend Cobscook Bay State Park, on US 1 south of Dennysville. Information about camping at Cobscook Bay can be obtained by contacting park headquarters between 9 A.M. and 3 P.M. on weekdays only:

Cobscook Bay State Park
RR 1, Box 127
Dennysville, ME 04628
(207) 726-4412
Instate: (800) 287-3824

Hazards: Moosehorn is open to deer hunting in November, so be sure to dress in bright colors if you are riding at that time of year. Be aware, also, that refuge vehicles occasionally travel the roads through the refuge.

Rescue index: The refuge headquarters, located in the northern half of the Baring unit, are one potential source of assistance, but their hours of operation are limited. Some traffic makes regular use of Charlotte Road, which runs through the middle of the refuge, and ME 191 is another potential source of assistance if you encounter problems in the southern portion of the refuge.

Land status: National wildlife refuge.

RIDE 73 · Snare Meadow

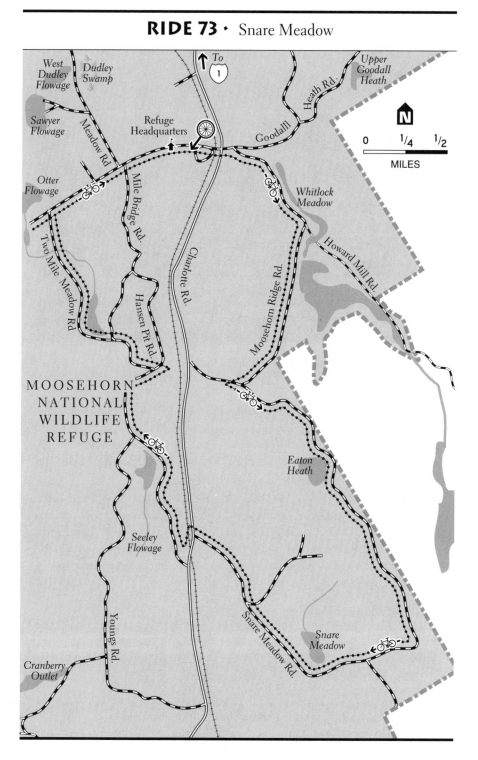

West Dudley Flowage

Dudley Swamp

To 1

Upper Goodall Heath

Heath Rd.

Sawyer Flowage

Meadow Rd.

Refuge Headquarters

Goodall

N

0   1/4   1/2
MILES

Otter Flowage

Mile Bridge Rd.

Whitlock Meadow

Howard Mill Rd.

Two Mile Meadow Rd

Hansen Pit Rd.

Charlotte Rd.

Moosehorn Ridge Rd.

MOOSEHORN
NATIONAL
WILDLIFE
REFUGE

Eaton Heath

Seeley Flowage

Snare Meadow Rd.

Snare Meadow

Youngs Rd.

Cranberry Outlet

Seeley Flowage. Moosehorn National Wildlife Refuge.

Maps: Maps of Moosehorn are available at the refuge headquarters (Monday–Friday, 7:30 A.M. to 4 P.M.), located off Charlotte Road approximately 2 miles south of US 1. An outdoor information center located at the refuge headquarters may also be stocked with maps if you are visiting the refuge before or after hours, or on the weekend.

Finding the trail: From Calais, travel south on US 1 for a few miles. After crossing the east branch of Magurrewock Stream, turn left on Charlotte Road. Drive down Charlotte Road to Headquarters Road and turn right, crossing the Maine Central Railroad. Continue on to the refuge headquarters, or park in the area next to the Woodcock Trail, where there are more parking spaces available.

Source of additional information:

> Refuge Manager
> Moosehorn National Wildlife Refuge
> RR 1, Box 202, Suite 1
> Baring, ME 04694-9703
> (207) 454-7161

Notes on the trail: From the parking area outside the Woodcock Trail, ride back to Charlotte Road. Cross the road and continue straight on the other side. At the first fork in the road, bear right and pedal down Howard Mill Road. After just half a mile, bear right onto Moosehorn Ridge Road. At the next intersection, a **T** junction with Snare Meadow Road, turn left. You will be riding in a southerly direction on Snare Meadow Road, until the road swings to the right and traverses the southern shore of Snare Meadow. At a second curve in the road, you will be traveling northwest toward Charlotte Road. At the intersection with Charlotte Road, turn left.

At this point in the ride, you can choose your return route, depending on how much distance you wish to cover. The shortest loop requires that you turn right off Charlotte Road and up Mile Bridge Road, for a ride of 8 miles. Alternatively, you can continue down Charlotte Road to the intersection of Youngs Road, South Trail, or Beaver Trail, and return to the trailhead along the perimeter of the refuge wilderness area. These options create rides of 10, 11, or 13 miles, respectively. With the map provided by the refuge, and the number of distinct landmarks throughout the refuge, it is nearly impossible to get lost.

AROOSTOOK COUNTY

The network of rail trails in Aroostook County is northern Maine's answer to the carriage trails of Mount Desert Island. Wide, well maintained, and free of automobile traffic, they offer access to the quiet beauty and rugged wilderness of Maine's northernmost county. The most striking difference between these trails and their southern counterparts is to be found in the number of people you may meet. From May through October, you will be more likely to encounter the tracks of moose, deer, or bear than you will the tread-marks left by a previous rider. Indeed, although these trails link some of the larger towns and cities of Aroostook County, they follow the paths once taken by trains through some of the more remote areas of the state. Though you may not be far from a road as the crow flies, the thick woods and wide rivers that border the trails make road access almost impossible except at marked junctions and intersections.

POTATOES IN AROOSTOOK

Aroostook County forms Maine's northern and northeastern boundary. "The County," as it is referred to, has been described as being a land entirely different from the rest of the state. It is Maine's "big sky" land, where large farms are nestled among hundreds of acres of cleared and cultivated land that provide wide-open views for miles. The County's 6,453 square miles extend across an area of rolling agricultural land and scattered mountains. One such mountain, the 1,660-foot monadnock named Mars Hill, is visible to riders pedaling north along the Houlton-to–Phair Junction railroad bed.

Other highlights of riding along this abandoned railroad bed are the track-side potato storage facilities. Potato farming is the major industry in this part of Aroostook County. These potato "houses" are a distinct form of agricultural architecture. Though they vary in size and design, they were usually built into hillsides to provide a cool, stable environment for storing potatoes. Potato houses evolved with the potato farming boom that followed the arrival of the Bangor and Aroostook Railroad in 1899. Prior to the railroad, most of Maine's potato crop was consumed instate. With the extension of the railroad, production increased dramatically and one half of all the potatoes raised were shipped out of state by rail.

In addition to potato farming, the logging industry has been a significant part of the County's industry, particularly along the St. John River Valley. The town of Van Buren was one of the larger logging towns along the St. John River. Houlton, the Aroostook County Seat, was a pioneer community and the first town in the county to be reached by the railroad in 1899. Caribou was the shipping center for Aroostook potato farmers, and near Caribou, Fort Fairfield, and Limestone, many small limestone quarries once operated to make lime for cement, mortar, and agricultural purposes.

In 1993 the closure of Loring Air Force Base, the largest employer in the County, sent an economic shock through the region. However, by aggressively reusing the space formerly occupied by the air force, the towns have returned to a state of relative prosperity.

RIDE 74 · Houlton-to–Phair Junction Rail Trail

AT A GLANCE	
ME	**Length/configuration:** 40-mile point-to-point
	Aerobic difficulty: If ridden in its entirety, this ride requires endurance
	Technical difficulty: Minimal; generally smooth, unobstructed trail surface
	Scenery: Everything that Aroostook County has to offer, including rolling fields, thick woods, and pretty rivers and streams
	Special comments: This ride makes a great tour of the potato farming industry

In 1894, the Bangor and Aroostook Railroad completed this 40-mile link between Houlton and Presque Isle. For decades, the economic lifeblood of Aroostook County flowed along this route. Passengers, potatoes, and, in later years, wood products were carried by the railroad. Eventually, an improved road system allowed automobiles and trucks to siphon business away from the railway. In 1978, the B&A announced that it was intending to abandon this section of railway. The tracks were removed in 1983.

Fortunately for bicyclists, the rail bed was acquired by the state for conversion into a state recreational trail. Today, the old route of the Bangor and Aroostook Railroad makes a dandy 40-mile point-to-point ride for cyclists of all abilities. It is probably most practical to park a vehicle at either end of the trail, or to select a portion of the trail as a shorter, out-and-back excursion. Alternatively, more adventurous cyclists can use this route as the start of a 160-mile back-roads tour of Aroostook County. Seventy additional miles of abandoned railway can be accessed by means of a 14-mile road ride to Mapleton or a 17-mile road ride to Washburn. (See Ride 75, Aroostook Valley Trail.)

Points of interest along the old railway include the high trestle over the Meduxnekeag River near Monticello, numerous potato houses, and several old mill sites. The rail bed passes through several wetlands that teem with wildlife. The highlight of our ride occurred on a portion of the trail near Westfield, as dusk settled over the woods. Ahead of us in the trail, a shadowy figure turned out to be a black bear collecting berries. True to their reputation for being shy animals, this bear quickly disappeared into the bushes.

General location: This linear trail passes through the towns of Houlton, Littleton, Monticello, Bridgewater, Mars Hill, Westfield, and Presque Isle in southeastern Aroostook County.

Elevation change: This is a former railway. The change in elevation is negligible.

Season: Early spring through fall is the best time to ride this trail.

Services: There are small grocery stores and/or restaurants in all of the small towns through which this trail passes. Bicycle repair facilities, however, are only available in Presque Isle. Vicious Cycle is a full-service bike store that is affiliated with Northeast Outdoor Adventures, an outfitter that offers pedal-and-paddle tours of the area. Vicious Cycle is located at 95 Parkhurst Siding Road (ME 205) in Presque Isle and can be contacted at (207) 764-5728 or (888) 881-7469. Another source of bicycle service and repair is Aroostook Bike and Sport (phone (207) 764-0206).

If you are camping, there are facilities at Aroostook State Park in Presque Isle. For further information, contact the park headquarters at (207) 768-8341.

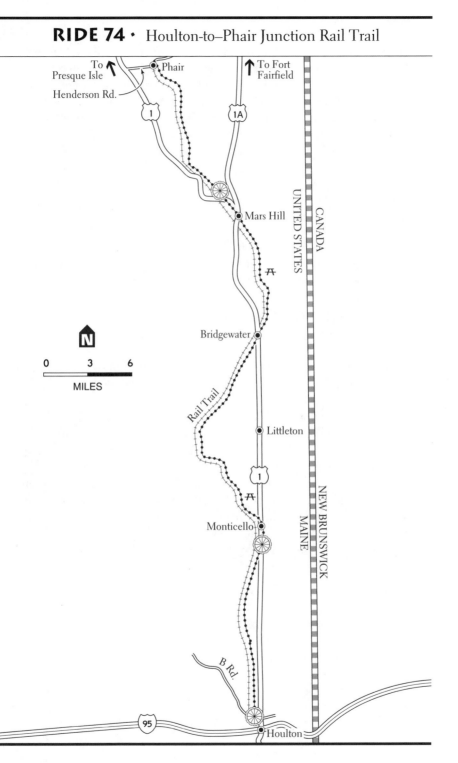

Hazards: The rail bed is in relatively good condition, although in some places there are remnants of the railway still in the trail bed. Watch for such things as ties and track spikes. Carefully check for traffic where the trail crosses roads. Some of these intersections are blind. You will share the route in the summer with all-terrain vehicles. They move along at great speed on the smooth, straight stretches of the trail.

Rescue index: You are rarely more than 2 miles from assistance, with one exception: the section between Harvey and Bridgewater is remote. We suggest that if you require assistance in this section, head toward Bridgewater. This section is also open to logging trucks. Get well off the trail if you hear one approaching.

Land status: State recreational trail.

Maps: This trail is depicted in the DeLorme Mapping Company's *Maine Atlas and Gazetteer* (map 53, section A-3; map 59, sections A-3 through E-3; map 65, section E-3).

Finding the trail: To get to the trailhead in Phair, head south on US 1 from Presque Isle. One mile after passing beneath a green railroad bridge, turn left on Jamieson Road. After 0.8 mile, turn right on Centerline Road. Drive for 1.5 miles before turning left on Henderson Road, at a four-way intersection. Continue along Henderson Road until you cross the old rail bed. Pull off the road to park. You will begin riding south.

To reach the trailhead in Houlton, take Exit 62 off Interstate 95 and follow signs for US 1 North. Immediately after leaving the highway, look for signs for the State of Maine Tourist Information Center. There is plenty of parking at the information center, though we would advise requesting permission if you plan to leave your car overnight. From the information center, turn left onto B Street and ride toward the railroad crossing, which is visible a short distance away. Just before crossing the railroad, turn right into a gravel driveway (there are signs for a Reload Facility at the entrance). Ride past a fertilizer plant on the right and continue following the road, keeping left at a fork. At a small gravel lot, cross some tracks and begin riding alongside them on the other side. This rail spur soon joins the main tracks that, after a short distance, have been pulled up.

Source of additional information:

Department of Conservation
Bureau of Parks and Lands
ORV Division/ATV Program
22 State House Station
Augusta, ME 04333
(207) 287-4958

Early spring
riding along the
recreational trail
between Houlton
and Phair Junction.

Notes on the trail: This trail is obvious and easy to follow. The first section alternates between passing through alder swamps and the wide-open potato fields of the type that used to cover all of eastern Aroostook County. Notice the ruins of the old potato houses in Littleton, Monticello, Harvey, and Bridgewater. The high trestle near Monticello can be safely crossed and provides a wonderful view of the Meduxnekeag River and the old dam that used to be at this location.

The trail swings west and then north after Monticello, with the landscape becoming more wooded and interspersed with beaver flowages. There are some big puddles along this section, which should be negotiated with care. After Bridgewater, you will encounter more users, as the trail is easily accessed from US 1. There are the remains of an interesting mill site at Robinsons. From Robinsons the trail follows Prestile Stream the rest of the way to Phair. This stream provides habitats to a variety of mammals and birds, including moose, beaver, muskrat, ducks, and herons. There are several open stretches of trail as it meanders through potato fields. These areas can be quite windy, particularly if there is an approaching storm.

Mars Hill is a good place to stop for a bite to eat, either in the form of a picnic at the town park (head north on US 1A approximately 0.2 mile from the trail), or at the local diner. From Mars Hill the trail becomes a wide road for approximately 2 miles, before narrowing again and passing the ruins of several potato houses as it enters Westfield Village. From Westfield it is a fast, pretty cruise to Phair Junction.

RIDE 75 · Aroostook Valley Trail

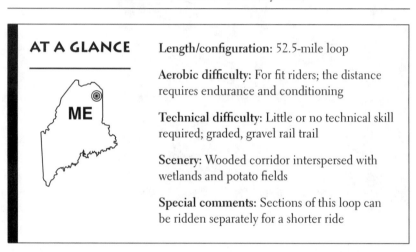

AT A GLANCE

Length/configuration: 52.5-mile loop

Aerobic difficulty: For fit riders; the distance requires endurance and conditioning

Technical difficulty: Little or no technical skill required; graded, gravel rail trail

Scenery: Wooded corridor interspersed with wetlands and potato fields

Special comments: Sections of this loop can be ridden separately for a shorter ride

Creating a circular tour through northern Aroostook County, this 52.5-mile journey allows bicyclists to pedal the old path of the Aroostook Valley Railroad and the Bangor and Aroostook Railroad. The loop follows a wide, graded, gravel trail that was constructed as part of the rails-to-trails initiative to create recreational trails along portions of abandoned railroad beds. This rail trail provides a level alternative to the hilly countryside surrounding it. Although the ride requires no more than a beginning level of technical skill, its total length is a challenge that only experienced riders in good physical condition should attempt. Riders familiar with self-contained bicycle touring may opt to use the trail as a starting point to explore the back roads of this part of the County. Camping facilities away from the lakes and major towns are virtually nonexistent, however, so campers should be prepared to rough it. Intrepid cyclists who attempt the whole ride should set aside the whole day to complete it.

The Aroostook Valley Trail passes through woods of spruce and cedar, past abandoned potato fields, and through countless bogs. Throughout this stretch of the ride, you will pass several rest areas where picnic tables have been set up. In Woodland, several miles north of Washburn, the trail crosses the Nature Conservancy Woodland Bog Preserve. The preserve was created to protect a variety of rare plants, including several species of national significance. North of Woodland, the trail ends and requires riders to pedal a few miles on pavement, before reconnecting to the rail trail in New Sweden. Farther north, the trail enters the small community of Stockholm and swings southwest to parallel the Little Madawaska River. This section of the trail follows the old route of the Bangor and Aroostook Railroad. It is common to see moose, muskrats, and beavers along this portion of the ride, which is more remote.

General location: This ride passes through northeast Aroostook County.

Elevation change: There is little appreciable elevation gain, as this trail uses abandoned railways.

Season: The Aroostook Valley Trail can be ridden between mid-May and October. Autumn is the best season in which to ride, as the weather is cooler and the black flies and mosquitos have abated.

Services: Services are scarce along this route. Groceries are available in Caribou, New Sweden, and Washburn. The nearest bicycle shop is located in Van Buren. Cyclists should carry all necessary supplies with them, including food, adequate water, and bicycle parts such as spare tubes and cables. Due to the remoteness of some sections of the ride, it is prudent to take the extra time to ensure that your bike is in sound mechanical condition.

Hazards: The trail surface is primarily loose gravel, with some sandy sections and others overgrown with grass. Although the riding is not difficult, you can be sent flying if you are not paying attention. All-terrain vehicles use this trail frequently and, particularly along wide, straight stretches of the trail, may be moving at very high speeds.

If you are planning to do the entire route, take plenty of food and water. Although water is plentiful along this route, it is of dubious quality, even if filtered or chemically treated.

The weather can change very quickly, particularly in the summer, when late-afternoon thunderstorms are a common occurrence. Bring enough clothing.

Rescue index: You will be far from assistance, as much as 10 miles along parts of the trail. Your best bet, if you need assistance, is to stay on the trail

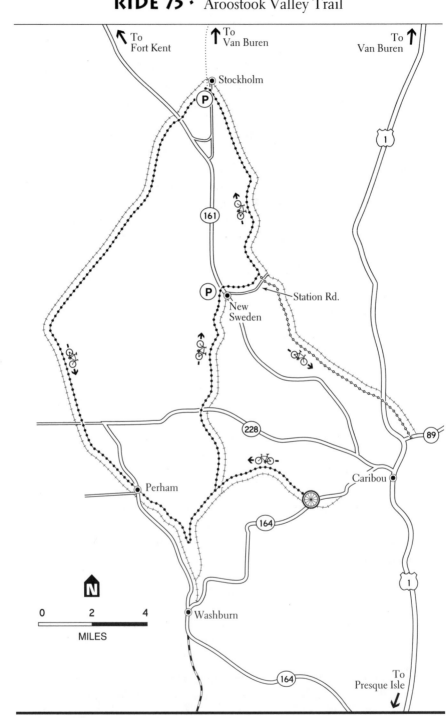

To
Fort Kent

To
Van Buren

To
Van Buren

1

Stockholm

P

161

P

New
Sweden

Station Rd.

228

Perham

Caribou

164

89

N

0   2   4

MILES

Washburn

164

1

To
Presque Isle

until you come to a farmhouse or road crossing. There are many woods roads that cross the trail. Blindly trying to follow one of these without knowing where you are will certainly make matters worse.

Land status: State recreational trail.

Maps: Although completely devoid of place names, the Department of Conservation's *Maine ATV Trail Map* is adequate. The entire route is shown in DeLorme's *Maine Atlas and Gazetteer* (map 64, sections A-4, A-5, B-4, B-5, and C4; map 65, section B-1; map 68, sections E-4 and E-5). *Note:* The DeLorme map incorrectly shows where the railroad grade passes through New Sweden. It does not pass through New Sweden village, as shown on the map, but actually crosses Station Road in the vicinity of East Road, approximately 1 mile east of where the map shows the grade crossing Station Road.

Finding the trail: The trail can be accessed from trailheads located in Washburn, Caribou, and Stockholm, as well as from many other points along the route. We chose to start the ride in West Caribou, where a parking area provides convenient access to the trail. To reach this trailhead, drive west on ME 164 from Caribou for approximately 4 miles. Just after crossing the Washburn town line, look for the Aroostook Valley Trail sign on the right. Turn right into a gravel parking area. Begin riding west.

Source of additional information: ·

Department of Conservation
Bureau of Parks and Lands
ORV Division/ATV Program
22 State House Station
Augusta, ME 04333
(207) 287-4968

Notes on the trail: From the West Caribou trailhead, begin pedaling west toward Washburn. You will ride past several picnic areas and cross several roads, including Creed Road and McIntire Road. After approximately 3.2 miles, turn right where another trail branches off on the right. Trail signs at this junction may direct you to New Sweden, Stockholm, and Colby. You will be traveling north. This trail is rough and grassy, and you will notice that ties remain from the railway that once traversed this route. Continue riding until you reach the end of the trail at West Road in New Sweden. Turn right onto West Road, which is paved, and cross ME 161, continuing straight on Station Road. You will ascend a moderately steep hill on Station Road (the views from the top are spectacular) and then descend steeply. At the bottom of the hill you will pass East Road on the right before coming to the railroad bed. This is the site of the old New Sweden train station. Turn left onto the trail, once again riding north. This trail is much wider than the Aroostook Valley Trail and thus presents more open vistas of the surrounding countryside.

A beaver lodge by the side of the Aroostook Valley Trail.

Continuing north along the rail trail, you will cross the Madawaska River as you reach Stockholm.

In Stockholm, there is a small grocery store visible from the trail to the right. This is the last opportunity you will have to purchase food or water until Washburn, 22 miles away. After riding through Stockholm, past a playing field on the left, you will come to a fork in the trail. The right fork continues to Van Buren, 17 miles northwest. You will want to stay left, following signs directing you to Perham and Washburn. Once again you will cross ME 161, after which the trail parallels the Little Madawaska River. The buildings at the intersection of ME 161 are the last significant buildings you will see for the next 16 miles, until you reach Perham. This portion of the ride follows the route of the old Bangor and Aroostook Railroad. Service along this line was discontinued in the early 1950s. The trail that now follows the abandoned route is quite wide and considerably more open than the first part of the ride. The trip to Washburn, though long, is an easy cruise, and you should be able to make good time. The easiest way to gauge your progress is to carefully note the many roads you cross as you proceed southward.

Sixteen miles after leaving Stockholm, you will start to encounter an increasing number of homes and other buildings close to the trail. We noticed that, after passing through Perham, the last 5 miles to Washburn flew by as the prospect of reaching a source of food and water grew closer! As you arrive in Washburn, notice the complex of abandoned potato houses that greet you as you enter what was once the old rail yard. Sights like this make one appreciate the magnitude of the potato industry in Aroostook County during the early part of this century.

To return to the starting point and to your vehicle, return to the railroad bed, heading back in the direction from which you came. Look carefully for the signs for the Aroostook Valley Trail, which will fork to the right. This is a pleasant trail, much narrower than the old Bangor and Aroostook Railroad trail, passing through a series of bogs and along the edge of pastures. This is also a great place to see wildlife. Eventually, you will reach the intersection where the trail heads north toward New Sweden, Stockholm, and Colby. Stay right, and retrace your tracks to your car.

Congratulations, you made it!

RIDE 76 · Van Buren–to-Stockholm Rail Trail

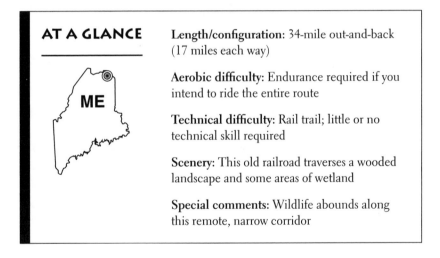

AT A GLANCE	**Length/configuration:** 34-mile out-and-back (17 miles each way)
ME	**Aerobic difficulty:** Endurance required if you intend to ride the entire route
	Technical difficulty: Rail trail; little or no technical skill required
	Scenery: This old railroad traverses a wooded landscape and some areas of wetland
	Special comments: Wildlife abounds along this remote, narrow corridor

From downtown Van Buren, a scenic and often remote rail trail extends southwest to the town of Stockholm. The complete ride adds up to a 34-mile round-trip, from Van Buren to Stockholm and back again. Alternatively, if you can arrange for transportation or leave a vehicle at either end, the ride can be pedaled as a 17-mile point-to-point excursion. Although the ride is best suited for intermediate-level riders in good physical condition because of the distance involved, the trail is perfect for beginning cyclists, large groups, and families who plan to ride just a portion of it as an out-and-back affair. The trail surface is hard-packed gravel and features virtually no change in elevation.

This rail trail provides a scenic link between two culturally distinct communities. Van Buren was settled by a community of French-speaking Acadians who fled to the St. John River Valley in the latter half of the eighteenth century, rather than pledge allegiance to the Crown and the Church of England after the Treaty of Utrecht granted Nova Scotia to Great Britain in 1713. The town prospered as an agricultural community and later became one of the larger logging towns along the St. John River. The railroad bed that this ride follows once served to transport the potatoes, lumber, and wood products that still form the economic strength of the town. The town is named for U.S. president Martin Van Buren, who once paid a visit to the area. Stockholm, on the other hand, bears its name because of the successful establishment of a Swedish community in Maine. The inspiration for this settlement project came from a Portland man, William Widgery Thomas, who was sent to Sweden in 1863 by President Lincoln. Thomas, impressed by similarities between Sweden and northern Maine, proposed a program to encourage the immigration of Swedish farmers. In 1870 his plan was approved by the House of Representatives, who voted to grant 100 acres of land to each family who immigrated to the townships now known as Stockholm and New Sweden.

General location: Northern St. John River Valley in northeastern Aroostook County.

Elevation change: As with most rail trails, you will not see more than a 2 percent grade along this route. Therefore, the change in elevation is minimal.

Season: The best conditions for this ride are usually from June to late October. The route is a popular snowmobile trail in the winter, so for those who never put their bike away, this is a good year-round ride.

Services: The Ski Shop in Van Buren is an excellent source of information about biking in the area and will satisfy all your needs for bike service and repair. Food and water are available in both Van Buren and Stockholm, provided that you are there during store hours.

In Presque Isle, several miles south, Aroostook State Park offers wooded campsites with tables and fireplaces. Other more primitive campsites are also available west of Stockholm, in Maine public reserve land around Eagle Lake and Square Lake. Access to this area is gained off Sly Brook Road, connecting with ME 11 at Soldier Pond in Wallagrass.

Hazards: Remember that you are sharing the trail with all-terrain vehicles, horseback riders, and hikers. Washouts are usually well marked, as are road crossings and any other potential hazards.

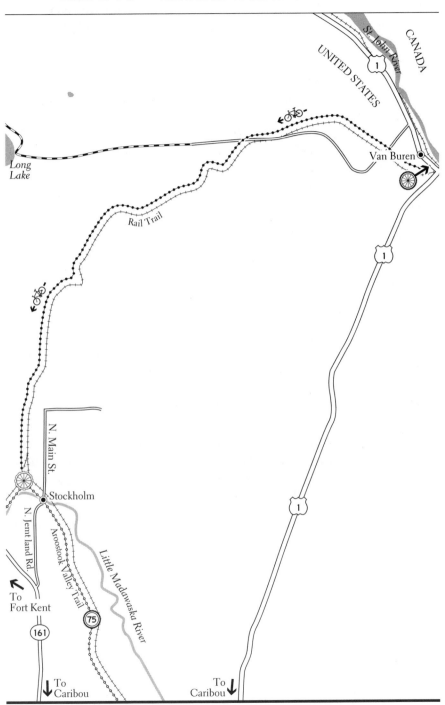

CANADA

UNITED STATES

St. John River

Van Buren

Long
Lake

Rail Trail

1

N. Main St.

Stockholm

1

N. Jemtland Rd.

Aroostook Valley Trail

Little Madawaska River

To
Fort Kent

161

75

To
Caribou

To
Caribou

Rescue index: At the farthest point, you will be 8.5 miles from both Van Buren and Stockholm. Although the trail does pass through some fairly remote areas, frequent road crossings provide potential access to assistance.

Land status: State recreational trail.

Maps: The *Maine ATV Trail Map*, produced by the Department of Conservation, is available at tourist information centers, or by contacting the Bureau of Parks and Lands, ORV Division/ATV Program, 22 State House Station, Augusta, ME 04333, (207) 287-4958. In addition, *The Maine Atlas and Gazetteer* (from the DeLorme Mapping Co., Yarmouth, ME) provides detailed maps of the entire state that include most old railways.

Finding the trail: The trailhead in Van Buren is located at the Tourist Information Booth situated next to the train tracks at the junction of US 1 and 1A. There should be ample parking here. The trail begins just behind the information booth.

Source of additional information:

The Ski Shop
31 Main Street
Van Buren, ME 04785
(207) 868-2737

The Ski Shop is a full-service bike store located just a few buildings away from the trailhead. The staff at The Ski Shop can provide you with information about the rail trail and direct you to additional riding in the area. In the summer, the shop is open Tuesday through Saturday.

Notes on the trail: Keeping the tracks on your left and an old gray storage building on your right, begin riding west away from US 1. You will ride through an old freight yard, past some warehouses, and along a narrow dirt trail that bears left over several sets of tracks. The main trail begins from Poplar Street (a dirt road that becomes paved as it enters town). Follow the rail bed as it heads out of town. The trail is obvious and crosses a few roads en route to Stockholm. Keep your eyes open for bear and moose, which are most often seen at dusk. As the trail enters the town of Stockholm, a large billboard indicates various routes at an intersection with the Aroostook Valley Trail. Continue straight to ride into Stockholm. Unless you have arranged for transportation, turn around and retrace your route back to Van Buren.

AFTERWORD

A few years ago I wrote a long piece on this issue for *Sierra* magazine that entailed calling literally dozens of government land managers, game wardens, mountain bikers, and local officials to get a feeling for how riders were being welcomed on the trails. All that I've seen personally since, and heard from my authors, indicates there hasn't been much change. We're still considered the new kid on the block. We have less of a right to the trails than horses and hikers, and we're excluded from many areas, including:

a) wilderness areas
b) national parks (except on roads, and those paths specifically marked "bike path")
c) national monuments (except on roads open to the public)
d) most state parks and monuments (except on roads, and those paths specifically marked "bike path")
e) an increasing number of urban and county parks, especially in California (except on roads, and those paths specifically marked "bike path")

Frankly, I have little difficulty with these exclusions and would, in fact, restrict our presence from some trails I've ridden (one time) due to the environmental damage and chance of blind-siding the many walkers and hikers I met up with along the way. But these are my personal views. The authors of this volume and mountain bikers as a group may hold different opinions.

You can do your part in keeping us from being excluded from even more trails by riding responsibly. Many local and national off-road bicycle organizations have been formed with exactly this in mind, and one of the largest—the

National Off-Road Bicycle Association (NORBA)—offers the following code of behavior for mountain bikers:

1. I will yield the right of way to other non-motorized recreationists. I realize that people judge all cyclists by my actions.
2. I will slow down and use caution when approaching or overtaking another cyclist and will make my presence known well in advance.
3. I will maintain control of my speed at all times and will approach turns in anticipation of someone around the bend.
4. I will stay on designated trails to avoid trampling native vegetation and minimize potential erosion to trails by not using muddy trails or short-cutting switchbacks.
5. I will not disturb wildlife or livestock.
6. I will not litter. I will pack out what I pack in, and pack out more than my share whenever possible.
7. I will respect public and private property, including trail use signs and no trespassing signs, and I will leave gates as I have found them.
8. I will always be self-sufficient, and my destination and travel speed will be determined by my ability, my equipment, the terrain, and the present and potential weather conditions.
9. I will not travel solo when bikepacking in remote areas. I will leave word of my destination and when I plan to return.
10. I will observe the practice of minimum impact bicycling by "taking only pictures and memories and leaving only waffle prints."
11. I will always wear a helmet whenever I ride.

Now, I have a problem with some of these—number nine, for instance. The most enjoyable mountain biking I've ever done has been solo. And as for leaving word of destination and time of return, I've enjoyed living in such a way as to say, "I'm off to pedal Colorado. See you in the fall." Of course it's senseless to take needless risks, and I plan a ride and pack my gear with this in mind. But for me number nine smacks too much of the "never-out-of-touch" mentality. And getting away from civilization, deep into the wilds, is, for many people, what mountain biking's all about.

All in all, however, NORBA's is a good list, and surely we mountain bikers would be liked more, and excluded less, if we followed the suggestions. But let me offer a "code of ethics" I much prefer, one given to cyclists by Utah's Wasatch-Cache National Forest office.

Study a Forest Map Before You Ride
Currently, bicycles are permitted on roads and developed trails within the Wasatch-Cache National Forest except in designated Wilderness. If your route crosses private land, it is your responsibility to obtain right of way permission from the landowner.

Keep Groups Small
Riding in large groups degrades the outdoor experience for others, can disturb wildlife, and usually leads to greater resource damage.

Avoid Riding on Wet Trails
Bicycle tires leave ruts in wet trails. These ruts concentrate runoff and accelerate erosion. Postponing a ride when the trails are wet will preserve the trails for future use.

Stay on Roads and Trails
Riding cross-country destroys vegetation and damages the soil.

Always Yield to Others
Trails are shared by hikers, horses, and bicycles. Move off the trail to allow horses to pass and stop to allow hikers adequate room to share the trail. Simply yelling "Bicycle!" is not acceptable.

Control Your Speed
Excessive speed endangers yourself and other forest users.

Avoid Wheel Lock-up and Spin-out
Steep terrain is especially vulnerable to trail wear. Locking brakes on steep descents or when stopping needlessly damages trails. If a slope is steep enough to require locking wheels and skidding, dismount and walk your bicycle. Likewise, if an ascent is so steep your rear wheel slips and spins, dismount and walk your bicycle.

Protect Waterbars and Switchbacks
Waterbars, the rock and log drains built to direct water off trails, protect trails from erosion. When you encounter a waterbar, ride directly over the top or dismount and walk your bicycle. Riding around the ends of waterbars destroys them and speeds erosion. Skidding around switchback corners shortens trail life. Slow down for switchback corners and keep your wheels rolling.

If You Abuse It, You Lose It
Mountain bikers are relative newcomers to the forest and must prove themselves responsible trail users. By following the guidelines above, and by participating in trail maintenance service projects, bicyclists can help avoid closures which would prevent them from using trails.

I've never seen a better trail-etiquette list for mountain bikers. So have fun. Be careful. And don't screw up things for the next rider.

Dennis Coello
Series Editor

GLOSSARY

This short list of terms does not contain all the words used by mountain bike enthusiasts when discussing their sport. But it should serve as an introduction to the lingo you'll hear on the trails.

ATB all-terrain bike; this, like "fat-tire bike," is another name for a mountain bike

ATV all-terrain vehicle; this usually refers to the loud, fume-spewing three- or four-wheeled motorized vehicles you will not enjoy meeting on the trail—except, of course, if you crash and have to hitch a ride out on one

bladed refers to a dirt road which has been smoothed out by the use of a wide blade on earth-moving equipment; "blading" gets rid of the teeth-chattering, much-cursed washboards found on so many dirt roads after heavy vehicle use

blaze a mark on a tree made by chipping away a piece of the bark, usually done to designate a trail; such trails are sometimes described as "blazed"

blind corner a curve in the road or trail that conceals bikers, hikers, equestrians, and other traffic

BLM Bureau of Land Management, an agency of the federal government

buffed used to describe a very smooth trail

catching air	taking a jump in such a way that both wheels of the bike are off the ground at the same time
clean	while this may describe what you and your bike *won't* be after following many trails, the term is most often used as a verb to denote the action of pedaling a tough section of trail successfully
combination	this type of route may combine two or more configurations; for example, a point-to-point route may integrate a scenic loop or an out-and-back spur midway through the ride; likewise, an out-and-back may have a loop at its farthest point (this configuration looks like a cherry with a stem attached; the stem is the out-and back, the fruit is the terminus loop); or a loop route may have multiple out-and-back spurs and/or loops to the side; mileage for a combination route is for the total distance to complete the ride
dab	touching the ground with a foot or hand
deadfall	a tangled mass of fallen trees or branches
diversion ditch	a usually narrow, shallow ditch dug across or around a trail; funneling the water in this manner keeps it from destroying the trail
double-track	the dual tracks made by a jeep or other vehicle, with grass or weeds or rocks between; mountain bikers can ride in either of the tracks, but you will of course find that whichever one you choose, and no matter how many times you change back and forth, the other track will appear to offer smoother travel
dugway	a steep, unpaved, switchbacked descent
endo	flipping end over end
feathering	using a light touch on the brake lever, hitting it lightly many times rather than very hard or locking the brake
four-wheel-drive	this refers to any vehicle with drive-wheel capability on all four wheels (a jeep, for instance, has four-wheel drive as compared with a two-wheel-drive passenger car), or to a rough road or trail that requires four-wheel-drive capability (or a *one*-wheel-drive mountain bike!) to negotiate it
game trail	the usually narrow trail made by deer, elk, or other game

gated everyone knows what a gate is, and how many variations exist upon this theme; well, if a trail is described as "gated" it simply has a gate across it; don't forget that the rule is if you find a gate closed, close it behind you; if you find one open, leave it that way

Giardia shorthand for *Giardia lamblia,* and known as the "backpacker's bane" until we mountain bikers expropriated it; this is a waterborne parasite that begins its life cycle when swallowed, and one to four weeks later has its host (you) bloated, vomiting, shivering with chills and living in the bathroom; the disease can be avoided by "treating" (purifying) the water you acquire along the trail (see "Hitting the Trail" in the Introduction)

gnarly a term thankfully used less and less these days, it refers to tough trails

hammer to ride very hard

hardpack a trail in which the dirt surface is packed down hard; such trails make for good and fast riding, and very painful landings; bikers most often use "hardpack" as both a noun and adjective, and "hard-packed" as an adjective only (the grammar lesson will help you when diagramming sentences in camp)

hike-a-bike what you do when the road or trail becomes too steep or rough to remain in the saddle

jeep road, jeep trail a rough road or trail passable only with four-wheel-drive capability (or a horse or mountain bike)

kamikaze while this once referred primarily to those Japanese fliers who quaffed a glass of sake, then flew off as human bombs in suicide missions against U.S. naval vessels, it has more recently been applied to the idiot mountain bikers who, far less honorably, scream down hiking trails, endangering the physical and mental safety of the walking, biking, and equestrian traffic they meet; deck guns were necessary to stop the Japanese kamikaze pilots, but a bike pump or walking staff in the spokes is sufficient for the current-day kamikazes who threaten to get us all kicked off the trails

loop	this route configuration is characterized by riding from the designated trailhead to a distant point, then returning to the trailhead via a different route (or simply continuing on the same in a circle route) without doubling back; you always move forward across new terrain, but return to the starting point when finished; mileage is for the entire loop from the trailhead back to trailhead
multi-purpose	a BLM designation of land which is open to many uses; mountain biking is allowed
ORV	a motorized off-road vehicle
out-and-back	a ride where you will return on the same trail you pedaled out; while this might sound far more boring than a loop route, many trails look very different when pedaled in the opposite direction
pack stock	horses, mules, llamas, et cetera, carrying provisions along the trails . . . and unfortunately leaving a trail of their own behind
point-to-point	a vehicle shuttle (or similar assistance) is required for this type of route, which is ridden from the designated trail-head to a distant location, or endpoint, where the route ends; total mileage is for the one-way trip from the trail-head to endpoint
portage	to carry your bike on your person
pummy	volcanic activity in the Pacific Northwest and elsewhere produces soil with a high content of pumice; trails through such soil often become thick with dust, but this is light in consistency and can usually be pedaled; remember, however, to pedal carefully, for this dust obscures whatever might lurk below
quads	bikers use this term to refer both to the extensor muscle in the front of the thigh (which is separated into four parts) and to USGS maps; the expression "Nice quads!" refers always to the former, however, except in those instances when the speaker is an engineer
runoff	rainwater or snowmelt
scree	an accumulation of loose stones or rocky debris lying on a slope or at the base of a hill or cliff

signed   a "signed" trail has signs in place of blazes

single-track   a single, narrow path through grass or brush or over rocky terrain, often created by deer, elk, or backpackers; single-track riding is some of the best fun around

slickrock   the rock-hard, compacted sandstone that is *great* to ride and even prettier to look at; you'll appreciate it even more if you think of it as a petrified sand dune or seabed (which it is), and if the rider before you hasn't left tire marks (from unnecessary skidding) or granola bar wrappers behind

snowmelt   runoff produced by the melting of snow

snowpack   unmelted snow accumulated over weeks or months of winter—or over years in high-mountain terrain

spur   a road or trail that intersects the main trail you're following

switchback   a zigzagging road or trail designed to assist in traversing steep terrain: mountain bikers should *not* skid through switchbacks

technical   terrain that is difficult to ride due not to its grade (steepness) but to its obstacles—rocks, roots, logs, ledges, loose soil . . .

topo   short for topographical map, the kind that shows both linear distance *and* elevation gain and loss; "topo" is pronounced with both vowels long

trashed   a trail that has been destroyed (same term used no matter what has destroyed it . . . cattle, horses, or even mountain bikers riding when the ground was too wet)

two-wheel-drive   this refers to any vehicle with drive-wheel capability on only two wheels (a passenger car, for instance, has two-wheel-drive); a two-wheel-drive road is a road or trail easily traveled by an ordinary car

waterbar   an earth, rock, or wooden structure that funnels water off trails to reduce erosion

washboarded   a road that is surfaced with many ridges spaced closely together, like the ripples on a washboard; these make for very rough riding, and even worse driving in a car or jeep

whoop-de-doo   closely spaced dips or undulations in a trail; these are often encountered in areas traveled heavily by ORVs *wilderness area*   land that is officially set aside by the federal government to remain *natural*—pure, pristine, and untrammeled by any vehicle, including mountain bikes; though mountain bikes had not been born in 1964 (when the United States Congress passed the Wilderness Act, establishing the National Wilderness Preservation system), they are considered a "form of mechanical transport" and are thereby excluded; in short, stay out

wind chill   a reference to the wind's cooling effect upon exposed flesh; for example, if the temperature is 10 degrees Fahrenheit and the wind is blowing at 20 miles per hour, the wind-chill (that is, the actual temperature to which your skin reacts) is *minus* 32 degrees; if you are riding in wet conditions things are even worse, for the wind-chill would then be *minus 74 degrees!*

windfall   anything (trees, limbs, brush, fellow bikers . . .) blown down by the wind

INDEX

ABOUT THE AUTHORS

SARAH HALE and **DAVID GIBBS** live in Yarmouth, Maine. Originally from Montreal, David grew up biking and hiking all over Maine and has completed many trips to the western United States. David's love of cycling began in the 1970s, with the acquisition of a Peugeot 10-speed. Committed to promoting bicycling as a form of alternative transportation, David commutes 25 miles a day to and from work year-round. He has toured extensively throughout New England and recently completed a bicycle tour in Alaska. David has attended both the University of Maine in Orono and the University of Southern Maine and has been employed as a forest ranger, fire fighter, and bike mechanic. He is currently the safety coordinator for the City of Portland and can be found most weekends hiking or bicycling around his cabin in western Maine.

Sarah moved to Maine in 1992, after a two-month cycling tour of France and Spain that opened her eyes to the exhilaration of traveling and exploring on two wheels. Born in England, she has also lived in and explored Switzerland, the northeastern United States, and Canada. She completed a degree in English literature and women's studies at McGill University in Montreal. Sarah currently manages Chintz-N-Prints, a retail store specializing in fabrics for home interiors. Thanks to a benevolent employer, she has been able to take frequent leaves of absence. Her most recent trip was a two-month mountain bike exploration of the Maritimes, which marks the beginning of her work on another book in this series—*Mountain Bike! Canada's Atlantic Provinces.*